REFORM JUDAISM:
A HISTORICAL PERSPECTIVE

REFORM JUDAISM:
A HISTORICAL PERSPECTIVE

Essays from the Yearbook of the
Central Conference of American Rabbis

selected, edited and with
an Introduction by

JOSEPH L. BLAU

KTAV PUBLISHING HOUSE, INC.

NEW YORK

1973

733261

SBN 87068-191-5

MANUFACTURED IN THE UNITED STATES OF AMERICA
LIBRARY OF CONGRESS CATALOGUE CARD NUMBER: 72-428

The Central Conference of American Rabbis proudly dedicates this volume to its companion organizations within the Reform Movement—the Union of American Hebrew Congregations and the Hebrew Union College-Jewish Institute of Religion—upon their Centennials.

FOREWORD

For more than eighty years, the Central Conference of American Rabbis has provided the rabbinical leaders of the Reform movement in American Judaism with a forum for the presentation of their ideas on a variety of themes. These presentations, addressed to professional colleagues, have often been more penetrating and more thoughtfully elaborated than other utterances of the rabbis, directed to more popular audiences. Here the young rabbi has made his mark, impressing his colleagues as someone to watch; here the rabbi approaching the end of his career has spoken his most mature private reflections on the cause he serves. For the most part, however, this has been a forum in which the rabbis who are in the prime of life and dedicated service have spoken of the problems that face Reform Judaism in its attempt to develop interpretations of the millennial Jewish tradition to meet the needs of twentieth-century Western man.

These presentations, carefully prepared before the conferences and often carefully revised to take account of criticism after the conferences, have been published along with committee reports and other official acts of the Central Conference of American Rabbis in a *Yearbook*. Dr. Joseph L. Blau (professor of religion and director of graduate studies in the Department of Religion, Columbia University, Chairman of the Committee on the History of Religions of the American Council of Learned Societies, and Vice-President of the Conference on Jewish Social Studies) has selected twenty-four essays from the full run of the *Yearbook* to illustrate the development of Reform Jewish ideas in the United States of America. He has arranged the selected essays in groups to illuminate Reform thinking on some central themes: The Nature of the Reform Movement; the place of Liberal Judaism in a Reactionary World; Theological Speculations; Ritual and Worship; Law and Authority; Israel—People and Land.

The authors included range from early European-trained rabbis through the first few generations of those trained in the United States to teachers in the Hebrew Union College-Jewish Institute of Religion and dominant figures in the pulpit and the organizational life of American Reform Judaism. These writers and thinkers of past and present are presented in a context that clarifies the significance of what they said for the history of the Reform Movement. Dr. Blau's full Introduction to the volume prepares the reader for understanding the individual contributions as representative of stages in this emerging history. In itself, the Introduction is an original interpretation of the creative tension between the ancient Jewish tradition and the demands of modern Jewish existence in the United States.

TABLE OF CONTENTS

Introduction

WHEN ISAAC MAYER WISE led in the creation of a Reform Jewish movement out of the scattered and independent Reform congregations spread across the United States, his work proceeded in three distinct stages. Each of these stages was dependent upon what had gone before; each provided a new dimension of the Reform movement. There had been stirrings of Reform Judaism as far back as the 1820s, in Charleston, South Carolina; these came to nothing in their immediate impact. From the 1840s, however, congregations in many cities were organized with Reform objectives. Some of them induced rabbis with a background in German Reform Judaism to come into their service; in others, members of the lay group conducted the worship of their fellow members. By the year 1870, there were Reform congregations in Baltimore (Har Sinai, 1842), New York (Emanuel, 1845), Albany (Anshe Emeth, 1850), Cincinnati (Bene Yeshurun, 1854; Bene Israel, 1855), Philadelphia (Keneseth Israel, 1856), Chicago (Sinai, 1860). Each of these congregations went its own way, making whatever changes in traditional forms of worship its members felt desirable, or following a prayerbook edited by its rabbi. The German background of these congregations was evident from their wide use of German for the keeping of their records, the translation of Hebrew prayers into German, and the persistence of German as the language of preaching.

1

The first stage of Dr. Wise's work, ably abetted by Max Lilienthal, David Einhorn, Samuel Adler and Samuel Hirsch, led to the combination of these congregations, in 1873, into the Union of American Hebrew Congregations. Had Wise been able to fulfill his deepest desires the Union of American Hebrew Congregations would have included more than the explicitly Reform groups and become the focal point for all American Jewish synagogal cooperation. This wider union was not to be, however, although in the initial stages of the work congregations other than Reform in orientation did participate. In its first years, a major activity of the Union was to prepare the ground for the establishment of the Hebrew Union College, where young men were to train for the rabbinical office in an American environment. The College opened in 1875, once more with the unrealized hope that it would serve the entire Jewish community of the United States and not merely the congregations fully committed to Reform Judaism. In its first years, Isaac Wise, with one assistant, carried on all the instruction at the Hebrew Union College as well as bearing responsibility for administrative routines and fund-raising. Without the financial and moral support of the Union of American Hebrew Congregations, even this limited program would have been out of the question. In this sense, the second stage in building a Reform movement, the establishment of a seminary, was dependent upon the first, the creation of the Union.

By the mid-1880s, the first graduates of the Hebrew Union College were serving in the active rabbinate, and other dynamic younger rabbis from Germany had emigrated to the United States and filled Reform pulpits. It was at this stage that ideological leadership of the nascent movement slipped out of the hands of Dr. Wise, into those of Dr. Kaufmann Kohler, a relatively recent arrival from Germany, a son-in-law of David Einhorn, and a more radical reformer than Dr. Wise. This shift of leadership was symbolized by Dr. Kohler's domination of the Pittsburgh Rabbinical Conference of November 16–18, 1885, and its declaration of the principles of the Reform movement in the form of the well-remembered Pittsburgh Platform. In later years, David Philipson, the young graduate of the

Hebrew Union College who had served as secretary to the Pittsburgh Conference, was to call the Platform "the most succinct expression of the theology of the reform movement that had ever been published to the world" and "the utterance most expressive of the teachings of Reform Judaism."

In the radicalism of the Pittsburgh Platform, however, the seeds of division between the "Eastern wing," of David Einhorn and his successors, and the "Western wing," of the more moderate group following Dr. Wise, were clearly evinced. That an open split did not occur may, perhaps, be the consequence of Dr. Wise's third stage in the organization of the Reform movement, the formation, in July, 1889, of the Central Conference of American Rabbis, the professional association of virtually all the Reform rabbis in the United States. For just over eighty years, as these lines are being written, the Central Conference of American Rabbis has held a plenary meeting every year, and its many committees and commissions have carried on the activities of the Conference between plenary sessions. Instead of a riven movement, leading possibly to a return to the catch-as-catch-can situation of an earlier period when, in the words of Rabbi Bernard J. Bamberger, "Each congregation was content to stagnate in its own way," the Central Conference of American Rabbis set up a forum in which differences of opinion with respect to ideas and to programs might be debated in a spirit of ecumenical cordiality if not of brotherly love.

To say this is not to imply that Dr. Wise foresaw the role that the Central Conference of American Rabbis would play in the later history of the American Reform movement, or even that his motives in moving toward its formation were irenic in intent. The time has certainly come when the legend of Isaac Mayer Wise can be laid to rest. It is quite possible that his actual intent was far more political. Wise had made earlier, unsuccessful efforts to organize rabbinical groups. Now he may have realized that the suitable time had come. His thought may have been that if there were such an organization, composed primarily of "his boys," the graduates of the Hebrew Union College, he would be able to maintain his hold on them, and through them his domination of the Reform movement. On the other hand, we should take note that Wise was aware of what the Central Conference of American Rabbis was actually accomplishing when he said, in his presidential message to the Conference in 1899 (the year of his eightieth birthday): "By this God-blessed organization, the American Rabbis were united in a bond of brotherhood, all feuds, strifes, quarrels and animosities which raged among us for many years vanished like the fog before the sun" (*Yearbook,* 1899, p. 18).

Over the years of its continuing existence, the Central Conference of American Rabbis has been, by design or by chance, many things to its members simultaneously. It has been a professional association or guild, where professional problems concerning the relation of rabbi to congregation and rabbi to rabbi have been ironed out. In this role it has been responsible for the inauguration and maintenance of dignified and suitable criteria for the contractual arrangements between rabbis and congregations, for setting up standards for temporary or trial periods of ministry, for making group provisions for the continuing care of rabbis incapacitated by illness and for pensions for rabbis who have become superannuated in service. From time to time, committees of the organization have entered, by request, as mediators and arbitrators, into situations that might otherwise have become open scandals. The Conference has served as a quasi-draft board, to assure that its younger members should share fairly in the obligations of the military chaplaincy. Through resolutions addressed to the President of the United States and to other agencies of government, the Conference has urged the passage of legislation or other governmental actions, and has thus adopted the role of a pressure group. By the publication of tracts and other materials, in cooperation with the Union of American Hebrew Congregations, the Conference has engaged in missionary activity to spread the message of Reform Judaism. The concern for Jewish education of the members of the Conference and the Union of American Hebrew Congregations has been manifested in so many ways and for so many years, that we might refer to the Joint

Commission on Education maintained by the lay and rabbinical groups as the Board of Jewish Education for the Reform movement. A special area of interest has been Jewish youth of college age who are cast into an atmosphere in which regard for all religious traditions is very weak.

The Conference has maintained a continued interest in and concern with the problems of adequate forms for worship to express the newer attitudes of members of the Reform movement. One of the first publications of the Conference was the Union Prayer Book, which was immediately adopted by most Reform congregations as a substitute for the regnant chaos and jumble of many voices. Among the aims of the Union Prayer Book was the provision of prayers that would reflect the beliefs of the twentieth-century worshipers rather than those of an earlier epoch in history. Another was the presentation of English translations of the Hebrew prayers in language more appropriate to modern times and to an ever-increasing number of worshipers whose native language was English. With each successive revision of the Union Prayer Book, there has been a closer approximation to the ideal toward which the editorial committees strive, but since the mandate of the editors requires appropriateness to the times, and the times are constantly changing, the process of revision will necessarily be a recurrent task.

The eighth paragraph of the Pittsburgh Platform affirms that:

In full accordance with the spirit of Mosaic legislation, which strives to regulate the relation between rich and poor, we deem it our duty to participate in the great task of modern times, to solve, on the basis of justice and righteousness, the problems presented by the contrasts and evils of the present organization of society.

Although the Central Conference of American Rabbis never explicitly adopted the Pittsburgh Platform, its members have been concerned, from the first, to follow the principle enunciated here. Much of the activity of the Committee on Social Justice (now called Committee on Justice and Peace) has been to study and to debate those causes that one or another of the members has thought worthy to be brought to the attention of the larger group, and to prepare resolutions expressing the sense of the members about the "just and righteous" dispositions that should be made in these matters. Individual members have gone beyond this to active participation in the agitations of their times. The reports of the Commission on Social Justice show a keen awareness of the problems of modern society and a clear "sense of injustice." These reports make it evident, however, that there is no comparable measure of agreement among the rabbis on the correct avenues of solution.

II

Despite the range and variety of the activities of the Central Conference of American Rabbis in the fields that have been mentioned, the point at which the program of the group can best be appreciated by the non-professional reader is to be found in the formal papers presented before the annual meeting and printed in the *Yearbooks*. In these essays, the rabbinic conferences approach most closely the character of scholarly meetings. Possibly they serve just such a function in the lives of the rabbis, many of whom have qualities of academic scholars that are never called forth in the day to day and year to year round of rabbinic duties. After all, the primary traditional characterization of the rabbi was as a scholar, and the emphasis on his pastoral role is a comparatively recent innovation. Rabbinic training programs in the seminaries still stress scholarly preparation; yet the young rabbi entering upon his first pulpit soon becomes aware that his precious seeds of scholarship are falling upon barren ground. He learns then that most important lesson of religious ministry, that one must temper the wind to the shorn lamb.

At the annual meetings of the Conference, his frustrated scholarly inclinations can emerge, in discourse addressed to an audience that is qualified to understand and appreciate his learning and that shares his concerns. These papers are not, however, purely scholarly dissertations, for the subjects touch not merely the mind of the participant but his deepest emotions as well. Each paper has some apologetic content and, perhaps solely because of weekly habit, most have some homiletic quality as well. It is for these qualities, as well as for their intellectual explorations, that these essays deserve to be read. They are not presented merely as exercises in dialectical ingenuity. They are contributions to an ongoing consideration of the central problem of the Reform movement and of the Reform rabbis: to define Reform Judaism as a separate movement within the history of Judaism in order to understand its relation to other living varieties of Judaism as well as to other movements, religious and non-religious, in the environing world. For, essentially, this is the key problem of any vital religious group, to remain relevant to the contemporary situation without losing contact with the roots of one's tradition.

The unifying feature in the two dozen papers selected from the eighty-year run of the *Yearbook* of the Central Conference of American Rabbis for reprinting below lies, then, not so much in the subjects treated, which are diverse, but rather in their common concern to build and maintain in health a movement that is both Reform and Judaism. All the contributors are keenly committed to the view that innovation is necessary if the religion is to remain in the mainstream of modern life. They are equally committed to the view that the religion for whose survival they are concerned is Judaism. The authors agree that a balance must be found between tradition and novelty; they differ on the question of how that balance is to be established. Which traditional elements are to be retained? which modified? which abandoned? What are the aspects of modern life that can properly be celebrated religiously? How can religious services be so designed as to appeal to an age that seems to have lost the knack of religious celebration? Which of the modern competing philosophies can be helpful in the rethinking of Judaism, and which must be combatted? Even when these questions are not explicitly discussed by the writers of these essays, it becomes clear in reading them that these are the underlying questions; these are the preoccupations of the rabbinical authors.

In selecting this group of papers for reprinting, the editor has been greatly disappointed to find that, especially in two fields of deep concern to the Reform rabbis, materials worthy of wider readership are lacking. The passion for social justice which has informed and adorned the Jewish tradition from the time of the pre-Exilic prophets (if not earlier) is inadequately represented among these formal papers. Among the possible reasons for this we may suggest that the age for verbal protestations of passionate commitment to social justice has passed. Words have a hollow ring save when they are the expression of active participation, and if one has already testified by his actions, words are no longer needed. Social goals for the modern world have been defined; to reiterate them may be politic, but it is hardly productive. As the world changes, new goals will emerge, to be stated in resolutions; but it is not resolutions that change the world.

Religious education, too, is a matter that has been focal in Jewish tradition from antiquity and remains of great importance to the rabbinic leaders of the Reform movement. Here, again, although there has been much labor in the production of curricula for religious schools, and provision of materials for study through critical evaluation and sponsorship of textbooks and classroom aids, and even some experimentation with newer techniques of education, the few essays on education in no way reflect the high quality of the work that has been done, or even the intensity of concern for education that has been shown by many of the Reform rabbis. Perhaps this, too, is the result of the fact that religious education can only be tested in the effects, so difficult to measure, of the classroom experiences in the later lives of the pupils. Later attitudes and later actions measure the effectiveness of educational practices; yet by the time these attitudes and actions are evinced, the times have changed so that generalizations from earlier experience may have no carry-over value.

For the rest, the papers selected here are truly representative of the range of subjects treated at the Conferences. The criteria for their selection have been the greater profundity or penetration of those chosen and the continuing interest of the discussion. These criteria, applied with as much consistency and acumen as possible, have produced a selection that does not completely represent the historical development of the Reform movement in America. That history falls into three periods. In the first, American Reform Judaism, though often verbally insistent on the desirability of giving Jewish expression to the distinctive character of its American *milieu* and its Americanizing clientele, was in reality a transplanted German Reform Judaism. Its outstanding leaders and the teachers at the Hebrew Union College were all trained in Central Europe, and for the most part held degrees from German universities. Their views were generally rationalistic; the reforms they proposed tended to be sweeping and thoroughgoing. They were in virtually total revolt against the "Talmudic-Rabbinic" tradition, and willing to discard without compunction the most ancient of traditions where these conflicted with "modern" ideas. Even circumcision which, whatever its ultimate origin, had been the "sign of the Covenant" since biblical times, was held to be dispensable; that the practice was not abandoned was probably a consequence of the fact that medical opinion began to consider circumcision valuable to health and, therefore, rationally justifiable.

They flirted with the idea of sacrificing the historic Sabbath to the patterns of Western economic life. Many congregations experimented with the holding of services on Sunday morning. Recommendations for a uniform transfer of the main service of the week to Sunday were never accepted by the total body of the Central Conference of American Rabbis, but the move to make this transfer was sufficiently widespread to induce the Conference to publish a special liturgy for congregational services on Sunday. An alternative proposal that did succeed, and that changed the face of Judaism in America, was to institute the "late" Friday evening service, a full length service on Friday evening, at an after-dinner hour, when families could attend together. These services included sermons, often disguised as "lectures," and even readings from the Torah, at least in English translation. This innovation in Reform Jewish practice proved acceptable not only to Reform congregations but also to many others, so that it has become all but universal in the Conservative movement and has been adopted by some Orthodox synagogues. The Friday evening service, under the conditions of twentieth-century American life, with its urban character, its sharp separation of the supportive economic life of the family from its residence and the consequent "absentee father," has had particular value in preserving the traditionally close character of the Jewish family, thus far. It remains to be seen whether it can continue to do so as the "absentee father" is increasingly replaced by "absentee children."

Any rationalistic movement will be faced with the problem of authority, for its very basis of organization is anti-organizational. Thomas Paine summed up the problem when he declared, "My own mind is my own church." If an association is to be fruitful, it must make some provision for internal discipline; when the association is based on voluntaristic principles, as rationalistic movements inevitably must be, like-mindedness tends to reduce to an agreement on the acceptability of differences of opinion. Charismatic leadership can temporarily obscure the problem of authority but even charismatic leaders die, and the problem recurs. In attempting to resolve the problem of authority, under perhaps the worst possible conditions, for not just modern rationalism but the whole modern ethos is in revolt against authority and the American spirit and example has been a leading force in this revolt, Reform Judaism explored the possibility of re-instituting some version of the ancient Palestinian "synod." In effect, this was to argue for a nineteenth-century German conception of a democracy in which all minds were equal, but some were more equal than others. The idea, though it was presented with considerable erudition and skill, was never accepted by the American Reform rabbis; if it had been, it would never have been accepted by their congregations.

Philosophically and theologically, the first period of American

Jewish Reform was almost totally dominated by the German idealistic tradition stemming from Immanuel Kant and his followers. There is considerable evidence that the discussion of evolution in the latter part of the nineteenth century had an influence upon the thought of the Reform rabbis. One reason is, certainly, that the notion of evolutionary change supplied a sanction for religious reform. Even the title of Isaac M. Wise's book, *The Cosmic God* (1876), suggests John Fiske's evolutionary *Outlines of Cosmic Philosophy*. But there is no sign that the rabbis of this time were aware of the revolution that was brewing in American philosophy under the spur of Charles S. Peirce, William James, and John Dewey. Of the Jewish thinkers of the nineteenth century, there is reference to Samuel Hirsch, Abraham Geiger, and Samuel Holdheim, but not much else until Zionism and Theodor Herzl become an issue. When Zionism begins to come to the fore, Caspar Levias was a rare, almost unique, instance of one who accepted and defended the idea of a restored Jewish nation.

By the time the second period began, after the First World War, virtually all of the earlier leaders had died or were too old to be very active. Leadership passed to a new generation, almost all of whom were American born, and of those who were not, most were educated in America. Reform Judaism was still the liberalism of the Central European Jew transplanted to America; although much was said about the possibility of making an approach to the Jewish masses who had migrated from Eastern Europe after the pogroms of the 1880s. There was even an attempt to have the "missionary" tracts of Reform Judaism translated into Yiddish, the mother tongue of the East European immigrants, so that they might not be discouraged by linguistic difficulties from learning about Reform Judaism. To a considerable extent, this was the crusade of a small group of rabbis in the cities on the East Coast of the United States, the receiving centers for the new immigration. The rabbis whose work was in the already Americanized heartland did not feel called to energetic attempts to convert the Yiddish-speaking newcomers.

The turning point from Reform Judaism's first American period to its second may have been America's entry into World War I, as an enemy of the German-dominated Central Powers. The American cultural environment, always prone to exaggerated postures and overstated, simplistic attitudes, turned with remarkable speed to an anti-Germanism reflected in such totalitarian excesses as the abolition of the teaching of the German language in schools, the programming of concerts with no German music, and even (perhaps an ultimate inanity) the re-naming of sauerkraut as "liberty cabbage." In the prevalent atmosphere it is not surprising that Reform Judaism, largely a movement of German ancestry, made every effort to present itself as a bulwark of Americanism. America had been a romantic element in German Jewish Reform even before its actual beginnings; in 1783 Moses Mendelssohn showed that he looked to America as already a land in which Jews might live a fully human existence. Later, this America of Jewish imagination was a major factor in the thought of Isaac M. Wise and Kaufmann Kohler. Soon after Kohler came to America he heard Wise preach in English and many years later he wrote, "I thanked God for having been permitted to come to America, the land of liberty and large opportunity to help, with the powers allotted to me, in the building up of American Reform Judaism, the religion of the future." Among the papers presented before the Central Conference of American Rabbis in the 1920s there are several that go to such extremes in identifying Judaism and Americanism that they are almost embarrassing to read.

In the larger picture, however, the effort to develop a program to Americanize Reform Judaism is more significant than the banality or naivete of any single contribution. One important factor in the shift was that, for the first time, an alumnus of Hebrew Union College, Rabbi Julian Morgenstern, was named president of that institution. American Jewish scholarship and academic prestige was certainly bolstered by this appointment. Yet it had its less fortunate aspect, too, for Morgenstern was a zealous Americanizer. The decade of the 1920s was, we must remember, a period of intense isolationism in the United States, and the Americanizing

Reform rabbis allowed themselves to be infected by this disease. Since the Reform movement had already discarded the concept of Jewish nationality in favor of the notion of a Jewish mission among the nations, the new isolationist attitude reinforced an anti-Zionist position that was, by resolution, the official stand of the Central Conference of American Rabbis.

A number of the members of the Conference did not accept the official stand as a guide for themselves, and Zionism was, throughout this period, more widely acceptable to the members of the Reform congregations than to the national bodies in which the Reform movement was organized. From year to year, Zionist members of the Central Conference presented resolutions designed to modify the anti-Zionist position but had no success until the middle of the 1930s. Perhaps the majority feared to compromise their hard-won status as one hundred or more per cent Americans by permitting antagonists to raise the question of double allegiance. Perhaps enough of the members were still enamored of the rational ideal of theological consistency to such a degree that they subordinated to it the irrational ideal of the brotherhood of all Jews. Whatever the reason or combination of reasons, the Central Conference did not alter its official position until after the rise of Nazism in Germany had made support for a land of refuge unavoidable. Once more, as so often in Jewish history, antisemitism succeeded in moving the Jews to a unity they were unable to achieve by themselves—but at what great cost!

The impulse to consistency, which had been of such vital concern to Reform Judaism of the earlier period, both in Germany and in the United States, faced challenge during the second period, as Jews of Eastern European background, with a different sense of religious priorities, began to enter the Reform community, both as lay members and as rabbis. Whatever the resolutions of the Conference and of the Union of American Hebrew Congregations might say about the exclusively religious character of Judaism, the notion of a resurgent nation restored to the ancient homeland exerted a strong emotional pull upon many Reform Jews. For this reason, the members of the Conference charged with editing a Hymnal for the Reform movement faced a difficult decision when the question of the inclusion of Naphtali Hirsch Imber's "Hatikvah" was at issue. By popular acceptance, if not in origin, "Hatikvah" was the "national" anthem of the Zionist movement, although it was not originally written for this purpose; for the Conference, committed by an earlier resolution to the non-Zionist position, its inclusion in the Hymnal would be inconsistent. Yet "Hatikvah" was the one outstanding example of a modern Jewish song, widely if not universally known, accepted, and loved; to have omitted it from the Hymnal would have amounted to a virtual denial of the brotherhood of contemporary Jewish life. Faced with this dilemma, the editors resolved their question by a sacrifice of consistency; "Hatikvah" was included in the Reform hymnal.

A similar problem arose over the continued use of the much-loved *kol nidre* prayer in the service for the Eve of the Day of Atonement. *Kol nidre,* a renunciation of all vows made during the previous year, had a clear function in the Judaism of the Middle Ages, when forced conversions were frequent. It gave the Jews who had been forced to take vows that they could not fulfil an opportunity to put themselves right with God, to clear their accounts. Yet, in the modern age, antisemites had seized upon the text of *kol nidre* to bolster their charge that a Jew's word could not be trusted. Moreover, as the European and American world had become increasingly secular and tolerant, forced conversion was most unlikely. In addition, the theological ideas, not only of the Reform Jews but of other more conservative Jews as well, had come to disapprove of the content of *kol nidre*. On the other hand, *kol nidre* had become so familiar an element of the service for the Eve of the Day of Atonement, so much the center of that ritual, that, in popular parlance, the service itself was called by its name, the *kol nidre* service. Not to have included this prayer of disclaimer would have been a disastrous failure to strike the note of continuity and warm familiarity. Once more, consistency of theological outlook gave way to an anticipation of popular demand. After the first printing, however, a compromise position was taken; the traditional chant was preserved, but the traditional words were removed.

In this period, too, the evidences of awareness of intellectual and religious currents in the American environment are many. The success of various forms of faith-healing cults, culminating in the considerable leakage of Jews into the Christian Science movement, worried the rabbis in the Central Conference. Some of them searched the Jewish tradition for evidence that faith-healing was not an alien importation and proposed that it be restored to significance in Reform Judaism; many of the rabbis became interested, but only a few went farther to establish a Jewish Science movement. It may well be that out of this study there developed something much more important than Jewish Science, namely, a concern for the latest knowledge in pastoral psychology and especially a more sensitive awareness of when to recommend psychiatric treatment.

The emergence, at this time, in the late 1920s, of a humanist movement, largely but not exclusively grounded in the naturalistic and pragmatic philosophy of John Dewey, aroused deep concern in many of the rabbis who presented papers before their colleagues in the Conference. The idealistic philosophy that had been the staple of the earlier generation was hospitable toward the use of traditional religious language, although the meanings it tried to convey in this language were quite often untraditional. The new humanism much preferred a language of everyday usage and of science and, therefore, seemed to mount an even greater threat to religionists than it actually did. Wholly apart from its language, humanism tended to interpret the world in categories of secular understanding. It was not the obvious enemy of religion, as was nineteenth-century materialistic rationalism, with its universe conceived totally in terms of matter and motion. Humanism, nevertheless, spoke in subtler tones of the universe as a process entirely taking place in time, composed of an infinite number of interlocking subsidiary processes. The beginning, if it could ever be known, would become known through scientific exploration, and the end, if it could ever be foreseen, would be predicted by scientific methods. Whatever might be the function of religion, humanism denied it any explanatory value. The Reform rabbis, acutely conscious that this scientific humanism was the dominant outlook in the colleges and universities, where an increasing number of their congregants' children were in attendance, devoted much consideration to ways of remaining in touch with youth of college age as well as directly attacking the humanist view in their papers before the Conference.

The third period of Reform Jewish history in the United States may, without too much inaccuracy, be said to date from the accession to power of Adolf Hitler in Germany. As early as 1934, Rabbi Martin Friedman warned his colleagues of the implications of Nazi antisemitism. At a time when most Americans, and many Jews among them, were insisting that Nazism was merely a temporary aberration of a noble, idealistic, and intelligent people, a disease from which they would soon recover, Friedman noted that it was precisely in the appeal to the idealism of the German people that the greatest danger of Nazism lay. It was at this time, too, that there appears in the essays printed in the *Yearbook,* the first indication that there were some among the Reform rabbis who were becoming aware of the newer versions of spirituality that were emerging from the existentialist current in European thought, especially in the work of Martin Buber. Some of Buber's reworkings of the legends of Hassidism had, it is true, been translated into English before this time, but his more philosophic writings were not available. Thus in an age when Nazism and depression marked the end of an optimistic and expansive mood in American Reform Judaism, there was a beginning of a turning inward, toward the individual, to seek to renew the roots of religious sentiment.

At this time too, as the fiftieth anniversary of the Pittsburgh Platform (1885-1935) came close, the Central Conference decided that it was anomalous for an organization that prided itself on its progressiveness and openness to change to remain totally identified with a statement of principles formulated half a century earlier, in a completely different cultural situation. The Program Committee, accordingly, set up a symposium format for the papers to be presented at the 1935 plenary meeting, with prepared papers followed by informal discussion on the three conventional subdivisions of Jewish religion: God, Torah, and Israel. Inevitably, the discussion on the first of these themes was not very stimulating, while the third led to a vigorous exchange on Zionism. In the discussion of the second theme, Torah, appears a clear statement of the widely accepted evolutionary interpretation of Torah as "progressive revelation," by Joseph Rauch: "Such an idea of revelation is as sacred . . . as any that has come from the past. . . . It explains even better than the traditional theory of revelation the halting spiritual progress of our people. It has the added advantage of being in harmony with the scientific theory of evolution" (XLV, 257). This idea of revelation as progressive probably would have been accepted by virtually all of the members of the Conference and was, in fact, incorporated in the "Guiding Principles of Reform Judaism" adopted by the Conference in 1937. It allows for the rejection of any doctrines or practices prescribed by earlier tradition as part of a now supplanted revelation, and at the same time gives authoritative sanction to contemporary decisions as the current higher form of revelation.

Apart from the years of World War II, there is little indication in this third period of the intense concern for American identification of the previous periods. The American character of the Reform movement is by now something to be taken for granted by the rabbis, not to be desired or to be proved. It is more the Jewish character of Reform Judaism that is asserted, and the need for a refreshing of the spirit at the wellsprings of the Jewish tradition. The "Guiding Principles" accepted by the 1937 Conference as a replacement for the now antiquated Pittsburgh Platform qualified the universalism of the earlier statement by referring to Judaism as "the historical religious experience of the Jewish people." The Principles regarded Torah as revealed truth, but asserted that "each age has the obligation to adapt the teachings of the *Torah* to its basic needs in consonance with the genius of Judaism." The last phrase clearly suggests the greater concern of the third period for the Jewishness of Reform Judaism. This concern is brought out most forcefully in the section of the Principles dealing with religious practice:

> Judaism as a way of life requires in addition to its moral and spiritual demands, the preservation of the Sabbath, festivals and Holy Days, the retention and development of such customs, symbols and ceremonies as possess inspirational value, the cultivation of distinctive forms of religious art and music, and the use of Hebrew, together with the vernacular, in our worship and instruction.

No longer on the defensive about their Americanism, the members of the Central Conference of American Rabbis seem, in the Guiding Principles of Reform Judaism, to have gone on the defensive with regard to their Judaism.

Relieved, by the neutral plank of 1937, of the role of actively opposing Zionism and, by a further, more positive resolution in 1943, admitting the full compatibility of Zionism and Reform Judaism, the Central Conference of American Rabbis and its members were freed from the most divisive issue in their history. They were able now to devote much time and thought to ways in which to redirect the attention of their congregants to such notions as that of *mitzva*, religious obligation, *halakha*, the way of life, and authority. They could attempt to discover ways of halting the erosion of the centrality of the synagogue in Jewish life and thus restoring a sense of communion, of religious community, which had been corroded into a sense of merely secular identification. The papers of the *Yearbook* since 1937 have been concerned with problems of this sort and are, therefore, much more relevant for the contemporary reader. There has been, in addition, a renewed concern with basic theological questions, faced now with a philosophic sophistication that was almost completely absent during the second period. It is from these papers that the bulk of those selected for this volume have been chosen.

III

To have arranged the twenty-four selected papers in a straight-forward chronological order would have had some value in giving the reader a sense of this historical development, but it would have failed to show that, underlying the periodization, there is a continuity of concern with certain themes that are basic to an understanding of any movement within Judaism. The order that has been followed is one that largely disregards chronology in the interest of a more systematic approach designed to bring out the persistent themes of discussion in the Central Conference of American Rabbis. Each theme is, however, treated from different standpoints and brought to varying conclusions by several authors. The arrangement is, thus, a demonstration of the vitality that pluralism introduces into the deliberations of even a religious organization.

Despite the conventional history of the Jews and of Judaism, pluralism has always been a factor in Jewish religious life. The Bible, the Talmud, and the Midrash all bear witness to the existence within Judaism at all periods of differences of view and conclusions. When we add the evidence of the divergences of the many forms of Diaspora Judaism, it is clear that the terms "Judaism" (like its companion-terms, "Christianity," "Islam," "Hinduism," "Buddhism") encompasses a range of alternative interpretations of a common core of attitudes and beliefs which is, itself, not monolithic. Neither in its differences from other varieties of Judaism in the modern era nor in its lack of internal uniformity is Reform Judaism an unusual phenomenon in Jewish life. Its pluralism has, perhaps, been strengthened by the pluralistic American surroundings in which it has had its most extensive growth and influence. There is, certainly, a difference between the (largely German-inspired) language of the Pittsburgh Platform of 1885, with its suggestion of a single view for all Reform Judaism, and the 1937

Guiding Principles of Reform Judaism, which claims only to suggest, not to define. Yet it is not to pluralism that we must look to understand the distinctive quality of American Reform Judaism.

That quality arises, rather, from the voluntary character of religious life in America. Other forms of Judaism have come into being in circumstances in which adherence to one or another religious group was a necessity for the life of the individual. The ultimate option of disaffiliation was not an open possibility. In the United States, practically from the beginning of its history, disaffiliation has been a "live option." This is, of course, as true for the other branches of American Judaism as it is for the Reform movement. It was Reform Judaism, however, that first broke through the unthinking (and uninformed) traditionalism of earlier American Judaism to a recognition of both the strengths and the weaknesses of the voluntary nature of religious organization in America. The very creation of the Union of American Hebrew Congregations was an exercise in voluntary-ism. The Central Conference of American Rabbis was only the second permanent rabbinic organization in Jewish history to have been established on a voluntary basis. It was preceded only by the German *Allgemeiner Rabbiner Verband* (1884). Again, other branches of Judaism have followed the lead of the Conference, and even outside of the United States, changed conditions in other countries have led to the formation of comparable organizations.

There are disadvantages, as well as benefits, in the voluntary situation. One is that leaders can lead only as far as their followers will follow. The role of the leader becomes, therefore, far less dominant; wholly apart from any general identity-crisis felt by people in the twentieth century, and from the identity-crisis of Jews in the modern world, there is, as the papers below attest, a special identity-crisis felt by rabbis in a voluntary synagogue. Each proponent of a way to restore a sense of religious obligation seems perpetually to be looking back over his shoulder to see whether anyone else is there. It is interesting to note that this is particularly true when the essays deal with more practical "performance" aspects of Judaism, rather than with theoretical aspects. The Reform rabbis, like their predecessors for many centuries, are free within the broad limits of the Jewish tradition to think as they will; they do not feel the same degree of freedom to act as they will, or to propose a type of action for the members of their congregations save on a voluntary basis.

As a result, the effects of this rabbinic "identity-crisis" are to be seen in the sections below that collect papers on ritual and ceremonies, law and authority. When, for example, W. Gunther Plaut, in 1965, discussed ways of overcoming "the attenuation of Sabbath observance," he asserted that this decay of the Sabbath tradition was "related to the popular confusion of Reform Judaism with extreme permissiveness" and advocated the compilation of a Reform *halakha*. Some years earlier, in 1942, in a mordant critique of the failings of Reform Judaism, William G. Braude suggested, as a means of stemming the tide of disintegration, the development of small voluntary groups within the synagogue membership of those who were devoted to restoring the spirit of holiness. Out of such groups, he thought, an organic *halakha* might ultimately emerge; these new "pharisees" would "build a fence around holiness" as the Pharisees of olden times had "built a fence around the Law." To attempt to produce a Reform *halakha* by action of an *ad hoc* committee of the Central Conference of American Rabbis would be an enterprise doomed to failure. Braude would take advantage of voluntarism to restore the sense of obligation, while Plaut would restore the sense of obligation as a means of controlling voluntarism rampant.

It seems evident that these are differences in tactics, not in strategy. They concern questions of what to do first, not what end is to be sought. The end is, from the earliest meeting of the Central Conference of American Rabbis in 1889 to its latest, as of this writing, in 1969, to forward the preservation of Jews and Judaism in a world that oscillates between the desire for Jewish survival and a hostility to it. There is a basic agreement among the members of this group of leaders of Reform Judaism that for Judaism truly to survive as a vital force *in* the modern world, it must be *of* the modern world. Ultimately the Reform rabbis would agree with Solomon Schechter that it is not Judaism that determines what the Jewish people is, but rather the Jewish people that determines what Judaism is—though it is only fair to say that they would not agree with him in their definition of what follows from this principle. Since some part of the Jewish people, that part which constitutes the public served by the Reform movement, is convinced that Judaism can be relevant in the world of the twentieth century only by a radical modernization of its practices and at least its peripheral beliefs, the thrust of most of the essays here reprinted is toward the definition of a modernization that is not alien to the spirit of the Jewish tradition. Thus, from another point of view, each of these essays attempts to come to grips with some prior aspect of the Jewish tradition and to learn from it how to reform—or at least reformulate—it.

In the end, perhaps, we may generalize the statement with which Samuel Atlas concludes his profound study of the contemporary relevance of Moses Maimonides: "The most significant lesson which the understanding of Maimonides' philosophy teaches is that with Maimonides we can supersede Maimonides." In the early years of the Reform movement in America it was the aim of the rabbis to supersede the ancient Jewish tradition by creating a new tradition based upon alien philosophies and wholly rational grounds. The newer Reform leaders speak otherwise, for they say that the most significant lesson which the understanding of the ancient tradition teaches is that it is only with the ancient tradition that we can supersede the ancient tradition.

ON THE NATURE OF THE REFORM MOVEMENT

An Early Statement of Radical Reform

WHEN EMIL G. HIRSCH, one of the outstanding preachers in the Reform movement at the turn of the century, agreed to present a paper at an early meeting of the Central Conference of American Rabbis, he felt himself very much on the defensive. He was the son of Samuel Hirsch, a philosopher and leader in the more radical wing of the German Reform movement. Samuel Hirsch came to the United States soon after the Civil War and began his American ministry at Philadelphia. With David Einhorn of Baltimore, the elder Hirsch stood for a continuation of radical Reform on the American scene, while Isaac M. Wise followed a more conservative line, hoping for a unification of American Jewry.

From the perspective of nearly a century later, the chief difference between the two factions, as it emerges from Emil G. Hirsch's paper on "The Philosophy of the Reform Movement in American Judaism," was not philosophical at all. It was the readiness of the radical group to transfer the observance of the Sabbath from Saturday to Sunday to conform to the prevalent patterns of employment in American economic life. Philosophically, both groups were firmly committed to rationalism, revealing a keen distrust of any mystical or even romantic ideas. Both groups placed their emphasis on the moral aspects of Judaism, dismissing the ritual and ceremonial laws as out of date. Both embraced ardently the notion that Judaism and all other religions revealed a progressive evolution through their history. And, finally, both rejected the nationalist idea, in firm commitment to Isaianic universalism.

23

THE PHILOSOPHY OF THE REFORM
MOVEMENT IN AMERICAN JUDAISM
Emil G. Hirsch
(1895)

... FROM ACROSS THE OCEAN speed to us congratulatory messages in words of despair and doubt over the conditions prevailing in the lands where they dwell that send the greeting. "America, American Judaism, thou art the hope of these days," is the common burden. From England, but during the last week, this encouraging and cheering acknowledgment reached me, and from Germany has often traversed the ocean similar apostrophe. And yet we, in America, during the last two years have begun to despair of our own situation. Things are going to the bad. Our religion, so runs the warning, is fatally contaminated with disease. The world is losing its idealism, and we are the first to yield the victory to treasonable doubt leaning towards materialism.

Some urge that things were better in the olden days. Were they? Have we cause to despair? Is the diagnosis of our situation based on facts? I doubt it. After periods of great activity always supervene dreary stretches of disquieting lassitude. The struggle for Reform among us has made heavy drafts on our spiritual forces. They could not sustain the tension. Fields must lie fallow in fixed intervals, that the yield shall be all the greater in after days. Religion, too, is under the law of the Sabbatical year. Priests cannot expect their tithes therefrom. The relaxation now upon us could have been foretold. It need not worry us! Besides the masses are never stirred. It is the few that carry the burdens always of every progress. This is, I apprehend, good Jewish doctrine. The "remnant," שארית alone will be saved. A "remnant" among us does, indeed, betray most solid activity. The flame of their enthusiasm does not burn low. One who would weigh the sacrifices brought as a free-will offering by the Jews in this country, in behalf of Judaism, cannot conclude, except in moments of bitter disenchantment, such as visit noble souls, impatient of the slow pace of shuffling feet where wings alone should flap with boldest stroke, that there is no balm in Gilead. I fancy most of us suffer from a most insidious deception. They are *malades imaginaires*. The ills we complain of are more fancied than real. The catalogue of our shortcomings, our disarrangements, is by no means so rich in variety, or so terribly suggestive of immediate fatalities as some famous physicans have declared it to be. The "tired feeling" will be overcome. A, by no means serious, cerebral congestion is not beyond relief. Why, then, advise suddenly that the treatment be changed from ice baths to hot vapor cure? Ice bags may perhaps not be indicated, but this cannot lead to the antipodal alternative of drastic tropical applications.

I suspect, more or less by sheer dint of habit, we fall into the minor key of Jeremiah, sitting by the ruins of Jerusalem and singing lamentations. Yet Jeremiah himself had predicted not merely the fall and exile. He had bodied forth in as fiery words the unshaken confidence that Egyptian deliverance would pale in the memory of men before the greater glory of the redemption from captivity. He himself had taught a God without a temple (היכל ה')! Modern Jeremiahs have undoubtedly as deep a cause to weep and to forget the stronger utterances of their former days. Finely spun souls, delicately strung harps vibrate easily to love's pathetic disappointment. The stronger their loyalty, the greater is their alarm lest harm befall the object of their solicitude. And the very intensity of their attachment leads them to detect symptoms of dreaded decay where the more hopeful eyes of trusting Isaiahs cannot for the life of them apprehend extraordinary danger. I make bold to say that among us there is no provocation for however honest and self-sacrificing a Jeremiah to intone lamentation. The old temple of medieval Ghetto Judaism may be in ruins, but the new one of Messianic Judaism is taking shape. It is true but little noise is made by its builders. But such is always the case, where true sanctuaries of God are constructed. While that of Solomon was rearing, no sound of hammer or axe was heard. God's architects work silently. The clanking of mallet, the shriek of chisel are hushed where they instruct the masons. If noise be sign of religious ardor, the shouting Derwish must be credited with the flush of healthiest heart, throbbing to the rhythm of religion's appeal. Am I mistaken when I say that the genius of Judaism is averse to this froth of religious fervor? Salvation-army-hallelujah-methods create the presumption of hectic fever; but never does the quiet disinclination of him who shrinks to *speak* the holiest thoughts, suggest a constitutional disorder. In religion, as in everything else, the day of loud things marks the barbaric age; as culture advances, subdued silence takes the place of erstwhile strenuous sound. I, for my part, see on all sides abundant evidences that a new Jerusalem is arising. Of course, not yet has it attained unto its ultimate stateliness: not yet crown altar and holy of holies the waiting hills; not yet ring out the Levitical choirs, nor make the circuit solemn, priestly bands. But even so, the workers are busy, and their zeal makes one forget that the lance of defense must keep company to the trowel of peace, in the hands of the artisans. Ah! indeed, a new life is budding forth! As in the world abroad, religion is ever more and more bidden complement what science lacks; as to her to-day poetry, philosophy, the arts begin again to minister; so in our own home a new morn is about to dawn. What will it bring? There be such as hope from it the restoration of the old order; there be others—and among these I range myself—that are confident that the new day will wake the new Jerusalem, the new Judaism child of the old, to greater opportunities. This divergence of hope need not surprise. Whenever men fall into brooding dissatisfaction at the conditions by which they are surrounded, two ways open before them, by either of which they may seek to be relieved. One is to face about, to coax the past to burst the portals of its tombs. This is both the method and the motive of what is technically styled Romanticism. It remains life into the dead. Religion is not the exclusive field for this play of fancy, though naturally it is most apt to be invaded thereby. Politics, philosophy, poetry and the arts were also exposed to the attack. Before the burst of mad 1848, Germany was under its dominion. No wonder that German Judaism was potently affected by its spirit. If Germany is the cradle of Reform, it is also the nurse of Neo-orthodoxy, as taught by S. R. Hirsch and the Romantic school that took its cue from him. The year 1859 dealt the philosophy of Romanticism its death-blow. Darwin taught us a truer appreciation of the function of the past as a conditioning, yet stimulating preparation for the future. No Gabriel may arouse from death-slumber what time has laid to rest, however loud his trumpets blare. Resurrection is wrought, not by repetition, but by growth; continued life in fuller measure immortalizes the parent germ of which it sprang. Romanticism, at all events, has failed most woefully to redeem its pledges. At its bidding, new life would not leap from the ruins. However it tried, in the arts and in the church, to spread the thought-atmosphere of the middle ages, the sun would pierce its artificially created gloom. Julian, the Apostate, had with the ebbing breath of his dying hour to acknowledge his defeat. As in his days paganism was out of reason and rhythm with the fuller needs of his generation, so in ours, Romanticism cannot bridge, except in its own conceit the chasm gaping between the nearing twentieth and the long-departed fourteenth centuries. In Judaism, Ghetto and American freedom cannot be joined in holy wedlock. Theirs is a case of *Killayim,* if ever there was one. Under the hypnotism of Romanticism a pretender draped in garments in which the true medieval spirit could not have found ease of movement or comfort, usurps the throne of a deluded hope. We paint in glowing colors the life of our forefathers, as we think it was before the wicked spirit of reform had run rampant, when radicalism was not yet known. Then indeed, so we hold, hearts were filled with God's love, homes were aglow with God's joy, young and old were strenuously pious and virtuous. We might make a test of the truth of this assertion. If we find it true, we shall follow the trumpet, though it sound not the advance, but in warning blare forth the retreat.

This test is not a matter of literary research. It is one of actual and easily obtainable experience. The resurrected or galvanized medieval Judaism we have at our very door. If we so wish, we may daily brush against it. In Chicago we need but cross the river to come into populous districts never invaded by radicalism, defended by time-knit bastions against the inroads of our skepticism in all its deceptive temptation. We pay our visit in an expectant spirit, but we find, to say the least, no higher morality than obtains among us but instead of religious ardor, mechanical drudgery and thoughtless habit. We find in bolder shamelessness those things of which we ourselves complain. Atheists and materialists swarm in these by-streets as numerously, to be moderate, as they are said to hive among the radicals. The "faith of the fathers" seems, then, not to be the all-sufficient sea-wall against the devastation that has visited us. According to the diagnosis of the men who are our Jeremiahs, weeping over the fall of Jerusalem and pointing to the Jerusalem that once was as that to be rebuilt by us, we should meet in our quest a different state of affairs.

But there is another way to overcome our natural sense of dis-content. It is not to look toward the past, but to look onward, upward, to the future. Why this dissatisfaction? It is not with us because we have departed too far, but because we have not ad-vanced far enough. Half-hearted measures never satisfy. Our inconsistencies have wrought their revenge. Of reform we have had not too much, but not enough. Onward and upward let us march! It is thus that we can cure whatever now puts us so ill at ease. This at least is my deepest conviction. What is the fundamental note of our reform movement? To state it briefly, its watchword and motive is "not out of Judaism, but into Judaism." Our burning passion is not to have less, but to have more of Judaism. Never has Reform Judaism striven after less of Judaism.

But, says one, what is Judaism? Give us a definition. Crystalize its content in a few concise words! May a process of three thousand

years of life, of suffering, of aspiration, of martyrdom, of missionary seed sowing in behalf of self and others, three thousand years
of heroism and yearning after the Highest, of thought on the deepest
themes of life and universe be defined in two or three lines? Moses
the Pentateuch and we—two lines of definition? The Talmud, folio
volumes in Babylon and in Palestine; and we—one or two con-
densed paragraphs? But Webster has a definition. Of course, if
Webster has a definition we ought to yield. But why a definition?
In order to guide your life accordingly? No! that lawyers may sue
out writs of *quo warranto* to deny to me, to you, to others the right
to the name Jew! A definition is asked for, not to invite into
Judaism, but to expel and exclude the best therefrom.

What is Judaism? If we reformers claim that we are actuated by
the holy desire, passionately to have more of Judaism, and not less,
we must know what Judaism implies. I know what Judaism is,
and many more, I am sure, are not in doubt. I knew one who
knew what Judaism is; what I know of it I learned from him. He
sleeps in Chicago. His grave is marked by a column, not erected
by his congregation but by that of his son; on the shaft is written
what for him, what for me Judaism inculcates, whence it issued
and whither it tends.

The road to the knowledge of Judaism's distinctive doctrine is by
no means difficult to find and to travel. The method of study is
simple. You who would ascertain what Judaism is, consult first its
literature and then compare what you discovered in the books with
what is known of other religions. By this method one cannot but
succeed in tracing the original contribution made by Judaism to the
wealth of religious ideas of the world; what Judaism has given to
humanity, what its genius has created, what its history has evolved,
what to-day it points to as the ideal of Jewish future,—this and
nothing else is Judaism. It is, indeed, not impossible to explain,
though it is to define, what Judaism is. A definition may indeed
be put in one's pocket and carried about ready for consultation, but
does this not recall the fetich worshipper who trundles about his
fetich and is careful to hide it when its presence and exposition

would be inconvenient? Let us then, pursue the truer method in our search for the one thought which runs through all Jewish literature; the one stream of tendency making one for all time the people and the religion that have created this literature. Would I find out what Rome was, even if Rome were swept from the face of the earth, I should invite Roman literature to speak to me. Would I have an insight into the Roman spirit, its writers would grant me my desire. If, as the ages follow one the other, I find that ever and again some fundamental note is struck and worked into new melody, this one fundamental note strikes for me the song deathless of the Roman spirit. At the same time it reveals the contribution made by Rome to the world that needed the message, and was made all the richer for it. In this manner, and for this purpose, I approach for Judaism, Jewish literature. What is the one stream of tendency flowing through all the ages and pages? It is the awful thought of God, in ever clearer and clearer lines, apprehended as the centuries expand.

It is a mistake to hold that the Jewish God-idea was identically conceived of, in all its diverse aspects by the successive generations of its preachers. Even among the prophets that recorded their stirring thoughts in the pages of Biblical literature, there is clearly discernible an unfolding of the conception tending from localization and anthropomorphism to universalization and spiritualization. Isaiah I. was, for instance, certainly convinced that Jerusalem and Yahweh were so interwoven that no fear for the destruction of the state's capital need be entertained; while Jeremiah had outgrown this stage of theological thought and Isaiah II. sets the God-conception to the music of an all-embracing humanity as wide as the inhabited globe. Again Philo's theology is not coincident in all its views with that of the wisdom-books, nor is it in one plane with that of the Talmudic doctors. Even in the systems of our mediaeval thinkers diversities abound, and these not always on minor issues, not to mention the Kabbalistic speculations which seem to have abandoned altogether the strictly unitarian basis. The unity of Jewish theology is nevertheless a fact. For from the first to the last, whatever the differences, Jewish God-conception involves a

high appreciation of man's dignity and destiny. The center of gravity
is not metaphysics but ethics. To explain the universe, the Jew
starts with the exploration not of the stellar sky but of the storm-
tossed human heart. The experiences therein culled, point the interpretation of nature and rob it of the question marks otherwise
unanswerable. If Greek philosophy was a "brilliant failure," it was
so because it began with the extra-human, and then would arrive at
man. Judaism, inverting the order, began with man and from him
rose to the cognition of God. This is the lesson of Genesis! Creation by the divine Creator is intended to lead up to—man that he
might find God. Man is the first in the idea תחלה במחשבה of God's
creative purpose, though he is the last, yea the end in the order of
its ascending realization סוף במעשה.

For this cannot be repeated too often: The Jewish God is more
than a mere affirmation of even the one in all and the all in one.
The Jewish God, according to Jewish teachers, has a sanctuary not
made of stone, a temple not built even of the stars that glow in the
night, not by the flowers that bloom afresh every springtide. His
testimony is not alone in the silvery rivers that rill in Runic rimes,
proclaiming God through field and forest, over meadow and mountain. The sanctuary of this Jewish God is the human heart. God
created the all, but creation culminates in man and him, made in the
image of God. This conception is basic to Jewish monotheism.
And man was created in the image of God not alone pristinely, but
for all time is he fashioned in the likeness of his Maker. Compare
with this fundamental proposition of Judaism what all other religions teach on this matter. You will discover that this fundamental
thought is original and distinctive revelation by the genius of Judaism, by the prophets immortal and uncompanied in the history of
all humanity. Before the prophets sounded this revelation's eternal
appeal, man was considered as but one of the many things moulded
under the law of death and dust, knowing no higher aim in life but
the elemental one of dust. Even after this prophetic message had
gone out to humanity, by systems and churches its import was not
grasped. The elemental man was wrecked when Greek thought had

culminated in stoic resignation and epicurean revelry. But the off-spring of both Judaism and Greece, theological Christianity dwarfed into a shadowy hope as it had degraded it to a terrible doom, the insistence on man's original divinity. One being alone was divine. All others had lost this rare gift. By faith in the one divine in his atoning death, alone could, and then for world to come, divinity be restored to humanity. Buddhism despairs of man altogether! Life is a fatal error. Its sympathy is negative. Its hope—nothing. Islam proclaims the one God five times each day in the muezzin's call to prayer. Yet what is man? God is supreme. His omnipotence leaves no room for man in this world. He has not the power to change himself or others. He must submit. The will of God is the sum of his philosophy—involving suicide of his moral self.

But Judaism proclaims that God is one factor in the moral universe and man is another. In every human heart God and man meet, for in man, divine creation finds its completion and interpretation, the song of eternity its temporal, yea, its eternal versification and verification. This assurance is the contribution of Judaism to religion. It is one of the cornerstones of our religious philosophy. But there is a second. It is the conception of the Jewish mission to proclaim this ideal of God and man to mankind. The prophets —revelation—were found by this truth. Their people God's grace had called to this service, as he had endowed them with the sight, to read aright the eternal problems of the universe and of human life and given them voice to teach the truth that had found them. The people of the prophets, "the people of the book," have in the economy of humanity this vocation, because they are of one family with these seers, of one historic race, I might say. This people had assumed the obligation in its own individual and social life to illustrate the truth of this discovery: God and God-like man. The historic consciousness that Judaism calls for this high exemplification of man's divinity, this fundamental precept and principle of our religion, is the other basis on which Judaism rests. This it is, the sentiment of responsibility for ideas and ideals revealed by seers in his books, which differentiates the Jew from the non-Jew. His it is to prove by his life the doctrine that man is divine, that the Creator has made man to be on earth what God is in the universe, to be in time what God is in eternity. The Jew will stand before the world in his own life individually and in the community with other Jews, to demonstrate the possibility of living out, in beauty and truth, this prophetic doctrine which finds God dwelling in every truly human heart. These two thoughts distinguish Judaism from every other form of religious thought. They determine our relations to Unitarianism. The Jewish conception of life does not event in false optimism. This world is to be unto beauty indeed, and human life is to be indeed perfection. But this world is not yet beauty, and the human life is not yet perfection. Jewish idealism is meliorism, it flowers in the consciousness that morality is aggressive, that the moral life means resistance to evil, conquest of evil, activity in behalf of common humanity to make life more real and the world more worthy. "Not לתהו ובהו for chaotic strife, atomistic selfishness was earth created; לשבת for habitation was it destined." This Isaianic proposition furnishes the key to the Ideograms of Jewish ethics. "Holy shall ye be, for I the Lord your God, am holy," is the first tone in the melody of Jewish ethics built upon the apprehension of God and man as at one. For the mission of Judaism is the illustration of this oneness of God and the at-oneness of man with his Creator ruling in time and in all the eternities.

Sanctification in the Jewish sense of the word, does not mean what so often we are told it does, a sort of—what shall I say?—airy heavenward etherealism. The claim that because we are made of dust and dusty, earth and earthy, we are not capable of reaching out after the divine; that life real is a burden, its healthy, natural throbbings are undivine, this Judaism, though it roots in sanctification, cannot concede. The Jewish saint will, therefore, never withdraw from life. God, according to the Jewish anthropology, creates man pure. Every babe that knocks at life's door, comes bathed in purity, not laden with sin; but the purity of man shall be changed by man into sanctity, his one glory, through struggle, through con-

stant effort and discipline, which will not end till life itself shall
cease, which will not end, I say, in yonder life, which, as I hope,
will be continuation in God of appointed service. "There is no rest
for the wicked," is true enough. But Judaism eclipses all other religious suns by teaching that "there is no rest for the righteous."
צדיקים אין להם מנוחה לא בעולם הזה ולא לעולם הבא,

Sanctification, in this or any other life, is through effort, pain
and discipline. It is not quietude, composure, resignation; it is
action, unrest, resistance, against evil in all its forms, besetting the
human heart. The flesh is not to be killed, it is to be conquered
that it might serve the higher purpose of mind and soul. Asceticism
has no foothold in Judaism. A healthy zest for life has always characterized its saints. If a cloud curtained the horizon of some of the
rabbis, it was not woven of imputed sin or the consciousness of
man's sinfulness. Theirs was the grief that Jerusalem was in ruins.
How could they sing for joy when the temple and Zion called for
mourning? For individual ethics, no better foundation has been
devised than the principle of sanctification, as inculcated by Judaism. The empty formalism of Kant's categorical imperative was no
advance beyond it, nor was it robbed of its legitimate rights, when
"sweetness and light" rehabilitated the debilitating dogma of Paulinianism in a most insidious way. Sanctification of the individual is
the portal to a social organization resting on justice, the second
emphasis of our ethical faith. Indeed, none other than Judaism
has clarioned the appeal for justice. It is the passion of our prophets, who are theological pathfinders simply because they are social
reformers. Righteousness, צדקה in the Jewish interpretation, is
conduct flowing from the recognition of his divinity in every human
being. The murderer's argument, "Am I my brother's keeper?"
has no voice in Judaism. According to Jewish anthropology one
man is the keeper of every other man. What he is, he is for others.
What he holds he holds for others, and he must so use what he has
received as to profit all humanity, he must bear in mind his stewardship to those who pilgrim along the same path of earth. Social
righteousness is included thus in Jewish monotheism, as is sanctity

as the principle of the individual life.

And the third deduction from these fundamental ideas wings the golden dream of the future. God's kingdom come—on earth. There have been men without dreams of the future. Yet the people die for lack of vision. Old nations located the perfect state behind them.

Other religions speak of a paradise lost to be regained somewhere beyond the clouds. Judaism points to a future to be won here, and not by one, by all humanity. It is true, the picture of the future state, as painted by the prophets and cherished by Israel in centuried exile, displays politico-national coloring. Yet even so, it abounds in tints glorifying the triumph of justice universal, simultaneous with national restoration. The latter was only an episode in the great oratorio of universal redemption. We have learned to forget the national incident personified in the Messianic king, in the grander outlook into the Messianic age of universal justice and worthiness ascendant. It has been well said, Christianity pivots on individual salvation, Judaism hinges on social redemption and regeneration. The *'Olam Habba* of our religion is not a state *in heaven*. It is God's Kingdom *on earth*. ימליך מלכותה his kingdom come has been the one prayer of all Jews. It is the source of their consolation, when death breaks a link in the chain of their family love. One is tempted to say, it is the confession of the Jewish faith as legitimately as is the solemn invocation of Deuteronomy; the "Sh'ma'."

These ethical principles, then, founded on the apprehension of God's unity, *i.e.,* the oneness of the universal purpose running through creation, its essential righteousness, and of God's and man's *at-one-ness,* are the characteristic contribution made by Judaism to man's wealth. They constitute the one pillar of Judaism, while the other is the self-consciousness of the Jew rooted in his sense of responsibility for the illustration and spreading abroad during days of good and bad report, by example, of these ideas original in his historic life. The Jew being in the historic line of descent, the heir of those who first learned to view man and God in such relation, receives by birth the duty to illustrate by his own life and his own conduct that man is divine, that sanctity is not denied him, that justice may be done on earth, to emphasize his belief in the final triumph of righteousness and love and humanity in the Messianic age, God's Kingdom come.

So Judaism is, after all, not a mere religion; it is more than a religion which one may accept or reject.

No Jew has the right to accept or reject Judaism. It is a call, a duty, that comes to him with the accident of birth from Jewish mother, or let me rather say, it is providential appointment! We cannot choose our parents; we cannot elect our duties. Some would desert; what boot to them? The curse follows them, haunts them. Blood in their case is a stigma which water will not wash. A Reform Jew will never abandon his historic post. He understands that the Jew is called to be the illustrator of prophetic fundamental conceptions and principles which solve the riddle of the universe and also answer the enigmas of the human heart. This Judaism, the radical believes in and would practice. It is this Judaism of which the radical wants more, not less. The radical realizes that to carry out their mission the Jews shall live lives of righteousness. If from righteousness they depart, they commit blasphemy; they deny God "Hillul Hashem." For it is only by the righteous life illustrating the divinity of man, that this divinity is verified. Judaism is under law —the law of righteousness; but in no other sense is the Jew under the law.

But how may we reconcile with this limitation to the moral law, the apparent justification by Pentateuch and Talmud of the Paulinian and our own orthodox construction, that Judaism and nomism are exchangeable terms?

Biblical criticism has come to our aid, though it is the bugbear of people who are afraid that its results are apt to shatter all belief in the unique character of Judaism and the Bible. Woe unto Bibliolatry afraid of Hebrew grammar. Bibliolatry is not Jewish. Bible was never the only source of Jewish revelation. Woe unto a theology that is so little sure of its truth as to dread the searchlight of scientific investigation. Does Biblical criticism destroy? You cannot destroy the Bible. It is here with us. It is the echo of the human heart, of the history of Judaism during two thousand years of its spiritual growth. Whatever criticism or construction you choose to pass or place upon these books not one tittle of their moral and spiritual influence may be impaired. Bible criticism, however, separates the Jewish element in the Bible from the originally non-Jewish. It establishes beyond the peradventure of a single doubt, the fact that Judaism, in its prophetic sense, was before the law was. Are the Milah, the sacrifices, the laws of Levitical purity of Jewish origin? Can they then be held to be essential and distinctive? Biblical criticism proves that they are not. Their application to body the prophetic message is Jewish, but this message is essential, its symbolic dress is not. God, says the prophet, and after him the Jew, must be served in the living righteousness; by the prophets of those days in theory, no ceremonial law would have been tolerated, no sacrifices would have been legalized. In practice, they had to make a compromise. They utilized originally non-Jewish rites to convey the essentially Jewish thought of sanctification and righteousness.

How later Jewish law developed, is a familiar story. Ezra, in his systematic effort to make the "seed of Abraham"—the "priest people"—could not but accentuate the legal levitical code, as guarding rigidly the "racial" purity of the sacerdotal community. Life nevertheless continued to insist upon recognition. Hermeneutics trestled the fiction that codes were still regulative, in the very act of twisting the letter of the law to new and wider applications. The struggle between Pharisee and Sadducee lent new impulse to ceremonialism, while Essene apparently moulded into shape the ritualism of the liturgy. Rome, the lawyer of the world, had easy play to confirm the legalistic preoccupation of the schools, while Christianity, denationalizing Judaism and developing the theory of love as opposed to the revelation of law, could not but arouse opposition lending new emphasis to the discarded legal and national range of Jewish thought. Exile and expatriation, hope of the ulti-

mate restoration completed the successive impulses toward legalism. The "fence around the law" was the surest rampart of safety
against national disintegration. Medieval scholasticism did the rest
to establish Jewish nomism. For all this, Judaism is not—law! It
is not so in the Biblical prophetic books; it is not in the wisdom
literature. It is not in the apocrypha, largely of Essenic predisposi-
tion; it is not even in the Talmud, the Haggadah being both universal and ethical in its sympathies and outlooks. Now, as in the
prophetic, in the wisdom books of the Bible, Judaism is not law;
as in the Talmud, in the Haggadah it is morality and humanity:—
So Reform Judaism is the jubilant reassertion that life, not law,
that justice and love for man is the best illustration of the principles
the Jew avows, in his faith in God. Of course, ideas, in order to
bring their influence to bear upon the will and the sentiments of
men, need the beauty of the symbol. The age of symbolism is by
no means spent. Those that so hold are strangers in the workshop
of the human aspirations! Even the soul needs crutches in its weak
moments of halting hesitation, and wings in the hours of its bold
upward flight. The radical indeed understands full well that the
paradisical age of nudity, if it ever was more than barbarism, has
finally passed away, even in the world of thought. What is language
but symbol? What is art but sentiment clothed in color and sound
or form? Important as the ideal is, itself without sign cannot wake
to the high spirituality behind and beneath. And should religion
not also come to its own? Certainly the radical, if he understands
the philosophy of his movement, cannot but feel the necessity of
finding for the fundamental principles of his religious faith and
hope, fitting outward expression. The Jewish radical is free from
the embarrassment besetting the pioneers of the onward movement in other religious families. For he may draw upon the rich
storehouse built, in the four thousand years of Jewish history and
experience, for song and ceremony to garment in beauty and holiness the deepest convictions and noblest aspirations of both mind
and heart. Thus radicalism and reform Judaism are not opposed to
symbolism. They are to legalism and dead formalism. If there be

one for whom the oldest ritualism symbolizes in the daily observances his Judaism—if the practices of the fathers recall to him his
own moral responsibilities let him observe whatever appeals to his
nature. He is though he may not know it, a true radical. The radical merely objects to the prevalent fact that many make of the
symbols and ceremonies the sum total of the message of our religion. He who practices merely to please God, in the assumption
that He commanded such observances and must reward the faithful, or because selfish fear tenants his soul, is out of harmony, as
we understand it, with the genius of our religion.

Whatever man does in religion he does for himself, for the quick-
ening of the sense of obligation, never for God. Nor must the ceremony be looked upon as a substitute for righteousness. The main
inspiration of the reform movement, fifty years ago, was indeed,
the sad certainty that many claimed to be religious Jews on the
strength of their fidelity to ritual law, who at the same time had to
be branded as moral wrecks not to say wretches. The symbol to
be effective, however, must speak a living tongue. Fossil or fetich
is silent. Soul cannot wing upward if it be fraught with weights.
The appeal from the heart and to the heart must ring out in tones
free from mystery. The radical, indeed does not deny that the
emotions have their functions in the economy of man individual or
social, yet, Judaism must oppose whatever leads to mysticism. If
the emotions supply us with the power that propels, reason still
must guide; nor can radicalism accord to the proposition that religion shall merely act as a balm to soothe wounded hearts, as an
opiate to make us forget pain, and grief, and disappointment. For
the Jew religion must act as a spur. The consolation it affords cannot come in the guise of visions, beautiful but unreal, which awaken
at the best only the *fata morgana* born of our torturing thirst as
we wander through the self-created desert, and lead ultimately to
death. Such emotionalism is after all weakening, not strengthening.
It smacks of selfishness and of sensualism; it is dangerously akin
to voluptuousness. At its best, it spiritualizes men into oblivion of
the real duties incumbent upon them. Would we deny that men

have gone forth to meet their death because before their eyes was a vision of things that were not as yet? This supra-natural, if so you must style it, force is among the most vital energies of progress toward liberty. The intoxication of the prophetic spirit was on every "caller in the desert." This God-intoxication, how often do we find its trace in the tear-stained pages of Jewish history! Was not the Jew himself a visionary, a dreamer in the world that knew him only to distrust and to distress him? Yet he believed in himself and in his future, and it is this belief, but in grander Messianic measure, that undoubtedly the symbolism of the synagogue and the Jewish home to-day must vocalize again from the emotional side of our nature as a glorious appeal. It must fan into a brighter blaze the enthusiastic recognition of our mission:—the responsibility for a golden future, the vision before our eyes, as well as the memory of our martyr past which gives us the right to claim that indeed into our charge was entrusted the keepership of the best treasures of humanity. For, friends, it is this consciousness, the fruitage of our whole history, that must be stirred into activity as it slumbers alas, so stolidly but potentially in the breast of every Jew in his feelings, in his thinkings, by the ritualism of the synagogue, of the home, even in private life. This consciousness is indispensable to Judaism. It is that which binds the latest future, the youngest present to the most distant past. It gives unity to Jewish literature, to Jewish history; it gives direction to Jewish thought and Jewish idealism.

This Jewish consciousness is radically different from the vulgar race-pride, content to claim for Judaism every great man or woman, every statesman and prizefighter, every author of mark and every actress of notoriety, but neglects to remember the obligations concurrent with historic distinctions. Jewish birth alone cannot make the Jew. The historic connection established through the mother with the child, is merely preliminary condition, as evolution works through the channel of descent, even in the development of the "Volksseele." The potentiality of birth must be realized in the actualities of convictions. This is often overlooked. There is such a power as the Jewish *"Volksseele."* Upon it pivots Judaism. But descent alone does not suffice. The "ethnic soul" is not mechanical, it is dynamic. Every individual and every generation must acquire anew, really to possess it; for without this re-acquisition, we are merely possessed by it.

But is then Judaism tied to a race; is it tribal, or is it universal? At all times in Jewish history, and every document of Jewish literature proves it, this perplexity was instant and insistent. From one point of view, Judaism is racial, tribal and religio-national. Yet from another it is universal and all-embracing. The radical to-day would smooth the rough edges of this historic inconsistency. Would he open your gates wide that others might come to him? Yea, he would, but he will not at the sacrifice of one single thought of his, at the expense or compromise of one single principle that is still vital for him and for the world. Let those that will, come to us in purity of heart. They shall be welcome.

Our position is like that of a political nation which is also the offspring of a well defined historic process, and always has a consciousness of its own. Those born in the household of the nation are by birth its destined citizens entitled to the privileges and appointed to the responsibilities of their national life; but even so, the nation accepts strangers from without by naturalization and furthermore confers, upon children born of strangers in the country of their temporary habitation, the prerogative of election between the nationality of their parents and that of the land of their birth.

The English language has no term to cover accurately the idea involved. The German *"Volk"* is much more forcible than our "nation." A nation, implying possession of national territory, we are not. But a *"Volk"* we are. The Jewish *"Volksseele"* sounds its message through us. As the Germans in America belong to the German *"Volk"* and have a German *"Kulturmission,"* so do we represent a *"Volks"* consciousness and by it are appointed to an historic task. We radicals would not blur this fact. Still we do not consent that this *"Volksseele"* acts mechanically. More than birth and blood; conviction, "spirituality," the "spirit" is needed.

And the "spirit" has power to confer the gift of the *"Volksseele"* to the stranger even. Judaism cannot consist in physiological, it must be recognized in its psychological elements. How shall we proceed to widen the stream without endangering its depth? The analogy of the political nations above developed seems to me to suggest the way out of the growing perplexity. Without "race" we ossify in dogma, as did Christianity. Without universal tendency away from the merely racial, we are doomed to fossilization. Freedom of movement we must guard in either direction.

This analogy seems to me to point the way to a solution of the perplexity now besetting us. Those who are of Jewish parents, are Jews by birth and should be influenced by us to become Jews by conviction. There are others, numerous indeed, but only rarely conscious of the fact, who are Jews in conviction, but not by birth. If they desire to join us freely, let us accept them! And then we have to-day many born within the household of Judaism though one or the other parent be not a Jew. As long as they reside with us spiritually, let their children become Jews if they choose. In this wise the radical would indeed lengthen the tent ropes of the Jewish tabernacle, and widen it to east and to the west, in order to enlarge with every day more and more the number of Jews by birth and conviction and in the spirit, that seek shelter under its canvas roof open to the light of God's own sun!

The highest symbol of Judaism is indeed the Sabbath. It is the diapason of the Jewish symphonic proclamation of the dignity of man and his divine character. It is the prelude of the Messianic fulfillment. Without the Sabbath, it has rightly been said, "there can be no Judaism," but is the Sabbath contingent upon one day? I can fully understand the feelings of those that do hesitate to concede to the radical the right to speak of his desire to give to Judaism once more the emphasis of the sabbatical symbol. They are in the position of the mother at the bedside of the darling child, hoping against fate and certainty to bring it back to blooming life and quick energy. Oh! that mother's heart, whatever the physician may foretell or dread, it will never cease hoping and believing that death is not near until the grave has covered from sight the mortal temple of the infant's soul. And yet that child dead must be buried. Show us the way to revive the child in the old form, and the radical will indeed unfold the flag and, taking it up, boldly step out as the leader. But is that the Sabbath which can only be observed by proxy? Were even our houses of worship ever better attended than they are, would listening to sermon or reciting of prayer be Sabbath? Read Isaiah's denunciation, the fifty-eighth chapter, and you must come to the conclusion that even this is not the Sabbath. The Jewish queen, the Sabbath bride, sat enthroned in radiant beauty in the home much more than she did in the synagogue. Work is as much an element of the true Sabbath celebration, the work of the preceding six days, as is the rest of the seventh, and in the western countries, who will deny that with thousands and thousands the observance or non-observance of Saturday is not a question of increased or lessened gain, but of commercial and professional existence involving for them the possibility to lead that righteous life, that life of usefulness, as men, and of devotion to humanity which is the fundamental tone in the message of Judaism. We, the radicals indeed, in making the day generally observed by choice and law by our neighbors in this land of the free, as their day of rest, also ours, do not disguise the fact that originally the Sunday was a symbol of ideas antagonistic and antithetical to those which Judaism distinctively entertains. And still with all this, and perhaps all the more on account of this difficulty, we would give this, our *de facto* day of rest, a Jewish religious character and celebrate it with true Jewish fervor. We want religion in our Sunday services, not merely lectures on all sorts of possible and impossible subjects. But religion is not outside of life. It is not a reservation stockaded off. Religion is either all—or it is nothing, said no less a thinker than [Hermann] Steinthal. Jewish religion embraces all of man's life. The distinction between sacred and secular is not Jewish. The state, business, profession, marriage, social reform, brim with puzzles which religion alone may solve. To speak from a religious point of view on these themes is only following the precedent of Pentateuch and the prophets and the Talmudic teachers. Of course, lectures on "Trilby" or on the "Parallelopipedon" are out of rhyme with a religious exercise, yet the sins of one cannot be urged against the earnestness of another; as little as the failure of the movement in one locality is argument against its possibilities in another. If failure be evidence, it would seem to me that the historic Sabbath is thereby also adjudged.

We want Judaism taught in the light of the literature of Judaism. If this constitutes us traitors to Judaism, then we shall accept unflinchingly the burden of the imputation, for we know that our conscience could not so chide us. And we believe that He who weighs the motives of men, who searches their innermost parts, will indeed judge us more justly than others who accuse us of intentions utterly foreign to us.

There is another phase of our Sunday movement which cannot be too strongly stated. Judaism is not known by our neighbors. Shall old errors go uncorrected, old prejudices uncombatted, old superstitions unnoticed? We talk much about the necessity of presenting Judaism in the right light, of proving the fallacies of pseudo-rationalism as boldly as those of Paulinianism. Both misconceive of Judaism. The Sunday service has in our experience, in Chicago, been a most potent factor in this campaign of education. My colleague, so earnest and so gifted, our Rabbi Stolz, as well as I, have spoken regularly on Sunday to hundreds of non-Jews about Judaism. Is this slight service in behalf of positive Judaism?

We, the radicals, know that the voice of revelation has not ceased in Israel; not merely at one Sinai did it sound. It sounded through Bible, it sounded through Talmud, it sounded through our thinkers of old, it spoke through our great pioneers, the leaders of the reform movement, and we do humbly ask today that its voice also appeal to us, and as it thunders forth its behests as its spirit comes to us in the words of the old prophets, we reverently bow our head, and obey the summons to go up, on, into the brighter land of a common humanity, where hatred shall be unknown and love and justice rule supreme, that land which God shall show us. . . .

A Program for the Twenties

After the First World War, it seemed to Julian Morgenstern, the President of Hebrew Union College, that what Reform Judaism needed was a program for action rather than a new philosophic orientation. He thought that the philosophy of Isaac M. Wise and his co-founders of the Central Conference of American Rabbis and, indeed, of the Reform movement was still adequate in most respects. Wise and the others had wanted to "Americanize" Judaism; they had been able to carry out this process only partially because they came out of German backgrounds and addressed themselves largely to congregants of the same stamp. Jews of other backgrounds coming to America were not helped.

Morgenstern advocated the development of a program of missionary activity and publication designed to carry the message of Americanization and Reform to Jews of East European ancestry. He thought that thus Reform Judaism could become the religious foundation of a unified Jewish community. He accepted the "melting-pot" concept of Americanization and assumed as a result the desirability of eliminating all residual traces of foreign cultures. The American Jew, except for his religion, was to become homogeneous with other Americans; his religion was to be "a positive fusion of Judaism and Americanism applied to the daily existence of the Jews of America." This transformation of Judaism into an American culture religion seems to have been all that Morgenstern meant by asserting the need for a more "spiritual" emphasis.

In those days so soon after the tremendous life given to Zionist hopes by the Balfour Declaration, Morgenstern's program could not be explicitly anti-Zionist. Yet he hedged even his moderate position. The American Zionist, he said, "is primarily an American, and only secondarily and altruistically a Zionist." If this primacy be granted, then he saw little point in arguing that to be both an American and a Zionist betrayed a lack of consistency. In effect, Morgenstern's compromise was to allow even the most Americanized Jew to work on behalf of a homeland in Palestine for those Jews who were unfortunate enough not to have been admitted to the United States prior to the restriction of immigration.

WERE ISAAC M. WISE ALIVE TODAY
A Program For Judaism In America
Julian Morgenstern
(1919)

Were Isaac M. Wise alive today! It is a stimulating thought. For the conditions which exist in American Israel today, and the problems which demand solution, although of far larger scope and complexity, are none the less practically the same as those of his day, which, through his foresight, breadth of vision, indomitable will and energy and organizing, creative genius, he solved for his generation. Nay, more; he laid down the basic principle and pointed the way of the only possible solution of these problems for all generations.

His problem was then, and our problem is today, to create a living Judaism in America, a Judaism which shall base itself firmly upon the eternal principles which revelation and history have established, but which shall likewise comport fully with American life, shall adapt and apply its eternal principles to American problems and needs, and shall thus assist the Jews of America to live both as loyal, devoted Jews and as responsible, contributing American citizens. This was the vision, the aim and the problem of Isaac M. Wise in his day; just this is our vision, our aim, our problem today. . . .

But is American Reform Judaism really American? Is it not, perhaps, merely an American adaptation of imported German Reform Judaism? It is a question difficult of final answer, and one upon which there will hardly be general agreement. Yet it must sooner or later be faced squarely and answered honestly and without reservation. The only correct answer can be found first, in the measure with which Reform Judaism in America enables and assists its adherents to live their daily lives as American citizens completely in accordance with the eternal, spiritual principles of Judaism, and second, in the measure with which it enables and assists them, living thus as Jews, and upholding the teachings and principles of Judaism as a religious system, to contribute to the solution of the moral, spiritual and religious problems which confront the American people as a whole, and the solution of which is essential to the upbuilding of American culture.

Reform Judaism was the offspring, rather tardily born, of the Reformation movement in Germany. It sprang from out a Protestant environment and reflected a Protestant point of view and a liberal, Protestant attitude toward ritual and the authority of tradition. It dealt at first, as was but natural, with superficial matters, with simplification of the ritual and ceremonial life and with closer adaptation of the practice of Judaism to the standards of German culture. This was in the main negative work, pulling down the old structure, but not yet building up the new. But before this positive work could be inaugurated systematically, the period of liberalism in Germany had passed. Reform Judaism there ceased its development, and for practically half a century stood absolutely still. Only recently has it resumed its onward course.

But here in America German Reform Judaism flourished. So long as the majority of Jews in America were immigrant Germans, German Reform Judaism completely satisfied their spiritual needs. It even expanded considerably because the spirit of early German liberalism accorded well with the spirit of Americanism. These German immigrants came speedily to feel themselves completely American. And as they saw their imported German Reform Judaism adapting itself readily to the liberal, non-ritualistic, and rather negative American religious point of view, they came to believe that they had Americanized their Judaism sufficiently, and that it was now American Judaism.

Actually, however, what has been accomplished? There has been a continuation of the negative processes of reform, a further reduction of ritual and ceremonial practice until almost the minimum has been reached. Many ceremonies still big with meaning have been hastily and ignorantly discarded. A few positive reforms making for modernization of the temple ritual have been introduced. A significant, positive advance has been made in the development of the ceremony of confirmation in connection with the Shabuoth festival. And, in conformity with a tendency of modernism, woman has been accorded, or rather has won for herself, a position of approximate equality and responsibility in Jewish congregational life.

The prayer-book has been translated into the vernacular, and simplified and beautified considerably. A prayer for the United States Government and a few new prayers of high spiritual worth, but none the less of conventional, non-committal type, have been inserted. But the spirit is still largely the spirit of the German Reform Prayer-book, and, with the exception of the language, hardly anything indicates that our Union Prayer-book is an American product.

The truth is that American Reform Judaism is American not much deeper than the surface. It is regilded, as it were, with a thin coating of Americanism, but the body and soul beneath are still the body and soul of German Reform Judaism.

Meanwhile there are vital problems deeply affecting our life as individual men and women, problems about God, the meaning of life, the divine purpose of suffering, the efficacy of prayer, the truth about the future. We are beginning to think about religion as individuals, with modern education and culture, and with a certain disciplined religious knowledge. We have lost much of the old, conventional conception of Judaism as a religion for the Jewish people as a group. We are beginning to demand that Judaism speak to us as individuals also in words other than the conventional phrases of pious dogma and theology, and that it satisfy our individual spiritual and mystical needs and cravings. For this reason the Kaddish has become the most effective and uplifting portion of our liturgy. It speaks to our inner soul and satisfies the longing for union with the departed. Undoubtedly for this reason also an increasing number of co-religionists, even while still sincerely professing themselves loyal Jews, seek personal comfort and help in Christian Science. It seems to them to offer something which they feel they need, and which Judaism does not give. What shall we do? We have denounced Christian Science Jews, and have even, in a way, read them out of Judaism. We have exposed with convincing logic the incompatibility of Judaism and Christian Science. Yet this has not checked one bit the drift of Jews toward that church. Might it not be that we have pursued a wrong course, and that we should ask, "What is wrong with Reform Judaism; is not something lacking in it, that so many of its adherents should feel compelled to turn to Christian Science?" In other words, does Reform Judaism in America minister completely to the daily spiritual needs of all its adherents? But this only by way of illustration.

Obviously, however, American Jews, children of American environment and culture, demand that American Judaism minister to the individual as well as to the group, that it answer the call of the heart as well as of the head, and that, instead of the language of cold theology and bloodless rationalism, it speak the language of warm feeling and emotion and enable its adherents, like Moses of old, to commune with God face to face, as a man communes with his friend.

There are likewise the various social and economic problems which today trouble, and even threaten, the structure of society, the problems of capital and labor, of the social evil, of the liquor traffic, of the rightful position of woman in society, of corruption in politics, of internationalism. What has Judaism in America to say authoritatively on these questions? To what extent has it determined its own answer as to the right and wrong in them, and sought to influence and mould the opinion of the American people accordingly? Many rabbis have spoken time and again on some, if not all of these questions, some hesitatingly and some boldly, some sanely and some demagogically. But has American Judaism, through this Conference, let us say, defined its official attitude on any one of these problems and announced this unequivocally to the world? On some possibly it has, but on the majority it has hesitated and temporized and drifted with the current. Not once has it been the first to speak and to take the lead in the application of Jewish ethical principles to modern problems and needs. Where is our boasted prophetic spirit and our dream of Israel's mission? And where is American Judaism's conscious and purposed contribution to American culture and ideals?

Above all, to what extent have we incorporated a positive attitude upon these and like questions, the attitude of supposedly American Judaism, into our prayer-book? A prayer-book is the real exponent of the spirit and ideals of any religion; it voices, or should voice, its innermost visions and aspirations. Where in our entire prayer-book do we find a single prayer for divine guidance in the solution of the specific problem of creative justice in the social and economic life of America, and for the spirit of unselfishness and breadth of vision which alone can bring about a real solution? Our nation is wrestling with this problem in its manifold aspects. But although Judaism first voiced for the world the unalterable principle of social justice, American Israel does not yet pray for it. Clearly it has not yet entered deeply into our religious consciousness. We are still so engrossed with praying the prayers which past ages have formulated to express their convictions and needs, with affirming in heavy, learned prayers theological principles and beliefs, that we find no time nor place to pray simply and directly for the specific needs of the present. We seem to have forgotten almost completely that help from God can come to us today as it came to our fathers in the past. And we fail to implore guidance and strength and wisdom to solve the problems of the present from God, who is as much the God of the present as of the past. We pray in the past as Jews; we work and aspire in the present as Americans. But we have not yet learned to properly correlate Judaism and Americanism, that we might live more fully as both Jews and Americans, or rather as American Jews. To this extent our Judaism is something imported and antiquated, German, or possibly largely pre-German, but not yet completely American. And it is therefore something relegated to a temple for at the most two hours each week, and not yet a potent, constant influence in our lives as American citizens seven days in the week.

And just as these earlier German immigrants brought to this country imported, liberal German Reform Judaism, so have the more recent Russian immigrants brought imported, orthodox Russian Judaism, orthodox not merely because of restrictions imposed by the Russian government, but orthodox and Russian because it sprang from out a Russian, unprogressive environment. Influenced partly by orthodox, Greek Catholic spirit and example, these immigrants lay emphasis upon the ritualistic and legalistic side of Judaism. At the same time they possess an appreciable knowledge of Jewish literature and reverence for Jewish tradition.

Unlike their German predecessors, they have not scattered throughout the country. They have settled for the most part in large groups in our great industrial centers, where they are able to continue their daily life and religious practice in much the same manner as in Europe. Yiddish continues to be the vernacular among the immigrants themselves, and among their children to an extent. A flourishing Yiddish press and Yiddish literature are their sources of information and education. One of their chief aims as a collective group is the preservation of orthodox life and practice. Relying upon their somewhat larger Jewish knowledge and their closer conformity to rabbinical law, they denounce American Reform Judaism, with rather intolerant zeal, as the product of ignorance of Jewish life and lore, and of the to them seeming attempt on the part of Reform Jews to shed Judaism gradually and gracefully and pass over by easy stages to the religion of the majority.

But the truth has come home even to many of them that orthodox Judaism can not flourish, nor even live long, in America. What
could satisfy their religious needs and impulses in Russia can not
endure in America with its altogether different life and standards.
The older immigrants have managed to live their orthodox Judaism
with comparatively little modification, but only at the tremendous
cost of remaining forever strangers and aliens. The younger immigrants, and particularly the first American-born generation, educated in American schools and imbued with American ideals, refuse
to pay this price. A very few, an almost insignificant percentage,
have found their way into Reform synagogs. A not inconsider-
able portion, misled by a peculiar, foreign habit of mind and study,
have passed over to agnosticism and atheism. Many, victims of
unbalanced cultural conditions, have made socialism a substitute
for religion, as if the two concepts were mutually antagonistic and
exclusive.

The vast majority, however, are merely drifting. Outwardly they
profess themselves orthodox Jews and affiliate nominally with
orthodox synagogs. But they visit the synagog and participate in
Jewish rites only seldom, and Judaism has become for them altogether formal and lifeless.

A few seek to work out their salvation by accepting certain
minor reforms, which American environment and education compel. With them a small, conservative element of early Jewish
settlers have made common cause. Together they are attempting
to evolve what is variously called reasonable orthodoxy or con-
ervative reform. The movement is foredoomed to failure by its
very principles. For it is founded upon expediency and compulsory
reform of externals, and not upon thorough-going, systematic
reform, based upon careful diagnosis and corrective prescription.
Not unnaturally this conservative reform, reasonable orthodox
movement is looked at askance by both strictly orthodox and
strictly reform Jews. Assuredly the future of Judaism in America
lies not with it.

Obviously there has been practically no contact and union of forces between the reform and orthodox groups. They stand almost as far apart today as thirty years ago. Why? It is largely because Reform Judaism has made no systematic effort to join forces with Orthodox Judaism and to make the adherents of the latter understand and accept the reform point of view. We gave charity generously. We established settlements, foster homes, orphan asylums and industrial schools. We organized classes and clubs, in which, we boasted, we were Americanizing our immigrant brethren. But all these activities dealt only with transitory conditions. Until we have complete union and cooperation for religious ends, there can be no true American Judaism. In the light of this self-evident truth our lack of constructive vision was inexcusable.

We are a people with a mission, we claim, yet we know not how to do missionary work among our fellow-Jews. We might well take a leaf from the home missions book of our Christian neighbors. We should make propaganda for our interpretation of Judaism, not at all merely in order that all Jews in America may think like ourselves, but because of our devotion to both Judaism and America; because of our supreme conviction that Judaism can live in America only by adapting itself to American life and ideals; because of our other supreme conviction that we can discharge our full obligation as American citizens of the Jewish faith only by cherishing and developing Judaism to the utmost, and making it contribute to American culture; and finally, because of the imperative need of evolving a unified American Jewish point of view as the basis for the future evolution of American Judaism. And if, as early comers to America, and therefore presumably more largely imbued with its spirit, we owed to our immigrant brethren any duty at all, a vital part thereof was the duty of Americanization. And Americanization means more than teaching a foreigner the English language, so that he might more easily earn bread and butter. An essential element of the Americanization of our immigrant brethren is the Americanization of their Judaism, to make it accord more largely with the American life which they must live. In this we have failed completely.

Failed! We seem never to have even dreamed that we had such a duty. For this work can be done only by education and active propaganda. And hardly ever has it occurred to anyone to present the principles and aims of Reform Judaism or to discuss the problem of Americanization of Judaism in a form and language which our immigrant brethren can understand. Some years ago it was suggested that this Conference translate its tracts into Yiddish and give them wide publicity among our orthodox brethren. It came to naught, chiefly because its full significance and necessity were not appreciated.

But, although much precious time has been lost, systematic, educational propaganda is indispensable, if union of the discordant elements of American Judaism is to be achieved, and if Judaism is to live and grow in America. If we believe that the form of Judaism which we have evolved is in greatest harmony with American life and spirit, and that American Judaism of the future must develop largely out of it, it is our duty to make propaganda for this form and principle of Judaism and to win over all elements in American Jewry to realization of this common need and to cooperation with us for this common good.

Another condition has materially increased the disharmony and group antagonism existing in American Jewry. German Jewish immigrants came to America as fully recognized German citizens, Jewish only in religion. They came with no idea other than to become complete Americans and American citizens, and to maintain Judaism only as a religion.

Russian Jewish immigrants came from out an altogether different political environment. The Russian and Roumanian governments were organized according to the national group system. Jews in those countries constituted a distinct national group, a small political unit within a larger unit. What few rights and privileges they possessed, they held as members of the Jewish national group.

Transplanted to America, many found it difficult to comprehend fully the American national ideal of a people one and indivisible, not split up into separate national or racial groups, but laying emphasis upon the facts and forces which unite and bind a people into one nation, with one common history and culture. And when they felt their orthodox Judaism slipping from them, they sought a Jewish substitute for it, through which they could give expression to their Jewish consciousness. Having no adequate knowledge of American Reform Judaism, and no sympathy with nor faith in it, they sought elsewhere, and found, or believed that they found, what they sought in Zionism.

This was perfectly natural. Zionism's fundamental premise of the distinctness of the Jewish people and its identity with the Jewish nation accorded fully with their political experience and education in their European home lands. It fitted into their conception of nationality and government much better than did Americanism, with its ideal of one indivisible American nation. Zionism, as a political and nationalistic theory, was a purely imported, European product. Among the immigrant Russian Jews and their children it has found the vast majority of its adherents in America.

There is no need to discuss here the merits or demerits of Zionism. There has been altogether too much of that, and it has led only to recrimination and dissension. But Zionism must be treated objectively as a historical fact and Zionists as a distinct group in American Jewry today.

There is actually for us only one question fundamentally at issue between Zionism and anti-Zionism. It is not the question of the establishment of a Jewish state in Palestine, and the evolution there of a specifically Jewish culture, and the influence of such a Jewish state and culture upon the fortunes of Jews and Judaism in other lands. This is, of course, the fundamental thesis and program of Zionism. But, except for the fact that it is the bone of contention between Zionists and anti-Zionists, and has contributed greatly to the division of American Israel into two camps, it has little direct bearing upon our main problem.

For us the vital question in the Zionist controversy is whether Judaism in America possesses the power of self-invigoration and self-perpetuation, or must eventually die unless it be given a prompt and oft-repeated hypodermic injection of national Palestinian Jewish culture and devotion. Many Zionists affirm that Judaism in America can not live, is doomed, without the constant stimulus of a Jewish state and a Jewish culture in Palestine; and even then its existence must be precarious and altogether dependent. This is certainly a logical deduction from the basic premises of Zionism.

One other conclusion also follows necessarily from these premises and this argument. If Judaism in America, just to continue to exist, requires the stimulus of a Jewish state in Palestine and a Jewish national culture, then we Jews in America, if we wish to remain Jews at all, must hold ourselves aloof and distinct, not only religiously, but also nationally and culturally, from the American nation and people. Contrary to what we have been taught to believe is the fundamental principle of Americanism, viz., American national unity and solidarity, we Jews in America must uphold the eastern European principle of national group organization and national group rights and cultures, and must refuse to incorporate ourselves completely with the American nation and to assume our responsibility and contribute our share to the evolution of American national culture.

If this be what is meant by assimilation, then we are assimilationists, and we accept the term as a title of honor and American loyalty. For we subscribe unconditionally to the principle of Americanism, which, while it guarantees full freedom of religious belief and worship, none the less demands that all American citizens, regardless of racial and national origin and previous culture, integrate themselves completely into the American nation and culture, and that even religion contribute of its spiritual treasures to the rich content of this American culture. In this respect we believe that Zionism is altogether foreign to and incompatible with Americanism and American Judaism.

But more than this, we believe with perfect faith that Judaism can live and perpetuate itself and expand here in America, entirely without the need of foreign stimuli, whether from Palestine or elsewhere. True, Russian Orthodox Judaism can not live here; and equally true, an unmodified German Reform Judaism can not live here. But neither of these is American Judaism. And in American Judaism and its power of life and growth in America we have complete faith.

And this question of faith or lack of faith in American Judaism is the real, vital issue between American Zionism and anti-Zionism. It matters little if one labors for a Jewish home land in Palestine, even as an independent Jewish state, so long as it does not affect his personal attitude toward Americanism, and his perfect faith in the future of America as a unified nation, and in American Judaism as a living religion in America. Provided he have this faith and labor for its consummation regardless of Palestinian interests and activities, he is an American and an American Jew in heart and soul.

And we believe that most American Zionists, so-called, are just this kind of Zionist, that their Americanism is in every respect unqualified and beyond question, and that their advocacy of a Jewish state or commonwealth in Palestine is entirely altruistic. What though there be a certain lack of consistency and logic in their combination of Americanism with Zionism. Very few men and women are perfectly consistent and logical in all their beliefs and works. Just this inconsistency and illogicality, we imagine, distinguish the American Zionist from the European Zionist. The former is primarily an American nationalist, a citizen of America; the latter is primarily a Zionist nationalist, a citizen of a Jewish state still to be formed.

But since the American Zionist is primarily an American, and only secondarily and altruistically a Zionist, he must have faith, not only in America and Americanism, but also in Judaism in America, in its power and in its historical compulsion to live and grow as American Judaism. As a Jew whose life in every way centers in America, he must integrate himself completely, as he does, with the spirit and works of Americanism.

If a Jewish state be ever established in Palestine, and a Jewish culture evolve there, and they be able to contribute anything, much or little, to the upbuilding and enrichment of American Judaism, as Zionists claim, surely we will not object. Undoubtedly American Judaism will receive certain stimuli from the Judaisms of other lands, with which, needless to say, it is, and will ever remain united by the strong bonds of history and religion. It will likewise undoubtedly contribute equally of its own knowledge and strength to those foreign Judaisms, even the Judaism of Palestine.

But upon all American Jews, Zionists and non-Zionists alike, whose home and whose faith are here in America, there rests the sacred obligation to compose all differences in the face of their common duty and their common goal, and to labor together to bring about union in American Israel, and to consciously, wisely, systematically build up a living, virile American Judaism, which shall root itself deep in American soil, shall grow and thrive in American atmosphere, and shall offer that spiritual pabulum which alone can satisfy the religious hunger of American Jewry.

The period of foreign groups and elements in American Jewry is passing. We have almost ceased to be Portuguese and German and Polish and Russian and Roumanian Jews. Those differences exist today only as rapidly disappearing survivals of an outgrown life. Tomorrow they will be gone entirely, and we will have become completely in fact, what we are already in spirit, one, united American Israel. Likewise the period of dominant foreign ideas and principles in the Judaism of America is passing. German Reform Judaism, Russian Orthodox Judaism, European Zionism, the day of all these in America is almost done. The new day of one, united, common American Judaism is dawning for us and our children.

What will this American Judaism be? We can only determine the tendencies of today, and from this attempt to forecast the future. The general principle is assured; American Judaism will be both Jewish and American, a positive fusion of the principles of Judaism and Americanism applied to the daily existence of the Jews of America. We know quite well what Judaism is. But Americanism is as yet only in the making. We are still largely a nation of immigrants. And as a nation we have acted with inexcusable shortsightedness. Congress has dealt with the problem of immigration superficially, by measures of restriction and limitation. Only today are we beginning to realize as a nation that there is another, far more logical and constructive solution of the problem, viz.: Americanization of the immigrant through education under government supervision.

This new movement is significant. Americanism has had a virtual rebirth. As a nation we have become impatient, and rightly so, not so much of things foreign in origin, but rather of the undue persistence of their foreign character in an American environment. We have, as a nation, resolved, unconsciously perhaps, but none the less positively, to cease our *laissez-faire* policy, and to begin to evolve a distinct, unified American culture. We welcome all foreigners who come in sincerity of heart and loyalty of purpose. But we refuse to allow them to continue too long as semi-foreigners. And even more, we refuse to allow a hyphenated Americanism to exist in this country. We must realize our national ideal of an American people and an American nation, one and indivisible, not only not divided into North and South and free and slave states, but also not divided into distinct, competitive groups, whether national, racial, economic, social or religious in origin and character.

Our soldiers sound the new note more positively, perhaps, than any other element of our population. A surprisingly large percentage, we are told, entered the army, either as foreigners or semi-foreigners in language and culture. But there was in them a latent germ of the American spirit; and that germ, warmed by the glow of sacrifice, wetted by the blood of life, fostered by deepening patriotism and broadening understanding, has flowered forth into an aspiring, creating Americanism.

These returning soldiers sound the note of this larger Americanism in all its particular phases and elements. And not the least important of these is religion. Religion can no longer be something distinct from and independent of Americanism, but must become an integral part thereof. Not that we will evolve anything at all suggesting union of church and state. Such union is abhorrent to

Americanism. But we will realize that life without religion is incomplete and uncertain, minus one important source of strength and guidance, like a wheel lacking one spoke. We will understand that Americanism touches upon the whole of life. And while it will never dictate religious creed or affiliation, it will assuredly determine the general attitude of all Americans toward religion, and will insist that all religious belief and practice in America be in perfect harmony with, and contribute to, the development of American culture and ideals.

We know now that the first, deep, religious fervor of our soldiers was somewhat exaggerated. As they became habituated to their service and to the thought of sacrifice, suffering and possible death, many ceased to rely upon religion for comfort and support to the same extent as at first. And yet, our religious workers tell us, something, even much, of this first faith remains, and our soldiers are returning with a more reverent and positive religious spirit. And their loved ones here at home, whose suffering was chiefly vicarious, also learned to trust and to pray as never before. In consequence we have become a nation with a larger religious consciousness and faith. Upon these we rest our hopes and plans for positive growth of religion in America and its integration with the American spirit.

But this new religious spirit in America has declared itself unmistakably. It is impatient of the formalities of creed, theology and ritual. In truly American manner it demands that we get down to fundamentals. It concerns itself but little with questions of dogma and ritual. But it asks one question, and it asks it insistently, "How shall we come close to God and pour out our hearts before Him, and find in this close and loving communion the inspiration, the strength, the wisdom, the guidance to rise above our trials, to grow strong and courageous, in order that we may live righteously, and may contribute according to our strength to the knowledge, the happiness and the blessing of our nation and of mankind?" This is the new religious spirit of Americanism. And only those creeds and churches which can breathe this spirit, which can reform and restate their essential principles in accordance therewith, can live and flourish in America. For the rest there must come sure and speedy end.

And not only does Americanism insist upon these fundamentals of individual worship, but it insists equally upon the fundamentals of collective worship and belief. It emphasizes the universal fatherhood of God and brotherhood of man and the spiritual, as well as the political, unity of the American people. And it demands that within its national limits, the American people as a whole live in accordance with these principles, that they emphasize, not minor credal and ritual differences, which separate and antagonize, but the fundamentals of faith and life, which all religions hold in common, and which must unite men in worship of their common God and Father. Religion, our nation demands, must be a positive force in the evolution of the one, united American people and of American spirit and culture.

To all of this Judaism gives unqualified approval. Even though it has evolved a complex ritual and an elaborate theology, it has never lost sight of the fundamentals of religious belief and practice. The knowledge of the common fatherhood of God and brotherhood of man has long been its cherished possession. Its prophets were the first to catch the vision of the golden age, when "swords will be beaten into plowshares and spears into pruning-hooks", and when all men will unite to walk in the law of the Lord. From Israel this vision has descended to America; and our nation has taken the lead in the present endeavor to make of this vision of Israel a living, world-wide reality. America has drunk deep of the life-giving wells of Israel's law and lore, and there is an indissoluble bond of union and sympathy and common aspiration between Judaism and Americanism.

But in this new period of positive religion in America, this spirit of sympathy and union must grow and deepen. Judaism in America, like all religions, must become more positively and constructively American, while America becomes correspondingly more deeply religious. Judaism must lay increased stress upon the practice and development of the fundamentals of religion. Theology and ritual must be relegated to their proper places as accessories, but not as the whole of Judaism. Judaism in America must evolve along the lines of simple, positive living, and must be a strengthening and creative force in the daily lives of all its adherents.

Yet it must remain Judaism. It must not lose itself and its distinctive message in the glittering generalities of mere ethics and abstract moralizing. It must never sever direct connection with its historic past, which lends direction, character and impulse to its present evolution. Nor must it forget that, even though theology and ritual are but accessories of religion, they are indispensable accessories. They are the language and philosophy of religion. Through them we give expression to our religious thoughts, define and guide our religious emotions and aspirations, and correlate our individual existences with God's plan and purpose of life. A vital and practical problem is that of preserving the proper, invigorating balance between theology and ritual on the one hand and simple faith and moral life on the other.

Just here is the task and privilege of the Jewish scholar and rabbi in America, to increase our knowledge of Judaism, to enlarge and deepen its spiritual content, and to guide its development and practical application, so that it may remain unconditionally Judaism, even while it identifies itself with and contributes to the growth of Americanism, and so that its adherents may remain conscious, loyal, zealous Jews even while they are conscious, loyal, zealous Americans. Such must the American Judaism of the future be.

This American Judaism will evolve out of no one single group or movement. Every group and every tendency in American Israel will undoubtedly contribute something to its upbuilding. Reform Judaism will probably contribute more than any other movement, since it is in fullest accord with Americanism. But it does not follow that American Judaism of tomorrow must flow directly and solely out of, and be the mere continuation of Reform Judaism of today.

If America represents a large melting-pot, into which various races and nationalities are cast to come forth eventually as one American nation, Jewry in America represents a smaller melting-pot, into which are cast Jews and Judaisms from various lands, with varying modes of Jewish life and worship and interpretations of Judaism, there to be thoroughly mingled and welded together until at last one united American Jewry and one united American Judaism will evolve. In this process all American Jews must meet upon the common ground of Jewish knowledge and devotion and American responsibility and patriotism, and discuss, exchange and test their beliefs, practices and ideals in tolerant, receptive manner. In this way alone can American Judaism be built up. Present tolerance among and eventual union of the present groups and movements of American Israel, and open-mindedness and constructive vision are its first, indispensable requisites.

But when American Judaism shall have fairly begun to evolve, what then? A very practical issue confronts us. Our present synagogs will not be torn down that new synagogs, devoted to the new American Judaism, may be erected in their stead. Nor will our present congregations and congregational system make way altogether for new congregations and a new system. Whatever Reform Judaism may contribute to its spiritual content and ritual practice, the actual physical organization of the new American Judaism must be largely upon the basis of our established congregational system. Into our present congregations eventual American Jews will seek admission. And they will come, not hesitatingly, as poor strangers, craving a welcome of any kind, just so they be allowed to enter, but they will ask admittance as honored guests summoned to congregational fellowship. They will demand admission upon terms of absolute equality of devotion, responsibility and privilege, as American Jews like ourselves. How shall we receive them?

There can be only one answer. Our congregations must be democratized sincerely and thoroughly. A spirit of Jewish fellowship must prevail. Absolute equality must be the right of all, and the responsibility and burden of administration must be borne equally by all in proportion to ability and means.

We have already endorsed the general principle of democracy in American Judaism in a way. We gave somewhat restricted and cautious expression to it in the model constitution for congregations. The principles of small, minimum, or even voluntary, dues and unassigned seating are finding constantly increasing support. More and more we are recognizing that congregations owe a duty to all the house of Israel, even to those not enrolled in their membership. The principle of democracy within the congregation and synagog is winning rapidly, and its future is assured. None the less, only a beginning has thus far been made. The complete democratization of the synagog is the second great need and problem of American Judaism.

Another problem of prime importance is that of efficient organization. Efficiency and organization are both American bywords. The churches of America are organized in a manner which daily becomes more efficient. The war has demonstrated the value of efficiency and preparedness in church organization. To us Jews it has taught this lesson at a particularly sad cost. For although it found us rich in organizations, it found us poor in organization. Other religions were prepared to discharge their obligation to their young men in the nation's service at almost a moment's notice. But the war was over before we Jews had barely begun to care for the spiritual welfare of our boys, even in a manner woefully inadequate and ineffective.

The time for recrimination has passed. It matters not who was to blame for this fiasco. Unquestionably the real fault was our over-organization and the attendant dissension and disorganization. We have countless organizations and institutions, many engaged chiefly in petty rivalries and squabbling for publicity and glory rather than in useful work. This is due in part to the present non-homogeneous composition of American Jewry, which has called into being many organizations duplicative and competitive in character.

With the evolution of a united American Jewry undoubtedly

much of this over-organization and duplication will cease automatically. But efficient and constructive organization will hardly evolve of itself. The problem must be dealt with directly and boldly. The blatant, self-seeking demagog must give way to the efficient consecrated leader, and competition and hostility between organizations must yield to cooperation and fusion.

Above all, the shameful spectacle of congregational rivalry must cease. It is a veritable חלול השם , absolutely unjustifiable and inexcusable. We must awaken to the pregnant truth, that while the congregation is the unit of Jewish life, the community, and not the congregation, should be the unit of local organization; or rather, the term congregation should be coterminous with the entire community, and not merely with a synagog and its membership. Within this large congregation there should be, when once we shall have evolved our common American Judaism, just so many synagogs and just so many religious schools and just so many Jewish institutions of any sort, as may be actually needed, each situated where it can discharge its obligations to its particular neighborhood most efficiently. With congregational organization such as this, there will be no opportunity for any Jew to fall into the present congregational interstices, and to escape integration with the rest of the house of Israel in the congregation of Israel. Proper, efficient, constructive organization within local Jewish communities and in the large community of American Israel is one of the most difficult and yet most urgent problems in the evolution of American Judaism.

There is likewise the problem of institutionalizing the synagog. It is a positive movement indeed, if we affirm, as we do, that the synagog is the center from which all specifically Jewish life must radiate and about which it must revolve. But in actual practice this problem is most difficult. Along what lines shall we guide this movement that it may make for a deepening and broadening of Jewish consciousness and Jewish life?

There is the grave problem of the relations of Jew to non-Jew and of Judaism in America to other religions. There are innumerable problems which confront us, and which must be solved positively and constructively before American Judaism can evolve completely. But we may not discuss these now.

One problem, however, this Conference must face squarely and endeavor to answer wisely and sincerely. It is the problem of the rabbi in American Judaism. Manifestly an American Jewry and an American Judaism, such as we have visioned, will need rabbis, yes, and in far greater numbers than at present. Whence shall they come, and how shall they be trained? Certainly, if our main thesis be correct, and a true American Judaism evolve and perfect an organization such as we have outlined, we shall need likewise rabbis or spiritual leaders, however they may be called, with varied and specialized training.

We shall need community leaders, men equipped with authoritative knowledge of Judaism, with large, constructive vision and organizing and executive ability, to coordinate and guide the complex life of the community. We shall need men preeminently preachers and popular expounders of Judaism, who will conduct the actual worship within the synagogs. We shall need pastoral and social workers, possibly to an even greater degree than now. We shall need teachers of Judaism in all its phases for all classes of our people. We shall need Jewish scholars, who will enrich our knowledge and interpretation of Judaism.

In the smallest communities the rabbi will necessarily combine in his one person as many of these varied activities as possible, just as under our present system. But as communities grow in size and complexity, these activities must be increasingly distributed among specialists. In this manner the work of the large congregation will be most efficiently administered. It will relieve the rabbi of the present, depressing compulsion, inimical to both efficiency and sincerity, of becoming, or far more frequently of passing as the final authority upon all matters, past, present and future, spiritual and material, religious and secular, Jewish and non-Jewish. The rabbi can then be himself, and being himself can work quietly and constructively in his chosen field. Possibly just here is our greatest need, the need of rabbis of deep spirituality and lofty idealism, rabbis who are above everything petty and ignoble, whose lives are an open book which all may read, whose deeds and service are an example and an inspiration, and whose perfect, living faith in God, in Judaism and in man must awaken an answering faith in the hearts and lives of all. In the hands of such rabbis the future of American Judaism is assured.

Naturally all these specialized rabbinical activities will have to rest upon the basis of authoritative Jewish knowledge, indispensable to all Jewish workers alike. Only after this education in the fundamentals of Judaism has been imparted and the requisite basic Jewish knowledge has been gained, can the specialized training begin. Our seminaries must attract worthy young men in sufficient numbers, and must prepare them thoroughly for their varying careers as Jewish workers. At the same time these institutions must serve as centers of Jewish knowledge and Jewish science. For unless American Judaism can contribute, through the scholars which it may raise up, to the increased knowledge of Judaism and the resulting enrichment of its spiritual content and religious values, it has no creative power and can have no future other than stagnation and death. Sincere, consecrated, efficient rabbis, creative Jewish scholars and all the complex apparatus of Jewish scholarship, ministration and spiritual leadership are absolutely essential, are, perhaps, the final and supreme requisite for a future of life and growth for American Judaism.

And that it has such a future we, spiritual children of Dr. Wise, founder of this Conference, by our presence here upon this historic occasion, solemnly affirm. A program for American Judaism, presented in all possible detail and with a solution for every problem that can be dimly foreseen, is beyond the limits of a simple prayer. The sage advice of Rabbi Tarphon is reassuring, לא עליך המלאכה לגמור ולא אתה בן חורין לבטל ממנה.   Though we might not complete the task with this one paper, we were not at liberty to desist therefrom. It suffices to have affirmed the supreme conviction that Judaism in America possesses the inherent vitality to perpetuate itself and to work out its own future of growth and expansion; and with this to have affirmed the fundamental principle, that Judaism in America, to live and grow, must become true American Judaism, founded upon the immovable rock of Jewish truth and Jewish historic continuity, yet adapted completely to American national standards and ideals and the daily life which we, as loyal American citizens in an American environment must live; and finally, to have affirmed the principle that this American Judaism can be evolved only through union and cooperation, upon absolutely democratic principles, of all the various, at present dissentient elements of American Israel. This is our main thesis. The additional problems, upon which we have ventured to touch, are mere incidents of this large program.

But this is no new program. It is in every essential detail the program and the vision which Isaac M. Wise proclaimed almost three quarters of a century ago, and for which he labored faithfully through all his long, constructive and beneficent life. And though he be not here in the flesh today, his spirit still lives with us, and we are all, whether or not we knew him personally and sat at his feet, his spiritual disciples. Upon all of us his mantle has fallen. The task is ours of carrying on the work which he, our master, began. What we may achieve will be his achievement; what we may create will be his creation; what glory we may win will be his glory, his fame, his monument. And as we hallow his memory today, we consecrate ourselves anew to his cause, American Judaism.

Looking Toward the Future

In 1958, some sixty years after Hirsch's call to a continuing rationalism and about forty years after Morgenstern's program for making Reform Judaism the culture religion of Americanized Jews, another over-all view of Reform Judaism was expressed by Bernard J. Bamberger. He concerned himself with three major issues, on each of which his position is clarifying though presented with proper tentativeness.

First, Bamberger saw in the actual establishment of the State of Israel a reason for revived concern to develop a Reform position that would eliminate any logical inconsistency between American patriotism and sympathetic devotion to the State of Israel. His simple proposal is that renewed emphasis be placed on the idea of the world-wide Congregation of Israel, and that support for the State be expressed within this larger spiritual unity. The active exertions of Reform Jews could be on behalf of all the Jews of the world, including those in the State of Israel. "This primary emphasis on the world Jewish community," he says, "greatly relieves the theoretical difficulty."

Second, he defends the desirability of maintaining the existing variety of congregational practices, even those that reveal "the emergence of a more colorful and distinctively Jewish pattern of practice." The stress of the early Reform leaders on de-Orientalizing the services of the synagogue seems to have lost its force for Bamberger. He opposes, too, the attempt to develop a codified Reform *Halacha*. The commitment of all Jews to accept religious and moral obligations is fine, but Bamberger argues that the liberal position requires that the people be encouraged to define those obligations for themselves, without dictation from a central authority. After all, he points out, the rabbis "have not been prepared to define and to follow scrupulously a Halacha that would regulate the moral aspects of our own profession."

69

Finally, the probability that liberal Judaism (in which Bamberger includes both the Reform and the Conservative movements) will become the main stream of American Jewish life, reducing Orthodox Judaism to a minority sect, leads him to stress the vital importance of developing a fuller and more effective educational program on all levels. Implied by this demand is the urgent need for the reformulation of liberal Jewish theology "in the light of all the changes that have taken place in the outer world and in the inner life of mankind during the last few decades."

THE DEVELOPING PHILOSOPHY OF
REFORM JUDAISM
Bernard J. Bamberger
(1958)

I

. . . Let us head at once for trouble: the relationship of Jewish nationalism to Reform Judaism.

Twenty-five years ago three views on this subject were possible and tenable. First, the traditional Reform attitude—that secular, particularistic Zionism was incompatible with the universal religious viewpoint of Reform; and that besides, Zionism was not really good for Jews.

The Zionists, on the other hand, argued not only that Zionism would help solve the Jewish problem, but also that it was needed to make Reform complete. The mission of Israel, they held, would be no more than a vague dream until there was a Jewish community of sufficient size and concentration to determine its own destinies. Only such a community could actually implement the mission by embodying the prophetic ideals of Judaism in concrete acts and institutions.

Third, there was the non-Zionist viewpoint. Its adherents could not share fully the messianic ardors of the committed Zionists; but they did not regard Zionism as a danger to Reform or a necessary denial of its basic premises. They were sympathetic to all positive

71

manifestations of Jewish life, especially to one that promised so much for the welfare of Jews. So they supported efforts to rebuild Palestine, cooperating with Zionists as far as they could; and where they dissented, they tried not to interfere with or handicap those who were working for their people.

This sympathetic non-Zionism has, I believe, become the dominant attitude among American Jews, including many who are enrolled in various Zionist organizations. But the mood and content of this outlook have changed. Instead of calling it non-Zionist, we may now title it simply "pro-Israel." The tone of detached philanthropy has diminished, to be replaced by a feeling of personal involvement with the State of Israel and its destiny. Most American Jews take pride in what the Republic of Israel and its people have accomplished; they are deeply concerned that the State should survive and flourish. But their own personal future is rooted in the United States, and they regard their Jewish identity as primarily a matter of religion.

The anti-Zionist philosophy has been rendered obsolete by history, and I shall not discuss the psychology of those who still adhere to it. But the Zionist position has also become more problematical than would once have been expected. Zionist spokesmen have been trying to define the role of diaspora Zionism in the present, but it is not easy to do so. Outstanding leaders of the Republic of Israel have pointedly asked what difference there is between a friendly non-Zionist and an avowed Zionist who does not intend to settle in the State of Israel. Still more difficult is the problem of fusing a positive Zionist approach with Reform Judaism, or for that matter with any religious interpretation of Judaism.

This did not appear to be an insuperable difficulty as long as the Zionist goal was still in the future. A great redemptive ideal, it was properly the subject of religious aspiration and prayer. Such a prayer was incorporated into the Friday night service of the Revised Union Prayer Book. This prayer is now out of date, since it contemplates the *future* establishment of a commonwealth. . . .

Nevertheless, there is a problem in the adjustment of patriotism and religion. But to bring positive Zionism and positive Reform Judaism into an organic synthesis is a still more difficult and complex problem. First, because we are not citizens of Israel, living in the land, sharing in the responsibility for national decisions and in the consequences of those decisions. Even more difficult, those who have attempted this synthesis want Jewish nationalism to be a central factor in their religious viewpoint and a prime source of Jewish religious dynamic. We do not assign such decisive importance in our theological thinking, in our liturgy, or in our religious education, to our position as Americans and our relationship to our national life and government.

In short, while we have a great store of emotional warmth toward the Republic and people of Israel, it is extremely difficult to articulate an ideology in which our religious outlook and our devotion to the State of Israel are combined in an organic and at the same time logical unity. It is such considerations, no doubt, which have led to great searchings of heart among American Zionists. A most impressive effort to think through this problem is the address which our colleague Leon Feuer, presented before the Conference last year under the title "Beyond Zionism."

The approach I now suggest is slightly different from his in emphasis, though it does not in any way contradict it. It is simply that we should strengthen and reaffirm the concept of the Congregation of Israel, a world community which is at once a living reality and a religious doctrine. We relate ourselves to it not only in the theological terms of covenant and mission, but also through the familiar principle that all Israel are fellows and that all Jews are mutually responsible.

In these terms we can teach and pray concerning our own existence as part of world Israel, our devotion to the material and spiritual welfare of all Jews, and our dedication to the ancient covenant. Within this framework, the people and State of Israel occupy a special place. First, because we have made so great an investment, not only of dollars but even more of concern and devotion, in the land of Israel. Second, because its people are in a unique situation which gives them special opportunities and imposes upon them special problems.

The proposal that we should view the State of Israel within the larger framework of world Israel does not mean that we should be less devoted to the State, but that we should recognize more fully and intensely our obligation to the other communities of the world. Surely we ought to give more attention to the Jews of Latin America, who by all accounts have great spiritual needs even though they do not want bread. We should not lessen our efforts on behalf of U.J.A. and Israel Bonds; but we may well exert ourselves more for that most pathetic of all the stepchildren of the Reform movement, the World Union for Progressive Judaism.

This primary emphasis on the world Jewish community greatly relieves the theoretical difficulty. For the Congregation of Israel has no treasury or military or diplomatic corps; it does not employ economic or political strategy. It is both reality and concept. We can recognize simultaneously the divinely ordained destiny of our people and their human limitations. The pattern for this is clearly set forth by the second Isaiah. He describes his people as God's servant on whom He has put His spirit, who is to be a light of the nations, to open the blind eyes and bring out prisoners from the dungeon. But a few verses further on, the prophet exclaims: "Who is blind but My servant? Or deaf as My messenger that I send?" On this prophetic model, we may affirm the spiritual destiny of our people in all its glory without chauvinism, and at the same time castigate their faults without the suspicion of being pro-Arab. Once more, my intent is not to downgrade the dignity or the dearness of the Republic of Israel, but to heighten and intensify our awareness of, and concern with, all Israel everywhere.

II

The proposal to codify or at least standardize Reform Jewish observance has been debated with a vehemence which I cannot share. I am not enamored of chaos, and the proponents of a guide do not alarm me. Yet it seems entirely in keeping with the spirit of our movement and not inherently dangerous that different congregations and families should display much variation in practice—some warmly traditional, others austerely simple, some frankly experimental.

Nor do I share the excitement of some colleagues over the emergence of a more colorful and distinctively Jewish pattern of practice in our synagogues. Personally I like such a style of worship: I was brought up on it in a classical Reform congregation in Baltimore! But the real issue here is not the amount of traditionalism which the contemporary Reform congregation will tolerate. It is the extent to which our people will recognize and discharge concrete religious duties. We have always proclaimed the basic Jewish concept that religion is concerned with deed rather than creed. But this statement itself tends to become a kind of thin creed: how can we give it life and substance?

Not, I think, by spelling out the particular duties which a Reform Jew ought to perform. First we must find a way to convince our people that they do have an obligation to Judaism, to their people, to their God—an obligation to be discharged in specific and definite acts. As a rule, when we are commending some sort of observance to our people, we point out to them the advantages that will accrue to them from it—the sense of release, of tranquility, of balance that comes from participation in public worship; or the psychological and spiritual benefits which their children will derive from Sabbath and festival observance in the home. Critics may object that Judaism deals not in folk ways and pageantry, but in *mitzvot*— divine commands. But we rarely talk in these terms to our people, because most of us are not prepared to use such terms.

Frederic Doppelt and David Polish, in the introductory chapters of their *Guide,* have attempted to justify from the Reform standpoint this approach to Jewish observance as the fulfillment of actual *mitzvot*. Their arguments are interesting and impressive, but not compelling. They are on solid ground when they insist that the

Reform Jew must acknowledge some sacred obligations; but they do not make clear why he must recognize as *mitzvot* the particular items they include.[1]

Halacha, as understood through the ages, had these two features: it was highly specific and detailed, and it was regarded as divinely ordained. Now most of us believe in a general way that the great ethical principles of the Torah and prophets are a divine revelation; the problem is to apply them in practice. Our ancestors could rely on the *Poskim*. But we, with the best will in the world, find it hard to believe that the rules codified in the *Shulchan Aruch,* or the specific regulations in any Reform Jewish guide, or the resolutions adopted by majority vote on the floor of this Conference are God's revelation and commandment to us. I see no easy theoretical escape from this difficulty. It seems to be inherent in our liberal concepts of revelation and authority.

All we can do—and what we must do—is to try to convince our people, not only by our words but by our total demeanor, that we Reform Jews have duties and obligations, the definition of which must be left ultimately to the individual conscience, but the compelling power of which is beyond question. We can then encourage them to consider, under our guidance and with the help of available literature, what specific duties they regard as incumbent upon them. Some experience with this procedure indicates that many of our people are thinking seriously about the matter and trying to arrive at some positive conclusions. More may be accomplished by encouraging them to work their problem out for themselves than by providing them with a formalized guide.

Obviously our own conduct is a crucial element in this situation. And of course Halacha has always included much more than ritual. It has involved the application of moral principles to specific instances. Yet up to this point we, the leaders of American Reform Judaism, have not been prepared to define and to follow scrupu-

---

[1] Doppelt and Polish, *A Guide for Reform Jews* (New York, 1957), pp. 12–47. See also J. J. Petuchowski, "Problems of Reform Halakhah," *Judaism*, Vol. 4, pp. 339 ff. (Fall, 1955).

lously a Halacha that would regulate the moral aspects of our own profession. We have not been able to accept a discipline on such matters as officiating at mixed marriages, the relationship between rabbis in the same congregation, and other serious issues.

I am not arguing for blind conformity on moral questions after deprecating conformity in matters of ritual: that would be indeed a betrayal of the liberal principle. But a law-abiding citizen is not inevitably a conformist. Indeed, to obey the law is sometimes a highly unpopular form of non-conformism. Yet even one who reserves the right of private judgment and decision can admit the desirability of general agreement on rules and procedures. It is gratifying to learn, for example, that our present pulpit placement system, even without mandatory provisions or the power to impose sanctions, is working reasonably well, and that most rabbis and congregations conduct their pulpit negotiations through this machinery.

Through the method of free discussion and the spirit of good will, and especially through the visible demonstration by rabbinic and lay leaders of their own readiness to abide by norms and rules which have proved generally acceptable, we may arrive at an increasing measure of agreement in the field of rabbinical and congregational ethics, in the area of social justice, and in that of observance as well. And I suspect that the more we practice with some consistency the things we honestly believe we ought to do, the more these acts will take on some of the emotional and perhaps even the theological qualities of the *mitzvah* in the older sense of the term.

III

Salomon Formstecher was known as the philosopher of Reform Judaism. Yet in his principal work, *Die Religion des Geistes,* he does not mention Reform Judaism by name. He describes the liberal trend as the direct and natural continuation of the development of Judaism as he has traced it through the centuries. In the same spirit, Abraham Geiger refused to regard Reform as a denomination or sect. That is why he several times refused the

invitation to become rabbi of the Reform Society of Berlin, pre-
ferring to endure the storms that beat about him as he served an
inclusive community. He expected the Reform tendency to become
dominant; and he hoped that this progressive tendency could be
made standard for all the communities of German Jewry by means
of an officially chosen synod. These expectations were not fully
realized; still, the liberal movement made such progress that the
extreme Orthodox group led by Samson Raphael Hirsch seceded
from the official community of Berlin, Frankfort, and a few other
places. For the first time, Orthodoxy appeared as a dissident
minority.

Isaac M. Wise followed a strategy much like Geiger's. He viewed
Reform as *the* Judaism of the future, not as a splinter party. He
worked for Jewish unity, even making concessions to tradition for
which he was severely criticized, because he was confident that the
progressive forces would triumph. And his dreams, too, were by no
means chimerical prior to 1880.

Subsequent events have conditioned us to regard ourselves as a
minority, a significant and even a growing minority, but still a
minority deviating from the main body of Jewish religious life.
Some of us seem satisfied and perhaps even a little relieved that
it should be so. For though Reform meets their personal needs,
they doubt that a totally Reform Jewish community could survive
on its own.

Such a view must be taken seriously when expressed by so
devoted an adherent of our movement as Dr. Solomon B. Freehof.[2]
He does not idealize the past; he knows that Jewish modernism
came into existence because the old Orthodoxy could not hold its
own children. He praises Reform for its independent, experimental
approach, and for its contributions in beautifying Jewish worship
and reformulating Jewish theology. But Reform, he fears, is not
equipped to preserve and transmit the heritage of Hebraic learning
which is indispensable to Jewish survival. The Orthodox day

[2] *CCAR Journal,* October, 1957.

schools and Yeshivot still prepare not only specialized scholars, but a substantial group of laymen as well, to know, appreciate, and perpetuate Torah-learning. He concludes that the survival of Judaism requires a contribution from all three denominations, though he notes with deep concern that none of the three has yet succeeded in reviving a deep spirit of worshipfulness.

Now it is right that we should respect all the philosophies of Judaism, acknowledge the contribution each has made, and learn from their experiences and accomplishments. But to rely on any other branch of Judaism to make good our deficiencies and to supply needs which we are failing to meet comes perilously close to irresponsibility. We dare not be that easy on ourselves. For liberal Judaism, I submit, is becoming—if it has not already become—the dominant position among committed Jews. In the generations ahead, men will look on liberal Judaism in the broadest sense as the standard, the norm, the direct continuation of the main stream of Jewish religious life—while Orthodoxy becomes a minority sect.

This may sound shocking, but it is born out both by the lessons of history and the facts of the present.

Of course Orthodoxy is still very much alive, and recently has manifested a marked increase of vitality. No doubt there will always be a place in Judaism, as in the world in general, for the orthodox authoritarian position. But consider these facts:

First, nearly all the new congregations which have been established since the end of World War II are either Conservative or Reform. Second, sociological studies which appear to be objective indicate that, though the most disastrous defections from Orthodoxy have already taken place, the Orthodox movement will continue to decline slowly while the Conservative and Reform groups are holding their own pretty well.[3] Third, we all know that a substantial proportion of those who are members of Orthodox congregations are not personally Orthodox either in belief or practice. It is true that in all the synagogues there are plenty of members who are not

[3] Marshall Sklare and Marc Vosk, *The Riverton Study* (American Jewish Committee, 1957), pp. 9–16.

enthusiastically committed to the doctrine and program of their denomination. Note this difference, however. The inactive members of the Conservative and Reform congregations may lack ardor, but they are in a general way sympathetic to the liberal interpretation of the Jewish religion. But there are many people who belong to Orthodox congregations out of family loyalty, sentiment, superstition, or force of habit, and a mixed multitude who make use of Orthodox facilities and functionaries on special occasions in their lives, who are utterly remote from that acceptance of authority which is the very essence of Orthodox Judaism.

In short, all indications are that the dominant form of American Judaism will be modernist. The rather large segment of unsynagogued Jews will probably continue to decline. Some of these wanderers will disappear from Jewish life; a great part of them will join synagogues—and it is safe to assume that of these most will join liberal synagogues. In the future Orthodoxy may be more effectively organized; certainly it will be more articulate; but its status will be that of a dissenting minority.

All this may seem startling; but it will not be the first time in our history that the main highway of religious life has taken a sharp turn to the left, with the result that what had been the standard version of Judaism became a sectarian deviation. No doubt the conservative, literalist, sacerdotal doctrine of the Sadducees was "the old time religion," while the Pharisees were the innovators and revolutionaries. No doubt it was hard for many people to accept the notion of a standard Judaism without sacrifice and without supreme authority centered in the priesthood. At various times, people with a sense of history must have been troubled at the thought that the Judaism of the future would ban polygamy, or admit novel philosophic and cabalistic doctrines, or introduce new-fangled prayers and rites of intercession for the dead. In the same way, there may be some among us who find it difficult to conceive of a standard Judaism which is not based on the supernatural origin of the Torah and which does not include such practices as kashrut —even though we personally do not accept them. Yet the decision

of history seems to be clearer every day; and it would be strange
if we should be unwilling or reluctant to accept a verdict in our
own favor.

But it is natural and proper that we should manifest a certain
awe and even anxiety, asking ourselves whether we are adequately
prepared for the enormous responsibility implied. Certainly the
issue which so troubled Dr. Freehof, the issue of our relatively thin
and insufficient educational program, must be confronted with all
seriousness.

The dimensions of this problem, however, should be indicated
a little more precisely. As to the preservation and transmission of
Jewish learning, I believe we can do our full share. American Reform has already produced a fair number of competent professional
Jewish scholars and scholarly rabbis. The number of the latter
group will surely increase when the present explosive growth of
our movement has slowed down, and American Reform Judaism
arrives at a new equilibrium. It should be remembered that ancient
Israel did not come to Sinai until after it had been liberated from
hard labor with mortar and bricks! When our rabbis are less pre-
occupied with the construction of buildings and the organization
of new groups and activities, they will surely give more time to
study.

But in the past rabbinic learning was not confined to specialists;
a considerable body of laymen also shared in the heritage of the
Torah. Let us recognize frankly that we will hardly see again the
kind of Talmudic scholarship that was once common among the
Jews of Eastern Europe. Our most hopeful expectations do not
include a *Hevra Shas* in our temples. But whatever our sentimental
regrets, we do not need that kind of erudition. Time was when
most women could spin; today the technique is known only to
antiquarians. So with the skills required in managing a great clipper
sailing ship. The type of learning once dispensed at Volozhin must
in the future be the province of specialists. On the other hand,
many a learned Talmudist had only the vaguest notion of the role
played in history by the prophets of Israel, or of the achievements

of the Maccabees. We need a far better educated Jewish laity, but the standards of education we must set are necessarily different from those of other countries and centuries. We may expect to teach less Hebrew lore than some previous generations, but there are other areas of Jewish knowledge which were of no concern to them which we must stress vigorously. Our standards, in short, are not to be lower, but different. The task of adult Jewish education is immense. But the magnitude of the problem is not an excuse for relying on some other branch of Judaism to do our job; it is a challenge to hard and earnest labor.

We are also working to improve the quality of elementary education and increase the amount of time devoted to it. I must add that we have never fully exploited the possibilities even of the one-day-a-week school. In particular, we have not offered enough to students who are willing and able to learn more than a minimum. This criticism, so much directed against the secular schools of late, applies also to us. In many of our schools the youngsters who wanted to learn something have had to twiddle their thumbs while slower and less interested children were relearning for the ninth time the meaning of Pesach and Shabbos. While providing a realistic curriculum for those who are not ready for more, we must give the eager children—and we have them!—a chance to progress, including more intensive Hebrew instruction.

We may, however, expect an improvement in the preparation and attitude of many religious school children. The alumni of our youth groups who have attended conclaves and institutes, and the young parents who are now attending study groups on how to introduce their youngsters to Jewish experience will be sending us children who have already learned some of the basic prayers and ceremonies, who know something of the vocabulary of Jewish life, and for whom we will not have to begin at the absolute beginning. There is thus a strong possibility that we shall see a reversal of the trend of the last few generations in which children had less Jewish knowledge than parents, and grandchildren still less. As a greater interest in Jewish study develops, as people grow up in a milieu where there is more Jewish information, we may even hope to see a greater readiness to learn Hebrew. But so long as the United States remains a monolingual country where the teaching of foreign languages is ineffective, we cannot hope for too much. The total picture is one of opportunity for progress, though nothing is assured and though the responsibilities are heavy.

It will have been noted in what I have been saying that I refer to "some form of liberal, progressive, Judaism" and that I have included both Reform and Conservative Judaism in that category. The relationship between the two liberal branches of Judaism has been repeatedly explored, and I have nothing new to add. I see no clear, sharply definable line between the two movements in terms of basic philosophy. But I see no prospects on the horizon for any kind of organic merger between them. The differences between us, indeed, are not merely organizational. They ought not be minimized, but certainly should not be exaggerated. Every effort should be made to promote cooperation between Reform and Conservative Jews in areas of common interest. Past attempts at joint action have not been invariably successful, though sometimes they have yielded good results. I am concerned, however, not merely with cooperation between national organizations and institutions, where considerations of political expediency may interfere, but with encouraging "the life of dialogue" between Reform and Conservative thinkers.

A happy example of what can be done in this respect was the Samuel H. Goldenson Lecture delivered recently at our Cincinnati school by Dr. Jacob Agus. It is gratifying that this distinguished rabbi should have been invited to lecture under our auspices; his scholarly and stimulating discussion on "The Prophet in Modern Hebrew Literature"[4] revealed the great area of theological agreement between the two wings of Liberal Jewry.

We should do our best to eliminate irritations, to encourage cooperative efforts, and to avoid overstress on petty distinctions.

[4] *HUC Annual,* Volume XXVIII.

But while we doubtless can learn much from all groups of American Jewish life, it is important that we ourselves should be discerning and critical in what we borrow. We shall not gain anything by blurring basic principles or watering down convictions in the hope of achieving some kind of mechanical unification. In the long run we shall do more for Jewish unity if we "pick up the occupation of our fathers," and raise a standard to which all the just and wise may repair. To many people, it must have seemed that the early reformers were troublers of Israel. We now see that by their bold and courageous proclamation of principle, they provided the rallying point around which modern Jewry could order its scattered ranks. And it is perhaps the most serious criticism of contemporary Reform that we, whose forebears pioneered in rethinking the basic principles of Judaism in the light of modern social and intellectual conditions, have not carried on their work sufficiently. Since the publication of Kohler's *Jewish Theology* at the close of World War I, the theological output of the Reform movement has been meager, save for a few notable essays delivered before this Conference.

Many of us have been deeply dissatisfied with the kind of theological writing that has appeared in the last decades from Jewish pens. We find the thinking of Mordecai Kaplan and his school too naturalistic and chilly; on the other hand, we are disturbed by the different versions of neo-Orthodoxy that have made a stir in our world and have been much applauded by some of our Christian contemporaries. But if we do not like these restatements of Jewish belief, it is idle to belabor their authors or to chant lamentations. The only satisfactory response to the newer theologies is to go to work on them with the tools of reason, learning, and positive religious conviction. There have been repeated calls for a reformulation of the liberal Jewish religious viewpoint in the light of all the changes that have taken place in the outer world and in the inner life of mankind during the last few decades. But thus far we have had little more than introductions to, or appeals for, such a rewriting of liberal Jewish theology. I do not believe that any task of the present is more urgent than this one.

Thus, whatever area of the problem of Reform Judaism we consider, we come back again to the challenges and obligations that confront each one of us as Reform rabbis. Of the three pillars which, according to Simon the Just, sustain the world, our colleagues have done marvels to keep in repair the third—*gemilut hasadim*. They have worked tirelessly for the benefit of their own congregants, for the welfare of their communities, for the relief and redemption of their people, for social justice and world peace. A small group of men have over the years made a great contribution to the life of humanity. Nevertheless, there are *three* pillars on which the world stands. And it is our responsibility to rebuild and strengthen the pillars of *Torah* and *Avodah* as well.

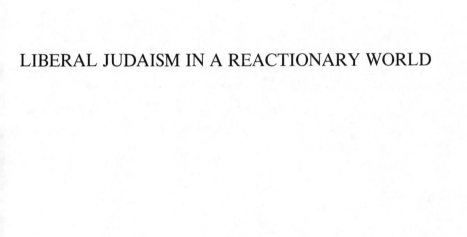

LIBERAL JUDAISM IN A REACTIONARY WORLD

Liberal Judaism in a Reactionary World

It is hard to conceive of two more different approaches than those presented by Levi A. Olan and William G. Braude to the question of the road ahead for Liberal Judaism in a world grown increasingly reactionary. This question was raised before the Central Conference of American Rabbis in 1942, amidst the rigors of the second World War. It was a time of stress and struggle, when no one could be certain that military victory would elude the forces of totalitarianism. Certainly no one could possibly have foreseen the extent to which the anti-liberal attitudes and philosophy of the defeated would be adopted by the victors. Yet it was clear that the fate of liberal ideas was at stake; and in a well-nigh classical manner the program committee of the Conference posed the question, What does this mean for the (Liberal) Jews?

Rabbi Olan rested his case on the universalistic tradition of liberal thought. He saw the various forms of reaction as belated attempts to restore a medieval authoritarianism, destructive of the freedom of the human mind and spirit. The future of Liberal Judaism he regarded as integrally bound to the future of liberalism in general. Consequently he advocated a continuing stress on the "fighting faith" of liberalism as the best guarantee of a future for Liberal Judaism.

Rabbi Braude declared this type of universalistic liberalism to have been proved bankrupt by events. He meant to include the events of the external world, of course, but he emphasized the internal developments in Liberal Judaism. With the forthrightness of a modern Jeremiah he described in mordant phrases "this active and extroverted religious community" and scathingly denounced the spiritual emptiness of Liberal Judaism and noted the failure of Jewish nationalism to fill the spiritual vacuum. His positive proposal was to develop within the Liberal Jewish movement, a group dedicated to spiritual revival, not in terms of the rabbinic dictum to "make a fence about the Torah" but rather in terms of the modified injunction to make a fence about holiness.

LIBERAL JUDAISM IN A REACTIONARY WORLD
(From the Point of View of Philosophy)
Levi A. Olan
(1942)

The philosophy of liberalism is under attack by forces external
and internal. Vast areas of our globe are populated by people who
are under the leadership of avowed enemies of the liberal spirit.
The very nation which was so instrumental in forging the intellectual pattern for the idealism of the nineteenth century is this day
dominated by the most violent force of reaction against it. Internally, liberalism is suffering from a confusion of philosophies.
Challenged by two world wars and the resultant flight of man to
extreme forms of salvation, liberalism has become a term without
meaning. The philosophy of irrational authoritarianism is spoken
for by an acknowledged liberal, and that of anti-empirical humanism is championed by an avowed catholic. This is confusion con-
founded as the liberalism of a hundred years ago tries valiantly to
maintain some semblance of respect and retain some measure of
public loyalty.

Liberal Judaism, being one of the constituents of general liberalism, finds itself today faced by the common problem. The approach
to an understanding of it may be made along more than one avenue
of analysis. In this discussion we shall limit ourselves by two arbitrary conditions. In the first place, by Liberal Judaism we do not
mean the general tendency toward liberalism which is inherent in

the tradition of the religion of Israel from the prophets' day until the Reform movement. That phase has been studied and described by many Jewish students. There is the unquestioned impulse toward a freedom from authority which has been well reported by one of the members of the Conference. By the term Liberal Judaism, we shall refer to that specific movement which took some definite shape about a century ago and is today represented by this Conference and affiliated bodies all over the world. In the second place, we shall further delimit our subject by discussing the general liberal religious problem without specific reference to the particular Jewish phase of it. This is done primarily because the attack upon liberal religion from the viewpoint of philosophy is essentially the same for all the component members. The problem of Liberal Judaism is fundamentally the problem of liberal religion everywhere, and, conversely, the problem of liberal religion everywhere is the problem of Liberal Judaism.

As a matter of fact, one of the failures of the study of Liberal Judaism has been that students have isolated it from the climate of opinions in which it arose. Unless one can view it in the totality of the liberal development, there is the danger of coming out with a picture hanging in an absolute void. Liberal Judaism was part and parcel of that historic movement which created the modern era, that era which is best characterized by the overthrow of authoritarianism in several areas of life. In politics it challenged the unquestioned right of kings to rule and gave rise to the concept of political democracy. In economics it stormed the position of the entrenched feudal classes and culminated in the French Revolution and the succeeding movements for a more equitable participation in the production and consumption of goods. In the field of thought, or specifically in religion and philosophy, it challenged the authority of a particular revelation and made way for the rationalism and empiricism of the newborn period. It can be asserted, with reasonable justification, that it was in this latter area, the revolution in thought, that the basic principle of liberalism was established. It is in the field of epistemology, the way of knowing truth, that the heart of this modern world is found. The change from authority based on revelation to truth sought by mind and experiment, plowed the soil in which the seeds of the political and economic revolutions took root and developed. If we are to understand liberalism at all, it is this basic change that must be clearly comprehended.

The task of supplanting divine revelation with human intelligence was no simple undertaking. To supplant magic and mystery with the methods of reason and science was not the labor of one man, nor of one generation, nor of one century. In point of fact, the struggle is still going on in many places of the earth. Beginning with Descartes in the seventeenth century who has the honor to be the first modern philosopher to affirm without equivocation the supremacy of reason, we had the first shot against the pillars which supported the world of thought until that time. By applying the methods of analytical geometry to the solving of all problems, the Cartesian creator injected the mathematical approach which was the basis for the rationalism that stormed the citadels of authority and tradition which had held the minds of men imprisoned since recorded time. When, in the next century, John Locke laid the foundations for an empirical philosophy, he forged the second of two forces which destroyed the old and created the new. Reason and experience were effective weapons for attacking the might of the past and discovering the potentiality of the future.

It is difficult for us to think of Isaac Newton as a revolutionary, for his creative work was neither thrilling nor popular. Yet, the modern world is inconceivable without the particular innovation which he brought forth. The term nature takes on meaning only as he reveals through his *Mathematical Principles of Natural Philosophy,* what it really is. The harmony and intelligibility of physical nature suggested that the natural could be discovered in other fields as well. Thus the chaos in the political field, as in the entire social realm, began to be contrasted with the order of the natural world. Religion, too, fell under the careful scrutiny of the naturalistic thinker, and men wondered whether the true form or the "natural," had not become corrupted with crude superstition and objectionable forms.

These three basic departures in methodology formed the triangular cornerstone of the enlightenment period which gave birth to the liberalism of the nineteenth century. This is not the place to trace the fascinating story of the development of these principles. One can only suggest that at the hands of David Hume and Immanuel Kant, George Wilhelm Frederick Hegel and others this evolution fought its way back and forth until it was concretized in the basic philosophic pattern of the mid-nineteenth century—an absolute moral idealism, the dominant philosophy of well-nigh a hundred years. Two essential factors characterized the achievement of this philosophy. First, and of increased importance to our day, was the emphasis upon the freedom of the mind in its search for truth. The victory against special revelation was decisive and the century following was markedly effective in employing and extending the techniques of logic and research. This freedom is basic to liberalism in all fields including religion. Second, was the creation of a philosophy which fostered one of the most hopeful and progressive eras in history. The supreme emphasis was on the moral nature of the universe, and from it followed the two potent corollaries of freedom and progress. Man came marching into the world as a free moral being assured that the universe was favorably disposed towards his sincere efforts to perfect his social and personal life.

This philosophy of moral idealism had a significant influence on the continent of Europe, which is not our concern at this time. It was in the United States that its most fruitful effect may be studied. Not only is there a direct relationship of our two basic documents of nationhood to such thinkers as John Locke and David Hume, but what is of even more immediate interest, the development of a philosophy of society that is stamped with the liberal philosophy of the nineteenth century. It was Emerson in 1836 who declared, "The moral law lies at the center of nature and radiates to the circumference." It was the father of constitutional thought, John

Marshall, who wrote "There are principles of abstract justice which the Creator of all things has impressed on the mind of His created man." This thought is made explicit by Mr. Justice Story in his *Commentary on the Constitution* when he said, "The rights of conscience are indeed beyond the reach of human power. They are given by God and cannot be encroached upon by human authority, without criminal disobedience to the precepts of natural as well as revealed religion." Here was the moral absolute set at the base of American democracy. This gave rise to a government of laws and not of men which secured the equality of rights for men. Under tyranny law was and is the chance whim of the ruler; under moral law it became the challenge to man to translate his individual and social law to conform to this higher moral dictate. As one student aptly phrases it, "moral order was really a doctrine of cosmic constitutionalism." The belief in progress followed naturally from this concept of freedom. Emerson epitomized it in a pithy sentence, "Liberty is an accurate index in men and nations of general progress." However, moral idealism waited patiently until the great commoner of American history chiseled it into immortal phrases which have become the beacon light for faith and freedom. "I have never had a feeling politically," said Lincoln in 1861, "which did not spring from the Declaration of Independence . . . I have often inquired of myself what great principle it was that kept this confederacy so long together. It was not the mere matter of the separation of the colonies from the mother land, but something in that Declaration, giving liberty not alone to the people of this country, but hope for the world for all future time. It was that which gave promise that in due time the weight should be lifted from the shoulders of all men . . . and that all should have an equal chance."

Here, then, was the rich ripe fruit of the seed sown at the dawn of the modern period of history. Here in the new world did the flowering of the enlightenment become real. Here did moral idealism become a faith justifying the revolution in thought which Rationalism ushered into the seventeenth century for the first time.

Here it was transformed into a dynamic faith that fashioned the political and social forces of a century of progress. Here, too, did Liberal Judaism find its most fertile soil for development. All of the pent up potentialities were set free on the shores of the new world where, nurtured by the liberal atmosphere, there evolved the most influential liberal Jewish movement in the world. It would be significant at this point to rehearse the ideas of the early preachers of Reform in America to demonstrate the integral relationship of the moral idealism of the country to the fervor of the liberal theology which they were creating. But this has been done by others and must be here assumed. Sufficient to our thesis is it that Liberal Judaism in America was a component part of the liberal faith which was to shape the certain progress of the future as man moved to fulfill his moral promise.

It is generally assumed that liberalism stood its ground until World War One. During the period of about a hundred years it was threatened several times by antagonistic philosophies but successfully weathered the attacks and arose stronger than before the combat. Thus, Darwinism was one of the early sources of serious concern to liberal religious thinkers, but not for long. Having accepted the evolution of religious history as it affected the Bible, it was not difficult to fit the evolution of man into the liberal theology. Whether one stopped with Fiske's famous pronouncement that evolution is the way God works, or went on to the more profound elaborations of Bergson or Lloyd Morgan with their creative and emergent evolutionary theories, the vital point here is that Darwinism was fully assimilated by liberal thinkers. From their point of view it made God greater than merely an argument from design and made man a more hopeful creature. In fact, it had the optimism of the era inherent in it.

The second threat came from the mechanistic materialism which was rampant during the last three decades prior to the First World War. It derived its theories from the Newtonian physics of Mass-Space-Time; matter moving in absolute space and time. This gave rise to the law of necessity in a universe of fixed patterns. In the flush of enthusiasm which their rigid determinism engendered, there hurriedly burst forth the hope that all life could some day be explained under these fixed forms. Indeed, even biology and psychology would be harnessed to the universal machine. The recorded pages of the struggle between theologians and mechanists now make amusingly sad reading. Time, through steady scientific research, has eliminated the problem for liberal religion. The revision of the concept of matter into the principle of Heisenberg's indeterminacy plus Planck's Quantum theory has made of determinism an interesting museum piece in the gallery of man's superstitions. When Einstein added insult to injury by transforming the fixed time-space theory into one of the simultaneity of time-space, the ghost of mechanism was unequivocally interred. This newer physics again supported the freedom of the human will and made way for the pragmatic theory of knowledge so ardently championed by John Dewey. Liberal religion hailed the modern naturalism a bit too fervently, neglecting the problems which arise from indeterminacy and relativity. But the atomistic threat against freedom was overcome and liberalism still stood its ground.

The last and most recent challenge has come from the textbooks of modern psychology. While it is true that the battle lines of its conflict with liberal religion are not as sharply defined as in the other two, yet a threat has been hurled and the struggle is still on. The most disturbing phase appeared in the form of behaviorism as represented by John Watson. This had its heyday from 1915 to 1930. Based as it was on the mechanistic physics which was doomed, it met an early and quiet demise. The scuffle was short-lived and never a very serious threat. In fact, the succeeding psychology of the Gestalt school of Wolfgang Köhler, which built its concepts on "wholeness" and "forms" of thought, comes very near intimating the objectivity of values in nature. It may even develop to be the complete repudiation of the mechanical interpretation from the viewpoint of psychology. However, it is the psychology of the "unconscious" as created by Freud and his disciples which arrests the attention of liberal faith today. That there are dangers in the idea of religion as a wish fulfillment, has been pointedly said many times. To explain God by an Oedipus complex is a definite challenge to the moral concept of life which is at the base of liberal religion. This is not the place to enter upon an evaluation of this problem save to point to one or two suggestions. In the first place, the disciples of Freud, especially Jung, are coming nearer in attitude, if not in thought, to the essential value of religion. Secondly, we must beware lest we accept Freudianism as a science. If we look upon it as a tool for research and take its valid findings we may discover that it will serve our liberal faith devotedly. The finality of Freud is absurd; the possibilities are vast. While we cannot say of Psychology, as we did of Darwinism and Mechanism, that liberalism stood stronger at the final mark, we are justified in positing the assertion that the essential tenets of liberal religion as it is here described have not been seriously affected.

Here, then, is the picture of liberalism in general and liberal religion in particular as it enters into the latest era, this period of our day which is so steeped in reaction. The two basic tenets, that of freedom of the mind in its search for truth and that of the moral nature of the universe in which man freely and progressively pursues his fulfillment, have successfully weathered the threefold blasts of Evolution, Mechanism and Psychology. That there have been significant changes during this century no one will deny. Certainly the pure rationalism of the Kantian school has given way to a greater emphasis on the empirical source of knowledge. The absolutism of yesterday has suffered some serious redefinitions. Yet, by and large, the essence of liberalism remains true to its original formulation of a hundred years ago. It is in our day that its basic tenets are being challenged both externally and internally and it is to this last phase that we now turn our attention. This aspect of the problem will be understood more readily if it is remembered that the First World War was its mother and the ensuing period of stammering peace was its nursemaid.

The most clearly defined formulation of anti-liberalism may be subsumed under the term fascism. This external threat to liberalism is so painfully arresting at this moment that it calls but for mention and not for elaboration. The threat to the social, economic and political foundations of liberalism is apprehended even by the untutored of all democracies. What is not grasped by many, but is the crux of this conflict, is the attack of all fascists upon the basic philosophy of liberalism. It is anti-intellectualism which characterizes these reactionary forces. "It is faith that moves mountains not reason. Reason is a tool, but it can never be the motive force of the crowd." That statement can readily be ascribed to any of the preliberal-era spokesmen. Actually it is a pronouncement of Mussolini. In the jumbled ravings of Hitler there are many attacks upon reason and science. Here is but one! "Faith is more difficult to shake than knowledge . . . He who wishes to win the broad masses must know the key which opens the door to its heart. It is not objectivity, i.e., weakness, but will and strength." Whatever else these words mean, they are aimed to discourage the use of man's mind and his powers of scientific research as a way of knowing the truth.

This anti-intellectual movement has its philosophers. Nietzsche is justly revered by all fascists, for not only does he sanctify a dominating class in the social scheme, but he sets the anti-intellectual basis in academic thought. Thus he wrote, "we must recognize untruth as a condition of life," or "the falsest opinions are the most indispensable to us." Sorel is another of the intellectual patrons of fascism. In his defense of myths he writes, "Science can help us little and parliamentary deliberations not at all. Hence reliance must be put upon intuition alone" as contrasted with "considered analysis." When we turn directly to the spokesman for fascism we catch the fruit of these philosophic labors. The Nazi Rosenberg expounds it in this fashion. "Just as nature and its happenings have nothing to do with reason or logical requirements, so also during great historical movements, the same forces of nature operating in the human soul overlap the confining wall of logic." In the more stentorian tones of Mussolini it appears as, "We have created a myth. The myth is a faith, it is a passion.

It is not necessary that it shall be a reality. It is a reality by the fact that it is a goal, a faith, that it is courage."

This irrationalism as a basis for faith finds its way into the more weighty academicians of fascism, Pareto and Spengler. Both of these build exclusively upon an anti-rational, anti-empirical epistemology. Their social theories are reared upon the basis of mystic revelations and authoritarian sanctions. The entire fascist ideology is so markedly a reversion to the pre-Cartesian age, that we are tempted to suggest that as the basis of the conflict of our era. It is a mistake to see in these reactionary forces only the political, social and economic challenge to liberalism. Far more important is the threat to the basic concepts of liberalism, the free mind and the moral universe in which it operates. Both of these are under merciless attack today, not only in Germany and Italy whom we have here cited. In justice one ought to point to Russia which basically supports an anti-intellectual philosophy, and to many people who live in democracies but whose mental climate is that of fascism. The authoritarian political and economic forms of modern totalitarian states and advocates of it are not separable from the intellectual authoritarianism which they accept. Just as in the pre-liberal era both were integrally related, so they are today.

It is in this sense that the liberal faith is involved in the present world struggle. The two basic tenets are being opposed by the most coherent forces that have appeared since their conscious formulation a century ago. Liberal Judaism is here inevitably involved as a member of the larger liberalism in religion, society and philosophy. Just as no liberal can compromise with the fundamental principles of his faith, so we are called upon to fortify our loyalty to the idea of a free mind in a moral universe. In this conflict between fascism and liberalism wherever it breaks out we are challenged to a profound re-affirmation of our progressive, idealistic heritage. Whether or not we emerge triumphant in this conflict depends on many factors inherent in our age. But that the liberal philosophy in which we were born and nurtured deserves our unswerving loyalty must be the supreme faith of all the component members of liberalism, including Liberal Judaism.

The internal threat to liberalism is in our discussion confined to the realm of religious thought. The absolute idealism which characterized the beginning of liberal religions is today no longer acceptable to large numbers of liberal thinkers. In point of fact, so diffused is the field of religious philosophy that to extract a clear philosophy for liberal religion from the blurred mass, appears as a hazardous undertaking. In the not too distant past one could enumerate the four great traditions in religious philosophy: Supernaturalism, Idealism, Romanticism and Naturalism. Most thinkers fell neatly into one of these categories. Today this procedure is impossible. The emphasis has been shifted to epistemology, thus creating supernaturalists who are naturalists, mystics who are empirical, and naturalists who are theists or humanists. This confusion cries out for a re-examination of the original philosophic formula which graced the birth of liberalism. The last two decades have produced more literature in the field of religious philosophy than any other period in the last century. A possible explanation for this increased interest may be found in Professor Wieman's distinction between theology and philosophy. When traditional religion is satisfactory we have theology, which is a clarification and systemization of accepted basic tenets. When traditional religion is not satisfactory, we have a philosophy, i.e., a criticism of the assumptions in theology. The unusual emphasis on philosophy of religion in our day may be a sign that our theology is not satisfactory and demands a critical re-examination. In this discussion we propose merely to indicate the general trend of thought and to present a bare outline of a possible philosophy for Liberal Judaism which is within the tradition of its liberal philosophic beginnings.

There are three modern philosophies of religion which fail to satisfy the standards of liberal thought. The first may be called the neo-supernaturalist, as represented by Kierkegaard and Barth on the continent and by the brothers Niebuhr in America. Here we are again faced with the authoritarianism of the pre-liberal era, and a genuine anti-intellectual approach to religious knowledge. Its main doctrine of God's absolute "otherness" which has no relationship with nature, reason, ideals, values, etc. precludes its inclusion in a philosophy of liberal religion. To say that God is in His heaven and thou art on earth as the Barthians of all shades do, is to ally oneself with anything but the liberal tradition. Since God in this instance reveals Himself as He chooses, a theory of knowledge is a meaningless concept. To accept the revelation of God by myth and paradox, which is the epistemology of this school, is, whatever its intrinsic value may be, opposed to the rational, empirical approach so basic to liberal thought. In general, its emphasis is upon an unknowable God and a helpless man. A theory of social progress such as is characteristic of the tradition of liberalism is logically impossible in this newest form of reactionary irrationalism. The slogan of this philosophy may well paraphrase a reverse Kantianism, that what is irrational is real and what is real is irrational.

A second school of thought which fails to meet the test of liberalism is that of modern absolute idealism or what is more pertinent as a description, the dualistic realists. The essential point of weakness in this group is its arbitrary ruling out of an objective reality which may be determined empirically. It derives its philosophy from Kantian idealism and Schleiermacher's "feeling of dependence." It is pure rationalism and unrelated to the nature and structure of the universe as revealed by the physical sciences. Its emphasis is upon religious value judgments as in the case of Ritschl or critical rationalism as in Ernest Troeltsch and Rudolf Otto. Driven to its final formulation, their philosophy expresses itself in some phase of religious agnosticism. Both Henry Mansel and Herbert Spencer accepted this Kantian dualism which precludes the possibility of experiencing the object of worship. Mansel arrived at authoritarian traditionalism and Spencer at avowed agnosticism. It is to be regretted that this school of rationalists which contributed so much to the birth of liberalism by emphasizing reason as opposed to special revelation hardened itself into a fundamentalism. By refusing to extend its methodology to the growing body of experiential knowledge, it severely limited its services to a philosophy of liberal religion.

A third school of thought which does not satisfy the standards of a liberal religious philosophy is what is popularly known as the pragmatic or the instrumental. Its forerunners are Feuerbach who made of atheism a religion; Lange who saw religion as poesy; Leuba who announced that the God idea is useful even if it is not true; and Vaihinger who stressed the concept of necessary fictions. The modern disciples of this philosophy vary in kind and emphasis from Jung who sees the therapeutic value of religion to Santayana who recognizes it as an expression of the moral needs and aspirations of mankind and stresses the feeling of piety found in the symbolic religious heritage handed down from the past. John Dewey is bolder in his pragmatic aims, proposing that man's creative imagination finds in nature the ends of life. Unlike Santayana, Dewey fears too much reverence for the past. This school goes from the non-theistic Hayden who speaks of religion as the cooperative quest of the good life, through Walter Lippman's disinterestedness, and Bertrand Russell's realistic humanism which concludes that outside human desire there is no moral standard. The essential weakness of this school is that its hope for man is set in a universe which is, at best, neutral and often hostile to his efforts. It should be pointed out that the advanced social program which every member of this philosophic school sponsors falls into conflict with a cosmology that does not support its successful fulfillment. Personal salvation may be achieved no matter whether the world is hostile or friendly. But a social good depends in the end on natural forces. The unpardonable finality and intolerance of this philosophy as to the possibility of an empirical study of religious knowledge is as fallible as that of authoritarianism. Whatever else be the merit of this psychological idealism, and its merits are considerable, from the point of view of liberal religion it is as unsatisfactory as neo-supernaturalism and absolute idealism.

The denial of a place on the program of liberal religion to these three schools of philosophy should not blind us to the constructive contribution that each has to offer to the totality of religious knowledge. The Barthian theologians of crises are incurably authoritarian, yet they remind us of the checks which our age must put upon the deification of man in humanism which has run so rampant in the last few decades. The humanists, who are essentially non-theistic or atheistic, are withal necessary signposts against a deflation of man before the unknowable but omnipotent deity. The absolute idealists who are consciously blind to the contributions of the natural sciences and their empirical methods, are, nevertheless, indispensable as a warning against the exclusion of the large area of religious experience inherent in mysticism as experience and reason as a method. Indeed, all of them possess invaluable aids to a suitable philosophy of religion from the standpoint of a modern liberal. Individually, however, we cannot follow them in their totality without losing the basic character of a liberal faith.

Our discussion should arrive at some principles for a philosophy of liberal religion. Four general characteristics are here suggested as a possible basis for definition and formulation. In the first place, we affirm our faith in the competency of human intelligence. It is in this aspect that fascism is so glaringly antagonistic and Barthianism so sadly irrational. Liberalism was born out of the discovery that man could progressively know more and more of God and the universe. Secondly, the epistemology of liberalism must be eclectic. Knowledge about the ultimate nature and character of the spiritual must be sought in mind, in experience and in nature. It may be suggested that Professor MacIntosh of Yale has here proposed a theory which deserves serious consideration. He speaks of empirical theology as a possible technique of experimentation in the realm of religious experience. The minute formulae for these experiments are suggestive of the emphasis which must be placed upon the method of science in religious knowledge. In the third place, liberal religion is meaningless without an affirmation of the validity of the objective reality that is God. It is in this field that pragmatism and humanism display the most grievous shortcoming. The nature of God need not and cannot be described with finality. The question of the attributes of the ultimate reality need not be settled dogmatically by liberal religion. There are suggestions from cosmological theists like Whitehead and his "principle of concretion," Brightman and his "supreme consciousness" or even Wieman and his "mode of behavior in the cosmos." The differences are subject to further research along the methods proposed in our article on method. Any philosophy without theism is essentially a social theory and not a religion. Lastly, the ethical beliefs both personal and social should be established on the first three principles. Religious ethics as distinguished from humanitarian ideals must rest upon the reality of basic laws in the universe. These are to be sought by all methods at man's disposal and should be held eternally possible of discovery.

These four principles, obviously, are not proposed as new dogmas for liberal religion. At best they are suggested minimal standards aimed at giving shape to a movement which is in danger of becoming all things to all people. The formulation of basic principles tends to dissolve the confusion which the undefined status of religion presents at this time. Certain philosophies of religion will be asked to forego the term liberal or even the word religion. The remainder will be small in size but consequently more dynamic in faith. Furthermore, these four principles are true to the spirit of liberal religion as it arose out of the enlightenment of the modern world. The emphasis is still upon a free mind in a universe of law. It is true that these have been re-defined and extended to include a century of development, yet, in their basic nature the essence of liberalism is paramount. It is well to remember that liberalism does not mean a middle of the road between progressives and conservatives. It rather aims to conserve the truth or good of the past, not the errors. Progress is the process of adding to what we conserve!

There are two obvious criticisms which can be anticipated and partially satisfied. The first deals with the failure to discuss Liberal Judaism specifically instead of liberal religion generally. The criticism is valid and is seemingly fatal. The answer lies in the assumption here made that the principles of liberal religion are basically the same for all faiths. That there are unique interpretations in Jewish tradition no one can or cares to deny. Our emphasis has been upon the common characteristics of liberal religion primarily because of the belief that, in the main, they are the essentials. It should be noted, however, that there is relatively speaking, a surprisingly small amount of published material in the field of modern Jewish philosophy. Compared to Christian theologians and philosophers, we are paupers.

The second criticism is directed against the move from the absolute to the probable. Here, too, we have a valid criticism, but one that arises from a narrow interpretation of liberal religion. Indeed, the faith of our liberal fathers was set in the pattern of idealism which was shaped by certainties already achieved, and not to be quested for from that day unto eternity. In this sense, the proposed principles for liberal religion extends the concept into a philosophy of theoretical relativism. As Professor Groos cogently argues this concept, "final proof, complete demonstration and logical certainty can never be reached by human skill on any matter whatever. No knowing leads to absolute certainty." Professor [E. S.] Brightman summarizes this idea poignantly . . . "it may be interpreted to mean that our most coherent hypotheses are, if not finally demonstrated truths, at least means of moving toward truth. They are not dogmatic revelation, but they fulfill the purposive function of leading man in the direction of the revealer of truth. They are, therefore, not certain, but they are heuristic. Such, at least is the faith on which progress in science rests; and it is not incoherent to suppose that a similar faith is valid in the realm of religious knowledge."

The faith of a liberal is undying. The periodic eruptions by reactionary movements have not extinguished the flame. Liberalism is essentially optimistic as it is practically progressive. It stakes its life upon the guarantee of a meaningful universe possessed of a God who assures the success of man's sincere efforts towards Him. If, at this moment in history, the forces of darkness are rampant, the liberal sets about to sharpen his weapons and reaffirms his determination. With certain ideas a liberal cannot compromise. That man is free to search and know God cannot be compromised no matter what the cost. That the universe will sustain man's highest hopes for the ultimate good cannot be compromised. The religion of the liberal is a fighting faith that draws its strength from the assurance that is given by the integrity and potentiality of the cosmic affirmation.

LIBERAL JUDAISM IN A REACTIONARY WORLD
(From the Point of View of History)
William G. Braude
(1942)

Out of the ruins of classic belief there slowly emerged Liberal Judaism as we know it. Men had begun to challenge transmitted tenets and to brush aside ancient practices. Many sought quick salvation at baptismal fonts. Akiba Eger and Raphael Cohen closeted in their four ells of Halakah did not see at first the stigmata of collapse. When they saw them they attempted to cauterize them with thunderclaps which struck no terror. Others like Israel Jacobson and Abraham Geiger, also concerned with the destiny of Israel, at first timidly and later boldly introduced reforms in worship, practice and belief. They and nameless others wrought the patterns of Liberal Judaism.

Their reforms were facilitated by the social, political and intellectual climate of the times. The Jew had begun to move fearlessly among his gentile neighbors and, to avoid conspicuousness, he clipped his beard and gaberdine without benefit of שאלות.[1] Everywhere there was talk of the rights of man and the Jew dared hope that he too might have a share in these rights. He was encouraged in this hope by a dizzy optimism filling the air. Rumania and Russia to be sure still had their Jewish question, as it was politely

---

[1] *She'elot*—Ritual Questions.

called, but everyone was certain that those lands cluttered with antiquated hatreds would through patient suasion be swept clean by the warm and luminous waves of progress and humanity. The few Jews who read the works and the periodicals put out by the pioneers of *Juedische Wissenschaft* learned that the Jewish religion was not a sudden fiat at Sinai, but a story of worldwide growth, of ever more pleasant evolution or dialectic in a kind of gradual theophany. Reading those works they thought they heard the steps of the Messiah coming ever faster and ever nearer. The European concert of nations was to bid the Messiah a ringing welcome. Soon, soon nations would no more strive for specious honor, for raw materials, for weapons of war. Instead they would vie with each other in the unfolding of their national destinies. Music and philosophy, reason and letters were to become the coins of international exchange. The people of Israel was to contribute ethical monotheism to this sweet harmony. It was a lovely vision which came to be substituted for the satisfactions of classic faith. To be sure, the intimate assurances of שור הבר,[2] of תחית המתים,[3] of God, the shepherd, piping אל תירא עבדי יעקב [4] were gone. But these losses were compensated by assurances of civil and political comity which were strongest, of course, in the United States.

God ceased to be the intimate companion of Reb Yaakob, but then God was at work in the larger world. He was busy revealing himself in the *Zeitgeist*. He was the *demiurgos* seen ever more clearly in the happier courses of human history.

Now inasmuch as civil and social adjustments were principal preoccupations of the nineteenth century, Liberal Judaism, its faithful child, was neither meditative nor mystical. Its chief expressions were directed כלפי חוץ.[5] Its major ambitions were externalized. Here, for example, is the testimony of Myer Stern sketching the history of Reform Judaism in America: "Magnificent

---

[2] The meat of the wild ox served to the righteous in paradise.
[3] "Resurrection of the dead."
[4] "Fear not my servant Jacob." Isaiah 44.2.
[5] "To the outside."

shrines rose all over America, showing the world that the fire which consumed Jerusalem's temple was not the death warrant of the wandering Jew, but that his staff had bloomed forth anew to hold out the promise of mankind's spiritual regeneration."[6] Note the phrases "magnificent shrines," "showing the world". These are visual words. And "the promise of mankind's spiritual regeneration" as read in the context is atingle with Messianic intimations.

In this active and extroverted religious community, glittering temples on main streets, dazzling interiors with no place for meditation or study, competent rabbis vying with journalists and politicians in their comments on public affairs took the centre of the stage.

Leading ideas in our religious arsenal were similarly externalized. In the limits of a paper, only the ראשי פרקים [7] of these ideas can be indicated. Take in illustration the virile hope, לתקן עולם במלכות שדי,[8] inadequately rendered as the kingdom of God and rapidly paraphrased as the universalistic impulse. Unquestionably ours is the first great missionary religion of the Western world. We were the first who sought to bring men תחת כנפי השכינה.[9] But we insisted that only by repentance could men—individuals, not masses of men—come to God. The rabbis were determined to put an end to the antinomian trend of which Paul was an outstanding example. For among Jews, too, some believed that the whole burden of the law need not be imposed upon converts. The rabbis, no less universalistic, to use the fashionable jargon, were determined not to compromise. Judaism was not to be whittled down. The Revelation could not be bargained with. No special groups recognizing it in different degrees were to be tolerated. Whereupon

[6] See *Rise and Progress of Reform Judaism in America . . . from the . . . Records of Temple Emanu-El*, by Myer Stern, New York, 1895, p. 130.

[7] "Chapter headings."

[8] "To perfect the world under the suzerainty of Shaddai." (*Shaddai* is usually translated, "almighty." The Englishing does not convey the overtones of tenderness and splendor.) The phrase occurs in the ancient *Alenu* prayer. See *The Singer Translation of the Daily Prayer Book*, 13th ed., London, 1925, pp. 76-7 and *The Singer-Abrahams Companion to the Daily Prayer Book*, p. lxxxvi.

[9] "Under the wings of the Shekinah." Shabbat 31a.

they proceeded with infinite detail and patience to assert and to prove by Scripture that the proselyte was bound to observe all the details of the Jewish law, that he was, in a word, "our brother in the Revelation and in the commandments."[10]

But we nineteenth- and twentieth-century Liberal Jews have annulled for ourselves and for others most of the commandments; we have paraphrased revelation as the religious genius of Israel; we were left essentially with the strident and clamorous plea that all men were brothers; we ardently hoped that our neighbors would echo our cry, slough their distinctiveness and merge with us into a vague and formless union. Kaufmann Kohler, for example, writes: "People crave for unity, for a faith which unites Protestant, Catholic and Jew, nay even Mohammedan and Hindoo Theists in a God who is the father of all . . . Is this not the God of the Bible, of patriarch and prophet . . .?"[11] Obviously, since the patriarchs did not exist and the daily religion of the prophets was lost beyond recovery, the God of the patriarchs and the prophets is a meaningless apostrophe. Note, too, the significant omission of sage and teacher. Are they out because they lend a distinctive, inescapably rabbinic flavor to the potpourri? Lesser men were even more outspoken in these aspirations.[12] We thus unwittingly reduced the dream שדי לתקן עולם במלכות[13] to a hollow non-sectarianism bristling with disavowals of strong faith. The classic Jewish tradition never sought formless unity. We sought to make men our brothers in the revelation. We were not content with externalized utterances. Our virile inwardness, our rugged belief in a בורא ומנהיג לכל הברואים[14] was not to be polished down to a pleasant doctrine of public relations.

Many people in our ranks, sensing the emptiness of fashionable

---

[10] *Midrash Tannaim*, ed. Hoffmann, p. 156 (on Deut. 24.7). See on this my *Jewish Proselyting*, Providence, 1940, p.98.

[11] The Mission of Israel in *Studies, Addresses and Personal Papers* by K. Kohler, New York, 1931, p. 192.

[12] See re Krauskopf, for example, *Reform Judaism in America* by Beryl Harold Levy, New York, 1933, pp. 10, 57–58.

[13] "To perfect the world under the suzerainty of Shaddai."

[14] "Guide and creator of all creatures."

universalistic utterances, came forward with a panacea—Jewish Nationalism drawn right out of the intellectual arsenal of the nineteenth century. In behalf of this cause much debating blood was shed on the floor of this conference. The protagonists of the panacea charged that the denial of nationhood was the original sin of Reform Judaism. Its reaffirmation, they declared, would infuse it with the elixir of life.

The controversy raged with all the fire of a liturgical יצמח פורקניה ויקרב משיחיה. [15] נצמח פורקניה פורקניה we shall bring our own redemption, shouted the nationalists. ויקרב משיחיה why bother? Zion is here in Berlin, in Cincinnati! responded the so-called universalists. The Hatikvah is now in the Union Hymnal, the highest officials of the Conference are Zionists and the struggle has lost its punch. It is now possible to survey it dispassionately. Without the nationalist ardor the epochal work in Palestine would never even have started and the Hebrew language would not have been modernized.

But our concern is religion. And here plain words ought to be spoken. Some men, impressed by the visible achievements of the nationalist idea, by the many colonies, the stacks of Hebrew books, the reams of periodicals, felt that it might perform the same miracle for religion—a hope typical of an extrovert, mechanically minded era. Indeed, some rabbis, disciples of the Spencerian positivist, Ahad Haam, have proclaimed nationalism as the matrix for religion. For a while, these men had considerable influence. Second thoughts on nationalism are now becoming articulate. Briefly they declare: Religion is not one of the phases of the national spirit. *Mizvot*[16] are not strips of metal in the national armor. עשו שרין קיום האומה [17] was never the concern of lawmakers. *Mizvot* as ethnic integrators cannot endure. Witness Eliezer ben Yehuda who began to observe them in that spirit and abandoned them ruth-

---

[15] "May His redemption sprout forth and the Messiah come quickly." The introduction of this phrase by a Hasidic precentor into the Kaddish was apt to cause great commotion in a Lithuanian synagog.

[16] Divine precepts for human discipline and sanctification.

[17] "The forging of armor for the survival of the nation."

lessly after a while. The present efforts by certain groups to develop a rationale for *Mizvot* as folkways, are likely to go back to the pulp whence they came.

We are beginning to feel that Jewish nationhood is not an absolute command. It is blasphemous to make God the unborn subsidiary to *natio,* to that which is born, and its transient urgencies. Most of the nationalist thinkers have been unbelievers. Synagogs were not houses of prayer in their eyes, but national monuments, בתי עם,[18] if you will. Jewish festivals were not manifestations of God's glory and power in the life of men. They were victorious days in the national calendar made more delightful by varied delectable dishes.

Listen to the words of Yechezkel Kaufmann—they crystallize a thoroughgoing analysis of Jewish History: "Ahad Haam's Spiritual Zionism, which propounds the Palestinian center, and Dubnow's Diaspora nationalism, which believes in Diaspora centers, rest on a specious diagnosis of the factors which have always operated in the history of Israel, to wit, an inaccurate evaluation of the religious determinant.

"The Jewish religion did not serve as an instrument for the national will to survive. Neither was it a storehouse of 'wanderer's impedimenta' which the national will to live used as it saw fit. Religion was the prime mover in the history of Israel. It isolated the nation from its environment, compelled it to persist in uniqueness. . . . Religion brought exilic autonomy into being and created the exilic centers . . . Religion provided the world-wide basis for national unity and existence . . . The need for a center itself was a religious one, and the capacity of the center to influence its perimeter was rooted in religion. The channels of influence which connected all the exiles into one religio-national complex were religious in character. For how and in what manner could the Jewish *Yishub* in Palestine that spoke Aramaic influence Greek Jewry except through the force and within the province of reli-

---

[18] "Houses for the people."

gion? . . . There is no historic evidence for the belief that a secular culture created anywhere—even in Palestine—could influence the exile and keep it unified . . . No secular culture of any people ever kept its sons from assimilation. In this respect Erez Israel does not differ from other centers. The strength of Erez Israel was in its sanctity and not in its being a nursery for national culture."[19]

This analysis is accurate. Kaufmann's sobering words should disenchant those who have been hypnotized by the plausibility and the glamor of the national idea. The social consequences of the national hope have been and will continue to be immeasurable. But like the contemporary formulation of our yearning במלכות שד י [20] it is externalized and fails to answer the inner problem היהדות מה תהא עליה?[21]

We shall consider briefly another dominant idea in our Liberal circles. I have in mind the quest for social justice.

Influenced undoubtedly by the teachings of Rauschenbusch in his Social Gospel, which gave expression to the educated young clergymen, who "demanded that social justice be defined in Christian terms,"[22] we began our adventure in Social Justice. We declared that at last we were taking up the fight of the great literary prophets for a better world. There is no doubt that Wolf and Israel had "a religious conviction that God is against oppression and (is) on the side of the weak."[23] But a survey of the work of our Social Justice Commission reveals a pattern of continuous lacunae. Unlike the Prophets of Israel, for example, we rarely pioneered. We generally followed in the wake of the Federal Council of Churches of Christ. We were more or less emphatic Amen-sayers, most fearless where our people or congregations were not directly involved—in the Centralia Strike, in the United States Steel controversy, or else where our people agreed, as in

---

[19] גולה ונכר, Tel Aviv, 1929, II.355–6.
[20] "To perfect the world under the suzerainty of Shaddai."
[21] "What of our religious life?"
[22] *The Course of American Democratic Thought* by R. H. Gabriel, New York, 1940, p. 325.
[23] Rauschenbusch, *op cit.*

birth control. I looked for specific utterances on labor conditions in department stores; on admission of Negroes into or their employment by our shopping emporia; on the plight of workers in our clothing factories, or other specifically Jewish concerns. It was a futile quest. Our advocates of social justice did not, in the Amos or Jeremiah manner, appear on the premises of the sinner if the sinners were members of our congregations. In the years when many of our younger men were in great need of help, the Social Justice Commission promised to investigate and issue recommendations but never carried through. The only incursion in Jewish industry that I found was the projected investigation of the *matzoth* factories. But here again I suspect that most *matzoth* barons by interest and inclination are pillars in Orthodox congregations.

Isn't it curious that the Social Justice Commission, the avowed follower of the revolutionary prophets, does not have a single martyr, does not even have one member whose situation in the rabbinate was worsened by his activities. The prophets of Israel as you know were, as a rule, *spurlos versenkt*.

The conclusion must be drawn that here, in the main, was another extroverted activity which was not religion in its classic and exacting form. The grand and apparently fearless pronouncements of the Social Justice Commission, especially in the days of severe unemployment, together with the frequent מי שברך [24] for the President, which interlarded them, gave debating satisfaction to the men who felt something ought to be done; gave the illusion that these resolutions were rebuilding the social order; conveyed to our men the feeling that they were lineal descendants of Buttenwieser's prophets of Israel. Those men who presented and discussed the resolutions on the floor emerged in their own eyes as embattled fighters for the Lord with a heightened sense of religious purity. The plain truth was that Social Justice as we have been practicing it has in the main been a surrogate for religion.

Thus we carried on in the lotus years of the recent past. Vague

[24] Invocation of divine blessing.

assertions of universalism which culminated in non-sectarianism as the chief dogma. Eloquent disquisitions on nationalism with קרן קימת לישראל [25] and עברית [26] replacing Torah and *Mizvot*. Between these two extremes there pranced the knights-errant of social justice reviving the pageantry of the ancient prophets but not their spirit nor martyrdom, all the while this extrovert company was housed in ever more splendid environs and ever more affluent circumstances.

The meeting of the World Union for Progressive Judaism, which took place in Berlin in the summer of 1928, marked in a sense the climax of this extrovert era. Dr. David Philipson writes of it: "The sessions of the convention took place in the Herrenhaus, the former Prussian House of Lords. How significant of the change that the years have wrought in the position of the Jews was this Jewish gathering in the hall of Junkerthum whose walls resounded so frequently with anti-Semitic tirades in the Imperial days."[27]

Dr. Philipson's glowing words bring to mind a poignant scene from the prologue in John Buchan's *Huntingtower*. The year is 1916. A young Englishman in a Petrograd palace is urging a Russian princess to flee Russia. "What nonsense," she protested, "where should I be safe if not in my own Russia, where I have friends—oh, so many, and tribes and tribes of relations? . . . My complaint is that my life is too cosseted and padded. I am too secure."

The young man happened to glance at a heavy casket of dark green imperial jade. It rested on three ivory figurines, a priest, a soldier and a beast of burden. "Look, Saskia!" he said, "If you were living inside that box you would think it very secure. You would note the thickness of the walls and the hardness of the stone, and you would dream away in a peaceful green dusk. But all the time it would be held up by trifles—brittle trifles."[28]

Well, Jews were rarely cosseted and padded even in the nine-

---

[25] *Keren Kayemet LeYisrael*—"The Jewish National Fund."
[26] *Ivrit*—"Hebrew."
[27] *The Reform Movement in Judaism* by David Philipson, New York, 1931, p. 431.
[28] *Huntingtower*, p. 14.

teenth century. But we did live in a world held up by "trifles—
brittle trifles." One by one they have been knocked out and where
the Jew survives in the battle zones, he survives as a beast of burden. The liberal *status quo ante* is not likely to be restored. If
Haman wins, we shall be pariahs. If he loses, we shall be paupers—
one step removed from the pariah.[29]

We must not soothe ourselves with false hopes. The lice and
typhus ghettoes of Warsaw and Lublin are not remote. Though we
are not in them, we are of them. Even if our statutory position
remain unaffected, our social position has already been shaken. We
shall be suspect because we will be helping poor relations and these
suspicions will feed on a rationale of attack which is even now being
perfected. Remember that our enemies on this continent have not
been converted. They have merely been silenced. Even in the
Russia of the Tsars the *Novoe Vremya*[30] and the Black Hundreds
were muzzled in the first days of World War I.

In a world where cruelty is recrudescent and men's regard for
truth has declined, in a world shaken in its optimism, dubious of
progress, suddenly aware that the Messiah will not be ushered in
through pulpit oratory, in brief, in a reactionary world, what of
Liberal Judaism?

The first honest answer that must come is, that in the main we
shall remain what we are. We cannot help ourselves, for we are
children of a liberal era. Even if ghetto walls should be built
around Avondale[31] or a ghetto mind-set should possess the entire
people of Israel, we should still be unable to accept תורת משה מסיני
בכל פרושיה ודקדוקיה.[32] God himself you will remember had to resort
to כפית ההר כגיגית[33] because the children of Israel were unwilling to

---

[29] In *World's Work*, in 1920, Burton J. Hendrick denounced the Polish Jews. They
were hunted and driven, poor and persecuted. Now that German Jews have joined
this ragged company, Albert Jay Nock in the *Atlantic Monthly* of 1941 pronounced
the Ashkenazi Jews as unwanted. He excepts the Sephardim from this judgment.

[30] Notoriously antisemitic newspaper.

[31] Fashionable Jewish quarter in Cincinnati.

[32] "Sinaitic revelation with all its refinements and commentaries."

[33] R. Abdimi said: "The Holy One arched Sinai over the children of Israel as an
inverted cask and warned them: 'If you accept the Torah it is well; if you do not
your burial will be there.'" Shabbat 88a.

submit. But not unless a new revelation come or perhaps another prophet rise and sweep all of us into a new passion for faith can we come to accept it.

Why are we here in Reform Temples? we children of Orthodox homes? Why for that matter did Isaac M. Wise insist on reforms in the synagogs he served? Because he and we have found the old forms antiquated. Because we have come to look upon them as burdens without a meaning. Because in a word, we have stopped believing בתורת משה מסיני בכל פרושיה ודקדוקיה 34.

Yet there survived in us sufficient attachment to ancestral ways, to the Hebrew tongue, to the Jewish people, to social ideals, to the land of Israel, to the old shul, to the betterment of the Negro to keep us within the synagog, the liberal synagog, to be sure, but the synagog nevertheless.

We and our forerunners sought feverishly to heal the inner breach by a host of extrovert activities, often extraneous to the religious life. Now we stand perplexed.

Is there a parallel for this era of inner and outer crisis? Yes, there is. The first five hundred years of the Christian Era provide a rough analogy for these days. In the fourth century, newly baptized Roman emperors claimed and appropriated for Christendom Israel's ancient gifts of grace and election, dethroned our ancestors from their theological eminence and through a hailstorm of edicts transformed them into pariahs among the nations. These rulers sought to carry the imperial cross beyond the Euphrates and snuff out the flames of Ormuzd. The river proved impassable for the legions of Rome. But ideas are peculiarly infectious. Jazdegerd II, a devotee of Zoroaster, felt that his divinity deserved the identic exclusive homage which Constantius II claimed for his. Before long half the Jews of Ispahan were put to death and Jewish children were taken away by force and brought up in the Zoroastrian religion. Both banks of the Euphrates became untenable. That moment marked the end of a hopeful chapter. At its beginning, Herod gaily fraternized with Roman patricians, Paul

---

34 "The Sinaitic revelation with all its refinements and commentaries."

proudly proclaimed "Civis Romanus Sum" and Judah b. Illai unstintingly praised the conquerors as bath and bridge builders.[35] As the horizon darkened the name of the procurator Tinneus Rufus was transformed to Tyrannus Rufus; Hadrian the impeccable cosmopolite became עצמות שחיק הדרינוס,[36] and one Tanna exclaimed: אם יהיו כל הימים דיו וכל היערות קולמוסים וכל בני [37] אדם לבלריים אין מספיקין לכתב הצרות הבאות עליהם "If all the seas were ink and all trees quills and all men scribes, they could not record the measure of our grief."

How did Jews react? I do not know what the merchants of Mahuza and the publicans of Pumbedita[37a] had to say. They may have engaged in hysterical defence work and in repairing political fences. At any rate their utterances did not survive. But the more sensitive spirits withdrew into the halls of Halakah and Haggadah and renewed their strength by a majestic כנוס הרוח.[38] The Talmud is the eternal monument of this כנוס. Those confused place names and events which are characteristic in the בבלי and ירושלמי,[39] are not marks of ignorance or *lapsus scriptorum*. They bear witness to the intense inwardness of the literature, its essentially meta-historical approach. The Yeshiva student in Bialik's "Ha-Masmid"[40] who swayed over his ständer while repeating the refrain, הוי, הוי, אמר רבא, אוי, אמר אביי [41] took hold of these symbolic pillars of כנוס הרוח [42] and out of them drew strength to continue in his own desolate world. He in his humble way glimpsed into the eternal secret of the Talmud.

---

[35] Shabbat 33b.
[36] Hadrian the Roman Emperor (117 to 138) who crushed the insurrection of Bar Kokheba. In rabbinic writings his name is frequently coupled with the imprecation, "May his bones be ground." *Wa-Yikra Rabbah*, section 25, and elsewhere.
[37] *Megillat Taanit*, End.
[37a] Two cities in Babylonia. Both had important Jewish communities.
[38] *Kinnus Ha-Ruah*—"Ingathering of the spirit." Intense concentration on religious life.
[39] *Bavli* and *Yerushalmi*. The Talmudim of Babylonia and Palestine.
[40] "A man dedicated to the study of the Torah." Name of a famous poem by Ch. N. Bialik.
[41] "Thus said Rabba, and thus said Abaye." a phrase found frequently in the Talmud.
[42] "Ingathering of the spirit."

Liberal Jews face the challenge of כנוס הרוח in the direction of
לאהליך ישראל.[43] But what, the skeptic will ask, is left in the אהלי
ישראל ?[44] Broken phylacteries, threadbare *tallesim,* beards full of
snuff have become the dominant contemporary symbols of the
אהל.[45] אדם כי ימות when a man dies his children go באהל.[46] Yet it
is possible to make לאהליך [47] a ringing cry and to transform the
Biblical verse into אדם כי יהיה באהל.[48] For one classic ideal survived the spiritual and theological wreckage of the nineteenth century, the ideal of קדושה.[49] Even an outsider like Rudolf Otto
sensed it, as you will recall. A visit on Yom Kippur in a tumble-
down Moroccan synagog gave him the first inkling of the tre-
mendum and led to the writing of his classic work the *Idea of
the Holy.*

Talmud Torah

The coming years are likely to bring a new appreciation of Torah
as אדמת קדש [50] as a sacred discipline. The classic ideal of Talmud
Torah may be revived. For over a century, Juedische Wissenschaft
had taken its place.

The slogan of Juedische Wissenschaft has been: analyze, break
down, seek development in all spiritual phenomena. Proceed on
the theory of spiritual evolution—the simple precedes the complex, the low precedes the high. The declaration אם ראשונים בני
מלאכים אנו כאנשים ואם ראשונים בני אנשים אנו כחמורים [51]"If our predecessors were sons of angels, we are sons of men; and if our
predecessors were sons of men we are like asses," was held up to
guffawing ridicule. The worst offender in foisting the doctrinaire
jacket of evolution upon a sacred text was that branch of Wissen-

---

[43] "To thy tents, O Israel." (1 Kings 12.16) Here it means, *"Ad fontes,"* to the
sources of classic inspiration.
[44] "In the tents of Israel's Torah."
[45] "Tent of Torah," or the synagog.
[46] Rendered here, "When a man dies . . . into the synagog." See Num. 19.14.
[47] "To thy Tents!" *"Ad fontes!"*
[48] "A man shall live within and through the synagog."
[49] "Holiness."
[50] "Holy ground." Exodus 3.5.
[51] R. Zera, a third century Palestinian Amora. (Shabbat 112b).

schaft known as Biblical Criticism— בקרת which Nachmanides
equates with הפקר.[52] Nachmanides had a prophetic eye, for Higher
Criticism has indeed broken away from Israel's moorings. The
obiter dicta of Marti, the *närrischkeiten* of Gunkel are pondered
over and served up as great delicacies in works bearing the imprimatur of the Hebrew Union College. But the names of Akiba
who weighed every את[53] in the Bible or of Ishmael who declared
that the Torah spoke the language of men are not even mentioned
in the indices of these books. And generations of rabbis have
been brought up in their spirit. פלשתים עליך ישראל.[54] They have
taken away the rabbinic arcana of millennia and left a book with
the label Made in Germany written all over it.

Ah, but you may counter with the Higher Critics' *shibboleth:*
"The traditional accounts of the origin of the Torah are ridiculous
in their reading of history and in their story of origins." Listen
then to what Yechezkel Kaufmann who has approached the Torah
as a Jew and at the same time went through the "unclean gates"
of arrogant German criticism has to say. "Investigation shows
that in the Scriptural tradition (concerning its origin) there is
much greater truth than what the school of Wellhausen supposes . . .
The Pentateuch must be regarded as the most ancient monument
of Israel's faith. It is the stage preceding literary prophecy. There
are proofs that even if the Canon of the Pentateuch was closed at
a much later time, its sources are very ancient not only in part or
in their general content but in their entirety, in their script, in
their language, yes, in their letters. This establishes the antiquity
of monotheism in Israel,"[55] and refutes the Higher Critics' pet
dogma that the universal God was the result of many centuries of
growth culminating in the prophets. It deprives the Higher Critics
of their chief weapon—the claim to historicity.

This revised approach comes much closer to the formulation con-

[52] Leviticus 19.20. Nachmanides *ad locum* renders *Bikkoret* not "inquisition" as
does the Jewish version, but *Hefker*, i.e., "lawlessness."
[53] *Et*, a Hebrew particle.
[54] "The Philistines are upon thee, O Israel." Judges 16.20.
[55] תולדות האמונה הישראלית, Tel Aviv, 1937, I. vi.

tained in the Talmud whose theories on the Bible have hitherto provided much amusement to anti-Semitic theologians and their Jewishly uninformed *Hofjuden*. This levity is not surprising in that arid and sterile discipline which is essentially in the category of [56] ‏אחות לנו קטנה ושדים אין לה‎.

At any rate, the Higher Critics' chief weapon is rapidly falling from their hands into those of the old-fashioned and much-derided rabbis. Pilpul used to be one Hebrew Union College professor's condemnation of everything he disliked. ‏כל הפוסל במומו פוסל‎ [57] No discipline depends on as many tenuous and subjective hypotheses as does "Biblical Science." The "Bible," God have mercy, which emerges from their anatomical methods is a logarithmic Bible. This is inevitable for they violate the solemn warning of a great sage: "You imagine that you can understand a book which has been the guide of past and present generations . . . and glance over its contents as if you were reading a historical work or some poetic composition."[58]

That is the besetting sin of the Higher Critics. To them the Bible is a historical work or a poetic composition. The Christian Higher Critics may not theologically be expected to regard it otherwise. Their Jewish camp followers lack the sensitivity to regard it otherwise. A robot, mechanical Bible is the result.

If you wish to get at the sense of the Bible listen to this: ‏ויצעק‎

---

[56] We have a little sister and she hath no breasts." Song of Songs 8.8.

[57] "With his own blemish he stigmatizes others." The Babylonian Amora Samuel in Kiddushin 70a.

[58] Maimonides in *The Guide for the Perplexed*, I. 2, Friedlander tr. In the *Zohar*, there are two interesting observations on biblical exegesis: 'Woe unto those who see in the Law nothing but simple narratives and ordinary words! Were this really the case, then could we, even today, compose a Law equally worthy of admiration. But it is all quite otherwise . . . Every word of the Law contains an elevated sense and a sublime mystery . . . The narratives of the Law are but the raiment in which it is swathed. Woe unto him who mistakes the raiment for the Law itself! It was to avert such a calamity that David prayed, "Open mine eyes that I might behold wondrous things out of thy Law".' Another passage states similarly, but even more strikingly: 'If the Law merely consisted of ordinary words and narratives like the stories of Esau, Hagar, and Laban, or like the words which were spoken by Balaam's ass or by Balaam himself, why should it have been called the Law of Truth, the perfect Law, the faithful testimony of God?' (*Zohar*, Sperling and Simon tr. vol. I, pp. xiii–xiv).

צעקה גדולה ומרה [59] is written concerning Esau. The same words are repeated in the narrative of the agony of Mordecai. Why the repetition of the identic words? Because Jacob deprived Esau of his birthright inflicting great anguish upon him. This anguish in God's economy had to be atoned. And so it was decreed that Mordecai of the stock of Jacob drink that cup of bitterness.[60]

But this, someone will say, is a Midrash. Yes, it is a Midrash. What pray is wrong with a Midrash, with seeking into the meaning of a sacred text? No, the Midrash does not resort to Patten's patter about Purim, to eponymous nonsense about Esau. It does not sit in judgment over the text. It seeks its spiritual meaning. Remember, the great command דרשו את יהוה וחיו,[61] too, is a Midrash.

That is Talmud Torah, that was the method of the Tannaim and Amoraim. They lacked, to be sure, what we call the historical sense but they had a pervasive sense of the God above history. They had no patience with those who temporized what by its nature was extra-temporal.

We liberals have of course paid lip service to the "permanent values in Judaism." We said, for example, that the prophetic ideals of justice and righteousness were imperishable in the midst of much legislation and opinion essentially transient. To say that justice and righteousness are the only imperishable elements is not enough. The literature in its entirety is אדמת קדש.[62] Intimations of sanctity may always be found in it if it is approached not with a scalpel but with a scapular. Does it really matter which came first? Is a fugitive line of scripture recoverable at all? Are we so sure that the ancients had the same ideas of prosody that we have? If we concede that they did not, can we be certain that we have come to understand them? Is it not of greater importance that these

---

[59] "When Esau heard the words of his father he cried with an exceeding great and bitter cry." Gen. 27.34.

[60] *Bereshit Rabbah* 67, ed. Theodor-Albeck, p. 758.

[61] "Seek ye the Lord and live." (Amos 5.6). Midrash is derived from the verb *d r sh* which means "to seek."

[62] "Holy ground."

ideas have lived together for millennia, that many of them have been revealed by God, that others have been inspired through the divine in man, that all of them have been hallowed through centuries of contemplation by mystic and sage?

That brings me to our major failing. Our extrovert preoccupations have destroyed the art of contemplative study. We have fallen into the snare of hypercriticism—which is Higher Criticism. Some of us have carried over the curious nineteenth-century notion that the Talmud is טרפה,[63] yes is *unser unglueck,* that much of it is a melange which has lost its savor unaware at the same time that the output of the Higher Critics is often less intelligible than an obscure Maharam Schiff,[64] unaware too of Leopold Zunz's warning, הדובר סרה על התלמוד בימינו מעשה משומד הוא עושה [65] "He who speaks wryly of the Talmud does the work of a renegade."

We must come down from our critical heights and strive to fulfil the command which we often quote and rarely fulfil: והצנע לכת עם אלהיך.[66] We should heed the tender warning of Maimonides: דברי תורה נמשלו כמים...לומר לך מה מים מתכנסים במקום מדרון, אלא נזחלין מעליו ומתקבצים במקום אשבורן, כך דברי תורה אינם נמצאים בגסי הרוח ולא בלב כל גבה לב אלא בדכא ושפל רוח.[67] "The Torah is like water. Water cannot remain on a slope. It flows down to gather in the pond below. So, too, the words of the Torah will not be found in the haughty and arrogant heart, only among the humble and lowly of spirit." Let study resume its sacramental character. Let it cease to be catalysis and strive for synthesis, with the spirit of של נעליך מעל רגליך [68] hovering over it. We, in the rabbinate, must do it, seek to reinstill that spirit into the college, perhaps even by sending a few students to one of the better *yeshivahs* for a year. We maintain relations with Protestant

---

[63] *Terefah.* unfit—the opposite of kosher.
[64] A seventeenth-century German rabbi whose comments on the Talmud are occasionally cryptic.
[65] Wolf Jabez's תולדות ישראל, volume 13, p. 128.
[66] "Walk humbly with thy God." Micah 6.8.
[67] *Hilkot Talmud Torah* 3.9.
[68] "Put off thy shoes from off thy feet." Exodus 3.5.

seminaries so they will not be contaminated through contact with a *Yeshivah*.

It is interesting to note that the most significant scholar in the ranks of the American Reform rabbinate, Hyman G. Enelow, found his תקון הנפש[69] in the מנורת המאור,[70] representing integrated, contemplative and devotional study. His last work was מדרש שלשים ושתים מדות.[71] The very name proclaims the classic ideal of Talmud Torah, involving as it does an appreciation of the whole of its *gestalt*. It intimates that it is not important, for example, to find out which colors were painted first in Levitan's[72] country scenes or how the music of וטהר לבנו[73] came to be written. What matters is the totality, the metahistory, if you will, of the Torah.

Franz Rosenzweig's aspirations are pertinent in this connection: "Our time calls for a 'new learning,' just as central for the life of our people as the old learning, but oriented in the opposite direction—a learning which is no longer directed from the Torah outward into the wide ramifications of life, but which begins from the periphery of life, the life of the secular world, knowing nothing of the Law, and moves toward Judaism. This learning is not to consist in apologetics, in uncovering 'relations' between Judaism, and some modern ideals, or in showing the 'contributions' of Judaism to this or that present-day institution. It is 'to find the means of entering the heart of our life. And to have the faith that this heart is a Jewish heart. For we are Jews . . . There is a center, where the light of Judaism glows eternally and there is a way to that center, open to all who seek it. 'We must seek the unity . . . and we must trust to find it'."[74]

[69] *Tikkun Ha-nefesh*—religious consummation.

[70] *Menorat Ha-maor*—an ethical compendium by the 14th-century Spanish rabbi Israel ibn al-Nakawa.

[71] *Midrash Sheloshim u-shetaim Middot*—Midrash of the thirty-two norms which deals in part with the hermeneutics of the Talmud.

[72] Isaac Levitan, a 19th-century native of Lithuania, was a great painter of Russian country scenes.

[73] *We-taher libenu*—an inspiring religious song with the refrain, "Cleanse Thou our hearts!" ·

[74] *Modern Philosophies of Judaism* by Jacob B. Agus, New York, 1941, pp. 141–142.

Mizvot and Maasim Tovim

In addition to Talmud Torah, and in some ways exceeding it in value as a discipline in קדושה,[75] there is the complex called *Mizvot* and *Maasim tovim*.[76]

We are increasingly aware of our secularism, of our remoteness from the high ideals we proclaim. We have begun to suspect that Liberal Judaism has ceased to be a way of life and has become a manner of talking. It is significant that while in former years a typical rabbi was seen on the way to the synagog, leaning over a folio or perhaps wrapped in a *tallis,* the typical (and I suppose the great) rabbi is now photographed with his mouth wide open before a microphone. הרחב פיך [77] has become our supreme *Mizvah.* כל המרחיב הרי זה משובח.[78] We all have come to feel more and more the inadequacy of this phenomenon.

It occurs to me that the ardent pacifist sentiment of former years may be explained in part by our unfulfilled yearnings for עולן של מצות.[79] Here many of us felt was one bit of sacred ground which we would not surrender to expediency. עד כאן.[80]

Symptomatic too of these yearnings have been the repeated cries: we need a code of practice, a new *Shulḥan Aruk,* a Guide for the Modern Jew. The trouble with this sort of talk is that it calls for a mechanical solution.

We ask an outside agency to come and deliver us from our spiritual vacuity. Rabbi Solomon Bazell of Louisville and Dr. Solomon Freehof of Pittsburgh dealt cogently with this subject[81] last year. Dr. Freehof suggested that an individual might attempt issuing a code of practice. But I dare say few individuals will have the temerity to do so. Perhaps five or ten might pool their experiences and strike out for the goal of *mizvot* and *maasim tovim*. Note that I do not use the words ceremony or ritual. Those have

---

[75] "Holy living."
[76] "Good deeds, ethical practices."
[77] "Open thy mouth!"
[78] "He who opens it most widely is to be praised."
[79] "The yoke of *mizvot*."
[80] "No further!"
[81] *C.C.A.R. Yearbook,* volume LI.

about them an air of controversy and dispensability, though in no
way do I disparage them. I emphasize *mizvot* and *maasim tovim*.
The motto עשו סיג לתורה [82] to be sure has lost its massive weight
since the Torah has ceased to be completely mandatory. But
עשו סיג לקדושה [83] is charged with sufficient religious emotion to
spur us in this drive.

This סיג לקדושה group, as I see it, would proceed without
formal organization, without written resolutions, without reports,
without extrovert paraphernalia. Its deepest concern would be the
triad of Torah, *mizvot* and *maasim tovim*. May I point out in this
connection that Henry Cohen, the איש חמודות [84] among our older
men, has not been primarily a battler for ethical monotheism, for
cultural nationalism or social justice. He never fell victim to
externalized slogans. He continued in his life the classical tradition
of Talmud Torah and its inevitable corollaries of *mizvot* and
maasim tovim.

Specifically this group would determine to refrain from לשון הרע,
from רכילות , from נבול פה and from הסגת גבול.[85] These norms of
behavior leave among many of us ample room for improvement.

We might begin every morning with a modified *Shaharit*.[86]
Perhaps the new *Mahazor*[87] which the Committee on Liturgy is
preparing will provide such a service. In the meantime, we shall
have to use selections from the old *Siddur*. We should reintroduce a
kind of שנים מקרא ואחד תרגום.[88] We should set aside one hour a
day for תורה לשמה [89] which does not provide direct grist for our
homiletical mill. We should read regularly ethical works like
Luzzato's *Mesillat Yesharim*[90] and devotional books such as Psalms
with Rashi whose commentary on the text remains unsurpassed.

---

[82] *Asu seyog la-Torah*—"Make ye a fence about the Torah!" (*Abot* 1.1).
[83] *Asu seyog li-Kedusha*—"Make ye a fence about holiness."
[84] "The man greatly beloved." Daniel 10.11.
[85] "Slander, tale-bearing, foul speech, trespassing."
[86] "Morning worship."
[87] A liturgical anthology.
[88] Regular reading in Scripture. The reading of two chapters a day which was initiated about four years ago in Palestine is a helpful procedure.
[89] "Torah for its own sake."
[90] Available in the Schiff Classics Series of the Jewish Publication Society.

There ought to be no question about a rabbi's fasting on *Yom Kippur* and *Tisha Be'av*.

We should observe the dietary laws at least in abstaining from the flesh of the swine. I know that the Pittsburgh Conference has annulled the P Code and all its works. But then Claude G. Montefiore who knew the P Code and whose Reform *zizith*[91] were beyond cavil was at least sympathetic to the retention of the dietary laws in modified form.[91a] At any rate the classic tale told of one prominent rabbi who leaned over and asked for another helping of ham and when reproached for this flagrant breach of Jewish practice rejoined with: "Well, Sir, Moses knew nothing of Virginia ham," has a certain cynical הרחב פיך [92] looseness about it which is worlds removed from the spirit of קדושה [93] which we seek to recover.

We must strive to make the Sabbath once again a day of חלוץ עצמות, of renewal and sanctification. We should not ride unless it be to go to the synagog or to visit the sick. We should not shop or engage in profane endeavors.

These are but suggestions. If such a group dominated by the imperative of עשו סיג לקדושה [94] were to come together, it would arrive at other and more acceptable norms of religious conduct.

We must be persistent in this endeavor. We must remember that actions not only express the religious experience of a man but that these actions in turn help in the creating and molding of those experiences. You recall that the *Perpetual Lamp* was not lit by a single kindling. The precept was: הוה מדליק עד שתהא שלהבת עולה מאליה [95] Keep kindling until the flame leaps up of its own strength.

Let us not be frightened or embarrassed by possible charges of a new obscurantist mechanism of salvation. Remember that consent is of the essence in the classic idea of the Covenant which in its turn is basic in the acceptance of Torah. We began our career as a

---

[91] Literally "fringes." Here it means "standing."
[91a] See his *Liberal Judaism*, p. 132.
[92] "Open-mouth."
[93] "Holy living."
[94] "Make ye a fence for holiness."
[95] Rashi on Exodus 27.20.

religious people with נעשה ונשמע,[96] "we shall do and understand," a voluntary declaration.

Throughout our religious history, the נדר and the נדבה, the voluntary abstention and the free-will offering, enjoyed the highest rank in the hierarchy of קרבנות[97] and *maasim tovim*. This evaluation culminates in a striking almost revolutionary קרי: אלה מועדי יהוה אשר תקראו אתם is made to read קרי: אלה מועדי יהוה אשר תקראו "These are the festivals of the Lord which *ye* shall proclaim."[98] אַתֶּם

Eager and deliberate consecration brings with it divine mutuality, for [99] כשהמקום מחדש מצוה על ישראל הוא מוסיף להם קדושה "whenGod renews or restores a *mizvah* for Israel he adds holiness unto them."

Liberal Judaism is at the end of a cycle. Its religious course is even now being redirected. Everywhere men are groping for inwardness and integrity. Everywhere men are becoming aware with the *Zohar* that "human beings live in confusion of mind, beholding not the way of truth . . . The Torah calls them day by day to herself . . . but, alas they do not even turn their heads . . . the Torah lets out a word and emerges for a little from her sheath, and then hides herself again. But she does this only for those who understand and obey her."[100]

---

[96] *Na'aseh We-nishma.* Exodus 24.7.
[97] *Korbanot*—sacrifices.
[98] Leviticus 23.2. See *Rosh Hashanah* 24a.
[99] *Mekilta*, ed. Lauterbach, III.157, ed. Horovitz-Rabin, p. 320.
[100] *Zohar, Mishpotim*, 99a, Simon-Sperling tr. III.301.

THEOLOGICAL SPECULATIONS

The Mission of Israel

While classical Reform Judaism dismissed the traditional teaching of Israel as the "chosen people," its spokesmen replaced the doctrine of chosenness by the view that every people has a special mission on earth, and that Israel's mission was to bring knowledge of God, in the form of ethical monotheism, to all the nations of the world. This teaching provided a rationale for the worldwide dispersion of the Jews, as well as an argument against modern Jewish nationalism.

Kaufmann Kohler brought his great learning and his theological ability to bear in arguing that the United States of America could provide the setting in which the fulfillment of the mission of Israel could be swiftly advanced, bringing nearer "the realization of our Messianic hope, the establishment of God's kingdom on earth." Here, too, we see the rational system of classical Reform which replaced the traditional belief in a personal, divinely ordained Messiah, by the notion of a Messianic era in which men would live together in truth, justice and peace.

Kohler wrote in an age of confidence, and the spirit of his words seems today almost arrogant. In the afterglow of the formation of the League of Nations and the assumption of the Palestine Mandate by Great Britain the future seemed far more roseate than it was to prove a decade later. After the Holocaust, no Jew, of whatever degree, could echo Kohler's faith in the readiness of the world to receive the mission of Israel. Yet perhaps the world's unreadiness is the reason why there is most need that the mission be reaffirmed.

125B

THE MISSION OF ISRAEL AND ITS
APPLICATIONS TO MODERN TIMES
Kaufmann Kohler
(1919)

It is a strange psychological fact—or shall we call it caprice?—
that the idea of Israel's mission, which forms the very soul and life
force of the Jewish people in its history and religious literature,
should need a defence against those modern spokesmen of the Jew
who deny or question it from mere opposition to Reform Judaism
which placed it into the foreground of Jewish belief. It is perfectly
intelligible and logical, if atheists of the type of [Max] Nordau and
[Horace] Kallen scoff at the idea, since for them no divine Providence directs the affairs of men, history being merely a haphazard
complex of events, a kaleidoscopic view of accidental happenings of
nations or groups of men. So may the pure scientist, bent only upon
investigating the laws of nature, say, in his conceit, as did the
astronomer Laplace when reminded by Napoleon of having left
God out of his system: "I do not need this hypothesis." Seeing only
the working of causes in the cosmic order of things, he fails to
discover purpose, except as far as man injects it, and, unmindful of
the necessity of a final or supreme Cause, he insists that evolution
does away with teleology. Thus he declares that, instead of the sun
having been created to give light and earth to produce life, as we
are taught in Scripture, these cosmic bodies become what they are

127

by the various degrees of motion and speed in their rotation through the infinite space. To be sure, where mechanism rules the cosmos, there is no room for purpose. Neither can there be any historic task for nations or races in such a system. As soon, however, as we realize that the wonderful harmony and order prevailing in the universe can not be the product of mere chance, but manifest an all-comprising design and forethought, both in nature and in human history, working in the one by compulsion from *without* and in the other through self-determination or freedom from *within,* so soon are we bound to observe the working out of higher plans, or historic tasks for the social or spiritual progress of life by the combined efforts of certain groups of men. Such tasks are in response to the call of a nation's spirit or genius, with more or less consciousness, accomplished by the various nations in history, each contributing its share to the work of human civilization. Accordingly we may ascribe to Greece the culture of art and philosophy as its mission, and to Rome that of jurisprudence and statecraft, and, going further back in antiquity, we would find astronomy and arithmetic first developed in Babylonia, and architecture and the beginnings of art and literature as the products of Egypt. Thus each prominent nation or race, ancient or modern, appears to have been fitted out for some specific task which it was, or is, in due time called upon to perform.

But here the question comes up, whether we have a right to call these chosen people—just as Israel is called *the* chosen people —as does Israel Zangwill in his interesting but at the same time half-serious and half-sarcastic article, "Chosen People," in the *Menorah Journal.* In other words, can, or should, we place the historic mission of all other nations or races on the same level as is claimed for Israel's world mission? Or shall we go to the other extreme and allow Asher Ginzberg, the much overrated imitator of Nietzsche, to tell us "the reformers" that we have invented the famous theory of Israel's mission among the nations? Surely this calls for our strongest possible refutation and protest. Notice the fact that in calling the Jewish nation a *Supernation,* exactly as

Nietzsche speaks of certain classes of men as types of the *Superman,* the philosophy of Ahad ha-Am exalts it at the expense of divine Revelation, ignoring all the historic evidences, that only its religious truth, its pure ethical monotheism as its dynamic force, ever growing and expanding under the influence of the various civilizations, made it great and "high above all other nations."

Of course, as long as prophetic universalism had not been attained or conceived of by the Jewish mind, as long as Israel's God was of a tribal and local character as was any of the heathen deities, the idea of a world mission could not be thought of. Neither could the idea of a world mission ever take hold of any of the great nations in view of their superior culture, since for them there existed no World-Ruler nor God of History to assign to them their task. For the Greeks or Egyptians, to mention only these, the other nations were simply the inferiors, despised barbarians or unclean foreigners to be shunned; not kinsmen, members of the same human family to be won over for their ideas or elevated by their superior knowledge and skill. The thought of a providential mission never dawned upon their mind.

Quite different was the attitude of the Jewish people when the great prophets—as God's heralds—and in their train the psalmists and sages, proclaimed to them their world-task and world-duty in view of the superiority of their religious truth. It is shutting one's eyes wilfully to the light of the scriptural and rabbinical teachings to say with Ahad ha-Am that the Jewish people was elected by God simply for the attainment of the highest morality for themselves on a territory of their own, without concern in the spiritual welfare of the world around. Can there be a more luminous and more definite enunciation of Israel's mission than the one that is given in the words of the great anonymous prophet:

"Behold, My servant whom I uphold,
  Mine elect in whom My soul delighteth,
  I have put My spirit upon him;
  He shall make the right to go forth to the nations . . .

I, the Lord, have called thee in righteousness,
And have taken hold of thy hand, and kept thee,
And set thee for a covenant of the people,
For a light of the nations." (Isaiah XLII, 1-6)

Or in the still more striking 49th chapter, where he says:

"Listen, O Isles, unto Me,
And hearken ye people from afar:
The Lord hath called me from the womb,
Yea, He saith, It is too light a thing that thou shouldst be
    My servant
To raise up the tribe of Jacob,
And to restore the offspring of Israel;
I will also give thee for a light of the nations,
That My salvation be unto the end of the earth." (vv. 1-6)

And far from claiming any greatness for Israel to boast of as a supernation, the seer addressed it as, "Thou worm, Jacob!" (XLI, 14) and reproaches it, saying: "Who is blind but My servant, or deaf as My messenger whom I have sent."[1] The highest title bestowed upon it is that of the "Servant of the Lord" (XLII, 19), with the special implication that he is to undergo suffering and woe, "to be smitten and bruised for the healing of the nations" (XLII; L, 6; LIII, 1). God declares Israel to be His "witnesses" (XLIII, 10-12), "the people which I have formed, that they might tell of My praise" (XLIII, 21).

Not general culture, such as the great nations of history imparted to mankind in various forms and in larger measure than the Jew ever could, but the religious truth, the prime source of all ethics centred in the Only One God, the God of Righteousness and Holiness whom Israel is to proclaim to "the ends of the earth" (XLV, 5, 21-23), as "the light by which the nations shall walk"

---

[1] משלם in the second part of the verse is a corruption of משלחי

(LX, 1-3): this is the gift of Israel's genius to the world. Yet only when the great prophets had risen to the high watch-tower of history to survey the destiny of the nations near and far, there opened before them the wide outlook upon the world to be conquered for their all-encompassing truth. Nay more. Only when the great seer of the exile (it matters not whether he lived in Babylonia or, as more recent research seems to show, in some Palestinian border town) had come within reach of the broader views and aims of the world-conqueror, Cyrus, and the larger mental horizon of the Persian empire, did he become imbued with the spirit of Israel's mission and behold the whole of humanity, "all the people on earth," as the object of God's care and of Israel's mission (see Duhm to Isaiah XLII, 5).

Also the glorious messianic prophecy in Isaiah II, 2-4, and Micah IV, 1-4, speaking of "the end of days when the nations shall go up to the mountain of the Lord, to the house of the God of Jacob, to be taught of His ways and learn to walk in His paths, for out of Zion shall go forth the law, and the word of God from Jerusalem" points to the larger view obtained in the Exile and voiced by Trito-Isaiah when he speaks of "the aliens that will join themselves to the Lord" and then continues: "Even them I will bring to My holy mountain and make them joyful in My house of prayer . . . For My house shall become a house of prayer for all peoples" (Isaiah LVI, 6-7). Instead of seeing Israel go forth among the nations to win them for its Only One God, these prophecies have the nations flow to Judea's capital, attracted by the truth taught there in order to make Israel's God their own.

In the light of this world mission announced by the one or the other prophecy was then the early history of Israel construed by the prophetic writer who has the giving of the Decalog of Sinai introduced by the majestic proclamation: "Ye have seen . . . how I bore you on eagle's wings and brought you unto Myself. Now if ye will hearken unto My voice, . . . ye shall be Mine own treasure from among all peoples, for all the earth is Mine. And ye shall be unto Me a kingdom of priests and a holy nation" (Ex. XIX, 3-6).

Let Zangwill in his above-quoted article declare this a mere fiction, the fact remains that the biblical writer wants to have it understood (as I said in my article on the Chosen People in the *J. E.*) that the Jewish people began their career conscious of their life purpose and world duty as God's priests, and as the teachers of a universal religious truth. Let Prof. James A. Montgomery, who certainly does not write from any Jewish bias, be heard on the subject: "I am not discussing the historic truth of this historic mission," he says in his beautiful sketch on "The Hebrew Religion," in the volume, *Religion of the Past and Present,* Lippincott, 1919, p. 110. "My point is that Israel regarded itself from early days as a people with a future and a destiny, and ultimately with a mission in the world. This idea appears in the antique odes called The Blessings of Jacob and of Moses, and the cycle of the Balaam poems (Gen. XLIX, Deut. XXXIII and Num. XXIff). It is by no means adequately explained from Israel's political or intellectual genius. Neither Egypt nor Babylonia produced such a consciousness. The likest to it is that of Greece and Rome, but the greatness of those people is the explanation of their claims. Israel's consciousness is due to its religion, to an original idea concerning its God's purpose which it never let go, and which it always amplified in historic connection with the past."

Indeed, the introductory chapters of Genesis, as far as they belong to the Priest Code, beginning with the first man and culminating in God's covenant with Noah, the father of the new humanity, indicate, as is well shown by Bertholet in his instructive work, *Die Stellung der Israeliten u. Juden zu den Fremden,* p. 175f, the universalistic spirit which permeated Judaism since the Exile. Ranke, the great historian, goes even so far as to say that the first ten chapters of Genesis, which form the groundwork of biblical or Israelitish history, did more than any literature for the interlinking of the nations to make mankind one. Upon this basic idea the hope could well be expressed by the later prophets that "the whole earth shall be filled with the glory of God as the waters cover the sea" (Hab. II, 14, comp. Is. XI, 14); or that, "On that

day the Lord will become King of the whole earth; on that day the
Lord will be One and His name One" (Zech. XIV, 9). But the
most important feature of post-exilic Judaism is its *denationaliza-
tion,* owing to the admission of the stranger under the name of
Ger (Proselyte) (Isaiah XIV, 1). It was rather a long process
which led from a mere political or civic to a religious incorporation
of this element of affiliated foreigners, but it ultimately became a
prominent factor in the missionary activity of Judaism of the pre-
Christian centuries. It opened wide the gates of the Synagog to let
the non-Jews enter, and in the words of Deutero-Isaiah (XLIV, 4)
to have the one say: "I am the Lord's, and another call himself by
the name of Jacob," in which also the Midrash (*Mek. Mishpatim,*
18) finds a mandate for proselytism. Still, regarding the condition
of admission of the non-Jew, the views seem to have differed from
the very beginning. The priestly or legalistic view prevailing in
Judea was that he had at least to bring an offering (קרבן גר) con-
secrating himself symbolically to the service of God, whereby he
became a גר צדק —a Proselyte of (the city of) Righteousness
(See *Jewish Theology,* 415), fully to enter into the Israelitish
covenant with all its ritualistic obligations. The more universalistic
view is expressed in the 15th Psalm (comp. Ps. XXIV, 3ff): "O
Lord, who shall be a guest (*Ger* or adopted stranger) in Thy
tabernacle? who shall dwell in Thy holy mountain? He that walketh
uprightly, etc." (See Cheyne's Commentary and Lucius, *d. Es-
senismus,* 116f). The observance of the ethical precepts as the law
of God is, according to this, to constitute the character of one who
wishes to be a true Israelite. It was this spirit which actually created
the class of "God worshipers" יראי יי alongside of the other three
classes of Jews, "the house of Aaron, of Levi and of Israel" (Ps.
CXV, 9-11; CXVIII, 19-20; CXXXV, 19-20). This class, called
later יראי שמים [2] played a great role, as we shall see, in the Jewish
propaganda of the Diaspora. But the Psalms in general, while exalt-
ing, in ever new strains of song, Him who dwells "enthroned on the

---

[2] Comp. the קהל גרים in *Sifre Deut.,* 247.

praises of Israel," echoed forth in mighty appeals Israel's mission
to proclaim God's deeds, His praise, His truth and mercy to the
nations near and far, as was pointed out by Bertholet (*eodem*)
and Bousset (*Relig. des Judenth.* 2, p. 94) (See Ps. IX, 12; XVIII,
50; XXII, 28; XLVII, 2; XLVIII, 11; LVII, 10; LXVII, 8;
XCIII; XCV; C; CII, 16; CV, 1; CXXXVIII, 4). And so is the
book of Jonah justly characterized by Bousset as a work written
for the very purpose of defending the right of Israel's mission
among the heathens.

Of course, all these sporadic conversions of heathen individuals
became frequent and systematic in the land of Hellenic culture, in
Alexandria and the various commercial colonies where Jew met
Greek. Here the great opportunity came to familiarize the heathen
world with the truth of Judaism and win it for Israel's God. It was
a question between the intellectual or spiritual superiority of the
one or the other mode of thought, between the beauty of Japheth
and the loftiness of Shem. The great step towards such a *rapproche-
ment* and competition was first taken by the translation of the
Scripture into Greek, which opened up the treasures of Judaism
to the cultured world in the popular idiom. Whatever fault a later
period found with the Septuagint, the idea that the Torah was
intended for all mankind and should be brought home to the
knowledge of all nations is reflected in the significant rabbinical
saying that the Ten Words of Sinai were flashed forth in *seventy*
tongues of fire in order to reach the *seventy* nations of the world—
a saying reechoed in the Pentecost miracle of the New Testament,[3]
and in the similar saying that the words of the Law were, in accordance with God's command to Moses, engraved in *seventy*
languages by Joshua upon the stones of the altar on the Jordan
shore.[4] A parallel to this is the Midrash (*Mek. Yithro.* I), "The
Torah was given in the wilderness, which is the common property
of all, in order that no nation might say it was not meant for us."
The great Jewish propaganda carried on by an astonishingly large

---

[3] *Shab.* 88b; *Ex. R.* V, 9; *Tanh. Shemoth* (ed. Buber); Acts II, 6.
[4] *Sifre Deut.* XXXIII, 2; *Joshua* VIII, 32; *Sota* 32; *Deut.* XXVII, 3 and *Targum J.*

literature, which made the heathen oracles such as the Sibylline
books and ancient Greek poets proclaim Jewish truths in order to
make the heathen world repent and turn it into proselytes observing the humanitarian, the so-called Noahitic, laws, must have
achieved great results, before the Christian Church took up this
mission work of the Jew and reaped its great harvest in the field
ploughed and sown by him. Nor can this activity of the Jews of
that period have been disregarded or underrated by the Palestinian
teachers, or else they would not have made Abraham the prototype
of a wandering missionary going about to win souls for his God;
he converting the men, and his wife Sarah the women (*Ber. R.* to
Gen. XII, 5), and in proclaiming God to his fellow-creatures,
"thereby changing the God of heaven into the God of the earth"
(*Gen. R.* to Gen. XXIV, 3). Henceforth the blessing: "In thee
shall all the families of the earth be blessed" (Gen. XII, 3; comp.
Gen. XLVIII, 20), was given a spiritual meaning in the sense that
by him, that is, *through* the truth he would disseminate, the world
should be blessed.[5]

Accordingly we find Hillel to have been active in making proselytes "to bring them under the wings of the *Shechinah*," following
the example of Abraham (*Ab. d. R. Nathan* [ed. Schechter],
p. 53f). And this view of Israel's mission seems to have been
especially fostered in the house of Hillel, as Simeon ben Gamaliel
handed down a Mishnah no longer contained in ours, stating: "If a
stranger (*Ger*) desires to espouse the Jewish faith, we extend to
him the hand of welcome in order to bring him under the wings of
the *Shechinah*" (*Lev. R.* II, 8), whereas Shammai and his school,
especially Eliezer ben Hyrcanus, opposed proselytism of all kind
(*Shab.* 31[a]; *Gen. R.* LXX, 5; *B. M.* 59[b]). Of course, the enforced
conversions of the Idumeans and Itureans by John Hyrcanus
(Josephus, *Ant.* XII, 8, 1), and similarly such as had political and
social advantage or fear as motive, were generally deprecated.[6] Still

---

[5] See Kuenen, *Prophets and Prophecy*, 373, 457 and Kohler, *Jewish Theology*,
337.

[6] See *Yeb.* 24b; *Niv.* 566; *Yer. Kid.* IV, 65b with reference to the גרי אריות
and גרי שלחן מלכים

the number of proselytes under King Herod and afterwards seems
to have been quite large among the very prominent class of
Romans, as shown by Graetz, *Die juedischen Proselyten im Roe-
merreich.* (Compare Bousset, *Relig. d. Judenth,* 2, pp. 90-97.)
Especially noteworthy is Philo's remark (*Vita Mosis* II, 20),
concerning "the power of attraction and conversion exercised by
the Mosaic Law on Barbarians and Hellenes, the people of the
East and the West, of Europe and Asia, the whole inhabited globe
from one end to the other." Nor was this due merely to the extensive Hellenic propaganda. The striking utterance of Jesus in
Matthew XXIII, 15: "Woe unto ye Scribes and Pharisees, ye
compass sea and land to make one proselyte" betrays a systematic
missionary activity also on the part of Judea's authorities. And this
has been confirmed by Jellinek's reference to Midrash, *Gen. R.,*
XXVIII, 5; *Cant.* R., I, 4, where the words of Zephaniah, II, 5:
"Woe to the inhabitants of the sea-coast, the nation of Kerethites"
are interpreted to mean that the inhabitants of the pagan lands
would be doomed to perdition (*Kareth*), were it not for the *one*
God-fearing proselyte who is won over each year and set up to
save the heathen world. We also possess a Halakic survival of a
rule concerning proselytism in *Sifre* to Deut. XXIII, 16-17 (comp.
Targ. J.), where the verses in question have been taken to mean:
"Thou shalt not surrender him who flees from his former gods to
make him again worship their masters, but assign to him a place
in one of thy gates or cities where he is to be supported as a semi-
proselyte" גר תושב. That such was the actual practice of former
times may be learned from Philo (*De Monarchia,* I, 7, and elsewhere), who tells of *hospices* prepared for the proselyte who comes
to espouse the truth of Judaism, having fled from the falsehood of
idolatry (comp. Bertholet *l. c.* 285-288; Schuerer, *G. V. Is.* III,
31ff, and Kohler, *Aseneth,* in *J. E.*). It would lead too far, were I
to dwell here on the origin and development of the two classes
of proselytes, the גר תושב called also גר שער "Proselyte of the
Gate" (probably after the Sifre just quoted comp. *Tos. Negain,*
VI, 2), and the full proselyte גר צדק who at an early period be-

came the object of a special prayer in the Eighteen Benedictions alongside of the *Ḥasidim* and the *Soferim*.

With the rise of Christianity the whole attitude of Judaism to proselytism changed. The Church took hold of the mission idea and mission activity of the Jew in the Diaspora, appropriating even the Jewish Manual for Proselytes (see *Didache* in J. E.) and giving it a Christian character. Especially did Paul, the Apostle of the heathen, as we learn from the Acts, take these very Synagogs of the Diaspora, in which "the God-worshipers" or semi-proselytes formed a conspicuous and most susceptible element, for his field of missionary activity, claiming to do away with the difference between the circumcised and the uncircumcised, and making them all one in his belief in the Atoning Christ. As the enmity sown by him against Judaism widened the gulf between the Jew and the Christian, and many of the latter turned during the Hadrianic war into maligners of the former, proselytism was altogether discouraged by the Jewish authorities. To compete with the powerful Church had become an impossibility. Proselytism had become a peril. The ancient Mishnah of R. Simeon b. Gamaliel quoted above was eliminated, and the rule adopted by the Synagog was given in the *Baraitha* (*Yeb.* 47a; *Mas. Gerin* I, 1), beginning thus: "If a person in this time desires to be admitted into the Jewish fold, he is to be acquainted with the sad lot of the Jewish people and their martyrdom and thus dissuaded from joining. Should he, however, persist, let him be instructed in the principal laws, etc." The gloomy view prevailed, owing to the ever-increasing hardship and oppression, so that R. Helbo of the fourth-century declared (*Yeb. eodem* and elsewhere): "The proselytes have become as dire a plague as leprosy to the house of Jacob," taking the word ונספחו as an allusion to ספחת —leprosy. What a striking contrast to the utterance of R. Eleazar ben Pedath, the disciple of Rab and R. Johanan, so emphatic in the enunciation of Israel's mission: "God dispersed the people of Israel among the heathen nations only for the purpose that they may win over so many proselytes; for this is what God said through Hosea, II, 25: 'I will sow her unto Me in the earth (land)'—that is to have a rich harvest reaped everywhere from Israel's spiritual seed" (*Pes.* 87ᵇ).

And yet the mission idea was never altogether lost sight of. R. Helbo's own disciple, R. Berechiah, as if in mere protest to his teacher, said: "The time will come when the proselytes will be even rendered priests in the sanctuary" (in accordance with Isaiah LXVI, 21), the word נספחו being an allusion rather to the word ספחני used for admission to the priestly function   (I Sam. II, 36). And there are numerous *Hagadic* passages speaking in words of high praise of the proselytes, which I need not quote here. Quite instructive in that respect is the remark made by both R. Joseph and R. Ashi in Babylonia: "You are too harsh of heart: with all your gathering for the Torah; with all your charity work you have not succeeded in making *one* proselyte" (*Ber.* 17ᵇ). Suffice it to state that, however narrow the outlook of the Jew became during the dark ages, his synagogal liturgy voiced the universalism of prophetic Judaism for him each year in the sublime New Year's and Atonement Day's prayer for "the time when all the people on earth shall form one bond of brotherhood to do God's bidding with a perfect heart," and again in the *'Alenu* prayer recited at the close of each service, which echoes the hope for the speedy establishment of God's kingdom, when all flesh will unite in the worship of the One God. Is there any further proof needed of the fact that Israel's religious mission was the very heart-throb and pulsating nerve of Judaism in the past? Or could there be a fuller recognition of Judaism's historic world mission than is presented by the great medieval authorities Judah ha-Levi, Maimonides and Nachmanides when they in unison declare that the Christian and Mohammedan religions were entrusted by Divine Providence with the task of preparing the heathen world for the final triumph of the pure Jewish monotheism in the Messianic Kingdom. (*Cuzari,* IV, 23; *Yad. H. Melakim,* XI, 41; and Nachmanides, *Derashah,* [ed. Jellinek], 5,). As a matter of fact, the mission idea is inseparable from the Messianic hope for the universal kingdom of God. The Messiah himself, says the Midrash, bears the name *Hadrak* (Zech.

IX, 1) as the one who is "to bring back" all the nations to God
(*Cant*. R. VII, 10).

II

Having thus far dwelt at length on the *doctrinal* side of Israel's
mission, we must now consider the *practical* side. "How did you
verify this claim?" ask our opponents. "What has the Jewish people
ever done, and what are you, Reformers, doing in fulfilment of this
mission? The Christian Church has gone forth as the great prosely-
tizer of the heathen and converted all Europe and Western Asia
to her creed. Mohammedanism, despite its national character and
its rigor, has won well-nigh all Africa and much of Asia for its
system of belief. Buddhism has conquered almost all Eastern Asia.
Judaism,—not to speak of the Hellenistic propaganda which was
the precursor of the world-wide Church mission, or of the sporadic
conquests in Africa or in the Crimea,—remained in its isolation,
allowing only individuals to join it, but never taking steps to win the
masses for its sublime faith. In the opinion of Christian writers,
such as Max Mueller, Kuenen and others, ours has ever been a
national, not a missionary religion." How, then, are we to meet the
challenge of our antagonists? The answer is not far to find, if we
only keep the one important fact in mind that our mission differs
in toto from what is usually understood by this term. The Church
in her efforts to conquer the heathen world was to a large extent
conquered herself by the heathen view. Having started in the name
of Israel's God, she had, in order to win the nations for her faith,
to enter into all kinds of compromise, whether in regard to the
unity and spirituality of God or in regard to the unity of mankind
and of the cosmos. So under the influence of the Egyptian and other
trinitarian systems God was divided into three personalities and,
in consequence thereof, also mankind into believers and unbelievers, and the Cosmos between the good and evil power represented by Christ and Satan. Thus faith and reason, religion and
science, the sacred and the secular were opposed to one another,

and instead of having religion made "the all-uniting mother leading mankind to God as the Father of All," as Maimonides calls it at the close of his *Commentary to Eduyoth,* it became a disuniting force for the human race. And the same holds, of course, still more true of the other religious systems. Against all this the Jewish people had, amidst oppression and persecution, the peculiar mission assigned to them of being "witnesses" to God in His absolute Unity and sublime Holiness. And to be witnesses meant, as the Greek translation "martyrs" suggests, to testify to the truth held forth by them by offering up their very lives in martyrdom for it. Noble as the heroic task accomplished by many a Christian missionary indisputably was, the task of the Jew during the dark medieval centuries of withstanding all the trials, the threats, and taunts, the *auto da fes* [sic] and the alluring baits of the Church was by all means far nobler and more heroic, and it was performed not by individuals, but by the entire people. It was a passive, not an active mission. Had they then gone forth among the nations to win the world for their teachings, they might have long ago been swallowed up by the surrounding multitude. Instead of this, the Jew proved to be the "Servant of the Lord" who "gave his back to the smiters," "the man of pains, despised and forsaken of men," "wounded and crushed because of others' transgressions," "like a lamb led to the slaughter who opened not his mouth," yet whose "stripes were to be the healing of the nations" (Isaiah L, 6; LIII). A two thousand years' history of martyrdom, a tragedy without parallel in the world and yet sustained by a faith which never faltered and with words of praise and sanctification of the Most High which resound throughout the centuries—this was the wondrous realization of the Deutero-Isaianic prophecy, for the grandeur of which our Nationalists have as little appreciation as have our anti-semitic enemies. Well may the words of the English poet be applied here: "They also serve who only stand and wait." And for what did the Jew wait all these centuries? Not for his mere national resurrection or for the rebuilding of a State like any other, but for the new and grander revelation of God's glory, for the establishment of God's Kingdom on earth.

Nor was the mission of the medieval Jew altogether a passive one. He stood out indeed as "a light to the nations and a covenant of the people." In the midst of the dense darkness that covered the nations all around, his lamp of learning shone brightly in the humblest hut and diffused its rays into the cells of the monastery and into the abode of the solitary thinker of Christendom. Jews, intermediating between Arabic culture and Christian Europe, held the torch of philosophy and science aloft to enlighten and nurture the minds of the scholastics and the pioneers of the universities, and usher in the era of the Renaissance and of the Reformation. So also did the Jewish men of commerce, while carrying material goods from land to land, transport the popular wisdom and folklore of the East to the West to interlink distant civilizations. Like Lessing's *Nathan the Wise,* the Jew, standing between Moslem and Christian, typified a broader cosmopolitan humanity. True, this was rather the achievement of individuals and cannot be characterized as the mission of the people in general. Nevertheless the fact remains that the Jew excelled everywhere by his zeal for truth, his love of knowledge and wisdom and, owing to his religious fervor, his study of the Torah to which he was trained from childhood up, he became actually the instructor of an illiterate environment.

But above all, he remained ever-conscious of the mission assigned to Israel as "a kingdom of priests and a holy nation." He led a consecrated life. In the midst of a world full of profanity and vulgarity, of coarse sensuality and drunkenness he displayed the virtues of chastity and modesty in his domestic and social sphere. His whole being was amidst all temptations and tempests of life anchored upon loyalty. The Law extending over all phases and functions of life disciplined him to render him sober and earnest, a veritable priest among the nations, however little recognized as such. Each Jew was a living protest against the dogmas of the Church which placed a man born of woman on God's throne, and defied human reason in order to save the soul. He was God's priest and prophet pointing to a better day, to God's Kingdom on earth.

With the downfall of the ghetto walls the relation of the Jew to the surrounding world changed, and no less so his whole aspect and mode of life. Emancipation made him a citizen in all the Western lands and placed before him the alternative of loyalty to all the laws and customs of his national past or of unreserved acceptance of the mandates of his newly acquired citizenship. It was a severe crisis he had to go through. Amidst the changed social conditions the Law upon which his life and his faith had so securely rested all these centuries, lost its hold upon him, however tenaciously the few still clung to it. To this outward cause there came the spirit of progress, of historical investigation and, above all, the general secular education with its appeal to reason and common sense, which undermined his traditional belief and his loyalty to a glorious past. He no longer could conscientiously pray and hope for the restitution of the sacrificial cult in the Temple at Jerusalem, nor for the restoration of the State to be fashioned again after the Mosaic Law. The whole of Judaism seemed to be swept away by the onrushing tide of new ideas. But there amidst the despondency, which had seized upon the faithful, and the apostasy which spread to an alarming degree among the would-be enlightened, the Reform leaders stepped in to check the evil by translating Israel's past, its literature and history, in the light of the new spirit of historical investigation. With a deeper insight into the prophetical writings and the *Haggadic* or philosophical utterances of sages, they laid all the stress on the eternal verities, the essentials of Judaism which remained the same amidst the ever-changing conditions.

This led them to bring the mission of Israel, thus long obscured and ignored amidst the legalistic view of medieval Judaism, into the foreground,[7] and to illumine the path, the life task and duty of the Jew in distinction to other religious sects. Nor must it be said, as we are so frequently told, that the doctrines of Judaism such

[7] See Geiger *Wiss. Zeitsch.* 1868. 18 and Union Prayer Book II, 332 and compare to the following the suggestive chapter "The Mission of Israel" in Claude G. Montefiore's *Outlines of Liberal Judaism*, pp. 156-170.

as its pure monotheism, its concept of man as the son of God, its cosmic Unity which has no place for a Satanic power of evil, or its ethical principle of holiness which includes all of life and demands disinterestedness in the doing of good and the shunning of evil, that all these are only for the theologian, the man in the pulpit to proclaim and defend, but not within the scope of the people at large. The average Jew still shows that he stands forth steadfast through the ages, as "the witness" to the Unity of God as the Father of all and to the one undivided humanity in the coming Kingdom of God. Moreover, liberal Christianity has fully come to the recognition of what the steadfast loyalty of the Jew to his sublime faith throughout the lands and the ages has done for the world. Never before was the outside world so eager and willing to listen to the view of progressive Judaism and to accept its doctrines as it is today. What Dr. [Isaac M.] Wise is reported to have said in his intimate circle to the effect that within fifty years Judaism's teachings will have become the common property of the American people seems to come more and more within the possibility of realization. Amidst the stimulating intermingling of ideas and exchange of thought in press, platform and pulpit, amidst the general enlightenment through education and the open forum of discussion which works for progress, liberty and democracy, the narrow ecclesiastical systems of belief and absolute forms of religious practice are discarded. Orthodoxy in all creeds is fast dwindling away and melting like the snow before the sun of spring. A wonderful transformation is taking place in the various Churches. The cry for reconstruction is heard everywhere. People crave for Unity, for a faith which unites Protestant, Catholic and Jew, nay, even Mohammedan and Hindoo Theist in a God who is the Father of all and hears the prayers of all, for a God in whom all find refuge in trouble, comfort and strength in hours of trial and death, a God who is the deepest and holiest experience of the human soul. Is this not the God of the Bible, of patriarch and prophet, the God sought and yearned for by the first man and looked up to in aspiration and adoration by the last, the God of

History, revealed to humanity by the religious genius of the Jew?
But then we are confronted with the question: What are your
credentials as a missionary people today? We certainly do not,
nor should we, aim at converting the non-Jew. Ever since R. Joshua
ben Chananiah uttered the beautiful words: "The righteous of all
nations shall have a share in the world of eternal bliss," our maxim
has been Conviction, not Conversion; Conduct, not Confession;
Deed, not Creed. But who will deny that the Jew who suffered so
much for the truth has still that passion and zeal for the truth
which cannot remain indifferent to what others think and take as
the great verities of life. His must still be that deep conviction which
works like a wholesome contagion upon others. His incomparable
history and literature must have endowed him with that religious
experience and religious devotion which would for all time render
him the trusted guardian and acknowledged defender of Israel's
heritage. And if the average Jew today knows so little of the great
treasures deposited in our matchless literature, and lacks all ac-
quaintance with the names and deeds of our heroes and martyrs,
our thinkers and poets, with our unique history of the ages, so as
no longer to burn with the desire to make his God the banner of
truth to rally all men around, the fault lies with our education, not
with the mission idea of Judaism. As a matter of fact, the modern
time requires modern methods of reading the Scripture and the
entire religious literature of both Judaism and Christianity. Israel's
monotheistic truth has not come ready-made from heaven, nor
from the brain of law-giver and prophet to be accepted in blind
belief. It is the product of a long process of growth, ever ripening
and expanding with the ages, the outgrowth of the religious genius
of the Jew which was still to some extent working in the founders
of the Church. Presented in this light of historic development as
the ripest fruit of the Jewish spirit at each epoch, the Jewish truth
cannot but arouse new love and zeal in the new generation to make
all zealous defenders and champions of a religion whose spirit is
perennial, as the God to which it testifies is eternal. And should
this mission of the Jew for his only God cease at the very time

when the world needs him most, and is actually waiting for him to present the truth of our seers and sages in its immaculate purity, cleansed from the alloys which depreciated its value in the eyes of all thinking people? Yet only in living and working *in* and *with* the world for his Only God can he achieve this mission.

And there is the other insistent cry of the age: Religion must be *life,* a life of *service,* not self-seeking solicitude for happiness, either here or hereafter. The all-comprehensive, all uplifting watchword of our time is social service, the working together of all forces for righteousness, for the readjustment of all relations between high and low, rich and poor, between the strong and the weak, between labor and capital, between the wise and the simple. And this grand principle is being extended today beyond the life of communities to the entire human family, to all the nations of the globe to unify them in the endeavor to establish righteousness and liberty, peace and concord everywhere and secure the protection of the small and the feeble by the big and the strong among the nations. But again we ask, where and by whom was this principle of life, this golden rule of ethics most emphatically voiced from the beginning and rendered the hope and the goal of humanity, if not by our great prophets of yore? And who has suffered and fought persistently and confidently throughout the ages for this glorious boon of liberty and justice as did the Jew, in whose innermost being this dynamic force still lives as a fire never to be quenched? Yes, the Jew is still the God-appointed champion of freedom and righteousness, the world's missionary of justice and liberty, all the more as he is still to battle and to suffer for them like no other class of people. And with such unparalleled experience as the Jew has had throughout the centuries, and in the face of the world's attitude today towards our prophetic teaching, will he dare think first and last only of his own political security, instead of realizing that, as "the Lord's Servant" his life must above all, as heretofore, be one of service for the entire human race? To help in the redemption of the world by righteousness is his Messianic mission. Nor is it sufficient to claim the title of priority for this principle of social justice. He must substantiate his mission by its practice in so large a measure as to become from a mere materialistic pursuer of weath, which he is often declared to be, the very banner-bearer of idealism to command the world's admiration and emulation. How did Abraham win souls for his God? the rabbis ask, and they answer, By taking all his possessions as having been entrusted to his stewardship and thus devoting his life to the service of God by his philanthropic work. So is the Deuteronomic verse: "And thou shalt love the Lord thy God with all thy heart," interpreted in the ancient Midrash (*Sifre Deut.* 32ff) to mean: "Thou shalt make thy God to be beloved by all thy fellow-creatures through deeds of love as did Abraham" לכל הבריות כאברהם אהבהו. The Jew's obligation and responsibility is accordingly a twofold one. He must take care of his own co-religionists and at the same time "hallow the name of his God" by promoting social justice in the ever-widening circles of humanity.

But there is a third point in Israel's mission which must not be treated lightly, either. We have been appointed in our Sinai constitution as "a kingdom of priests and a holy nation," and, therefore, many laws were imposed upon us intended to distinguish us from the rest of mankind. Such laws were the laws of diet and dress and of levitical purity, which only the priestly castes had to observe elsewhere. They were gradually dropped by the modern Jew, not from frivolity, nor even for mere convenience, but in consequence of his closer contact with the surrounding world, from which he could, or should, not forever keep aloof, if he was to win it for his truths. Whether the Palestinian Jew will again observe them when there is no cause for discarding them, is a question which does not concern us. At all events the spirit of these priestly laws expressive of Israel's sanctity should be maintained to render him the model and exemplar of life's holiness. There is above all the sanctity of the home, of marriage, of the relation to sex in which the Jew at all times excelled, and which wrested from the heathen seer of yore the exclamation: "How goodly are thy tents, O Jacob, thy dwellings, O Israel!" (Num. XXIV, 5). This ought to cause each Jew and Jewess still to stand out as priest and priestess at the domestic shrine to present to the world around him patterns of purity and chastity. It is not enough to avert from our children the danger of sinking to a lower level amidst the many allurements of the environment. The Jew today should, in realization of his priestly mission, be foremost in endeavoring to lift the generation from the mire of coarse sensuality with which the so-called social evil with its concomitant free love and other modes of licentiousness threatens to engulf it, and invest the bond of marriage and the home with the highest possible sacredness binding for all classes of men. Let it be understood that just as in summing up Jewish ethics in the three words :"Only to do justly, and to love mercy, and to walk humbly with Thy God" the prophet addresses not Israel, but *man:* "It has been told thee, O man, what is good" (Micah IV, 8), so does the Law in giving the divine ordinances regarding marriage refer not to Israel only, but to man, saying: "Mine ordinances which, if a man do, he shall live by them" (Lev. XVIII, 5; comp. *Sifra* to the passage).

But holiness in the Jewish concept comprises much more. There is nothing so common or profane in all of life's functions that should not be hallowed by religion. "The bells of the horses shall bear the imprint: 'Holy unto the Lord'," says the prophet (Zech. XIV, 20). This is Jewish spirituality. Not a view to the world to come, but this world with all it offers and contains should be comprised by the idea of God's Kingdom. . . .

But there is another important viewpoint which must be set forth in all its clearness as being essential to Israel's mission. It is the forward-looking attitude, the real Messianic element of progressive Judaism. The allegation frequently made that Judaism stood still for the last nineteen hundred years is far more true of the Christian Church. For her all the Messianic prophecies have been fulfilled in Jesus of Nazareth, who is looked upon as the highest possible type of human perfection. Yet this retrospective attitude is contrary to our very idea of historical progress, to the principle of evolution. Judaism has been through the various periods of history growing and expanding philosophically and ethically, and its Messiah has ever been looked for as coming to realize the prophetic dreams and visions. True, Orthodoxy awaits a Messiah from the house of David to come and restore the Temple and State of Judea in accordance with the Mosaic Code, and is therefore backward-looking instead of favoring progress and accepting the principle of evolution. As the stars in heaven are moved along their heavenly track by both a centrifugal and centripetal force, so Judaism seems to require the centripetal force of conservatism, lest the centrifugal force of progress and reform sweep it off its historic path. This accounts for Orthodoxy, and as genuine Orthodoxy could not withstand the disintegrating force of the new age, it has now made a common cause with Zionism. The prophetic outlook and forward-pressing force of Reform Judaism, however, points insistently to the Messianic goal which gives it universal character, as voiced in our pulpits and our prayers. But then it should not be confined to the synagog. It should go out and challenge the non-Jewish world. Too long have we remained on the defensive. We must become aggressive in asserting our birthright. Too long have we been mis-understood and misjudged. Lectures and tracts are not sufficient. We need an extensive popular literature for general enlightenment. Let the world learn our view of Christianity and its founder. Let the New Testament teachings be shown in the true light of histori-cal development and the so-called Christian civilization presented from the Jewish point of view. We need not, and should not belittle or depreciate any creed or rite, but we should by all means dissipate the erroneous notions concerning the Jew and Judaism prevalent among the masses, and set forth in impressive and lucid form the virtues of loyalty to country and home ever fostered and the intellectual and moral forces engendered by the teaching and training the Jew received in all the lands and ages. The cry for the Reconstruction of humanity stirs all hearts today. A new heaven and a new earth are the prophetic promises of our statesmen and seers. Who can be in closer sympathy with the stupendous plan of a world peace built on justice and liberty in which the leaders of the nations are engaged in these days, than is the descendant of the prophets and psalmists, the Jew whose scriptural truths built up the American Republic, and whose prophetic dreams and visions of yore are made the sponsors of a new humanity today? Decades, nay, centuries may pass before the lofty ideals will have become a reality; but we have learned to wait. Not for a Zion which is within easy reach, which is purchased and made a matter of diplomatic bargaining. Zion has for us a spiritual meaning. It is the symbol of a united humanity, of the realization of mankind's highest ideal at the end of time.[8]

Let Palestine, our ancient home, under the protection of the great nations, or under the specific British suzerainty, again become a center of Jewish culture and a safe refuge to the homeless. We shall all welcome it and aid in the promotion of the work. Let the million or more of Jewish citizens dwelling there amidst the large Christian and Mohammedan population attached to their own sacred spots, be empowered and encouraged to build up a commonwealth broad and liberal in spirit to serve as a school for international and interdenominational humanity. We shall all hail the undertaking and pray for its prosperity. The historic task of the Jew is not to be, and cannot be, accomplished therewith. This would never be the solution of the great enigma of Jewish history, nor a satisfactory end to the awful tragedy. Call Israel, as did Judah ha-Levi, the great lover of Zion, the heart of mankind whose life sap was to flow through the arteries of the nations, or compare it, as was repeatedly done, to the Gulf Stream, whose warm currents run through the ocean to calm its wild waves, the Jew will ever remain an international force influencing the world, as it has been influenced by it on its course through the lands and the ages. His place is *not* among the *League of Nations,* but among the *League of Religions,* as already indicated by the last of the prophets when he says: "From the rising of the sun even to the going down

---

[8] See my "Jewish Theology" with reference to *Pes. R.* 144b and *Mid. Teh.* **Ps.** XXXVI, 6.

of the same, My name is great among the nations . . . saith the Lord of hosts" (Mal. I, 11).

Of course, before going outside for this missionary activity, we must begin within our own circle, and in concert with all our brethren, conservative or progressive, endeavor to make the modern Jew again a zealous lover of the Torah. We must first regenerate our own people before attempting to regenerate the world— קשוט עצמך ואחר כך קשוט אחרים . Morover, in hearty cooperation with all liberal and liberalizing forces around us, we should strive to broaden as well as deepen, to elevate as well as humanize religion so to make it everywhere the high road to the great Temple of humanity, "the house of prayer for all nations."

Not in haste, nor running the risk of being lost on the way shall we perform our mission among the Gentile world, but with due regard to our sacred heritage and our character as the priest people. "For ye shall not go out in haste, neither shall ye go by flight, for the Lord will go before you and the Lord of Israel will be your rearward" (Isa. LII, 12). Not a Church Universal, nor a uniform religion for all, but the divine truth reflected in many systems of belief and thought, just as the diamond reflects light by its many facets, a religion ever progressive on lines of historical continuity, but never finished or final, leading all the nations and classes of men to the mountain of God—this is Judaism's aim, the realization of our Messianic hope, the establishment of God's kingdom on earth.

Yet at no time and in no country has the opportunity come to the Jew to again mount the watchtower of prophecy, and in working out his mission to unfold the banner of the highest idealism for all humanity as at the present great turning-point in the world's history, and in America, to whom a disrupted and disjointed world looks to be reset on the firm and lasting foundations of justice, liberty and peace.

An Approach to Theology

Much of philosophic thought in the twentieth century has been concerned with an attempt to move from an abstract rational universality to the recognition of the concrete particularity of the individual thinker in his life situation. To the extent that theology is an application of the insights of philosophy to the interpretation of religious teachings, theology has also moved from abstract system-building to the personal search for meaning. Two major figures in recent Jewish thought, Franz Rosenzweig and Martin Buber, have led the way toward just such a reshaping of Jewish theologizing.

Lou H. Silberman, in this paper that starts from one of Rosenzweig's basic ideas, examines what it means to be a theologian in these terms. Silberman sees that the Jewish theologian (whether of the Reform movement or of any other persuasion) must begin by confronting the whole tradition of Judaism in its integrity rather than any one limited segment. It is not enough to say, arbitrarily, it is in the work of the Prophets that the heart of the Tradition is to be found; therefore one must study the Prophets. All the rest is outworn and of merely antiquarian concern. Only by studying (as far as is humanly possible) the entire range of the Tradition can one determine what, for him, is living Judaism, what of the Tradition he can affirm, "not as abstract, disembodied spirit, but for and by him as this living man at this point and place in history." A theology cannot be propounded by a committee. It must be born in the meeting of the concreteness of the Tradition and the particularity of the person.

151

THE THEOLOGIAN'S TASK
Lou H. Silberman
(1963)

An Introductory Admission

In his challenging open letter to Buber, *"Die Bauleute,"* Franz
Rosenzweig acclaimed his friend for his creative disclosure to that
generation, of the nature of Torah, "the Teaching." "You have," he
wrote, "saved the Teaching from the splendiferous poverty of basic
principles to which the nineteenth century—not the first but the
most practicable and far-reaching attempt—sought to reduce it."
No distinctions *a priori* were to be countenanced; the whole of the
Tradition, not a predetermined segment, became not only the
object of study (*Lernstoff*) but became potentially Torah, to be
actualized by choosing so that it became truth.

This understanding of Torah has been almost from the first
moment I read that essay the basic methodology of my own studies.
It has formed my interests and informed my concerns. It has, sadly
enough, uprooted loyalties and unwillingly brought about alienation. But it has opened for me vistas previously shut off and granted
me insights previously denied. I report this so that in what follows
you may recognize the working-out of a point of view that is not
arbitrary and disjoined, but is, I earnestly hope, grounded in just
such an approach as that described above.

152

I. *A Critical Appraisal*

Ten years ago as a part of a symposium on "The State of the Reform Movement," I read a paper before this Conference dealing with "The Recent History of Reform Philosophy." It was critical in its approach, negative in its conclusions, and avoided complete pessimism only by following the tradition of ending on a note of eschatological hopefulness. The intervening decade has, sadly enough, not softened the criticism nor erased the negativism. It has, however, deepened the pessimism. . . .

Yet when, within the last generation, a total repudiation of the bourgeois definition of the nature of the people of Israel espoused by the Reform movement was forced upon us by the tragic history of our times, we replaced it with that melange of Western European romantic nationalism and Eastern European messianism which we call Zionism, and submitted uncritically to its emotional appeal. Time after time, like all tired liberals, we have clung tenaciously to positions regarding issues that have moved through and beyond their crucial stages. The positions may or may not have been sound; their present failing is that often they are irrelevant. Nor is what I have said limited in any way to the particular segment of the total Jewish community we represent. Irrelevancy is not our possession alone; we graciously share it with all our brethren.

I do not, however, intend to belabor this point nor to become bogged down in debating yesterday. My own concern and, I hope, your concern is with the urgencies of today and the hopes of tomorrow. Nothing that anyone can say will change that which lies behind; and though to face today and to move into tomorrow one needs to understand yesterday, to make of that task more than a prolegomenon is to fall back into academic desuetude.

II. *The Problematic Nature of the Undertaking*

The task I have set for myself in this paper is the examination of a program of study and work that can lead to a meaningful statement of Judaism intellectually sound and spiritually relevant in and for the generation to which it is addressed. There is, unfortunately, a frustration built into the enterprise from the start, for one does not face a static body of given propositions that is merely to be rearranged or restated. One is caught up in a dynamic process which constantly shows forth new meanings, so that in a very real sense whatever one manages to say is rendered obsolete in its saying. Rosenzweig in the letter quoted above wrote: ". . . Torah [this is what he means by *die Lehre*] itself is not known once and for all but is always something in the future. Thus the question of him who asks for it today is perhaps already a part of the answer that will be given to another tomorrow and certainly at some time in the future will become the keyword of the answer given to him who today is the questioner." One must reckon at the outset with the dissolution of his statement at the very moment of uttering it, and must do so bravely and indeed thankfully.

The point of departure for this journey is, as I have already suggested, the open confrontation of the Tradition in its vastness, unfettered as far as humanly possible by prejudgments as to what is essential and what is peripheral. It is quite clear at once that the fulfillment of such a task is beyond the competence of any living man today, but this inability does not render invalid the basic presupposition, namely, that one dare not make unsupported prejudgments. One must be prepared to say yea as widely as possible, embracing contradiction and paradox, not for the sake of contradiction and paradox, but because this is the very stuff of the Tradition that one must face, so that it may become his truth.

This is what *die Wissenschaft des Judentums* must mean. It is not to be the drawing up of accounts and the closing of books as some nineteenth-century scholars imagined, bringing to an end and dismissing to dusty shelves large areas of the Tradition. It is the opening up of ever new realms that have been hidden under the dust of centuries, so that we may know again the magnitude of our past and thus be challenged to an equally broad tomorrow. One must be ready to face the multiplicity and complexity of the

Tradition and as scholar seek to penetrate into and to understand and to make one's own that which is encountered.

At this point, it seems to me, one must acquire that methodology so forthrightly exhibited by Leo Baeck, the technique of *Nacherleben* derived from his teacher Wilhelm Dilthey's *Verstehende Psychologie,* in which one seeks to understand a totality, a *Gestalt.* Here, recognizing the polarity of the Jewish religious experience, one affirms the tension and makes it one's own. This requires that one throw into question the choices and conclusions of yesterday, not arrogantly, but with the humbling knowledge that nothing is his until he has made it his.

III. *History And Dogma*

As a theologian, then, one begins with history, for there it is that one beholds the affirmations and the refusals made by and within the people of Israel confronted by God and His Word. These affirmations and refusals as action in political, economic and social life, affirmations and refusals made in the field of legal structure, in worship, in prophetic utterance and popular response, in historian's narrative and poet's art, in mystic's contemplation and philosopher's dialectic, in legend and in song, these affirmations and refusals are the "stuff," the material with which the theologian labors. This it is he needs to know, for this it is that through the risk of his own affirmation and his own refusal becomes in his life, and perhaps through him in the life of others, Torah. To affirm or refuse, not in isolation, not cut off from the community, but in its midst, or truer, with it, demands that we know what it has affirmed and what it has refused in its existence.

These affirmations and refusals are, and one must not cavil at the word, the dogmas of Judaism. By dogmas I mean *'emunot,* which, as Alexander Altmann has pointed out, is Ibn Tibbon's translation of Saadya's Arabic *'amanat* and denotes doctrines "accepted by an act of religious faith." I do not intend to enter upon what is for me the discussion of a side issue in the field of semantics. The whole question of dogmas has been so beclouded by "apologetic thinking" that only the most determined effort can wrench us loose from our so-called liberal prejudices. We have been so thoroughly bemused by formal considerations, so naively entrapped by nineteenth-century bias, that we have failed to recognize that our literature is shot through from the very beginning with theological affirmations. Where these occur and what they are thus becomes a crucial part of the theologian's task.

IV. *Liturgy and Dogma*

One of the most important contributions of contemporary Biblical scholarship has been the recognition of the role of the *Credo,* the liturgical confession in the Bible. One may find as do I the use of the term *Credo* not entirely satisfactory, but a mistake in labeling does not change the nature of that labelled. Yet what else is that most familiar passage in Deuteronomy at the beginning of *Ki Tavo* (26:1–11)? One is commanded to come before the Lord and to say: הגדתי היום יהוה (אלהיך) אלהי כי באתי אל הארץ אשר נשבע יהוה לאבותינו לתת לנו—"I am making a declaration unto the Lord (your) my God today because I have come into the land which He swore unto our fathers to give to us." What does he declare? He narrates a story: ארמי אבד אבי—the story of his people that is at the same time his own story. In the course of it he makes three theological affirmations: וישמע יהוה את קלנו—"He heard our cry"; ויוצאנו ממצרים—"He brought us forth from Egypt"; ויבאנו אל המקום הזה—"He brought us unto this place."

Here we see the *Sitz im Leben,* the living situation in which the theological affirmations of the Israelite community were made, the liturgical or cultic act. Here too we learn the structure or the form in which these affirmations are clothed, the historical narrative. This form, although it does not conform to our expectation that dogmatic creedal statements be framed in abstract propositions, is explicitly a creed, a normative affirmation of the Israelite community. Thus this passage and others like it provide one with the clue to the discovery of the dogmas of Judaism and the recognition that the superbly articulated narrative that begins with the opening verses of *Bereshit* and culminates in the stirring covenant-making scene in Joshua 24 is a great theological affirmation proclaiming the Creator God who is the Lord of history and the *Melekh* of Israel.

It is against the background of these affirmations that the prophetic movement in Israel gains its meaning. Only in a community where the dogma of a Creator God who rules history and is Sovereign of the people is accepted and affirmed, does the pattern of prophetic warning and promise make sense. Both the warnings of punishment and the promises of restoration are but workings-out of the meaning of divine lordship over history and divine sovereignty over Israel. While at the same time the narrative of the מצרים יציאת —the going forth from Egypt—is the paradigm of fulfillment, for He is a God who saves.

These affirmations grew up and continued to find their expression within the liturgical structure of Israel or in literary forms that reflected that structure. Israel's worship of God expressed what Israel affirmed about God. In contemporary New Testament scholarship it is a generally accepted position that the earliest theological formulation of nascent Christianity is the *kerygma,* the *haggadah,* the proclamation of the acts of God. The apostolic preaching was quite clearly a brief narrative of what the Church understood to be the crucial act of God in history. C. H. Dodd has pointed out that it is in the great liturgies of the Church that this *kerygma,* this proclamation, is retained in its purity. This but underscores the contention that it is in this direction that one must seek for the basic formulation of Jewish dogmas; dogmas already explicit in the whole of the *Tanakh,* now provided a clear and unmistakable structure.

Fifty years ago Ismar Elbogen wrote: *"Das Schma enthält das Bekenntnis, den Kern des Glaubensbestandes des Judentums . . ."* He was, of course, referring to the whole complex of prayers and Biblical passages that is gathered around the Deuteronomic verses.

In masterful fashion he demonstrated the development of this, the original form of public prayer. As this liturgical structure took shape, it provided for the normative expression of Israel's theological affirmations; it was the creed of Pharisaic-rabbinic Judaism. It proclaimed יוצר —Creator הבוחר בעמו ישראל באהבה—Lord of history and sovereign of Israel; it rejected multiplicity and affirmed uniqueness—אחד ; it commanded unconditional love, loyalty and obedience–ואהבת; it promised reward and warned of retribution— והיה אם שמע ; it made explicit the promise of redemption by reference to the past—אני יהוה אלהיכם אשר הוצאתי אתכם מארץ מצרים להיות לכם לאלהים —affirming in its earliest form— צור ישראל וגואלו — Israel's Rock and his Redeemer.

This is the way in which Pharisaic Judaism brought together and made explicit its comprehension of Israel's theological affirmations; the way in which the Scriptures themselves had time and time again done the same thing: through liturgical formulation. But, as indicated earlier, the form of expression in no way militates against its dogmatic content. Indeed, the very form underscores its dogmatic and binding nature. Professor [Louis] Finkelstein has shown that the various prayers of the *Tefillah,* too, serve the function of dogmatic definition. In discussing the role of the second benediction *Geburot,* he wrote: "The emphasis on the Resurrection in this benediction is too clear to be missed, and it can only be taken as a confession of faith in Pharisaism as opposed to Sadduceanism."

Elbogen put the whole matter succinctly when he wrote that the service of worship "expressed that which the community held in common, the confession of faith. The formulation of belief that united all the members of the community provided the primary element of the public liturgy around which the other elements, as around a natural center, ranged themselves." Thus, there can be no doubt but that the order of worship was indeed the basic statement of belief of Pharisaic-rabbinic Judaism, not derived from philosophic propositions but proclaiming as existential truth the various ways in which Israel had been confronted by God.

These were not only Judaism's dogmas; this was, contrary to

Rosenzweig, who has written: *"Judentum hat . . . nämlich zwar
Dogmen, aber keine Dogmatik,"* Judaism's dogmatic, a systematic
and integrated statement of the fundamental affirmations of Pharisaic-rabbinic Judaism, resting ultimately on the authority of Scripture. While the exact date of the emergence of this formulation is
uncertain, there is every reason to believe that it took place before
the rise of Christianity. With its establishment was set the direction
and task of that tradition within Judaism that became normative.
In a very real sense, what one may call Jewish theology is a vast
commentary upon the affirmations here set down. Anyone who is
at all concerned with an intellectually sound and spiritually relevant
statement of Judaism must, therefore, begin with a recognition and
acceptance of the dogmatic structure of Judaism. Each theologian
does not, of course, necessarily deal with all of these affirmations;
he may, indeed, limit himself to a discussion of one or several; but
whatever he deals with must be thought of with the consciousness
of the presence of all.

V. *The Dogmatic Undertaking*

The task of the theologian at this point is the discovery in all of
its details of the explicit and implicit meaning of these affirmations
within the Tradition. Methodologically, he is required to investigate and chart the route or routes by which this statement of the
faith of Israel emerged out of the encounter and dialogue between
God and the people of Israel. Beginning with what scholarship can
demonstrate to be the earliest full articulation of the liturgical-
creedal structure here outlined, he is obligated to disclose by a
meticulous *explication du texte* the possibilities and probabilities
that lie within it, recognizing all along the presence of ambiguities
and lost nuances. Thus Scripture and its interpretation, Midrash,
must be carefully scrutinized in order to recognize how the Pharisaic-rabbinic community understood the language which was embodied in its theological formulation.

For example, one would begin with the familiar eulogy יוצר אור

ובורא חשך עשה שלום ובורא את הכל and, recognizing that it is a quotation of Isaiah 45.7 with the substitution of את הכל for the Biblical רע, attempt first to understand the phrase in its original context, particularly what רע meant, and then seek to discover the theological motivation for the displacement. One would be led to examine the explanation for the shift found in the *Gemara* (*Ber.* 11b), and relate that interpretation to the far larger problem involved in what seems to be the rabbinic reluctance to reaffirm boldly the Biblical assertion that God is בורא רע "Creator of *ra*," again necessarily penetrating as far as possible into the Pharisaic-rabbinic understanding of the denotation and connotation of that word.

It is clear that here we have a crucial theological problem in the process of definition and we are obligated to understand as exactly as possible what the eventual affirmation was intended to convey. Once assured of at least a sound understanding of the theological function of this phrase, the theologian must turn to the subsequent theological activity within the community in order to discover, again as far as possible, the line or lines of development along which this question of the relation of God to *ra* moved. He must allow himself to be confronted by the Tradition in all of its variety.

At the end, having before him, in theory at least, the dominant direction this affirmation has taken in its functioning, together with a map of the side roads, cul-de-sacs, detours, etcetera, he is able to make a statement about the authentic position of the synagogue that will not be a homiletic conceit, a partial truth, hence partially untrue, or even a well-informed guess. He will have disclosed with all the rigor of scientific methodology the structure and the dynamic of a fundamental affirmation of the synagogal tradition as it has emerged.

The methodology here sketched thus opens the way toward the construction of a systematic statement of the Tradition, which will, should it follow the liturgical dogmatic outline above, begin with the doctrine of Creator and creation, of God and man, and move to the doctrine of the Lord of history and His covenant with the people of Israel, which will include the doctrine of commandment (*mitzvah*) and response, i.e., the whole *halakhic*-ethic structure of Judaism; and will culminate in the doctrine of last things, i.e., the redemption of history and the renewal of creation.

VI. *The Existential Risk*

In doing this the theologian's own suppositions and presuppositions will have been called into question. He will have been called upon to affirm or refuse. He will have had to take the risk, put his own relation to the Tradition in jeopardy. Where he is able to say yes, to say it with humility; where he must say no, to say it with candor and with courage.

One needs to remind himself over and over again of this, the situation of his study. It is, as I said above, "not in isolation, not cut off from the community, but in its midst . . . with it," that one learns, affirms, refuses. Nor is this done in isolation from the rest of one's self. He who faces the Tradition, he who enters into this crucial conversation with it, does not come to it unencumbered; he is not merely the sensitive plate of a camera recording all that is encountered. He chooses and refuses, says yea and nay out of the situation in which he stands. It is within and through his own life that the stuff of learning becomes Torah. His standing within the community confronts him with the Tradition he must affirm or refuse. The community's standing within the world, its meeting with the variety of the world's thought, sets the situation in which he affirms or refuses. Our contemporary theologian with few, perhaps with no exceptions, moves not from within the Tradition outward to meet the world's thought and subdue it. He begins most often not entirely outside and not entirely within. He begins in a dynamic situation in which the relationship between the fields of his existence is ever in motion, ever changing, ever forming new constellations and clusters of meaning. Torah is always becoming, for he is always becoming. He is always becoming, for Torah is always becoming.

VII. *The Philosophic Challenge*

Recognizing this, we can ask ourselves some questions about the various ways in which this relationship occurs. It is clear that there is always an incommensurable quality rooted in the uniqueness of each person; it is equally clear that as space- and time-bound creatures, yes, as finite beings, we are involved in finite possibilities. Indeed, the limits at any one time seem rather narrow. Yet though the options may be few, they are real.

This brings us back in a way to a consideration of the strictures I indulged in a decade ago. What concerned me then as now is the fact that in addition to or perhaps because of the limitations we impose upon the relevancy of the whole Tradition, we break off the crucial and constructive conversation between the Tradition and the world. The limitation actually inhibits any truly creative confrontation; in very fact the limitation is the acceptance of the world's judgment upon the Tradition. But more than this, the liveness of the option toward which the liberal movement turned its understanding of even this truncated Tradition has been a fading one. Only Hermann Cohen dared anything like a grand confrontation of the Tradition and what was for a time at least the vigorous option of neo-Kantian thought.

But it has not been this option that has in our day faced the Tradition, to become its dynamic partner in the becoming discussed above. Rather has the Tradition been faced by that revolutionary break with rationalist philosophy that had its origins in the late Schelling, found its early Christian theological expression in Kierkegaard and flowered in Nietzsche, Bergson and what has loosely been named the existentialist school. Indeed, this later meeting has provided the basis for almost the entire development of European theology, Christian and Jewish, during the last half century. Few other options have been offered, or rather, few other philosophic positions have existed that have been ready and willing to enter into conversation with the Tradition.

On the American Jewish scene only one notable confrontation

took place, that between the Tradition and the pragmatic instru-
mentalism of Dewey—a particularly American form of existentialism. But its full impact was vitiated by the transformation of the
Tradition's ontological affirmations into sociological functions. For
the most part we have been unable or unready, first to relinquish
our limited view of the Tradition, and second to enter into the
conversation at all. We have assumed an anti-intellectual stance
that has regarded theology as at best a luxury, at worst, sheer drivel.
Hence the present task of the theologian.

Existentialist theologies have made it evident that one theologizes
from one's situation. This has been the unmistakable thrust of this
paper, its ground and direction. But it has become ever more apparent to me that merely to stay with this necessary subjectivity is
ultimately to defeat oneself. As theologian my subjectivity is confronted by the stuff of the Tradition and I am called upon to thrust
myself into it in learning. In Rosenzweig's words: "to rivet oneself to the chain of the Tradition as latest link." But this thrusting,
this transforming from "stuff" to Torah—the living word of God to
me—does not take place, and here I paraphrase Rosenzweig,
because I wish it but because I have the capacity for it. Whence
the capacity? To ask this question is not to dismiss but to honor
subjectivity by recognizing it as the legitimate source of the
theologian's task without making it his answer.

It was in answer to just this question that R. Moses b. Maimon
wrote to his pupil R. Joseph ibn Aknin in the letter that serves as
the Introduction to the *Moreh Nebukhim:* "I perceived that you
had acquired some knowledge in these matters [metaphysics]
from others, and that you were perplexed and bewildered; yet you
sought to find out a solution to your difficulty. I urged you to desist
from this pursuit, and enjoined you to continue your studies systematically; for my object was that the truth shall present itself in
connected order, and that you should not hit upon it by mere
chance." How was the disciple, yes, how was the teacher himself
to affirm within the sphere of human reason, the truth of Torah?
The question is not bookish, for the language it uses carries us

into the human situation as defined by existentialist thought: "he is lost in perplexity and anxiety." ". . . he would be left with those errors which give rise to fear and anxiety, constant grief and great perplexity." The whole of the *Moreh* was the answer laid out in terms then accessible to human reason. It sought to give to the perplexed the capacity for affirmation.

The task of the contemporary theologian is none other. He must acquire the capacity for affirming and must affirm what he has the capacity to affirm. "I do not presume to think," wrote the Rambam in clear recognition of human limitation, "that this treatise settles every doubt." But that he had to grapple with doubt in terms that doubt presented itself was for him indisputable.

VIII. *The Theologian's Task*

The theologian is then concerned with the question of what makes it possible for him to affirm the Tradition and what makes it possible for the Tradition to be affirmed by him, not as abstract, disembodied spirit, but for and by him as this living man at this point and place in history. It is this Tradition, this Tradition in its scandalous particularity, not in abstract general principles, he struggles to affirm. Once we recognize the double nature of our task, we are escaped from mere subjectivity on the one hand and sheer objectivity on the other. But again we need remind ourselves, this recognition insists, that there is no *a priori* way of affirmation. At the very same time that Rambam worked through the architectonic rationalist structure that made it possible for him and his disciples to affirm the Tradition, the speculative mystics were engaged in the exploration of quite another intellectual structure directed toward the very same end, the affirmation of the dogmas. It is, of course, one of the limitations of liberalism that it has consistently refused to recognize the intellectual achievement of speculative mysticism, of *kabbala,* and to understand it as a valid mode of theological construction. In saying this I in no way make claim for it in our present situation, but I do not at the same time accept the liberal bias of *a priori* denial. This is, however, a side issue. The central concern of the theologian is not how the problem has been dealt with before (although it is indispensable for him to know this) but what are the tools at hand in his present situation as he looks toward the future. Are they those that have proved so valuable for European theologians? the *Existenzphilosophie* of Heidegger, Jaspers and some others? Are they those that are beginning to emerge within the English philosophic scene as linguistic analysis moves away from its earlier positions and directs its attention toward areas of human activity previously considered unproductive? Or will the promise of a renewal of the classical philosophic tradition, duly chastened, of course, in the manner of Tillich, develop into a real movement so that the conversation either broken off in the nineteenth century or generally unproductive in the twentieth may be renewed?

The answer lies not with any official body, not with organizations, commissions and conferences, but in the life of the single one who is in actuality the creative field in which Tradition and world meet and struggle to relate. The answer comes out of the risk he takes. The risk? He dares to say what he dare not say, to do what he dare not do. The reason? There is a passage quoted in Buber's *Ten Rungs* that sheds light on this:

> In the Book of Elijah we read: "Everyone of Israel is duty bound to say: 'When will my works approach the works of my fathers, Abraham, Isaac and Jacob?'" How are we to understand this? How could we ever venture to think that we could do what our fathers did?
>
> Just as our fathers invented new ways of serving, each a new service according to his own character: one, the service of love; another, of stern justice; a third, of beauty; so each one of us in his own way should devise something new in the light of the teaching and of service, and do what has not yet been done.

It is this that is the theologian's task, we hope, his bread, his tears, his trust.

Ideas of God

Historically, Judaism has centered not upon definitions of God, but on the "never ending effort to make more precise the definition of how God would have us live." The Halakha, the prescriptive code for Jewish living, was authoritative as a guide for action, but made no attempt to control thought. It is to the literature of Aggada, then, that we must turn to find the tentative, partial, human theological speculations in Judaism.

But Aggada is not, and was never meant to be precise and definitive. Thus there is no single conception of God to be found in Jewish tradition. There are, rather, many limited insights into the nature of God, each claiming for itself no more than that it expresses the faith of one Jewish thinker. Superficially, this seems to permit a total anarchy. Two factors, Eugene B. Borowitz suggests, restricts this anarchic tendency. The first is that any idea of God that may properly be called Jewish "must be such as to make possible . . . the life of Torah" in its widest sense. Here we have a functional and pragmatic criterion of the Jewishness of an idea of God: "In Judaism an idea of God is judged by the way it operates in the life of the individual Jew, and . . . in the life of the Jewish religious community."

The second factor is history, not so much of the past as of the future. The testing of any idea of God is the ongoing history of the Jewish people. The idea must, of course, be "an authentic development of the Jewish past." It must have the appeal of reasonableness in current Jewish life, as well. The final court of judgment is, however, the continuing vitality of the idea in the Jewish life of the future. From this critical perspective, Borowitz argues, Reform Judaism must search not for "the Jewish idea of God," but for "more or less acceptable Jewish ideas of God."

166

THE IDEA OF GOD
Eugene B. Borowitz
(1957)

לדור ודור נגיד גדלך
ולנצח נצחים קדושתך נקדיש
ושבחך אלהינו מפינו לא ימוש לעולם ועד

. . . [I]t is clear that Judaism requires a belief in God, but what kind of idea of God, what sort of mental construct or intellectual picture of Him does it deem necessary? What is the Jewish idea of God?

The answer to that question would seem, at first, to be the purpose of this paper. But I am troubled by a question which logically demands prior consideration. How will we recognize the Jewish idea of God when we find it? Among the concepts proposed by Mordecai Kaplan, Martin Buber, Hermann Cohen, Eric Fromm and others, how shall we judge which may properly be called Jewish? What are the criteria by which we may determine whether this formulation rather than that is truly the Jewish idea of God?

This crucial question, as far as I have been able to ascertain, has rarely been dealt with in our day. Yet unless our standard of judgment about the idea of God is first made clear, unless we can establish with reasonable certainty what Judaism requires of an idea of God, our partisanship of this or that concept is equally meaningless. Hence I must request that it is to the question of the proper form of the idea of God in Judaism, not to the delineation of its correct content, that I may devote what I hope will seem to you the less-than-eternity that I have been given.

Where shall we begin this investigation of ideational form? We must, I think, first find the place of the idea of God within the structure of Jewish religion as a whole, remembering that it is not belief in God, or the reality of God, or the existence of God with which we are concerned, but only the idea of Him which we create. Once we have found the relationship of this idea to the other elements of Judaism, we will then be able to establish the criteria which we seek.

We turn, first, to the place of the idea of God in Judaism.

It will, I think, help us clarify our perspective to begin with a brief look at how some other religions have dealt with this matter.

In Christianity, it seems clear, not just belief in God, but one's idea of God is crucial. This is not due simply to Christianity's early conquest and absorption of Greek philosophy. The idea of God has been of vital significance to more than Christian theologians alone. Paul made faith in the crucified and risen Christ central to Christianity. It is through his faith in the Christ that a man becomes a Christian, that he lives as a Christian and that he achieves salvation. But the Christ is God, God become man, God who suffered and died, God who saves us from our sins. Not every faith will save a man. It is the specific content of his faith which determines his Christianity, and his salvation for all eternity.

It is no wonder then that for its first five hundred years Christianity devoted a major part of its intellectual energies to defining its idea of God. The great controversies and heresies of those years all center about the precise meaning of God in Christianity. With but a small stretch of the imagination one might view all the intellectual history of Christianity as one continuing effort to define its idea of God. The Protestant rebellion, for example, is, intellectually, basically a dispute as to where the body of Christ, the indwelling presence of God in our world, is to be found: in the Roman church, the gathered church, the church spiritual, the Spirit acting in the church, the heart of the believer, or the like.

The very term Christianity uses for an exposition of its faith, "theology," literally "the science of God," shows that for it there can be nothing of greater importance.

But because this is so emphatically true of Christianity, we should not be misled into thinking it must be true of all religions. To Theravadin Buddhism, the school of the older, more authentic Buddhist tradition, the idea of God is totally irrelevant. Its concern is the universal suffering of mankind; its goal, to overcome that suffering. The means of doing this the Buddha discovered and proclaimed. He taught four noble truths: that all is suffering; that suffering comes from desire; that when desire is ended, suffering is ended; that desire can be ended by following the eightfold path. But as to God, he maintained what the Buddhist sages have called a "noble silence." On this subject he did not speak, for as he is reported saying about such matters, "Because this profits not, nor has to do with the fundamentals of religion, therefore I have not elucidated this."

Theravadin Buddhism has no place for the idea of God because it has no place for God Himself. The four noble truths were not revealed by any God. They were the product of the Buddha's own mental achievement, his inner enlightenment as he sat under the famous Bo tree at Budhgaya. The eightfold path does not at any step depend upon the grace, the mercy, or any other help from God. They are all acts which man by his own effort can do, if he will. No wonder then the Buddha could maintain a noble silence about God. Let Him be there or not—it makes no difference to your escape from suffering. Let Him be this or that—it does not matter in your search to find release.

And what of Judaism? What is the place of the idea of God within our religious faith? Clearly we are not religiously agnostic as are the Theravadin Buddhists. We are more like their brothers of the other Buddhist school and would insist that God is indispensable to our religion. But what place do our ideas of Him have within the structure of our Jewish belief? Shall we say it is the same one Christianity has assigned to the idea of God?

To answer this we must ask ourselves a most difficult question. Christianity is focused upon redemption from sin as Buddhism in both branches is devoted to release from suffering. What is it that Judaism is centered upon? What is the axis, the pivot, of the Jewish religion? I think we must respond, not an idea of God, but the life of Torah. The root religious experience of Judaism, it seems to me, is not the negative one of escape from sin or suffering. It is the positive one of hearing God's commandment that we serve Him, as a people and as single selves. It is the sense that God wants us to act in Godlike ways. It is the feeling of mitzvo. It is Torah.

Torah in its widest sense is the substance of that continuing Jewish religious experience, elaborated on many different levels. Here I use it in the narrower sense of the content of the commandment and its explicit application to all of life.

Is it not Torah in this sense that almost all the great Jewish controversies have centered about? Not concepts of God, but the implications of Torah separated the ethically sensitive prophet from the ritually centered priest; the pioneering Pharisee from the reactionary Sadducee; the law-loving Gamaliel from the antinomian Paul; the evolutionary rabbanite from the reductionist Karaite; and in our own day, it is their concepts of Torah, not their ideas of God, that separate Reform, Orthodox and Conservative Jews.

It is to Torah in this sense, to the never ending effort to make more precise the definition of how God would have us live, that the Jewish intelligence has dedicated itself. Until modern times it is almost impossible to find a Jewish book whose major purpose it is to expound the idea of God. Even the works of medieval Jewish philosophy seem to deal with the idea of God rather as a prelude to their discussion of Torah, as a requirement for establishing the origin and authority of Torah, and in this way the truth of Judaism.

Nor should we be surprised to note, therefore, that it was in the area of Torah, and here alone, that Judaism chose to make exact decisions and to exercise religious discipline. The official definition of Torah was binding upon the Jew and carried behind it all the power the Jewish community could muster, from fines to whipping, from excommunication to death. The closest thing Judaism had to the authority of Christian dogma was the rigor of the halacha. The nearest thing Judaism had to the Christian creed was the accepted code of law.

But the halacha is clearly limited to questions of action, which Judaism considers primary. It does not embrace the field of thought, which in Judaism therefore is secondary. Ideas of God as such do not come within the domain of the halacha. Their place is in another realm of discourse, the realm of the aggada.

The halacha strives for completeness and precision. The aggada gives these up in advance for illumination of the partial and brief insight into the whole. The halacha insists on resolving opposing views. The aggada is quite tolerant of apparent contradictions and will not coerce the assent of either "a" or "non-a." The halacha labors to fix the authoritative path for all to follow. In the aggada the Jew is always free to seek an ever more adequate expression of the meaning of his faith. He may spend all of his life in this quest confident that, except for certain minimal conditions, Judaism will not demand of him ideas he has not reached on his own, nor legislate him out of Israel by the adoption of an authoritative code of beliefs. Judaism has given the aggada, its world of ideas, an extraordinary freedom. Though the aggada abounds with ideas about God, we may not expect to find in Judaism one systematically integrated idea of God.

This placement of the idea of God in Judaism within the realm of the aggada is not a historical accident. It is rather a basic decision with regard to that kind of theological structure which would alone be true to the Jewish religious experience.

To have placed the idea of God in the realm of the halacha would have meant that Judaism believed the human mind as capable of reaching authoritative decisions about God as about Torah. The Torah does say of the commandments that it is neither too hard for us, nor too far for us. It is not in the heaven nor over the sea, but very nigh unto us that we may do it. The halacha,

Judaism feels, is clearly within man's power to understand and extend. Yet the Torah does not speak this way of God. Indeed it emphasizes rather the opposite, that though we may know the will of God, we may not see His face and live.

Judaism purposely confines the idea of God to the realm of the aggada because it knows the limits of human reason in this regard. The aggada should not then be thought of in a negative way, as only that which is not halacha. In the aggada, Judaism created a unique structure of thought, a special realm of discourse, complete with its own distinct standards and style, its own proper logic and language. By this ingenious mental architecture Judaism allows reason to extend itself continually, without the danger that it might overextend itself and its authority. Or to put it more positively, Judaism invented the aggada as the proper vehicle for Jewish religious ideas because its respect for reason did not transcend its awe of God.

Even medieval Jewish philosophy, whose language sought for something like the precision of the halacha, must be considered a branch of the aggada, specialized and sophisticated though it be. We see this clearly, for each philosopher felt he had complete freedom to reject and reformulate what his predecessor had thought were the required beliefs of Judaism. And despite Maimonides' immense authority, his creed down to our day is but a voluntary addition to the service, except as it occurs in the more overtly aggadic form of song.

Thus in Judaism, we must conclude, all efforts to speak of God must be understood as aggadic speaking, and all Jewish theology must be conducted in this domain. The freedom of the aggada, then, makes it a contradiction in terms to speak of "the" Jewish idea of God. Judaism has but one God, but not one idea of Him.

Hence our original decision not to speak of the content but of the form of an idea of God in Judaism has by this very investigation been justified. To have spoken here of what seems to me or to someone else the essential ingredients of an idea of God with contemporary relevance would have been to substitute a Jew's view for a Jewish view of God and to strive for the authority of the halacha in an area which requires the humility of the aggada. How much so-called Jewish theology has been of little lasting worth because its author's thought was structured in alien categories!

In the aggada Judaism created a form of thought which anticipates in essence what modern philosophy of religion has now come to. Through the positive emphasis of Kant and Cassirer on the way in which reason necessarily shapes knowledge, and through the negative criticism of the logical positivists that propositions are meaningful only insofar as they are verifiable, a revolution has taken place in our understanding of philosophic language and meaning. Gone are the days when philosophic propositions, particularly in reference to ethical or religious issues, could be taken at face value as accurate statements of fact. Today it is generally conceded that such language is a symbolic form of speech. The significant phrases, ideas or events around which religion centers carry their meaning in a way which cannot be taken literally or understood denotatively, but must be recognized as reaching a level of reality otherwise closed to us by pointing to something beyond themselves, in which they at the same time participate.

The most philosophic of contemporary Christian theologians, Paul Tillich, has been able to rear so lofty an intellectual structure only because he has been one of the foremost investigators of the meaning of symbolism for philosophical theology. From my outsider's point of view, it is this philosophic insistence that the word of God when spoken by man must be understood symbolically that will increasingly split contemporary Christian theology into two wings. Many now speak frankly in the realm of philosophic myth as Tillich does, treating the Christ as the ultimate symbol. Others, following Karl Barth, reject philosophy entirely and speak only of the Kerygma, the message of the New Testament, whose burden is the real, if rationally inexplicable event of the God who truly became a man in history and died that those who would believe in him might be saved. This "scandal" needs preaching, not philosophic exposition, for it seeks faith, not understanding. These differences are deeply troublesome to Christian thinkers because they tend to result in two views of the Christ. This is a matter of the highest intellectual importance to us since one of these views may be surprisingly liberal. It therefore seems to me no less than an intellectual felony to hear Jews indict these Christian thinkers indiscriminately (sometimes with Jewish thinkers thrown in among them). And why is this done? So that we may pronounce them guilty by their association with ideas we will not take the time to understand, because we are so eager to hang the witches of Existentialism.

Protestant theology may indeed be in great turmoil because of symbolic philosophy. Jewish theology, when it is true to its historic roots, when it remembers that it is part of the aggada, need not tremble. It has already known this wisdom.

Yet, though Jewish theology is relatively free, it is not formless. Despite the many contradictory statements of the aggada, what Solomon Schechter so perceptively called "a complicated arrangement of theological checks and balances," it has a kind of cohesive inner structure. The masters of this form of expression, Kohler, Cohon, Moore, Schechter, and the others, have by their researches elucidated the great central tendencies, the basic drift inherent in the prodigious number of ideas in the aggada. But as to what is crucial to our quest, these core ideas themselves cannot constitute the criterion of acceptability for a Jewish idea of God.

The criterion which we seek cannot be intellectual, for in Judaism thought, as aggada, is essentially free. Our criterion must come rather from the primary realm, that of action or life. It must, because of the centrality of Torah, be a functional criterion, not an intellectual one. In Judaism an idea of God is judged by the way it operates in the life of the individual Jew, and, by appropriate additional standards, in the life of the Jewish religious community. Let us then look at this criterion in some detail.

For the individual Jew, first, his idea of God must be such as to make possible for him the life of Torah. It is not enough to think about Torah. The Torah must be done, continually. A fully adequate Jewish idea of God would move the Jew to fulfill the Torah by showing him the cosmic authority from which it stems and the deep significance of the acts it requires. The more completely an idea of God motivates the performance of Torah, the more acceptable to Judaism it may be said to be. The limits are reached in the opposite direction. When a Jew begins to think of God in such a way that it keeps him from fulfilling the commandments, then he may be said to have an idea which is not a permissible Jewish conception of God. That is to say, an idea of God which keeps a Jew from observing Rosh Hashono or from giving to charity or the like is not a Jewish idea of God.

We Reform Jews, out of courage born of conscience, have reformulated the traditional conception of Torah, but we have not dispensed with it. Because we believe Torah is dynamic, not static, is not to say that there is no Torah here and now. We still believe that "our lives should prove the strength of our own belief in the truths we proclaim." We would agree, I think, that an idea of God which kept us from social action, prayer, study and the rest of what we know Torah is for us, had moved to the border of Judaism or beyond.

If this part of our criterion seems vague, it is because we have kept our definition of Torah vague. We do not hesitate to chide our Conservative colleagues over their failure to show that Jewish law can do justice to the *aguno,* but having declared that there is continual revelation, what have we done to guide our people to what we believe has been and is being revealed to us here and now? Just what is it that Reform Judaism feels the Lord doth require of us specifically and concretely? When we have fulfilled our age-old rabbinic responsibility to make the Torah clear and understandable in our day, then, and only then, will we have more certain standards by which to judge our God-ideas.

Yet the Torah is not meant to be carried out in isolation. It is given to a community, to a people, to Israel. A Jewish idea of God must also then imbue the Jewish mind with an assurance of the value of the continuing existence of Israel, the Jewish people.

The secularists will deny that the existence of Israel has anything to do with God. It is a people like all other peoples, they will
assert, and has the same biological right to life and self-expression.
The logic of these theoreticians would speedily doom all Jews outside the State of Israel to sterility and decay, while it would seek
to make the Jewry of the state itself just like the non-Jew. But this
was not the inner logic of our people from its birth in the Exodus,
through the trials of the Diaspora, down to the continuing birth-
pangs of our own emancipation era. It was Torah, not genetics, that
transformed the Hebrews into Israel. It was Torah, not politics,
which kept Israel alive and unified, which fashioned its distinctive
character.

But why should Israel have the Torah and be a people of Torah?
Because Israel felt that between it and God there was a mutual
pledge, a bond, a Covenant, by virtue of which Israel became somehow His people, and He became their God. Israel exists as Israel
because of its relationship with God. Whatever the Jew understands
by God, it must make some kind of Covenant between that God
and Israel possible; it must make Israel's continuing dedication to
Him reasonably significant; it must explain Israel's suffering and
make it possible for the individual Jew to intertwine his destiny
with that of his people. To the extent it inspires him to be faithful
to the Covenant among the Congregation of Israel it is an acceptable Jewish idea of God—but let his idea of God be such that it
negates the value or significance of Israel as a continuing religious
community, and it moves outside the sphere of Jewish belief.

Yet one thing more his idea of God must do for the individual
Jew—it must make life with God possible for him, not just as a
member of Israel, but as an individual as well. Life with God—
the life of piety, when we see all our experiences in the perspective
of their Divine dimension; the life of faith, when despite what happens to our plans and hopes we know His rule has not been broken
and we are not deprived of His presence; the life of prayer, when
we turn and speak to Him out of the fullness of what we are and
long for, knowing we shall always find His strength and inspiration.

An idea of God which will not let us speak to Him, nor let Him be of help to us in meeting the varied experiences of life is not an idea for Jews. But insofar as it makes possible for us a rich and intimate relationship with God, the idea is welcome within Judaism.

The life of Torah within the congregation of Israel in the presence of the Lord, this is what a Jewish idea of God must make possible. This is the standard by which an individual Jew's idea of God is judged.

It is not hard to see that the God implied in this standard would have the characteristics the scholars have found generally attributed to God in the aggada. A God whose relationship with man could be by way of Torah must be a God who cares for man, whose standards are ethical and whose nature is holiness. A God who could call a people to His service must be a God who trusts in man's powers, who is the master of history because He is its author. A God in whom man may confidently trust must be as present as He is distant, as forgiving as He is just, as revealed to the eye of faith as He is hidden to the eye of reason. Yet though our criterion implies a content for the Jewish idea of God, we must always remember it does not legislate one. The content itself is at issue only as it affects the way the Jew lives Torah. As long as it makes this possible, its elaboration may be naive or philosophic, simple or extensive. This is his private privilege.

Yet while one does not need to be a theologian to be a believing, practicing Jew, there are many persons for whom ideas form an important part of their lives. For them systematic thought is basic to motivation, and they feel obliged to think out their faith clearly and logically or else abandon it. It is with them that Jewish theology is born. They send their ideas from the private into the public domain, and in the process must meet new criteria. These cannot any longer be naive and unreflective concepts and hope to endure the scrutiny of the community. They must now come forth with a maturity equal not just to the best that Israel still contains, but to that which it still remembers.

Israel, on its part, needs such persons and their theological activity for it is only through their ideas that its faith is made clear and manifest, subject to analysis and criticism, open to creativity and intellectual progress.

It is here that Judaism gives reason its full due. Judaism exalts reason as the corrective of unreflective faith, questioning its consistency and coherence. In the rabbinic period when the direct intervention of God through miracles to decide issues of halacha was sought, the rabbis insisted that miracles could not replace logic. In the same way, Maimonides used every philosophic means to expose the superstition of those Jews who insisted on the corporeality of God. We Reform Jews have gloried in the important role assigned to reason in our faith. Unfortunately we have often tried to make it the whole of Judaism. Reason is significant in Judaism as the corrective of faith, but Judaism makes history the arbiter of both.

Any public idea of God in Judaism must stand not only before the test of intellectual coherence, but before the test of Jewish history as well.

No basic idea comes to Israel now as a complete surprise. We have a long history of theological thinking behind us in which no significant aspect of life has been omitted. Israel will always want to know how this modern concept relates to what has been thought before. As aggada it need not be a duplicate or exact derivative of what has gone before, but it must somehow appear to be a meaningful continuation of the Jewish past or Israel will deny its Jewish relevance. This is particularly true of areas in which Judaism, challenged by rival systems of thought, filled the aggada with its vigorous affirmation of its own belief, as in the struggles against dualism and gnosticism.

But here a bridge is set up between the aggada and the halacha. Not infrequently this reaction was sufficiently strong to pass over from the aggada into the halacha and from a matter of thought, become a matter of law. Thus the aggada is more than a domain of formulation and criticism. It is in due course the intellectual breeding ground of the halacha. It is because aggada can on occasion be transmuted into halacha that even the individual Jew is limited in part in the freedom of his God idea, by the experience of the Jewish past built into his practice of Torah.

Yet the final arbiter is not past history with its literature and its law, but history yet to come. The generations yet to be, they will finally decided the adequacy of this idea for Israel. They will decide it by testing it in their lives. They will live it for a century or more wherever life may take them, no matter what it may bring. Then perhaps they will reject it as they did the idea of original sin, or accept it as they did that of life after death, or continue to struggle with it if they find it meaningful though incapable of resolution, as with the problem of human suffering and the justice of God.

History is the laboratory of Jewish theology.

This is why reason has never triumphed over life in our religion. This is why Judaism at its best has not been afraid of the freedom of the aggada or the discipline of the halacha. It has them yoked in a dynamic tension which keeps them both alive, and it relies on the experiences of history to lead them both closer to the truth.

An idea of God set before Israel must then meet the criterion of history past, present and future. It must demonstrate it is an authentic development of the Jewish past. It must be logical enough in contemporary terms and standards to make the present generation want to live by it, and its content must be such that this life is recognizably Israel's life of Torah before God. And it must be willing to stand before the judgment of the lives of the generations yet to be. Past, present and future; the aggadic freedom is given— but the responsibility is great.

Such, it seems to me, are the standards Judaism sets before an idea of God. To make certain that we understand them and their implications, let us briefly apply them to some of the great public formulations of our day. There are not many.

Despite the Pittsburgh Platform's emphasis that "Judaism presents the highest conception of the God-idea," none of the great early leaders of our movement ever expounded it with the systematic philosophic attention we would require. They devoted their research to the history of the God-idea in Israel, assuming that by showing this, they were clarifying its present difficulties and establishing its meaning to our generation as well. While their research is still of enormous value to us, to know the history of an idea is one thing, and to be convinced of its validity for our time is another. The contemporary theological task was but peripheral to their interests, hence we must turn elsewhere for our examples.

Mordecai Kaplan has devoted himself to the exposition of his idea of God with a thoroughness unique in Jewish history—and with similar individuality he has not hesitated to define God. God is the Power that makes for salvation. By power is meant those real processes of nature which operate so as to produce salvation. By salvation is meant the maximum fulfillment of man's capacities and abilities both in an individual and social sense.

Kaplan derives this idea from the life experience of most men as well as from the motifs he finds implicit in the Torah. The origin and need of Torah itself he derives not from God, but from Israel. Our people as a historic entity can fulfill themselves only through living out the values they have created in the past, as these continue to have meaning. But the group also requires the belief that carrying out its Torah has real value in our universe, and so an idea of God is created to supply this.

In defining Israel's traditional concepts in this way their inner relationship to one another has changed, and Kaplan, for the sake of relevance, does not lack the intellectual courage to invert the traditional structure—where God once chose Israel by giving it the Torah, here Israel creates the Torah and chooses for it a suitable idea of God. This is aggada of unusual creativity and ingenuity.

In the generation since its enunciation this idea has drawn many fine and sensitive individuals to Torah, both in study and practice, made them loyal to Israel and eager to take leadership in its affairs, and helped them live in piety with their God.

As a public idea it has been charged with being too great a departure from the Jewish past. It is true that Kaplan uses familiar

words in a new and highly individual way, but the desperate need
to translate Jewish theology into modern idiom inevitably requires
the development of a new or renovated Jewish religious vocabulary.
To attempt this is precisely the poetic freedom characteristic of
aggadic discourse. While he may have stretched aggadic freedom
to its limits, there can be little question that our generation must
say אלו דברי אלהים חיים .

What the future generations of Israel will have to say of his
loyalty to the past, or, which is more important, his meaning to
them, we cannot now know. Let me only indicate why this one Jew
finds this idea of God intellectually confusing and functionally
obstructive.

While Kaplan refers to God in the singular, "The Power" as
such, as a single entity, has no individual existence. It is merely a
singular usage. The unity of God means only the oneness my mind
imposes on the diverse natural forces which make for salvation.
But if God, insofar as He is objectively real, refers to what are but
fragmentary forces of the universe, whence did these come, and
what is their relation to those other forces which exist about us
and which do not make for salvation?

If God as a unity is the creation of my needs and my imagination,
how can I know that He is as real in the world as He is to my
mind? Where will I find the certainty, which alone will make me
act, that He is indeed dominant in the universe? Why should I do
His bidding against much of my will when I know that His will is
but another part of mine?

To me, it is a contradiction in terms, or at least an enormous
paradox, that a "power" or a "process" should make for moral
ends. The terms "power" and "process" are useful precisely because they are natural, that is, objective, impersonal, mechanical.
But moral ends are inevitably tied up with personality, with freedom, will and choice. If God, insofar as He is an objective reality,
is somehow personal, we can understand how He can make for a
salvation which is intimately personal. But what is real in the
universe in this idea of God are natural forces or processes which

are by definition impersonal. How then can we understand them as making for moral ends and stake our whole existence on the outcome?

I find I cannot pray to this God, particularly in the language of the tradition. Shall I address forces that cannot hear? Shall I speak to myself and my ideas about the universe and call this prayer? I cannot even say a simple blessing like the one for the Chanuko candles when my mind, without which I cannot pray, understands by the Hebrew words: ברוך אתה יי אלהינו מלך העולם אשר קדשנו במצותיו וצונו להדליק נר של חנוכה, "I acknowledge those processes in the universe which make for my highest fulfillment, which predominate in it, and to which our people has been devoted, thereby creating activities which help the individual and group achieve self-fulfillment, one of which ennobling activities is to kindle these Chanuko candles." To this I cannot say "Amen."

Martin Buber, on the other hand, has said far less about God, though far more about how God may be known.

Most of our knowing is of things. We inspect them, peruse them, gather our sense impressions and unify them into concepts about things. Most of the time we know persons in this way—their hair, their height, the birthmark on the cheek. But not always. On occasions we cannot predict or produce at will, we meet them not as objects, but as selves. At such times all that I am and all that you are, Buber says, stand over against one another in complete mutuality. No words need pass between us and yet there is real understanding. No data or concepts are communicated for what I now know is you, as you know me. It is a separate kind of knowing characterized by its immediacy, intimacy and privacy. It is the kind of knowing in which I participate as a whole or not at all. Hence it cannot be observed or accurately recorded, but only experienced.

We know God in this way, meeting Him even as we meet other persons, encountering Him in the midst of life. Though we may not often find Him, each time we stand in relation to a "Thou" we meet something of Him. Though they must speedily become an "It" for us, He never can. He is the Eternal Thou. I know Him as a person, or what I know is not God.

To know God in this way is not to indulge in mental delusion. This is the same means which tells me you, not just your body, is real.

Nor is this some kind of mystic union or absorption into the great ineffable One, Buber would insist. I do not disappear as a self when I truly know you—indeed it is just this experience of being addressed as a person by you which brings me to know that I am a self, that I as "I" really am.

Nor is the fact that one cannot put what he has experienced into literal terms or exact ideas to be taken as sign that this knowing was simply irrational. Persons cannot be reduced to strictly rational terms. We cannot define our mothers, or give the concept of our wives. More than reason is involved here for reason is but part of a person—but reason is involved as well. To leave my reason behind would keep me from being myself in any relation. Hence reason participates in the meeting, though not autonomously. And after the event, it is indispensable in helping me understand clearly what it was that happened and what I now must do.

Thus Buber rejects all definitions of God, even refusing to say that God is a person. We know only that we meet Him as we meet persons; that, *kivyachol,* He lets Himself be a person for the sake of the encounter.

As the knowing of other persons makes us wish to do things for them, so the encounter with God leaves us with a sense of commandment and commitment. This is a particularly liberal understanding of Torah, for God is the Eternal Thou, who may be met in every age.

Israel's covenant with God was the result of such meeting. In the history of man, only Israel had such an encounter with God as a people and not merely as a collection of individuals. Israel pledged itself as a people to proclaim in history the Sovereignty of God, by serving Him alone. From generation to generation Israel renews its continuing commitment to God and their covenant.

Yet though this makes the role of Israel in history unique,

Buber's primary religious emphasis is on the individual's personal relationship with God. To pray to this God is to reach out for the dialogue, or at least to speak to One we know is real and near. To have faith in Him is to know between the moments of encounter that He is not lost, that in another moment we may meet Him again as the Source of all that is.

Though spoken of in modern times, this God Buber points to is not so different from the God pictured in our tradition. Future generations may well reject this formulation, but never on the grounds that it created a barrier between them and their God. Its greatest virtue is its self-transcendence. It does not show us God, but only where He may be found. It is aggadic, not only in form and language, but in its very content as well. Then surely we must say to him, ‏ואלו דברי אלהים חיים.

Time will not permit us to apply our criterion to the rationalist God-idea propounded by Hermann Cohen, the enlightened humanist strivings of Eric Fromm, or the ideas of others. Our purpose, however, was only to make the standards of judgment clear. Now let each one refine the instrument that he may use it in his own search for the most adequate Jewish idea of God. To test further will lead us only to more or less acceptable Jewish ideas of God, not to "the" Jewish idea of God.

Can we be content with the emphasis upon form rather than content? Can we be satisfied religiously with only the search and not the solution? We can, if we will remember that the search cannot be ended now, for history is not yet ended. Jewish theology will have the solution to all of its problems one day, the day Elijah comes preceding the Messiah, and answering all our questions. On that day Israel's great aggadic search will cease, for on that day, and on that day alone, the Lord shall be One and His name shall be One.

And until then?

Until then, as best we can

‏לדור ודור נגיד גדלך ולנצח נצחים קדושתך נקדיש
‏ושבחך אלהינו מפינו לא ימוש לעולם ועד ברוך אתה יי האל הקדוש

Reform Theology and Naturalism

The tendency shown in essays like those of Lou Silberman and Eugene Borowitz to introduce a noble subjectivism into Reform Jewish theologizing did not sweep all before it. Other members of the Central Conference of American Rabbis, in varying tones, pleaded for a return to a more rationalistic approach, closer in spirit to the methods of the nineteenth- and early twentieth-century founders. The position of the religious naturalist was given vigorous and forthright statement in Roland B. Gittelsohn's plea to the Reform rabbis that there should be "no retreat from reason."

The heart of Gittelsohn's argument rests upon the assertion that, throughout its history, whenever the faith of Judaism has been confronted by newly-discovered facts that contradicted it, Judaism has followed the facts and developed and grown. At every stage in its evolution, Judaism has created a new synthesis of "the insights of theology, philosophy and science." In such a confrontation today, Gittelsohn affirms the immanence of God in nature will be stressed, since nature need no longer be thought as exclusively physical. "The religious naturalist neither denies God nor diminishes Him. He simply enlarges his concept of nature enough to include Him."

Other conclusions that follow from the position of the religious naturalist include the conception of God as the Creative Reality responsible for natural law, which operates in the moral and spiritual realms as well as in the physical world. Naturalistic religion excludes neither revelation nor mysticism, but requires that both be understood as manifestations of natural law. Naturalism can, he maintains, supply the basis of a faith that does not violate reason, and yet provides a firm anchorage in the universe, an enriching experience, and a role for man in the divine cosmic plan.

NO RETREAT FROM REASON!
Roland B. Gittlesohn
(1964)

It would be dishonest and disingenuous to deny at the outset what would in any event soon become apparent: that this is in substantial part a paper of protest and rebuttal. Last year's Conference program included four discussions on theology, three of which could properly be called position papers. These three were in remarkable concurrence in presenting a unified point of view, the essence of which I shall in a moment attempt to summarize. Before doing so, however, let me assert in utmost candor that two of them bespoke a spirit of intolerance—almost of contempt— toward divergent views, which ill suits the liberal spirit of Judaism in general, of Reform Judaism in particular.

One spoke of possible dissenters as "wilfully low-brow circles," and of the attempt to synthesize the insights of theology, philosophy and science as "shoddy adulteration òf the disciplines concerned." The other referred to the theological concerns of this Conference in the preceding decade as "the intellectual wasteland in which our organization has set up its tents." Subsequent to last year's convention, the nadir of decent respect for divergence was achieved by one among our members whose boldness in identifying himself fails to match the brashness of his opinions. In publishing his theological

186

views under the pseudonym of Ben Hamon, he scorned "the intellectual shallowness . . . the religious superficiality of the rationalism-humanism which passed for theology among Reform rabbis in the past decade" as well as "the out-of-date and ill-informed latter-day term-papers that passed for theology in the *CCAR Journal* and meetings."

I submit to you, gentlemen—these are not the terms in which we should be comparing our respective points of view on theology or any other topic. I respect those of my colleagues with whom I disagree. I respect them and their opinions, even those which I am unable to accept for myself. My own attitudes are offered here not as dogma to which all must subscribe, but as a viable alternative, a version of our faith which is no less authentically Jewish than that to which we listened a year ago.

Let us hope to avoid not only an impoliteness in our polemics but also the dilemma of the Boston bookseller who some years ago was importuned by a customer to procure two rare religious works, Dean Farrar's *Seekers After God* and Cardinal Manning's *Confidence in God*. Unable to locate either volume locally, the merchant contacted his agent in New York. The following week he was astounded to receive the following telegraphed reply: "No seekers after God in New York. Try Philadelphia. Manning's confidence in God all gone!" Whatever differences there may be—and indeed, should be—in our interpretations, we are, all of us here, seekers after God and will, I trust, retain our confidence in God.

The Plea for Tradition

Very well, then, what was the point of view so skillfully and eloquently expressed last year? First, that the tradition of Judaism must be our primary postulate, our starting point and rock of reference. It is not vulnerable to refinement at the hand of any other discipline or criterion. Whatever correctives are to be applied to it must come from within itself. Eugene Borowitz put it this way: "I want faith in Judaism to come before any other faith, and I want to make this priority of faith in Judaism my methodological starting point." Steven Schwarzschild agreed that Jewish tradition must be approached "without prejudgment, prior philosophical comment, or earlier determination of any kind as to what is to be found and what must eventually turn out to be true, essential, and viable."

The second emphasis projected last year was that the empirical evidence yielded by science and the logic produced by reason are not reliable avenues to the divine. They can be of only subsidiary value at best. Faith merits priority over both science and reason. When the fruits of science and reason concur with the assumptions of faith, we are to accept them. When they conflict, we must reject them in favor of faith.

Third and finally, it was implied in last year's papers—even if not quite explicitly asserted—that God conceived in natural rather than supernatural terms is a limited God, therefore is not and cannot be the God of Judaism.

Now before spelling out the terms of my dissent from these views, let me first acknowledge a large and significant area of agreement. For me, too, Judaism is the methodological and substantive beginning. I, too, am anxious to retain every bit of Jewish theology I possibly can. I, too, "want faith in Judaism to come before any other faith . . ." Having thus acknowledged my agreement, let me at once turn to my dissent.

The Nature of Judaism

Perhaps the place to begin is with this Judaism, which we are agreed is to be our starting point and—hopefully—our conclusion as well. There seems to be an assumption in much of our recent theological speculation that Judaism is a given, static whole—a self-contained system which was supernaturally revealed in the past and must be the norm by which all truth is to be measured in the future. I can understand such a doctrine emanating from our Orthodox colleagues; it makes very little sense to me coming from members of our own Conference.

Are we ready to renounce the view that Judaism is a process, a becoming, a constantly growing and evolving syndrome of beliefs and practices? That it always has been and within the human purview must continue to be a compound of attitudes, some of which are permanently valid while others are transitory, hence subject to replacement? That, indeed, even at a given moment of time there have always been aspects of Judaism which are mutually contradictory; and that our Tradition has been inclusive and flexible enough to contain them all? If this is still our position—and I shudder to think what would be left of our liberal faith if it ever ceased to be—then how can we reasonably insist that Judaism is a fixed point by which all other positions are to be judged?

Or how can we forget that science, philosophy, and reason—the discipline and methods and tools which some of us would now relegate to positions of only incidental importance—have already insinuated themselves into the warp and woof of that very Jewish Tradition which is so precious to all of us? Our Judaism is stronger, not weaker—more tenable, not more tentative—by virtue of the impact which science and reason in particular have made on it in the past. If we are to protect the alleged pristine purity of our Tradition against the inroads of influences from outside itself, where do we begin and where do we end? Would we not have to make such protection retroactive—first exorcising that which has already become an organic part of Judaism?

It seems to me, moreover, to be the most specious kind of reasoning to insist that when we undertake to refine the Tradition with the instruments of the laboratory and the mind, we thereby denigrate the Tradition, giving priority to the instruments. Perhaps an analogy will help here. If, as a chef, I aim at preparing a clear consommé, and if, in order to accomplish that, I make use of a strainer to remove the vegetable greens, does that mean I give priority to the strainer over the broth? Or am I not resorting to the strainer precisely and only because the most important thing is the end result? To me, science and reason provide the most useful strainers I know for the necessary removal of that which was essential to Judaism at an earlier stage of its development but which may now need to be removed or at least refined if our faith is to be kept viable for the future.

Faith and Fact

I do not propose to give any other faith precedence over Judaism. On matters of faith I accept Judaism with all my heart and mind, because I am convinced that it offers me the most persuasive, inspiring, all-encompassing approach to reality and truth of which I am aware. But that does not mean that everything Judaism has ever embraced was valid or that it cannot accept correction from outside itself. The conflict we must be prepared to confront is not between one faith and another, but between faith and fact.

Where the two are in harmony, there is no problem. Where they are inconsonant, we must make a clear choice. My choice in such instances is unhesitatingly for fact. This is the choice Judaism has always made, is it not? Our ancestors believed on faith that earth and all its precious cargo were created in six days—believed that firmly and unquestioningly until it was proved in fact to be impossible. Thenceforth they stopped believing it, or at least the liberal among them stopped believing it. It begs the issue to protest that faith in a six-day creative process is not part of the essential core-message of Judaism. The point of importance here is that at one time it was essential, that it ceased being so only when it became demonstrably false. This is precisely how Judaism has grown in the past and precisely how, in my judgment, we must permit and encourage it to grow in the future.

Let me return for a moment to my consommé and to the strainer or strainers used in its preparation. A few weeks ago at the American Academy of Arts and Sciences I participated in a seminar on *Sources of Authority in the Search for Truth by Religion and Science.* During our deliberations a Harvard Divinity School theologian held up a Bible and said: "If you were to ask me whether any statement on page 437 of this book is true, first I would answer *yes,* then I would open the book to see what is said on page 437." I find it impossible to believe that any member of this Conference would agree with him. If I am correct in this, then every one of us has in fact accepted certain criteria of truth, emanating at least in part from outside the Tradition of Judaism, by which to evaluate and in some measure to modify that Tradition. In doing so, we have enhanced, not demeaned the priority we give to Judaism.

A *caveat* is both desirable and necessary here. Reason and science can be wrong. Both have been mistaken in the past; both will unquestionably be mistaken in the future. But so has revelation by means other than the mind or the laboratory been mistaken. While it is true that faith has led man to some of his most accurate and inspiring intimations of reality, it has also caused some of his most egregious aberrations in both conduct and belief. The plain, often uncomfortable, yet simultaneously invigorating fact is that there is no absolute certainty available to mortal man. No certainty and no guarantees—by the devices neither of faith nor of empirical evidence nor of reason. We must therefore be prepared to utilize all three of them, with prior and exclusive monopoly granted to none, as checks and balances in our unending search for the one goal which alone is entitled to unqualified priority—truth! We have said as much in our prayerbook, have we not? "O Lord, open our eyes that we may see and welcome all truth, whether shining from the annals of ancient revelation or reaching us through the seers of our own time." It would be presumptuous in the extreme to assume that theologians are the only seers of our time.

Sometimes it will be science or reason which will correct Judaism. At other times it will be Judaism which will qualify science or reason. Each conflict in our quest must be faced when and as it presents itself—without immovable, *a priori* assumptions from any source—and resolved according to the very best combination of faith and knowledge we can muster at that moment. This does not mean that science and/or reason must grant an imprimatur in advance to that which we believe on faith. It does mean they retain the right of veto at those junctures where faith conflicts with fact.

In the words of our Conservative colleague, Ben Zion Bokser: "Faith must often take over where knowledge halts, but faith is not a substitute for knowledge."[1]

Science and reason have not impaired any of the really essential insights of Judaism. I do not believe it likely that they ever will. But I must admit at least the theoretical possibility that even that which is most precious to me in Judaism could conceivably at some point along the line be proven to be inaccurate or impossible. Should that unhappy day ever come, I would be untrue to the very intelligence which God gave me were I to cling to the demonstrably absurd.

Back to Judaism

We began with the nature of Judaism, then turned to a consideration of the proper relationship between faith and fact. Now let us go back again to Judaism in the hope of discovering just how far removed my understanding of that relationship is from the Tradition itself.

Surely there is no need to elaborate at length before this assemblage on the rationalism of Saadia, on his doctrine that the contents of divine revelation and of human reason respectively are identical. For Saadia the purpose of revelation was only to obtain instantaneously those truths which reason would in any event have disclosed eventually and to make those truths accessible even to men who lacked the necessary reasoning power.[2] Bachya wrote: "Study man, and when we arrive at an understanding of man, much of the mystery of the universe will be clear to us."[3] Maimonides implored his generation to study physics as well as metaphysics if they would truly know God.[4] When asked what he would say about the Torah account of Creation if science were one day to

---

[1] *Judaism: Profile of a Faith*, p. 24.
[2] Guttman: *Philosophies of Judaism*, p. 63.
[3] חובת הלבבות ; 2.5.
[4] *Guide for the Perplexed*, I:55.

prove that the universe was infinite in time and therefore could have had no beginning, he responded that in that event it would be necessary to understand the Torah differently![5] Not to repudiate science because of a prior commitment to faith, but to understand *the Torah* differently! He asserted also that every expression in the literature of Judaism which is inconsistent with reason must be interpreted as a figure of speech. Gersonides said that the student of science is not to be hampered by preconceived religious notions, and added: "The Torah is not a code that compels us to believe in falsehoods."

There is no need to overstate the case, to pretend that these scientifically oriented rationalists spoke for all Jews or for the whole of Judaism. But neither is there need or right so to misinterpret our past as to rule them out completely. The fact is that a religion of rationalism, a religion of tension between faith and reason in which neither is by definition always and in every confrontation superior to the other—such a religion has been and continues in our day to be an authentic alternative within the Jewish Tradition.

We are indebted to our distinguished colleague and teacher, Solomon Freehof, for the reminder that when David Nieto in the seventeenth century was accused of demeaning God by identifying Him with nature, he was defended by no less than the Ḥacham Zvi on the ground that God's punishment and rewards do indeed come to us על דרך הטבע, by means of nature![6]

No one has expressed the treasured uniqueness of Judaism in this respect more perceptively or persuasively than the late Milton Steinberg: "Recognizing the presence of something unintelligible in all intelligibility, Judaism does not close its eyes to the intelligible where it exists. . . . It has the daring to admit that while man can know little, very little, about God and himself, he can and does know something.

"From my point of view, religious truth is properly achieved not

---

[5] *Ibid*, II:25.
[6] *A Treasury of Responsa*, pp. 177 ff.

by reason alone—because reason alone is unavailing. Religious truth, however, is not discovered by faith alone—certainly not in our time . . . We are equipped with reason, we know the power of reason, and it is our most potent possession as human beings. Reason cannot be repudiated or denied. It cannot be stifled or put asunder. . . . The real dialectic of the religious life is not a plunge into faith or a descent into inwardness, leaving the intellect behind. The real movement of personality is a continuous alternation between faith and reason."[7]

A Naturalistic Understanding of God

What, then, is the position of the religious naturalist in Judaism? That God is to be found within nature, not acting upon it from outside itself. This involves, to be sure, a much deeper and broader understanding of nature than may formerly have been the case. Men once thought of nature as being only physical. Acting on that premise, it became necessary for the religious among them to assume the existence of a spiritual entity outside nature to account for that in human life which is manifestly extra-physical. Today it is possible to think of nature as encompassing in itself both the physical and the spiritual.

Perhaps the most wondrous accomplishment of science in our time is its increasing propensity to see existence as unified and whole. The old boundary lines have been breached. George Russell Harrison, Dean of the School of Science at M.I.T., writes: ". . . the more closely one examines the borderline between living and non-living matter, the more is one forced to conclude that there is no boundary that is definite, no place where a breath of life comes sharply to inform matter."[8] As it is with the organic and the inorganic, so it is with matter and energy, with unconsciousness and consciousness, with the physical and the spiritual. They are aspects

---

[7] *Anatomy of Faith*, p. 213 and pp. 230 f.
[8] *What Man May Be*, p. 65.

of each other. Where one preceded the other in time, the ultimate eventuality was potentially present at the inception.

What glorious overtones modern science has added to the watchword of our faith! As God is one, so the universe is one, life is one, man is one! That which is spiritual in man—his soul—has evolved out of his protozoal beginnings no less than his spine or hand or brain. And such evolutionary development was possible because there was Soul in the universe from its beginning. The religious naturalist neither denies God nor diminishes Him. He simply enlarges his concept of nature enough to include Him.

The religious naturalist believes in natural law which manifests itself both physically and spiritually. He believes that God is the Creative Reality responsible for that law. He sees God no less in the inevitable collapse of corrupt societies than in the fall of a dead weight in response to the force of gravity. He is only now beginning to perceive how even our noblest and loftiest ethical ideals are also rooted in reality. You will forgive the immodesty if I say that for me the most important chapter of *Man's Best Hope* is one which received very little attention from reviewers, that in which the earliest adumbrations of our moral values were traced to the very physical structures and functions of nature.

The aim of that chapter was to show that evolution has tended in five significant directions: from chaos to order, from competition to cooperation, from conformity to individualization, from mechanism to freedom, from the purely physical to the spiritual. If this insight is valid, it bespeaks an inner thrust in the evolutionary process, something more than just a combination of random mutations plus natural selection.

When we act in accord with that thrust, our behavior is ethical. When we ignore or defy it, we are unethical. The Ten Commandments are authentic not because they were supernaturally revealed to Moses, but because they correspond with the inherent law of the universe, which is both physical and spiritual. Ethical conduct is rewarded and unethical conduct punished, not because a supernatural God is jealous of His prerogatives but because in the long run only conduct which is consistent with the nature of the universe can succeed. This, to the religious naturalist, is the meaning of the rabbinic comment: "When Israel does His will He fights for them . . . and when Israel does not do His will He fights, as it were, against them."[9]

Here is one of the crucial and exciting junctures at which the creative partnership between faith and science holds so much hope for the future. It was the geologist, Kirtley Mather, who wrote: ". . . biologists and paleontologists have been increasingly impressed by the importance of the role played by mutual aid and co-operation in evolutionary development. . . . Especially with respect to man's lineage, evolution tends toward the development of ethical behavior in complete harmony with the high principles of the best religious traditions."[10]

From the theological side of the equation, Mordecai Kaplan has said almost the same thing: ". . . moral laws come from the same source as the laws of gravity, light, electricity . . . they reveal a side to nature which is not only materialistic, nor only subject to the law of physical cause and effect, but also purposive, spiritual or divine. Moral and spiritual values are as much a part of nature as are our pains and pleasures."[11] To my knowledge, Robert Gordis has not identified himself as a religious naturalist. Yet it would be difficult to state the naturalistic creed more succinctly than has he: ". . . the moral order is rooted in the universe and the natural order is the matrix of morality."[12]

Some Objections

There are some among us who will protest—in fact, who have already protested—that this seems to eliminate the transcendency of God, to make Him only immanent. Indeed it does. But let us

---

[9] *Sifre* 59b.
[10] H. Shapley (ed.): *Science Ponders Religion*, p. 39.
[11] *Jewish Frontier*, March, 1962, p. 27.
[12] *The Root and the Branch*, p. 164.

not too hastily reject the naturalistic interpretation of God for this reason. Our ancestors needed a transcendent view of God because they had so limited a view of the universe. A cozy, self-contained little universe—consisting of earth, sun, moon and a sprinkling of stars—is too small to encompass the divine.

But ours is an incomparably different kind of universe. Where our fathers knew of only one sun, we are aware of millions. Where they believed the light which emanated from the sun reached us almost immediately, we know that it takes eight billion years for light waves to travel from one end of the universe to the other, assuming that the universe has ends. We know that if our earth were reduced to the size of a period punctuating this sentence— which means to say, to a diameter measuring one-fiftieth of an inch —our sun would be nineteen and a half feet away; the nearest star would be removed by 1,005 miles; the farthest known galaxy would be 81,830,000,000 miles away! Is it really an affront to God to suggest that perhaps today heaven and the heaven of heavens can contain Him? God is transcendent to humanity, yes. He is transcendent to our galaxy, yes. But I am not so sure that it remains necessary to think of Him as transcendent to the entire universe of nature, as we know it today and will know it even better tomorrow.

Some scientists have suggested that perhaps the universe itself is infinite. If this should prove in time to be true, will it then be insisted by some among us that there are degrees of infinity—that an infinite God is more infinite than an infinite universe? Or will it not then be necessary, in the spirit of Maimonides, to understand the Torah differently?

Is there room for revelation in a naturalistic understanding of Judaism? Of course there is, though this too must eschew supernaturalism. Last year Steven Schwarzschild objected to our striving after divine truth "by applying entirely human tools to entirely human material." Aside from the fact that our material of inquiry and speculation, in my interpretation as in his, goes far beyond the entirely human, let me ask in the name of common sense and reality: what kind of tools can we possibly have that are not human? What tools other than human ones were used by the authors of Scripture and Talmud? When a man says "God said to me" or "God told me" or "God revealed Himself to me," he is expressing with a human tongue affirmations reached by a human heart or intuition or mind. And being human, he may be mistaken at least as often as he is correct.

At the moment when any human being claims to be the recipient of divine revelation, the content of his message can be tested only by the judgment of the most spiritually sensitive men of that generation on the degree to which this new affirmation squares with what they know about the nature of reality. Where there is no basis for such judgment in previous knowledge and insight, the only test is time.

In short, God reveals Himself to men through men. Such revelation can take place in the laboratory or the space capsule, at the artist's easel or the composer's desk, as often as on the mountain top or in the sanctuary. It can come through mystic speculation, through intuition, through reason, through the study of empirical data or through a combination of these. It can be—whatever its source—a promising truth or a painful delusion. Whenever a human being, in contact with the Ultimate Essence of Reality, rises to a level of creativity or comprehension never reached before in the pursuit of truth, beauty, or moral excellence, then and there the Divine has revealed itself to man again. Dr. William Etkin, biologist and anatomist, spoke a truth in his own field of competence which I would apply more generally: "When we learn to comprehend a new geometry, a new chemical concept of gene structures, a new statistical analysis of the evolutionary process, a new theory of instinct, or any other of the great theoretic triumphs of contemporary science, we recognize that somehow we are in tune with the Creator and His Creation."[13]

[13] *Judaism*, Spring 1963, pp. 179 ff.

More Questions

A wide variety of additional questions has been raised about religious naturalism, mostly by men and women of good will for whom this relatively new way of understanding faith represents, precisely because of its newness, a threat to the very existence of religion. Though I cannot hope to do even half-justice to them in the short time which remains, neither have I the right or the desire to evade them. One such persistent question has been: does a naturalistic view of Jewish theology rule out the mystic approach to God? Though I must confess in all honesty that my disposition and metabolism are such as to allow for only a minimum of mysticism in my own religious experience, I do not see why this has to be true of others.

Arrogance is surely not a component of religious naturalism. All the knowledge we have or are for a long time likely to have will not eliminate the mysterious and the unknown from the universe. We shall be fortunate at best just to nibble away successfully at the outer edge of our ignorance. Even as there are some among us who are more sensitive to the reality of God through reason or scientific investigation, so others may have a special capacity for the mystic experience. As yet we have no naturalistic explanation for such talent; we just don't know enough about it yet. Many a phenomenon which our ancestors could understand only as supernatural, we today perceive to be the expression of natural processes. Perhaps the same thing will be true one day of the mystic experience.

Naturalism does not necessarily mean that mysticism is either irrelevant or spurious. Neither does it mean, however, that every mystic intuition of God is authentic or the content of every alleged mystic revelation of His will accurate. Some day we may know enough to explain this kind of sensitivity, too, by natural means. Meanwhile, let us listen to the mystic respectfully, reverently, but always with an awareness that he could be wrong.

It has been said that the religious rationalist deals with a concept

of God, not with God Himself. Permit me to confess that I find
this line of argument extremely difficult to follow. All of us have
concepts of many things. When these concepts square with reality,
they are valid. When they are at variance with reality, they are
illusions. How can a rational human being, whose endowment includes a mind, not struggle for a concept of God? Whether he be
rationalist, mystic, naturalist, supernaturalist—whatever his disposition or inclination, so long as he is a thinking human being
he will have to deal with God and with his concept of God. At best
the concept will coincide with the reality. Even at worst, however,
both will exist.

Perhaps the crux of the matter here is a suspicion that the
rationalist worships a God of his own creation. If he does, he is no
longer a *religious* rationalist. The fact that I have a concept of God
does not mean that God is therefore a construct of my own mind.
I have a concept of gravity, of chemical reactions, of protons and
electrons and atoms. This does not mean that I have invented all
these; only that I have been able to conceptualize that which objectively exists in nature. Even so—though, of course, with far
less certainty or precision—my ability in part to project a concept
of God in no way diminishes His reality in the universe. When my
heart and my mind both lead me in the same direction, why should
I deliberately spurn the promptings of either? I am convinced that
God exists in the universe, that he pre-existed mortal man, and
will survive any possible demise of man. We do not differ here on
the existence of God as a reality. We differ only on the means best
calculated to help us understand God and follow His will.

It strikes me as odd that the rationalist and naturalist should be
accused, so to speak, of "inventing" God, when it is precisely he
who has striven most zealously to find tangible evidence of God
outside himself. If there is in fact a danger that men will harbor
concepts of God which are products of their own imaginations,
which do not correspond to objective reality, it seems to me that
such danger is greater by far among those who rely exclusively on

mystic intuition than among those who attempt to correlate the products of intuition, of reason, and of science into a unified and balanced whole.

Closely connected to the foregoing is the suspicion that the partnership between science and reason can lead only to a God of cold abstraction. This need not be true in religion, any more than it is in marriage. Both are—and forever will be—for the most part emotional experiences. There is no more danger of emotion being dethroned in religion than in the love relationship between husband and wife. There is danger in both, however, of emotion taking over so completely that reason and fact are evicted. When that happens, we are in trouble.

When a man and woman wed on the basis of a purely emotional and physical infatuation, without stopping to evaluate, logically and factually, whether their personalities and values are compatible, the probability of success in their marriage is minimized. There are, of course—and should be—non-rational factors in every marriage. If the union is to bring happiness to its partners, there should not be irrational factors. A proper admixture of reason and fact, far from diminishing or endangering the emotional commitment of marriage, enhances it.

Even so, religion is to a large and necessary degree an emotional commitment. Here too, however, there are times when the microscope and the mind must say "no" to the heart. The intelligent man can be emotionally committed only to that which is an aspect of truth. His commitment must be rational and realistic. If not, he flirts with illusion and runs the risk of becoming spiritually psychotic.

One more question begs for consideration before we bring the formal part of our evening to its close. Is there room in a naturalistic and rationalistic theology for prayer? Will it help toward an answer if I attest that here is one naturalistic, rationalistic, religious Jew who prays every day of his life? Who prays, moreover, out of deep conviction that his prayers can have major consequences.

Who believes that within the natural order of things there is something in the universe which is responsive to his prayers.

I resort to analogy once more, aware of the fact that all analogies are imperfect. The main difficulty with this one is that it makes God seem impossibly mechanical and cold. Yet perhaps it will nonetheless clarify what prayer can mean to a naturalist. At various locations in my home, as in yours, there are faucets. Each of these is the terminal point of a pipe, which leads back to a water main, which in turn is connected to a pumping station. When I in my thirst seek a drink of water, does the engineer in that pumping station respond to my need? Not in the sense that I petition him for water and he, on the basis of my past conduct or of his affection for me, decides to grant my request. Not even in the sense that he is directly aware at that moment of my thirst. But in a larger and more significant way, the engineer does respond to my need; in fact, he has responded to it even before I myself was aware of it. He has created a system which makes it possible for my need to be met provided that (a) I understand the nature of the system, and (b) I understand the nature of myself and my relationship to the system, and (c) I assume my share of responsibility to activate the system. Lacking these three requisites, I can stand before the faucet all day long, piteously begging for water, and my thirst will not be slaked.

With all its admitted imperfections, this comes close to expressing a naturalistic concept of prayer. It holds that God is a spiritual Force or Power—throughout the universe and in each of us—which makes it possible for us to rise above our ordinary understandings and accomplishments. God is there, whether we pray or not. God performs His necessary work in sustaining and operating the universe, whether we pray or not. Our words of worship in no way alter God or change His course of conduct. They can, however, alter us. They can make us aware of spiritual potential of which we are otherwise oblivious. And by helping us—if you will forgive the commercial terminology—by helping us to capitalize on that potential, they can change our lives immeasurably. In short, prayer too can be understood as a natural phenomenon, as a meaningful relationship between nature and the individual, as a natural bridge between Ultimate Reality and myself.

Conclusion

Let me return now at the end to the place where I began. I would not pretend that this kind of religious orientation will be adequate for all of us, nor would I make any effort to force it upon any who resist it. But I would insist, with all the vigor of which I am capable, that this is an authentic, legitimate, Jewish religious view which can bring enrichment and value into the lives of many. For me there is no need for the supernatural, no dichotomy between religion and science, no requirement that I divide my life into separate categories or compartments. I refuse to surrender the insights of science or to retreat from reason or to abandon my faith.

Thus far, thank God, that faith has been firm and enduring enough to sustain me in the most shattering crises of my life. But this has been true precisely because my faith has never been insulated from the rest of my experience as a human being, has never made a claim to a province or domain where it is inviolate.

Within nature itself, consistent with reason and the findings of science, my faith gives me anchorage in the universe, shows me where I belong in the cosmic scheme of things, convinces me that in my moments of disappointments and grief no less than in those of exultation and ecstasy, I can contribute to God's universal plan. Though my connotations may not be exactly the same, it enables me to say, with as much deep conviction and commitment as any man in this Conference: והוא אלי וחי גאלי וצור חבלי בעת צרה.

ON RITUAL AND WORSHIP

Rethinking Jewish Ceremonies

Jewish traditionalism, it has been noted often, is less an orthodoxy than an orthopraxy. The "doxy" of Judaism, its creed and
essentials of belief, has always been minimal, while its "praxy," its
precepts and essentials of practice, has constituted the heart of the
religion. Even Moses Mendelssohn, so often and so erroneously
considered the grandfather of Reform Judaism, argued that all
the fundamental beliefs of Judaism were available to all mankind
through the use of reason, and did not, therefore, constitute the
special revelation to the Jews, which was entirely of the ceremonial
law. To develop a firm attitude toward the traditional ceremonies
was, accordingly, one of the first orders of business for the nascent
Reform movement at the beginning of the twentieth century.

The central significance attached to the enterprise of rethinking
the attitude of Reform Judaism to traditional ceremonies is surely
indicated by the fact that Dr. Kaufmann Kohler spoke to this
question at the annual convention of the Central Conference of
American Rabbis in 1907. Kohler, one of the most learned of
the American rabbis, was the permanent successor of Isaac M. Wise
as president of the Hebrew Union College. He lacked some of the
organizational skills of Wise, but his scholarship was of a far higher
order and he had a sounder and profounder theological mind.

Kohler's essay on "The Origin and Function of Ceremonies in
Judaism," follows a method its author was to employ with distinction in his book on *Jewish Theology* (1918). A full-scale historical
resumé, based upon traditional sources but interpreted in the light
of what was then the best of recent academic scholarship, occupies
most of the text. It is noteworthy that Kohler's emphasis on Persian
influence in the transition from "Mosaic" to "Pharisaic" Judaism
would today be considered an overstatement whereas, in his own
time, it was thought a very sound line of interpretation. The final
section moves from historical exploration to theological exposition
and sets forth a consistent view of the place of reformulated ceremonial in Reform Judaism, resting his case on the dominant
(Spencerian) theory of progressive evolution.

THE ORIGINS AND FUNCTIONS OF CEREMONIES IN JUDAISM
Kaufmann Kohler
(1907)

The significance of ceremony in the religious life of the Jew forms one of the main points at issue between Orthodoxy and Reform. To Rabbinical Judaism the Sinaitic Law, written or oral, is immutable (compare with Maimonides' ninth article his Code H. Yesode ha-Torah ix), each of the 613 commandments being regarded as fundamental (David ben Zimra, Responsa i, 344). The distinction made between moral laws dictated by reason and ritual laws which rather baffle reason and common sense (Sifra Ahare Moth xiii; Yoma 67b) does not imply that the former are of greater importance, nor does the latter classification of the Mosaic laws into rational or social and divinely revealed ones (Saadia, Emunoth iii. 1-2, Ibn Ezra to Exod. xxi. 2 and Kuzari II/48; iii. 7, 11) place the former class higher than the latter. "The divine precepts, whether their purposes are intelligible to us or not, demand unreserved obedience" says Maimonides (Moreh iii. 26, with reference to Yoma 67b, Sanhedrin 21b, Bereshith Rabba 44, comp. Berakot 33b). Nay, more. While dividing the Mosaic laws into universally human or social and specifically Jewish or religious precepts, Maimonides expressly assigns to the latter a higher rank in view of their ulterior spiritual aims and purposes. (Moreh iii. 27 and Mishnah Commentary Peah. i. 1). Nor do Simeon Duran (Magen Aboth at the beginning) and Albo (Ikkarim iii. 25) take a different view when speaking of the ceremonial laws in contradistinction to the moral and social or juridical statutes, since for them also the former as the religious or divinely revealed ones claim a higher place as constituting the Jewish mode of worshiping God. Viewed in this light, Moses Mendelssohn was in perfect accord with tradition when, rationalist as he was, he declared the ceremonial laws to be the essential portion of the Mosaic legislation, whereas the ethical laws of the Pentateuch, being dictates of reason and commonsense, are the universal property of mankind. . . . This well-known view presented by Mendelssohn in his *Jerusalem,* says Zunz in his *Gutachten ueber die Beschneidung,* 1844, prevailed for some time, and Zunz himself as well as Reggio, whom he quotes, shares it in so far as both lay all stress upon the ceremonial law as being peculiarly Jewish and bound up with the memories and hopes of the Jewish people. It is, however, a great inconsistency on the one hand to denounce submission to an imposed creed in the name of liberty of conscience and on the other hand to demand blind submission to imposed forms of practice which no longer have any meaning for us. It is perfectly logical for him who believes in a supernatural revelation to maintain that, no matter whether they appeal to our understanding or not, the ritual laws demand obedience as "the decrees of the great Ruler of Life concerning which scrutiny is not permissible." On the part of such as deny the authenticity of the Pentateuch—and here Zunz and Graetz are on the same side as the adherents of the Kuenen-Wellhausen school—blind adherence to usages that have no justification in themselves is, as Dr. Geiger, in his *Wissenschaftliche Zeitschrift,* 1839, so well characterized it: "Hunde-Gehorsam," slavish practice without conviction, unworthy of thinking men. The whole Reform movement, indeed, as is so lucidly shown by Dr. David Philipson in his scholarly work: *The Reform Movement in Judaism* (see especially 6-13; 332 f.) hinges on the question whether Judaism is a system of ceremonial observance as binding upon the Jew as is the system of dogmatic belief upon the Christian, or whether Judaism is a system of religious and ethical truths, the ceremonies being only the means to higher ends, not ends in themselves.

It is not the object of this paper to follow up the warfare waged by the leaders of Reform against ceremonialism. It is fully recognized today that Holdheim far overshot the mark or, as Dr. Philipson aptly expressed it (p. 91 *eodem*) "he made the serious error of quite underestimating the place of ceremony in the religious life," when he declared the whole ceremonial law to be the outcome of Israel's national life and, therefore, of no validity for Judaism as a religion. Far more correct was the attitude of Einhorn and Samuel Hirsch at the very outset when, in opposing the vagaries of the Frankfort Reform Verein, they emphasized the need of ceremonies as symbolic expressions of the priest-mission assigned to the Jewish people (see *Allgemeine Zeitung des Judenthums,* 1844, p. 88 f.; 123 f.; 134 f. compare Aaron Chorin *Rabbinische Gutachten ueber die Vertraeglichkeit der freien Forschung,* 1842, p. 28). But in how far the ceremonies are to be regarded as essentially Jewish and therefore to be unalterably maintained, and in how far they present only adaptations from older non-Jewish life and accordingly permit of modifications, alterations, and radical changes is a question concerning which opinions still widely differ. In order to reach positive conclusions, a historical review of the ceremonies in their various stages of growth is required, and the principles underlying their development in the different phases of religious life must be investigated and established.

The Origin and Development of Jewish Ceremonies

When speaking of ceremony, we must dismiss the notion we moderns have that it is a mere conventional form without intrinsic value and meaning. To go back to the Latin, *caerimonia* signifies reverence and awe like the word *religio* with which it is frequently coupled, while the plural *caerimoniae* denotes religious rites, which in Rome had a magical rather than a symbolical character. That is to say, the Roman ceremonies were believed to have a coercive power over the deities. For the pagan mind in general the ceremonies constitute religion, which is viewed simply as a mode of worship void of ethical purposes. In the course of time, however, the original object of these ceremonies is forgotten, and they become empty forms until upon a higher stage they are invested with new meaning and made to convey higher thoughts. There is, consequently, a singular affinity noticeable between the ceremonies of various people and classes, since, as a rule, they have a common origin in primitive life. Ceremonies are never the creations of individuals; they grow and change like languages. They are, as Edward B. Tylor in his *Primitive Culture* and his *Researches into Early History of Mankind* calls them, "the gesture-language of theology." The people that crave for rain, for instance, would in solemn manner pour out water before the heavenly power to suggest what it should do for them, and henceforth water libation becomes part of the sacrificial ritual elsewhere. Each ceremony may thus be traced to its origin in primitive time. When the Occidental lifts his hat before a superior today, he is unaware of the far older form of showing submissive self-surrender by stripping oneself of all armament and equipments which, of course, included the headgear. This corresponds with the Oriental custom of taking off the shoes, as Tylor has shown. On the other hand, it is regarded as disrespectful in the East to receive, or be seen by, strangers bareheaded, and it stands to reason that it is considered by Orientals still more derogatory to the honor of God to stand bareheaded before Him in prayer or in sight of the sanctuary. (See Mishnah-Berakot ix, 5, where the words: *"Lo yakel et rosho beshaar ha Mizrah"* can only mean "One should not bare his head in sight of the Holy of Holies," exactly as the Roman priests officiated only with covered heads. Compare Hughes *Dictionary of Islam*, s. v. Head; and *Jewish Encyclopedia*, s. v. Bareheadedness). You observe at once the pivotal question at issue: Are we as Jews in Occidental life to be Orientals in the house of God, or are we Occidentals in every respect?

So are forms of greeting mere questions of politeness to us. But when the Mishnah in Berakot, just quoted, dwells at some length upon an ancient Pharisaic institution to the effect that, contrary

to the rule prohibiting the use of the sacred name of God for profane purposes, men should distinctly pronounce the holy Name
when meeting each other, as did men in Biblical times, we must
come to the conclusion that this usage had a more serious motive.
No doubt, the fear of malign influences such as that of the evil eye
and the various evil omina prompted these greetings (comp. Psalms
cxxix. 8; Ruth ii. 4) the real meaning of which gradually fell into
oblivion.

Robertson Smith in the introductory remarks to his *Religion of
the Semites* says: "Behind the positive religions which . . . trace
their origin to the teaching of great religious innovators who spoke
as the organs of a divine revelation, lies the body of religious usage
and belief which cannot be traced to the influence of individual
minds. No positive religion that has moved men has been able to
start with a *tabula rasa*. A new scheme of faith can find a hearing
only by appealing to religious instincts and susceptibilities that already exist in its audience, and it cannot reach these without taking
account of the traditional forms in which all religious feeling is embodied, and without speaking a language which men accustomed to
these old forms can understand. . . . The precepts of the Pentateuch
did not create a priesthood and a sacrificial service on an altogether independent basis, but only reshaped and remodelled, in
accordance with a more spiritual doctrine, institutions of an older
type which in many particulars were common to the Hebrews with
their heathen neighbors. Every one who reads the Old Testament
with attention is struck with the fact that the origin and *rationale*
of sacrifice are nowhere fully explained; that sacrifice is an essential
part of religion is taken for granted as something which is not a
doctrine peculiar to Israel but is universally admitted and acted on
without as well as *within* the limits of the chosen people." These
observations have their bearing upon the whole Mosaic Code with
its purity and dietary laws. Of course, the orthodox Jew of the
type of David Hoffman in Berlin for whom the Mosaic Code with
its traditional interpretation is divinely revealed and the sacrificial

and Levitical laws only temporarily suspended until their reinstatement by a divinely ordained power, can only assign mystical, or at best symbolical, reasons to all the ceremonies prescribed by the Torah. We, who behold in religion an ever-progressive force working through the inner consciousness of man, first collectively and afterwards individually, must ascertain the origin and purpose of each and every ceremony in order to find out whether by appealing to our minds and hearts it fulfills a religious function or whether it has become an empty shell with the kernel gone. In doing so, we must discriminate between the ancient ceremonies of Biblical times which are still influenced by primitive notions, the Rabbinical ceremonies which received their mould and character under the influence of conscious but authoritative forces, and modern ceremonies which still lack more or less the authority of historic powers and specific Jewish characteristics.

1. The Mosaic Ceremonial

The Mosaic ceremonial system, impressive as it is with the authority of divine legislation and with the grandeur of a great world-wide historic power, speaks to us, nevertheless, in a religious language not our own. We have to retranslate it into our own mode of thinking and feeling. It is based upon sacrifice against which our religious consciousness revolts. It rests upon notions of priestly holiness and purity which we reject. It confines the worship of the Most High to the priesthood and the sanctuary and fails to bring God nigh to the people and home to each heaven-aspiring soul. Mosaism, with its temple cult, is to us—and this is the essential difference between Reform and Orthodox Judaism—only the preparatory stage to Rabbinism with its Synagogical life and to Modern Judaism with its many-centered religious life. Those who call us Karaites or Mosaites know neither what Karaism was nor what Reform Judaism stands for. We believe in the ever-working laws of historic evolution and see in assimilation the force ever at work in Judaism's progress. The entire *sacrificial* cult of the Pentateuch is the result of a powerful assimilation. . . . The fundamental principle that all the sacrificial and priestly practices should, by various degrees of purity and sanctity, lead up to and culminate in the divine ideal of Holiness, in a Holy God whose sacredness is to eradiate from the sanctuary and impart itself to the people over the land, at once lent the system a peculiar and lofty character; but the system itself as a religious machinery was borrowed from its environments. The central idea which pervades the entire sacrificial service is the same that underlies the Semitic, if not primitive religion in general, and that is, that only *blood* as the vital power of man and beast *unites* and *reunites* men and God. Only blood possesses the power of *atonement* (see Lev. xvii. 11). Only blood seals a covenant and reconciles an angry deity. Only the signs of blood protect the houses, the men and the flocks against malign spirits. . . .

We must bear in mind that antiquity knew of no other form of worship than sacrifice. However bitterly the great prophets in Israel condemned the heathen mode of bribing deity by the blood and the oil poured upon the altar while Israel's God demanded righteous conduct, they could not abrogate the sacrificial cult. Nor did they intend doing so. They did not accord to prayer and song a higher place in the service. Even the great seer of the Exile, when giving utterance to the glorious vision of the time when the house of God would become a house of prayer for all the nations, still beholds the pillars of smoke rising from an altar decked with holocausts and other blood offerings. And so does the incense of sacrifice offered to God from the rising of the sun unto its setting betoken to the last of the Prophets the universality of religion. Only the Hasidean Psalms xl and l echo forth the clear note of dissent, ushering in a new era of religious life during the Exile, as we shall see. In the Mosaic system the priestly ritual, dominant in all sanctuaries, is the only legitimate one. Prayer, and confession of sin are admitted as occasional outpourings of the individual, yet only at the outer parts of the sanctuary. Even the inspiring song and music of Levitical choirs find no place, or mention, alongside of the primitive horn (Shofar) and trumpet.

In all likelihood this simplicity is intentional. It was to form a striking contrast to the seductive orgies of the Canaanite. This would also account for the strange lack of ceremonial prescribed for the different holy days. Only the old shepherd festival of spring, Pesah, transformed into a memorial feast of the Exodus, has a more elaborate ritual. The three agricultural festivals still appear in a rather shadowy form except insofar as the number of sacrifices is concerned. Obviously, the lawgiver is concerned only with the regulation of the official cult. As to the popular festivities, we only learn that the poor, the widow and the orphan, the stranger and the Levite were to participate in the joy of the harvest and vintage and to receive the corners of the field at the ingathering of the crops. From other sources, especially from comparative studies of religious practices, we learn that certain portions of the field were consecrated by the people to the gods of fertility amidst religious processions of a half-lascivious and half-austere character; and we at once comprehended the meaning and the high ethical purpose of the Mosaic law assigning the corners of the fields to the poor. Also in regard to the Sukkoth festival and the palm, myrtle and willow branches specified in connection therewith, there are several indications in Scriptural passages that the festivities of the water libation held in the Second Temple originated in ancient times; only the priestly legislation had no interest in a public ceremonial outside of the sanctuary.

In the Atonement Day ceremonial we have a peculiar combination of a primitive Semitic and a purely monotheistic rite of expiation. The scapegoat sent out to Azazel, the goat-like demon of the wilderness, as Ibn Ezra sagaciously explained the name, belongs to the same category as the bird sent out to carry the disease of the leper into the wilderness (Lev. xiv. 53) and has many analogies in ancient Semitic usages (see Robertson Smith, *Religion of the Semites,* p. 402 note, and comp. Orelli, *Religionsgeschichte,* p. 760; and art. "Azazel" in *J. E.*). This archaic rite meant for the inhabitants of Jerusalem originally the removal of physical evil for the new solar year (xi. 1 and comp. Lev. xxv. 9-10). The priesthood,

on the other hand, expatiated on the rites of expiation for the sanctuary, the effects of which only indirectly affected the people for
whom the day was made a fast day. The whole ritual has an exclusively hierarchical character which was changed only at the hands of
the Pharisees in their combat with Sadduceeism. These only gave
it the character of a grand symbolic act of purification and divine
atonement.

The only day which stands out as a genuine Jewish institution
without parallel in paganism is the *Sabbath*. It is emphatically declared to be the sign of the covenant between God and Israel (Exod.
xxxi. 16-17). Unlike the Babylonian Sabbath which figures as
a day of austere stand-still for the royal representative of the
nation, the Mosaic Sabbath is a day of rest and recreation for the
whole nation, including the slave, the stranger and the beast. It is
a testimonial to God as the Creator of the Universe as well as the
Liberator of man. Still a ceremonial of a positive kind is prescribed
only for the priest who, besides the additional sacrifice, places the
new shew-bread upon the golden table each Sabbath day while taking home the old (Lev. xxiv. 8-9).

As the great memorial day of the deliverance from Egypt, the
Passover feast also occupies a central position in the Mosaic number of holy days. Many ceremonies cluster around it to become
reminders of important religious and ethical laws, the unleavened
bread of primitive time (See Tylor's *Anthropology*, p. 267) having
been rendered symbolic of the hastened exodus of Israel from the
land of bondage.

There remain for discussion, then, those ceremonies particularly
enjoined as signs for the body. The most important of these is the
sign of the Abrahamitic covenant. Here, too, the pedagogical tendency of the Mosaic law becomes evident as soon as we compare the
rite prescribed in Genesis xvii. 11f. with the one in use among all
the other tribes in Arabia, Africa and Australia, and find traces of
the older primitive form also in ancient Biblical time. I refer to
the stone knives used by Zipporah and Joshua which, as shown by
Tylor (*Early History*, p. 217) point to a cruder age, and to the

connection of the rite with marriage in the story of Shechem (Gen. xxxiv). It is the consecration of manhood at the approach of puberty and before marriage that is intended by the practice in primitive life, and the painful ordeal becomes a test for the youth, as in similar savage customs. Obviously, in assigning the tenderest age of infancy as the time for the performance of the rite, when the pain, or consciousness of pain, is minimized, whereas Ishmael, the father of the Bedouin tribe, is circumcised at thirteen years of age, the act is elevated to the dignity of a solemn initiation of the child into the Abrahamitic household. The solemnization of the act by a public festivity, however, as is done by the Moslem who calls it "the feast of purification" (comp. Joshua v. 9 and the art. "Circumcision" in the *J. E.*) came into use only in post-Biblical time. Whether the Deuteronomist (Deut. x. 16; xxx. 6; comp. Jeremiah iv. 4 and ix. 24), in symbolizing the rite, accepts the view of the priestly Code or deprecates it, is a matter open to controversy. There is no doubt, however, that the idea of the Blood Covenant prevailed also in relation to this rite, as may be learned from its relation to the Passover feast (Exod. xii. 44-48). And this leads us to the "sign" on the hand and between the eyes mentioned in this connection in Exod. xiii. 9 and 16. Rabbinical tradition refers this to the Phylacteries introduced in post-Biblical time. But Samaritan practice to this very day helps to elucidate the passage. The blood of the Passover lamb slaughtered on Mount Gerizim is put on the arm and the forehead of the children, as has been witnessed by Petermann, *Reisen in Orient,* I, 137; Stanley, *Eastern Church,* I, 561 and others. Out of such custom which has talismanic character, the Tefillin or Phylacteries developed, just as the Mezuzzah grew out of the other talismanic practice of bedaubing the doors with blood in the shape of a hand and the like. The Deuteronomic law-giver (vi. 8-9; xi. 18-20) suggests by way of symbolism "the binding of the words of the Law on arm and forehead and the inscription of the same on the doorposts," a practice met with among Moslems today and among Christians of old; and this became a fixed ceremonial law, although the talismanic character of both the Tefillin and Mezuzzah is occasionally alluded to in the Targum and the Talmud (see my article in *Monatschrift,* 1893, p. 445 f.). The Zizith, too, which in Deut. xxii. 12, appear to be merely enjoined as a lesson of public decorum, are in the Holiness Code (Numbers xv. 37-41) prescribed as a ceremonial practice of a religious nature, though the talismanic character of the purple blue thread upon the fringes is generally assumed by modern commentators and seemingly confirmed by Talmudic utterances. (See Tosefta Berakot at the close and Midrash Tehillim to Psalm vi.)

A real consecration of the entire people of Israel as God's holy priest-nation is expressed in the dietary laws, the priestly origin and character of which cannot be doubted by the student of comparative religion. Whether R. Smith's theory of the totemic significance of the unclean, or tabooed, animals, be accepted or not, the fact that the laws of the Hindoos, of the Persians, the Babylonians and the Egyptians forbade the same classes of animals to the priesthood and that the Mosaic Code itself takes it for granted that the distinction between the clean and the unclean animals dates back to the oldest, the Noahidic, times (Gen. vii. 2), proves that the underlying principle is not a social or hygienic but a specifically religious one as stated (Lev. xi. 44; xx. 25 f.; Exod. xxii. 30; Deut. xiv. 21, comp. Ezek. xliv. 31 and Judges xiii. 4; and the art. "Dietary Laws" in *J. E.*). It is the great legislative attempt to carry into practical effect the prophetical idea expressed at the Sinaitic Revelation: "Ye shall be unto Me a kingdom of priests and a holy nation." It was, however, on a higher stage, in a more congenial religious atmosphere that this great plan could be brought nearer to its realization, and this was the period of Hasidean or Pharisaic and Rabbinical Judaism.

2. The Ceremonies of Pharisaic and Rabbinical Judaism

The difference in the religious life between pre-Exilic and post-Exilic Israel is so marked and so amazingly great that the rabbis could account for it only by the legend that the founders of the

Synagogue, "the Men of the Great Assembly," had seized the Yezer ha-Ra by magic and exterminated him from the earth so as to make an end to the idolatrous propensities of the people (Yoma 69b; Sanh. 64a). The fact is that with the rise of Persia a new spirit entered the world and brought about a great change especially among the Jewish exiles. The higher conception of deity which lent to life in general a moral purpose, though based on dualism, demanded of the Parsee a purer form of worship. The rising and setting sun, the waning and waxing moon, the various phenomena of nature presenting the combat of light with darkness, and of life with death, were greeted with invocations and prayers rather than with bloody sacrifice. The sensual worship of the lascivious Baby-lonian deities made way for an adoration of the god of light whose heavenly court appeared as the prototype of the court of the Persian King of Kings. Again it is the principle of assimilation which is at work in the shaping of the Jewish religion. Alongside of the temple with its sacrificial cult attended to by the Sadducean hier-archy, the Synagogue arises as a new centre of religious life created by "the humble" or "pious ones," the saints of the people, impreg-nated with the prophetic truths and echoing forth their lofty aspira-tions in the psalms and then in a liturgy shaped after Parsee models. An intense, religious enthusiasm which finds its resonance in the people's heart is awakened by these Hasidim, of the type of Daniel, and expresses itself in ceremonies of a far higher order than is the priestly ritual. The latest writer on the Jewish liturgy, Dr. Elbogen in the *Monatschrift,* is quite at a loss to explain the origin of the recital of the Shema with the preceding benediction praising the Creator for the light of day and Israel's Only One for the light of the Torah. Yet Rappaport and Schorr, as I indicated in my article above referred to, pointed out the way of tracing it to Parsee influ-ence. It was not *imitation,* as our anti-Reformers would say, but *assimilation* that prompted this and many other great improvements upon the old priestly cult. Yes, the Anshe Kneseth ha-Gedolah, the founders of the Synagogue, were reformers in adopting the Parsee ceremony of greeting the orb of light at its rise every morning and

every evening at its setting; but whereas the worshipers of
Ormuzd with their magic formula hailed the sun as deity, the Hasidim invoked God as the Creator of Light and Darkness, expressly
accentuating the monotheistic doctrine in contradiction to the dualism of Persia. I cannot here go further into detail. Let me merely
call your attention to the fact again overlooked by Dr. Elbogen,
that, in order to give expression in due form to "the acceptance of
the yoke of God's Kingship"—Kabbalath Ol Malkut Shamayim, as
is the term for the Shema recital—the ceremony of putting on the
Tefillin and of wrapping the head into the Zizith (ornamented shawl
or Tallith)—were made regular parts of the morning prayer, for
which also the Parsee custom offers an analogy. In fact, most of the
morning benedictions are adaptations from the Parsee ceremonial.
I will single out the one recited at the crowing of the cock, the
sacred messenger of the god of light. The solemn greeting of the
new moon is undoubtedly also an adaptation of a Parsee practice to
the Jewish faith. Nay, more. As has been shown convincingly in the
seventh and eighth volumes of Schorr's *He-Haluz,* the whole
Pharisaic principle of investing life with ceremonial observances
and corresponding benedictions is taken over from Parseeism.

The leading idea of the epoch ushered in by the Persian dominion
was the assertion of the right of the individual in the religious life
of the nation. And of this the Synagogue became the powerful exponent, revolutionizing religion by instituting in place of the sacrificial priestly pomp a simple service fervent with true devotion and
rich in instruction to appeal to all hearts. God stepped, as it were,
out of the darkness of the Holy of Holies, to which only the elect of
the priesthood had access once a year, into the full daylight of reason and knowledge to become in reality the God and Father of all.
The Torah in the hand of the scribe, the teacher and preacher was
to become the property of all; and around the ark containing it and
the desk from which it was read and expounded to the congregation,
sprang up ceremonies full of meaning and impressiveness. The
Torah lent to the Sabbath and holy days a significance they could
not have had in ancient Israel; it gave to each season of the circling

years a new charm and rhythm. Out of the heart of the religious community blossomed forth the ideas which transformed the three agricultural feasts and the feast of the temple expiation on the tenth of Tishri with its herald, the day of the Shofar blowing, into the great awakeners of religious thought and sentiment, and around each there began to cluster specific ceremonies of soul-stirring beauty and grandeur.

But here, too, we must not lose sight of the historic law of evolution. It is always the few elect who usher in new ideas. Such, in the epoch we are speaking of, were the Pharisean brotherhoods which, in reclaiming for their assemblies the sanctity of the priesthood guaranteed to Israel in the preamble of the Sinai Constitution, gave a new solemnity to their Sabbath and holy-day meals by the Kiddush and Habdalah ceremony, made the Passover night resonant with the joyous strains of the Haggadah, transformed the farmer's feast of the firstlings into a memorial day of Sinai and created the great autumnal season of religious revival for the Jew. The daily meals were also lifted out of the commonplace and invested with priestly holiness by these brotherhoods. Seated around a common table they began and finished with benedictions and other ceremonies in imitation of temple practice and that of other religious fraternities. In like manner, social events, such as weddings and funerals, or the initiation of youths into the study and practice of the Torah, the Bar Mizwah celebration, were made specific religious solemnities. (See art. "Bar Mitzwah"; "Benedictions," "Essenes" and "Pharisees" in the *J. E.*). Gradually a new factor of religious life enters and opens a new sphere for ceremonial observance. Woman as builder and guardian of the home is more and more recognized, and the rigor of the Mosaic purity laws as well as the austerity of the Hasidean saint gives way to the dictates of common sense. Henceforth, the Jewish home is emblazoned and enriched with new ceremonies which accord to woman a prominent place in religious life. The kindling of the Sabbath lamp and the baking of the Sabbath bread, and the like, invest domestic life with new means of sanctification. In the same measure as the Jew with-

draws from the political arena to form an exclusively religious community in the midst of the nations, his life from the cradle to the
grave becomes a round of ceremonial observances distinguishing it
from his surroundings. Yet as the real purpose and origin of all
these rites and ceremonies are forgotten, the impression obtains
that separation, distinction of the Jew from the non-Jew, is the sole
object, and non-Jewish habits, even of the most innocent kind, are
condemned as included in the Mosaic prohibition of Hukkat ha
Goy, which refers only to the lewd practices of the idolatrous
nations.

But such is the power of assimilation working unconsciously in
Judaism that almost every age and country added customs and
ceremonies of pagan origin and superstitious character. Such a one
is the rite of Kapparoth, the waving and slaughtering of a cock,
respectively hen, for males and females, on the eve of Yom Kippur,
a sort of vicarious sacrifice met with also among Mohammedans
and likewise the ransoming of the dangerously sick, "Pidyon ha
Nefesh" (see Curtiss, *Primitive Semitic Religion,* 28, 233). . . .

In thus reviewing the entire system of Jewish observances as they
have come down to us through the centuries, we find them to be
indispensable forms of expressing the religious feelings prompted
by the various events of life. As we advance in culture, enlightenment and refinement, these various ceremonies may appear to us
as empty shells void of meaning, but we must never forget that
nothing grows on the tree or in the soil without the shielding leaf
and husk. Abstract truth and ethical practice fail to satisfy the
religious craving of man. He needs ceremonies that impress him
with the nearness and the holiness of the divine. And while the
Mosaic Code placed the sanctuary and the priesthood into the foreground, often ignoring the life of the people, we see Pharisaic and
Rabbinic Judaism creating new ceremonies or transforming the old
so as to impress the Jew on all occasions with his priestly sanctity.
He rejoices in the multitude of observances which surround his
life like so many guardian angels. Unlike his Christian neighbor,

who from fear of the Satanic powers of evil surrenders to blind dogma, he sees his path of life lined with ceremonies which secure to him the divine favor.

The question for us today, however, is: Can these ceremonies of traditional Judaism still occupy the same place in our life? True, they have accomplished much for the Jew of the past in offering a wondrous discipline which drilled him to do soldier's duty in defending the ancestral inheritance and in shunning no sacrifice to uphold it against a world of bitterest enmity and intolerance. Still, they have long ceased to impress us with the idea of priestly holiness and have become "the work of men inculcated by rote." Rabbinical ceremonialism has become as unbearable to us as the sacrificial sacerdotalism was to the prophets of old. It is just as much fetishism for us to wear the Tallith and the Tefillin, though the Talmud consigns the head not adorned by Tefillin to Gehenna (Rosh Hashanah 17a), as to have the Aaronides still chant the Priestly Blessing in the synagogue. The dietary and purity laws, whether Mosaic or Rabbinical, are dead and buried for us, and no power in the world can resuscitate them. And this is the case with many other ceremonial institutions deemed fundamental by the law-observing Orthodox. We cannot shut our eyes to the fact that, as our entire *Weltanschauung* changes, so must our religious views necessarily change. In order to have a positive religious value and significance, ceremonies must either directly or symbolically express thoughts and feelings that appeal to us while elevating, hallowing and enriching our lives. Romanticism which only loves ancient practices because they are picturesque representations of a dead past is not religion, which must above all be the voice of a living truth, a living God.

3. The Ceremonies of Modern Judaism

Before discussing the need and the function of ceremonies in modern Judaism, we must be clear as to what we would call Modern, or as it is commonly termed, Reform Judaism. To most people, some of our Reform Rabbis included, Reform appears as something arbitrary, as a sort of eclecticism which singles out such of the laws and institutions of Judaism for observance as appeal to reason and common sense and suit our convenience, more or less, while disregarding or rejecting the rest. Moreover, they find it to be paradoxical to disclaim the authority of the written and oral Law and at the same time lay claim to loyalty to the Torah as divine revelation. It is unquestionably this very perplexity which has induced many Reformers to seek refuge in Nationalism. The fact is, Reform Judaism is just as much the necessary outcome of our historical age of research as was Rabbinism the result of blind belief in authority. The principle of evolution offers us the key so to reread the past as to enable us to see its continuity in the present, no matter what changes altered conditions have brought about. Looking beneath the surface of the letter and the form, we find the same laws that have been at work both in the Mosaic and in the Rabbinic period of Judaism to be still at work in the modern epoch; only with the essential difference that in the former stages the work was done by unconscious forces of the Jewish genius for which the religious terminology is revelation and inspiration, God working through the chosen organs and authorities, whereas in our age of reason the religious progress is achieved by us in response to the dictate of our own religious consciousness. The recognition of the fact that both Mosaism and Pharisaism have been borrowing and adopting forms of religious practice from their surroundings in the shaping and reshaping of the religious life of the Jewish people, entitles us to pursue the same method of the remodelling of the present Judaism in order to revitalize and quicken its forces. Of course, innovations and reforms at first militate against the justly venerated authority of the past, and it requires a successive period of tacit assent to legitimize them and render them integral parts of the whole system of religion. No doubt, to the prophet Elijah as well as to Hosea xii. 10 the Solomonic Temple with all its sacerdotal pomp appeared as an imitation and assimilation of Phoenician worship, while in the priestly Code this very sacerdotal cult is represented as divinely patterned. Exactly so will much that is now decried as Christianization by our short-sighted retrogressionists, viz.: our Reform temple with its organ and female singers, its family pews and all its Occidental characteristics, receive its full acknowledgment as Jewish by coming generations who will no longer know of the former dissent. Each age creates its own divine authorities, is the maxim voiced in the Rabbinical saying: "Jephtha the Judge in his age is the same as Samuel the prophet in his." Life is bound to assimilate forms as well as ideas and will sanction such assimilations as have strengthened and vitalized the religious idea.

Now there can be no question as to the need of ceremonial practices in our age. Doctrine alone, however lofty, does not stir the soul and bring it in touch with the great Fountainhead of Holiness and Love. Religious acts do. They awaken and deepen, as Lazarus says in his *Jewish Ethics,* the sense of duty in us. They develop our spiritual faculties because they appeal to our emotional nature. They impress us with the holiness of life much more than abstract truth can. They bring all the lessons of religion home to us in striking, persuasive and attractive form. The skeptic who remains cold when he hears arguments, however convincing, is moved to tears when some ceremonial act brings back to him long-forgotten memories roused by associations of thought and sentiment connected therewith. No religion can be without such memorial "signs"; least of all, Judaism with its wondrous history of achievement and of endurance. Ceremonies are the educators and monitors of the people; they speak to old and young, to sage and simpleminded alike the language of faith, of hope and of loyalty. When the Torah scroll in its time-honored garb of splendor is held forth before the assembled congregation, the words: "This is the Law" resound in our ear and heart with the glorious tale of the centuries of Jewish heroism and martyrdom, with the worldwide message of its perennial truth. So should each ceremony be another appeal to lofty aim and noble action. It comes to us as a means of sanctification of life and of consecration to duty. Every event or experience in life, each turning-point in nature and history should link mortal man to the throne of the everlasting King and invest the commonest incidents of daily existence with the dignity of divine service. This is the underlying idea of ceremonial law in Judaism, and our strenuous age of worldly ambition and greed can least afford to be without this educating influence.

The question is, however, in how far do our inherited religious practices fulfil this aim and object? There is no dispute among the most radical that the Sabbath and festival days are still most potent ceremonial institutions performing the function of educators for the Jewish community, the home and the individual. They revive the dormant soul of the Jew ever anew, giving rhythm, pathos and charm to the life of all and each. But, then, are the ceremonies connected with each real signs and testimonies symbolic of the truths they are to convey? Do they speak an intelligible language to the young for whom they are, according to Scripture, chiefly intended? Here is the place where Reform has to step in and render the old ceremonial attractive, suggestive and impressive for the new generation. We all realize today that the ceremonies for the home have not received sufficient attention. The importance of hallowing and enriching the Jewish home life has not been fully appreciated. Dr. Berkowitz has made a good beginning with his Sabbath Eve Kiddush. A corresponding Kiddush ceremony we shall soon have for each of the holy days, something similar to the Passover Haggadah. But there is no need of stereotyped traditional formulas. We ought to create fitting expressions of the ideas suggested by the day. It is unnecessary to say that the older generation ought to reintroduce the beautiful parental blessing at each family reunion or Sabbath and holy-day eve to render the whole more impressive. It must be placed to the credit of the Reformers that the ceremony of the kindling of the Hanukkah lights has been revived in homes where the Christmas tree threatened to captivate the young hearts and lessen their pride in their ancestral faith. Yet much more ought to be done by us to awaken the sentiment of loyalty and love in the young by the introduction of new appropriate forms where the old ones have lost their impressiveness.

At present we need means of strengthening the self-respect of the Jew, of arousing his Jewish consciousness. Especial emphasis must therefore be laid upon the ties that bind him to his past which alone will fill his soul with pride in his great heritage. In religion especially, where reverence plays so prominent a role, the ancient institutions must be treated with regard and awe, and as long as any religious observance proves helpful it should be retained. We can herein learn from nature never to cast off the old before the new is strong enough to weather the storms. If the wholesome effect made by ceremonies upon the parents is observed by the child, they will not fail to work by the mystery of sympathy upon the latter in the plastic time of youth. Upon the much neglected home of the Jew, then, the ceremonial system should be centered. Religion should stand as sponsor at the naming of the child and should solemnize each important event in the life of the household, thus rendering the home a true sanctuary, and father and mother its priest and priestess, as of yore. Even the recital of the Shema each morning and evening might be transformed into a solemn domestic service to leave its ennobling and hallowing impression upon each member of the household.

We must bear in mind that we are in a great transition period. The yoke-bearing age is behind us. Formerly the ceremonies were to be observed as divine command; for us today they must have an intrinsic value in order to be of binding force. Religion must first of all voice the innermost craving of the human soul as a child of God. Ceremonies which assign to woman an inferior rank according to Oriental notions are out of place with us. Reform Judaism recognizes woman as man's equal and sees in her deeper emotional nature, which is more responsive to the promptings of the spirit, the real inspiring influence for religious life in the household. Accordingly all the ceremonies in the domestic life today should be Occidental rather than Oriental in form and character.

In this connection let me speak of the Bar Mizwah ceremony to which many Reform Congregations still adhere. By so doing they ignore the plain fact that the calling up of the thirteen-year-old lad to read from the Torah is a mere survival of the calling up of all the members of the congregation to the Torah reading. The original significance, which was to indicate thereby the admission of the lad into the membership of the congregation, has been forgotten and consequently the usage today is meaningless. The moment the Oriental notion of the superiority of man over woman in religious life was abandoned, a form of consecration for the young of both sexes was instituted in its place and the beautiful rite of confirmation was adopted. As a befitting conclusion of many years of religious instruction it exerts a potent influence upon the young Jews and Jewesses, while it has lent new attractiveness to the Shabuoth festival which otherwise lacked a specific or characteristic ceremony in traditional Judaism. Of course, it ought to be simple, a sincere outpouring of the hearts of the young; we must not allow it to degenerate into an empty display. Another feature in our religious life of today should be mentioned here. In the same measure as our age refuses to blindly follow the past, realizing the wide difference between our mode of thought and that of our forbears, the need of giving fuller expression to the sentiment of piety has made itself felt. Greater stress than in former days is laid upon the recital of the Kaddish and similar tributes of affectionate regard for the dead. True, such emotional piety can never replace true, religious sentiment. Nevertheless there is a brighter side to it of which account must be taken. The crude belief in resurrection of the past which has been the source of fear and superstitious practices, has made way for the belief in the immortality of the soul. And this has lent new solemnity to that part of the service called Commemoration of the Dead—a liturgy which, while emphasizing in classic form the inherited trait of Jewish reverence and piety has invested the Yom Kippur with new luster for the Jew of today.

But above all the Jewish religion must be presented as a factor of life in humanity's work, in order to win all hearts today. It must accentuate the universal, the human and the practical side of life. It must train man for the service of mankind. By this standard alone is religion judged and estimated. Will Judaism be found inferior to other religions before the forum of humanity? This ethical concept of religion is the Jewish one ever since the great seers of Israel hurled their scathing denunciations against sacerdotalism, demanding individual rectitude and social righteousness. The world is coming ever nearer to the lofty prophetic view. Are our ceremonials vocal of this prophetic truth? I am far from believing that Reform's work is accomplished by a mere remodelling of the Sukkah and Lulab or the Shofar to harmonize them with our advanced aesthetical or artistic taste. Reform must become constructive and positive, aggressive and boldly self-confident, more imbued with the creative spirit of the religious genius of Judaism. It is by no means sufficient to have symbols bringing home to us the glorious memories of the past. We must have such as hold before us the great hopes, promises and ideals of the future together with practical lessons for the present. The feast of redemption must tell us of the redemption of an oppressed world and of the great universal plan of liberty allotting its burdens and its tasks to each and all. So must the Maccabean feast of lights proclaim the ultimate triumph of truth and justice over falsehood, intolerance and wrongdoing everywhere. So will each festival, the Day of the Giving of the Law with its lesson concerning Ruth and the Proselyte, and Sukkoth with its peace offerings for the seventy nations of the world, lead us out of the narrowness of the national self to the broad outlook of cosmopolitan humanity with its practical aims. And as the great New Year's and Atonement Days preached since well-nigh two-thousand years the religion of manhood and of broad humanity, may they not become also powerful instrumentalities of uniting and reconciling all classes and races of men by practical modes of readjusting the inadequacies of social life suggested by symbols taken from the Yom Kippur Haphthara (Isaiah lviii) and the Jubilee idea connected with the Yom Kippur (Lev. xxv)?

It has been said that in emphasizing our mission to preach pure ethical monotheism we are fast losing our Jewishness which is maintained only through separatistic Jewish observances of the Oriental type. It seems to me that they labor under a great delusion who earnestly believe that the Occidental Jew in general will ever fashion his social life differently from that of the people amongst whom he lives. And if he were to do so he would merely lessen the great opportunities offered him by this age of ours of rendering his religion "a light to the nations" and "a blessing to all families on earth." To me Judaism is an ever-progressive religion, and in a congenial atmosphere of freedom and moral greatness it is bound to expand, and its symbolic rites will be commensurate in suggestiveness and intrinsic value. No fear, then, that the Jew may lose his identity when he aspires to the highest aims of life, buoyed up with the consciousness of his mission for the world. In order to impress the Jew with the greatness of his task and his responsibility as mankind's priest we should have certain ceremonies. It is for this that new symbolic forms may have to be created expressive of the Jew's world-duty as God's chosen one, since the mere prohibition of intermarriage or the Abrahamitic sign of the covenant is not sufficiently indicative of Israel's priest-dignity. . . .

"Break the barrel but let not one drop of the precious wine flow out!" This is the way the Rabbis characterize a seemingly impossible task. Such is the problem Reform has to solve. Under the influence of time the old forms crumble and fall. We have to see to it that the fragrance, the spirit of the old be not lost as we pass on to the new.

Restoring the Sabbath

The Sabbath, the seventh day of rest, may very well be the oldest institution of Jewish life. Its origins lie so far back in antiquity that historians can only speculate about its beginnings. Yet under the conditions of modern life, especially in the nineteenth and early twentieth century, maintaining the Sabbath tradition was one of the most difficult tasks in all branches of Judaism. The Reform movement experimented with the transfer of Sabbath observance to Sunday; this experiment was successful only in a handful of congregations. Far more successful, and widely imitated in the Conservative movement, was the transformation of the Friday evening service into the major service of the week. But while this brought fairly large attendance, it has never been regarded as a complete answer to the problems of preserving the Sabbath as a day of sanctity.

W. Gunther Plaut, in 1965, reexamined the history of Sabbath observance in the Reform movement with particular attention to restoring the centrality of the Sabbath morning services. He attributed their weakness partly to the "weakness of worship feeling" in the modern age, but also to the "erosion" of the concept of Sabbath sanctity. His proposals for reinvigorating the Sabbath include taking advantage of the residual sense of obligation and *Halacha* to eliminate the feeling of total permissiveness in Reform Judaism. The *mitzva* of worship does not stand alone; yet without it, the other aspects of Sabbath sanctity cannot be restored.

THE SABBATH IN THE REFORM MOVEMENT
W. Gunther Plaut
(1965)

Only once in over fifty years did our Conference take time out to devote itself to the subject of the Sabbath. Such silence and self-restraint practiced by our usually vocal and often volatile body have surely not been accidental.

Was it because there were other, more pressing problems? Hardly. Our discussions have dealt with the esoteric as well as the ephemeral and the marginal.

Was it because the Sabbath was so secure in our midst that, like Motherhood, it needed only a friendly nod? Hardly that—and besides, we did discuss Motherhood from time to time.

Or was it because we deemed the Sabbath issue beyond our power of confrontation? The suspicion persists that this motivation was not altogether absent. We talked on matters *surrounding* the Sabbath: attendance at services; Bar and Bat Mitzvah; dances and committee meetings on the Sabbath; we discussed how to deal with school and social parties on Friday nights; we deplored that stores were open—and we returned to debating how to increase attendance at services. Attendance: there has been at least this one consistent concern. But the student of the record must note that even this concern touched primarily on issues other than the

Sabbath: we spoke about prayer and its place in modern life, about social habits, about attractive sermon topics, stimulating forums and pleasant Onge Shabbat.

But we avoided the Sabbath qua Sabbath. We did not ask questions of substance and, since 1937 when our colleague Israel Harburg dealt with the matter, the Sabbath question as such has not appeared on our agenda—not once.

What becomes then of the sentiment which Ahad Ha-am phrased so memorably: יותר משישראל שמרו את השבת, השבת שמרה אותם "More than Israel has guarded the Sabbath, the Sabbath has guarded Israel?"[1] For one thing, we emended the axiom officially. Our *Union Prayer Book* now proclaims as a self-evident truth: "Even as Israel has kept the Sabbath, so the Sabbath has kept Israel."[2] It is a *quid pro quo,* and has a sad, penitential ring. But the older saying was closer to reality. The Sabbath has done more for us than we for it. In fact, it continues to exercise this guarding function, more so than we realize.

It is to an exploration of this problem that our paper is devoted, i.e., to the mutual relevance of Sabbath and Reform Judaism. We will not undertake an exposition of the traditional Shabbat, its history, its halakhah, its customs, its special mythos and midrash, except where such investigation may help us arrive at a better understanding of our own present situation and potential. We will, in fine, attempt to present notes toward the definition of a liberal, realizable Sabbath for our time. . . .

III

In its earliest years Reform was concerned primarily with worship improvement and education. Alterations in the traditional modes of prayer had aroused the most violent opposition from the Orthodox, which in turn led the proponents of Reform to believe

---

[1] על פרשת דרכים, part III, ch. 30 (new ed., Jüdischer Verlag, Berlin, 1921. vol. 2, p. 78). Ahad Ha-am's formulation was based on earlier statements such as Abraham ibn Ezra's polemic poem in his אגרת השבת: למען, שמרתיך בכל ימים, שמרתני מאד מימי נעורים.

[2] *Union Prayer Book,* newly revised ed., vol. I, p. 31.

that, if only the prayers were shortened, beautified, and translated, Judaism could make its full adjustment to the new era. The liberalizers were of course mistaken. Forces were at work which did not and could not yield to mere worship reform. This applied especially to the Sabbath. Already at the Breslau meeting of the liberal rabbis, in 1846, the discussions concerning the Sabbath occupied a major portion of the conference.

There was no question about the need to do something. The Sabbath was being violated, people were working, stores were open and services were poorly attended. Valiantly the Reform rabbis tried to maintain the principle of Sabbath rest, but there were no quick remedies to be had. The new principle was: *Maintain the Sabbath according to tradition if you can; but if you are unable, do what you must.* "Where it is a question of one's total material welfare, where one's total possessions or the means of one's future existence are in question or threatened, a Jew (said Bernhard Wechsler) would not be transgressing a religious duty if he takes remedial measures and, where others cannot assist him, attends to them himself."[19] He quoted the rule of tradition: מוטב שיחלל שבת אחת ואל יחלל שבתות הרבה, "It is better to desecrate one Sabbath so that one should not be forced to desecrate many Sabbaths"[20]—but alas, no argument availed and many Sabbaths were desecrated. Nor could the ingenious *pilpul* of a Samuel Adler prevail—the same Adler who later came to New York as rabbi of Temple Emanu-El —who tried to rescue the Sabbath on the shaky distinction of כל מלאכה and כל מלאכת עבודה . His effort was as ineffective then as it would be today. It was, in fact, already then an anachronism.[21]

Whatever one may think of Samuel Holdheim and his many aberrations, he certainly had ideas. He resuscitated the dual emphases on מנוחה and קדושה, on Sabbath rest and sanctification. The

---

[19] W. Gunther Plaut, *The Rise of Reform Judaism* (WUPJ: New York, 1963), p. 188.

[20] I have not found the source of Wechsler's quotation. In *Mekhilta, Ki Tissa* the text reads: חלל שבת אחת כדי שתשמור שבתות הרבה See also *Yoma* 85b, and Mark 2:27–28.

[21] Plaut, p. 189 f.

former he declared to be of symbolic and therefore of time-bound importance; only the latter, the sanctification of the Sabbath, was to him a timeless command. Sabbath holiness was the goal, Sabbath rest a means to achieve the goal. The goal was unvarying, the means was not. If necessary, the latter could be altered or dispensed with altogether. How to hallow the Sabbath was therefore left to the individual Jew: "We must leave it to his conscience how far he will by himself try to reach the purpose of religious exaltation on the Sabbath, even though he does not celebrate it as a general day of rest, and we must avoid judging him in this respect."[22]

Not only did Holdheim thereby give sanction to complete הפקרות, which some naively called eclecticism, but he drew a further conclusion: the command, he said, merely asked that man sanctify himself *once a week*. To do it at *some* time was center of the demand; the actual day of sanctification was quite secondary in importance. If it no longer could be the seventh day, let it be the first day of the week. To Holdheim and his Berlin Reform Association it mattered not *when* but *that* the spiritualization of time took place. Holdheim became the father of the Sunday services which in the 120 years of their existence have had a checkered and often embattled career.

But for the time being, in Germany as in North America, the old Sabbath remained the problem child. In 1871 the Augsburg Synod proclaimed its brief Sabbath amendments to the Shulhan Arukh. They are worth repeating for on the whole they represent the position which now, a hundred years later, is taken by the Conservative movement:

If the distance from the residence to the house of worship, or age and delicate health prevent attendance at divine service, it is permissible to remove this obstacle by riding to the place of the communal worship on Sabbath and holidays, either on the railroad or in a vehicle.

[22] *Ibid.*, p. 192.

This permission extends also to the practice of charitable acts in such cases where delay would be dangerous.

The same permission holds where the purpose is educational or recreative.

An Israelite is permitted to play the organ in the house of worship on the Sabbath.[23]

While in mid-nineteenth century Germany the Reformers had already given up on such questions as work and business activities on the Sabbath, and restricted themselves to the more malleable halakhot which surrounded synagogue worship, their American colleagues still had high hopes for some more thoroughgoing observance. Bernard Felsenthal, first rabbi of Chicago Sinai Congregation, concerned himself less with prayer innovations and instead attempted to tackle the "widespread evil," as he called it,

> ... that Sabbath and holy days which ought to be dedicated to the life of the spirit are also used as business days and thereby these days miss their purpose altogether. To be sure, some people visit religious services for one hour during the morning, but then hurry into their stores and offices and attend to their business. ... Here in America ... it is possible for everyone to find his livelihood without making the Sabbath into a weekday. ... It is possible to observe the religious law, to withdraw the Sabbath from weekday work and to utilize it for the advancement and sanctification of the spirit, and therefore it must be observed. If one knows and recognizes this law then it must also be possible to bring a sacrifice to fulfil it. To know the law and yet to disregard it, if observance is possible, merely shows rottenness in his spiritual nature. For that act

---

[23] *Ibid.*, p. 195. Cf. *Proceedings of the Rabbinical Assembly of America,* vol. XIV (1950), pp. 112 ff.: "One should refrain from all such activities that are not made absolutely necessary by the unavoidable pressures of life and that are not in keeping with the Sabbath spirit, such as shopping, household work, sewing, strenuous physical exercise, etc." (Responsum by Morris Adler, Jacob Agus, Theodore Friedman.)

is immoral and unethical, which is in contrast to our convictions.[24]

That same year Isaac M. Wise and Max Lilienthal motivated several Cincinnati business men—Reform Jews all of them!—to sign a public resolution which stated that they would unite their influence

> to persuade all business men of our creed in this city, to observe the Sabbath by abstaining from all business transactions. RESOLVED, that we in signing our names . . . declare that we pledge our word to each other and to all, to keep our places of business closed during every Sabbath of ours; to transact no business ourselves, nor allow any of our clerks, bookkeepers, or any other person in our employment to transact business for us on that day on our premises.[25]

There was only one condition. This compact, forerunner of a modern חבורה, was to take effect only if 25 wholesale houses which were not presently observing the Sabbath would join themselves to the signatories. I have reason to believe that the full 25 were never found, which spelled the end of a noble venture. It also marks the one serious effort on record to find a new voluntary discipline for Sabbath observance within our movement. Perhaps it is decreed by fate that we should make another effort a century later in this very city.

For a hundred years now the question of how to return the Sabbath to a day of rest, a day on which no labor would be done, has been avoided by Reform leaders. Even our official platforms are vague on the subject and with obvious embarrassment look the

---

[24] *Kol Kore Bamidbar, Über jüdische Reform* (Chicago, 1859), p. 10. See Plaut, *The Growth of Reform Judaism* (WUPJ: New York, 1965), Ch. XIV, #5.
[25] Plaut, *loc. cit.* See also I. M. Wise, *Reminiscences* (Leo Wise: Cincinnati, 1901), p. 289.

other way. [26] Instead, we attempted to tackle the one aspect of the observance which seemed to lie within our rabbinic reach, and that was attendance at Sabbath worship. The pews were emptying or empty, and no rabbi could overlook this all too obvious fact. Two radical remedial measures were the consequence of this dilemma, and both were for some time the cause for bitter intramural controversy. I refer to the institution and ultimate rejection of statutory Sunday worship (which was a sort of negative rescue if you will), and the other was the innovation of holding Sabbath services on Friday night.

Isaac M. Wise claimed for himself the distinction of having first proposed the institution of Sabbath eve lectures and services at a fixed time. Whether this is so or not I do not know; in any case no one else came forward to dispute his claim. But while Wise may have thought of it first, he did not succeed in the beginning to persuade his own congregation to adopt his idea. Benai Yeshurun turned down its rabbi's request, but two other Reformers, Leopold Kleeberg of Louisville and Jacob Mayer of Cleveland introduced the innovation in their communities, apparently with good results. By 1869 the board of K. K. Benai Yeshurun relented and permitted Wise to establish a 7 p.m. Friday night service. For some years thereafter Wise advocated the experiment with great vigor, describing its advantages in detail, suggesting topics for discussion and even tackling the already pesky problem of members attending theater parties on Friday nights.

It has been objected [he wrote] that many prefer the theater and the opera to the Temple, and will go to those places of amusement in preference to the house of worship. Good-bye to you, ladies and gentlemen, we will see you again. Persons who have no higher than fictitious ideals, who prefer play to reality, self-deception to self-elevation, fiction to truth, amusement to instruction, the fleet shadow of the moment to the

[26] The German "Guide Lines" of 1912 were an exception. See below, note 33.

rock of eternity, persons who worship selfishness in lieu of the Eternal God, will go almost anywhere. But we do not suppose we are mistaken in the bulk of our coreligionists, if we maintain that the vast majority of them will visit the temple, when opportunity offers and go to hear artists some other evenings, if they wish to hear them. Managers of theaters and operas will have to put off their gala evenings from Friday to Saturday evening.[27]

In his enthusiasm Wise thought of every conceivable argument to bolster his new project. He reminded his readers that in ancient Jerusalem sacrifices were held at the twilight hour, that during the summer months the morning heat was oppressive, that Gentiles too could come at night, that working people could not come in the morning, that a fixed hour was advantageous, and finally he was led to exclaim that in any case "evening services are much more impressive and solemn than the day service."[28] He encouraged the use of Friday · nights for adult educational lectures[29] and was pleased to record a few years later that the Sabbath eve worship idea had been widely accepted and, in his congregation at least, was a success. Already in 1873 Wise, who was then engaged in battling against the rising tide of Sunday services, exhorted his readers with this apotheosis: "Take care of Friday evening, and it will take care of Judaism to be preserved intact."[30] We who have taken care of Friday night can, alas, no longer be as sanguine about the Jewish future as was Wise.

Not everyone was, incidentally, enamored of the great innovation. That the Orthodox would ridicule it was to be expected,[31] but they were not alone in opposing it. Wise claimed that only the

---

[27] *The Israelite,* Dec. 31, 1869, p. 8. His later recollection (*American Israelite,* Nov. 8, 1898) that Friday night worship was introduced in 1867, was erroneous. James G. Heller, *Isaac M. Wise* (UAHC: New York, 1965), p. 383 f., quoting a still later source, errs equally by placing the original date in 1865.

[28] *Ibid.,* Dec. 31, 1869, p. 8.

[29] *Ibid.,* March 31, 1871, p. 8. Wise credits Mayer with this idea.

[30] *Ibid.,* July 11, 1873.

[31] *Ibid.,* March 25, 1870.

supporters of the Sunday-Sabbath would have no part of the Friday night service, but he also failed to convince men like Joseph Silverman and Kaufmann Kohler who even in this century thought that our total effort should continue to be directed toward strengthening Sabbath morning worship.[32] In this respect these men remained closer to the European tradition. There, Friday night services neither achieved the prominence they had in America, nor did they replace the morning worship as the chief service. The Guide Lines of 1912—which were German liberalism's Pittsburgh, or rather Columbus, Platform—still stressed total Sabbath observance and counseled that "all workday labor must be avoided," where possible.[33] A rabbi in a small community suggested that all members of the community should voluntarily assume a "Sabbath watch" and promise to attend one particular Sabbath morning a month, thus assuring the congregation of a minyan.[34]

The historic fight over the Sunday-Sabbath which began in America during the 1860's and lasted for 50 years was, if one was to believe the proponents of the shift, an attempt to rescue Jewish worship and thereby Judaism itself. They claimed that, with daily prayers having disappeared and Saturday services ever more poorly attended, the only recourse was to attract Jews to a Sunday service. Holdheim was the father of this idea, but while in Europe he found almost no supporters, the Sunday service movement spread in the United States and Canada. While the opponents did not deny that one could get larger attendances on a Sunday morning, they believed that once Reform instituted Sunday as the chief worship day, two consequences would be inevitable: whatever little was left of Shabbat would be further attenuated, and there would be a real danger of Reform Judaism becoming a schismatic sect. Moritz

[32] CCAR *Yearbook*, vol. XII (1902), p. 145–46; vol. XV (1905), p. 62. Kohler called it "an innovation of dubious character," and Silverman warned that "by some peculiar reasoning people believe that if they attended synagogue for thirty minutes Friday evening, they are then keeping the Sabbath." See also Eugene Mihaly's critique of evening worship, *Journal* of the CCAR, April 1965, p. 19 f.

[33] Plaut, *The Growth of Reform Judaism*, Ch. XIV, #5.

[34] Siegfried Gelles, "Ein Vorschlag zur Sabbath-Heiligung," *Liberales Judentum*, vol. 6 (1914), Nos. 6–7, pp. 152 ff.

Loth, a founder and the first president of the UAHC, was so emphatic on this point that he advocated the adoption of

> a code of laws which are not to be invaded under the plausible
> phrase of reform; namely, . . . that the Sabbath shall be ob-
> served on Saturday and never be changed . . . ; that any Rabbi
> who, by his preaching or acts advises . . . [Jews] to observe
> our Sabbath on Sunday has forfeited the right to preach before
> a Jewish congregation, and any congregation employing such
> a Rabbi shall, for the time being, be deprived of the honor to
> be a member of the Union of Congregations.[35]

On the other side were equally sincere advocates of regular
Sunday services. Some, like Hyman G. Enelow, took up the old
Holdheim argument and argued for an official transfer of the day of
rest to the first day of the week. To this Conference he quoted the
midrashic rule: לא מן השבת מתירא אלא ממי שפקד על השבת, "Fear
not the Sabbath but Him who instituted it."[36] Others who advocated Sunday services did so from pragmatic rather than theological motives and, while they wanted to retain the seventh day as
Shabbat, nonetheless felt that it would be—as Kohler said at the
Pittsburgh Conference—"the most cruel and stubborn, the most
stupid and fanatical blindfoldness of mind and heart to deny these
hundreds of thousands of poor Jewish employees (who have to
work on Saturday) the privilege of divine service and religious
instruction on Sunday. . . . The responsibility of their religious and
moral shipwreck falls upon us."[37]

For some years the argument surged back and forth, occupying
this Conference for more than a decade. The discussions make instructive reading even today for much that was said then can be

---

[35] UAHC, *Proceedings of the 1st Council,* p. 1. Loth made his statement on
Oct. 10, 1872, in an address to K. K. Benai Yeshurun, of which he was president.
He gave the observance of Shabbat equal weight with that of שחיטה and מילה .
[36] *Sifra* on Lev. 19:30. Enelow's address is found in CCAR *Yearbook,* vol. XIII
(1903), pp. 168 ff.
[37] *The Jewish Reformer,* vol I (1885), No. 1, p. 5 and subsequent issues.

and is being said today, and while for us the issue is not the Sunday-Sabbath, it is the neglect of Jewish practice and it is the same Judaism with the survival of which we are occupied. Especially rewarding is a study of the long and carefully reasoned address by Jacob Voorsanger who reported as chairman of a special committee on the Sabbath question.[38]

In the end it was not our Conference but our congregations who saved us from the horns of the Sabbath dilemma. The Conference agreed to publish a special separate prayer service for Sunday worship and in fact proceeded to do so. But either the pamphlet, separated from the *Union Prayer Book,* appeared as a sectarian offshoot, or the Sunday movement had already passed its peak; in any case our only official attempt at a Sunday prayer book found no favor, the booklet saw no second edition and instead was given an unostentatious burial in our Reform cemetery of experiments. Sunday services continued, of course, but in ever diminishing numbers. This did not, alas, betoken a revival of the Shabbat: the seventh day remained as little observed as ever. The outcome of the Sunday controversy meant, however, two things: one, that Friday night had (literally speaking) carried the day; and two, that Shabbat remained for us, in principle at least, the weekly day of holiness. "However we may interpret the statement of its divine holiness," said Voorsanger, "that institution is indissolubly interwoven with other elements that make up our religious system."[39] In the sixty years which have passed since then, this Conference has not changed its position.

But while we have not changed we have also not done anything about it. I have already indicated that only once in this time span did we put the complete Sabbath question on our agenda. In 1936 Felix Levy, then President of the CCAR, recommended that the matter be studied,[40] and the following year, in Columbus, Israel Harburg delivered an address which occupied 25 pages of the

---

[38] CCAR *Yearbook,* vol. XII (1902), pp. 103 ff.
[39] *Ibid.*
[40] *Ibid.,* vol. XLVI (1936), p. 157.

Yearbook and which I recommended to you for most profitable reading.[41] He traced the reasons for the silence of our movement on the subject, and he made a number of cogent observations which are as relevant to day as they were then. "First and foremost," he said, "we should free ourselves and others of the prevailing notion that Sabbath observance means exclusively attendance at Temple service." He reminded us that more than worship practice or ceremonies was at stake, but our whole attitude toward mitzvah and halakhah. The Sabbath was the keystone of Jewish life, he reiterated, and what we did or did not do with it would spell out the success or failure of our movement.

Perhaps it was because in 1937 we were concentrating on our new Platform (which speaks politely of the need for the preservation of the Sabbath), or because Jewish existence in Europe was rushing toward its nadir, and because the cataclysmic events of the next decades left little room for truly fundamental reconsiderations of the type which Harburg had submitted, that we turned our collective face almost entirely away from שבת קדש

Almost, but not entirely. Two apparently disparate developments, each representing an important aspect of the Sabbath, occupied us in the intervening years.

One was the dramatic and unforeseen return of Sabbath morning services to our Reform movement. They came dressed in the garment of the Bar Mitzvah and presented us with new and different problems. We did not and do not always like what comes along with this reincarnation, but I say frankly that it may turn out to be the formerly unwelcome Bar Mitzvah who with his breaking voice, imperfect Hebrew and his man relatives and friends has given us an entirely new lease on Sabbath celebration. The least he will have done is to have given us a new basis for development, for he has reopened the doors to synagogue on Sabbath mornings and, even more important, has caused Jews to remember the Sabbath in ways they had not remembered it for some time. This situ-

41 Vol. XLVII (1937), pp. 324 ff.

ation has also pointed up sharply what we have known for some
time: that we no longer have the same people in our movement as
we had 60 years or even 30 years ago, and that we therefore have
opportunities of which our predecessors could hardly dream.

The second development is closely related to the first. It is the
great increase of interest in guiding principles for Reform Jews,
highlighted by the growth of our Responsa literature and, specifically, of responsa concerning the Sabbath. The *Yearbooks* of our
Conference bear less testimony to this than the writings of our
teacher Solomon Freehof.[42] Jews still—or is it, *again?*—want to
know whether certain procedures are allowed or forbidden, whether
one may or may not keep a gift shop open or whether committee
meetings are permissible on Friday night, and so forth. "Allowed,"
"forbidden": we have not heard these words for a long time in the
meetings of the CCAR. We have heard that some practices were
beneficial and others were not, that some were in the spirit of
Judaism and others were not, but we shied away from calling anything "forbidden" if we could possibly avoid it. Now the concept
is back in Reform Jewish life and it is back for the Sabbath also and
gives it a dimension it has not had for us in a hundred years. It is
none too early.

IV

These then are the history, the ideas, the problems which have
formed the Sabbath as we have it today. Before we can speak of
the future we must first properly ask: Just where are we now? How
much or how little is *really* observed in our movement? We all have
of course our impressions and I have the feeling that perhaps we
prefer not to know with too great precision what our people do
or do not do. But now that the matter is once more before us we

---

[42] Of older responsa see e.g., CCAR *Yearbook*, vol. XXXVII (1927), pp. 203 ff.
(Lauterbach); vol. XLII (1932), p. 82 f. (Lauterbach) vol. LXII (1952), pp.
129 ff. (Bettan); Freehof, *Reform Jewish Practice*, 2 vols. (1944, 1952); *Reform
Responsa* (1960); *Recent Reform Responsa* (1963); all published by HUC Press,
Cincinnati.

have to look at the contemporary observance of the Sabbath by Reform Jews as it is, and not as we think, hope or fear it is. . . .

V

The facts spell out a significant failure in the two areas of Sabbath worship, Sabbath rest and sanctification. The failures are related, but they are far from identical.

The weakness of Sabbath worship is of course only in part attributable to our neglect of Shabbat. It is our whole modern attitude toward prayer which is involved, our theology and deology, our ambivalent relation to our own sense of worth, our externalization of values—in short, the decline of worship is a fundamental aspect of our western civilization. We Jews who live at its periphery react more quickly to the swing of the wheel, we are less rooted and therefore, spiritually as well as physically, the most mobile element in our society. This is the subject which our new Joint Commission on Worship will tackle. It would be presumptuous for me to anticipate its research and recommendations, but some matters must be obvious to all of us.

One is, that the fond dream of the founders—that a beautiful understandable service will bring the Jew back into the synagogue —has not and will not become reality. It was based on the misconception that esthetics and philosophy, properly presented, are the bases on which worship is founded. It was as fallacious as the Talmudic prediction that it would always be rainy on Friday and sun-bright on Saturday[44] (although some rabbis still believe this is so and thus explain the poor Friday-night turnout). We will of course revise our prayer books from time to time, our Liturgy Committee will carefully scrutinize each word, rabbis will worry about their sermons and think of many ways to attract the multitudes, they will have baby namings and installations and boy scout nights and Onge Shabbat and forums, concerts and films and youth dances—in vain, none of these hallowed devices will by itself produce worshipfulness and devotion. The malaise lies deeper.

[44] *Ta'anit* 8b.

We will get farther perhaps if we ask not why we *fail* but why we *succeed* on any level. Why *do* some people come to Temple on Shabbat? In part because of various external stimuli, certainly; in part also because they do have an inner urge to satisfy their spiritual hunger, however ineffectively they manage to do this at our services. But there is one other reason, and it is often overlooked. *Many people come to Temple because it is Shabbat.* They may not be aware of it at all times; still, they often have a residual sense of obligation. Have you not heard the most recalcitrant absentees of your congregation say: "Yes, I know I ought to be there, but . . ." There is more of a sense of ought in our members than we realize. Search deeply enough and you will find that the knowledge of mitzvah is still present on some level.

I hold therefore that strengthening our feeling for worship is only one side of the coin. Strengthening the feeling for the Sabbath is the other. In fact, we would have little worship left were it not for Shabbat. It is not, in my opinion, our worship which has saved the Sabbath, but exactly the reverse: it is the Sabbath, weak and emaciated though it is, which has saved our worship. (The few surviving Sunday services, based on local traditions and attractive lectures, do not prove the contrary.) We have been entirely too one-sided in our approach. We have said: Make the service attractive and people will return to the Sabbath. Now I present the other side: *Make the Sabbath attractive* as a precondition for people returning to the services. This point of view has a direct bearing on the recommendations we will make.

Before I turn to them, however, I must address myself to a related matter, an additional reason which has determined our Sabbath failures. I refer to the erosion of the concept of mitzvah, of any sense of obligation vis-à-vis the Sabbath. We are reaping here the fruits of permissiveness which have grown, ripened and have inevitably turned rotten. Our own awareness of halakhah is so attenuated that it is hardly alive at all. Out of the 150 replies to the questionnaire there were not 10 who made a demand of Sabbath observance—and some of these added in a postscript: What

good would it do? They are right, of course. Short of some resolve
by this Conference to introduce a level of halakhah into Reform
Jewish life, short of some understanding that even Liberals must
submit to obligation, be it theological, historical, national or even
congregational in origin—short of this there will be only frustration
and further decay. Our "mental health" approach to the Sabbath
is a failure. The fact is that the rabbi's opinion of Sabbath observance as "desirable" and "good for the Jew" has not been convincing.
Why not recognize this? Of course, the rabbi cannot suddenly
make Sabbath demands when the foundation for making *any*
demand has not been laid.

Has the time not come, my colleagues, to make the turn which
has been overdue for a hundred years? It is my suggestion that this
Conference which will ineluctably proceed to a reconsideration of
Reform halakhah begin its labors in the field of Sabbath observance. For I hold that with all the erosion which has taken place,
there remains—along with the total residual power of the Sabbath
—a basic respect for halakhah which we have utilized all too rarely.
But when we do we are aware that there are possibilities.

Let me refer you to two familiar aspects of לא תעשה. None of
you officiate either at a funeral or at a wedding on the Sabbath. If
your members complain of inconvenience, you say No. You would
perhaps not mind making הבדלה while it is still light, but you will
wait with קידושין until it is dark. You yourself may smoke, ride,
shop, work or violate the Shulhan Arukh in a hundred ways, but
you will not assist in a celebration of nuptial holiness or say the
relevant blessings on Shabbat. Why? Because you don't want to
write a כתובה you don't use anyway? Because suddenly you don't
want to assist in a business transaction? Or because you don't want
to transgress the principle אין מערבין שמחה בשמחה?[45] Yet you say
No and firmly so and, *mirabile dictu,* your members respect your
stand. You say "It is Shabbat," and the people understand. They
may not know the word halakhah, but they respect it vaguely *if*

---

[45] *Mo'ed K.* 8b. In its traditional setting the principle refers of course to weddings during the festival week.

you will help them respect it. Perhaps there is something in the midrashic text which says: אין שבת בטלה מישראל, "The Sabbath will never disappear from Israel" (because God called it "a sign forever").[46]

Let me summarize this section by repeating its main propositions:

1. The weakness of Sabbath worship is only in part due to the weakness of worship feeling in our time. It is due also, and in greater measure than usually recognized, to the erosion of שבת קדש. Conversely, what feeds the existing observance of Sabbath worship is only partly the pervasive human need for prayer, or the various time-bound attractions provided by rabbi and synagogue, but in greater part than realized the residual strength of Sabbath feeling. It is the Sabbath which keeps communal worship alive as much as worship keeps the Sabbath alive.

2. The attenuation of Sabbath observance is related to the popular confusion of Reform Judaism with extreme permissiveness, which is in turn caused by our failure to formulate a Reform halakhah. What is true in general is true for the Sabbath. But here as elsewhere there does remain a rudimentary respect for halakhah which, when we bring it into play, has surprising depth. There still is Sabbath law, and perchance it can be of regenerative power.

VI

What then can we do? Does the future hold any promise for us? Two premises are necessary for any kind of program: we must have definite goals, and these goals must be realistic.

Premise one. We must resolve that the Shabbat problem is of lasting concern to us and not merely of passing interest. It is inconceivable to me that we should continue to disregard this question and thereby contribute by our silence to the neglect of the Sabbath. Shabbat must remain on our agenda. *I suggest that this Conference resolve to establish a permanent committee to define goals for the observance of Shabbat and to delineate ways and means to approach these goals.* After some years of thought and discussion we

---

[46] *Mekhilta, Ki Tissa.*

may be ready to suggest to the UAHC the establishment of a Joint Commission. It should be clear that the new Joint Commission on Worship is not the agency to deal with the Sabbath. The problem of worship exceeds the limits of the Sabbath, and vice versa.

Premise two. Our goals must be meaningful in the context of Reform Jewish life. We do not aim at the re-creation of the traditional Sabbath. Both the theological and the sociological foundations of such a return have disappeared. Our goals must reflect devotion and imagination of our own movement as well as the springs of tradition. We will have to choose those elements from the wealth of past Sabbath treasures which may serve as the ingredients for a new and viable structure. They will be drawn from those ideas which we presented earlier: there will be שמור and זכור, there will be emphases on homes as well as synagogue, the individual as well as the people; our Sabbath must be celebrating the specifically Jewish as well as the broadly universal; and, last but not least, it must make demands and speak of עשה and לא תעשה.

No one's single thought can anticipate the multitude of ideas which will come out of such cooperative study. We merely make a beginning today, and this paper will now proceed to indicate some areas for discussion and some possibilities for new approach patterns.

Friday Night

I venture to say that a test of free association with the words "Friday night" would produce one overwhelming response amongst rabbis and another amongst our members. When *you* hear "Friday night" you think, quite naturally, of services. The majority of our members, if they think in Jewish terms at all, will probably associate Friday night first and foremost with candles and Kiddush, or more likely, with family, and only then with services. I have tested it often enough to state this with confidence, and I draw an important conclusion from it.

Friday night as a family night, with or without some mitzvot performed, *is still a reality amongst many of our people.* What have we done to give this feeling a meaningful mode of expression? Next to nothing. Our *Union Prayer Book* allots two and a half pages in the Appendix to it and assumes *ab initio* that a Reform Jew will not or cannot recite more than one line of Kiddush.[47] The less said of our *Union Home Prayer Book* in this regard the better. We leave it to the National Federation of Temple Brotherhoods to devise a more effective home service, we leave it to the Joint Commission on Ceremonies to create a havdalah service in experimental pamphlet form, and we leave it to the ingenuity of our colleagues to mimeograph, multigraph or otherwise reproduce some substantive suggestions for other rich and prayerful home worship.

The reason for this studied underplay of Friday night observance at home is obvious: We do not want to compete with ourselves. We want our people to light candles, yes; we want them to say Kiddush and a prayer or two, yes; but not too long, not too much, because we also want them to get through with dinner and hurry to Temple. We even put our emaciated ברכת המזון some place else, lest they spend too much time at home.[48]

But suppose they do not want to come to Temple or cannot come for valid reasons? What do we do for them? Nothing, they are left to their own devices. So are the families of those congregations which do not have a late Friday night service. And what happens during the summer when we don't even want the people at Temple? Nothing.

I suggest that we create a full book for use on Friday nights at home. It should contain a service to be used by people who that evening—for whatever reason—will not come to Temple. It should have appeal for young and old; it should speak about the Sabbath and its opportunities; it should contain some guidance for Sabbath observance; and it should contain diverse readings. In other words, just as we have been able to produce a Haggadah for our

[47] The first edition of our prayer book had the full Kiddush for home use; the second edition abbreviated it to one line; the last edition restored the full Kiddush—but in mutilated form and to the synagogue service only.

[48] The first edition of the *Union Prayer Book* still had a respectable Hebrew ברכת המזון

movement, so can we produce a Sabbath Book and then set about with all our persuasive power and energy to get it accepted.

But, you will say, what happens to our service? Our service will not be affected, certainly not adversely. The 10 or 20% of our congregants who now put in an appearance will continue to come and, if need be, eat a little earlier. I am thinking of the 80 or 90% who rarely come and whose Sabbath needs we have almost completely disregarded. We have said, in effect, "Temple or nothing, take it or leave it." Yet, where is it written that one can truly observe the Sabbath only at Temple on Friday night? We owe our people an alternative for Temple attendance, especially since this alternative is steeped in Jewish tradition and sentiment.

Even if I would be convinced that a concerted Friday night home service program would be superlatively effective and eventually diminish my Friday night attendance to the vanishing point, even then would I gladly proceed with my efforts, in fact I would redouble them. I would then happily abandon my Friday night services and concentrate on Shabbat morning, as my traditionalist colleagues in Toronto have done. There, all Conservative and Orthodox synagogues have closed down their late services on Friday and instead record increased attendances on Sabbath morning. Their members come from the same neighborhoods as mine and belong to the same occupational and social strata. For them Shabbat morning is a possibility—but only because they no longer have Sabbath Eve services. Meanwhile, for most of us this will not be the immediate problem, although I think that we ought to consider the reascendency of Shabbat morning most seriously.

In any case, our Friday night worship hours are in no danger from a resuscitation of home observance. Of course, there will be no overnight success in this effort. But we must start. Our Brotherhoods are already on record as favoring this enterprise and surely we can enlist our Sisterhoods for a task which is so well fitted to their purposes. What is needed, and I repeat it once more, is for us to cease considering Judaism a Temple activity. None of *us* believes that it is, but by inadvertence and circumstance we have led our members to accept this as תורה למשה מסיני. In the area of social action we have already magnificently demonstrated our capacity for making Judaism effective beyond the synagogue; now let us do for Jewish observance what we have done for social action. Instead of making our congregants come to us, let us go to them into their homes with our treasures of Jewish life. And if we go to them they will also come to us.

"The matter is not too far from thee." We do not start from the zero point. Friday night still has reality for many whom we never see at Temple. Perhaps the subject is, like Torah, dependent on *our* mouth and *our* will כי קרוב אליך מאד בפיך ובלבבך לעשותו

SATURDAY

Again, I will not treat here of our worship services nor of the Bar Mitzvah conundrum, nor of related problems, such as the holding of religious school on Saturday mornings. I will address myself now to the question of Saturday as a part of Shabbat. We are here, alas, at the point of unawareness. If our people still remember Friday night on some level, they no longer grasp that Shabbat has 24 hours. They have, in the style though not the sense of the ancient rabbis who reduced all commandments to one, reduced the Sabbath to Friday night, if not worse. The morning, the afternoon, no longer carry even a reflection of holiness. They are part of merely another weekday. To this especially, my colleagues, we need to address ourselves.

I do not blame the people. I need look no farther than our own movement to find a שעיר לעזאזל. We have failed to give direction to our people. How can they know what is expected when we steadfastly refuse to tell them? Vague pronouncements about "observing the spirit of the Sabbath" are about as efficacious as talking about "being good" or observing "a spirit of charity." I am of course talking about a guide for Shabbat. Say No to such a guide and you will by your negation condone our present הפקרות.

We have talked long enough about the pros and cons of a Reform guide, its advantages and its dangers. I belong to those who strongly feel that without a clear presentation of some Reform halakhah we will have ultimately no Reform Judaism left. But I am also aware that this Conference is not ready to undertake a far-reaching project. I therefore suggest that you consider nothing else but *the creation of a Sabbath guide.* It will serve as a pilot project for the larger, more comprehensive guide. It will tell us much about the potential of discipline in our movement; its success or failure after a decade of application will instruct us about the expansion, alteration or abandonment of similar experiments.

The often heard objection that a guide will establish minimum norms which will therefore reduce Reform Judaism to a level of minimal practice is surely not applicable in the area of Sabbath observance. How much more minimal can we become?

It will be objected that it is impossible to create a guide which would not be motivated by a clear philosophy or theology and which would be able to define its position. True, this Conference could not at this time reach agreement on such motivation. Some of us would say: "This is how we understand God's will for us," for there can be no מצוות without God, and no God of Israel without מצוות ; others would speak of such practices as "sancta" in Kaplan's sense, as means for our people's survival; still others would plead for personal discipline; others would appeal to a historic sense of unity; and we certainly have scores of colleagues who would advocate such rules as good mental health measures. Some would support the rationale offered by Doppelt and Polish or the Reconstructionist *Guide*[49] and others would not. No matter—in order to create a Sabbath guide our Conference could present all of these motivations in a preface and leave the theology to the individual, or it could omit such a statement altogether. We only need to agree that in our opinion this ought, and this ought not, to be done.

We have ample precedent for this. The Joint Commission on

---

[49] *A Guide for Reform Jews* (Bloch: New York, 1944), pp. 12ff.; *A Guide to Jewish Ritual* (Reconstructionist Press: New York, 1962). This latter Guide deals in some detail with the Sabbath and does so from a liberal point of view.

Synagogue Activities in 1954 published a volume called *Responsa* in which no fewer than 229 official pronouncements made by the CCAR between 1890 and 1950 were collected.[50] Our last ten *Yearbooks* have carried further decisions. What are these responsa but guides to rabbis and congregants? And what of specific resolutions of the Conference on scores of matters, some of which are reprinted in our *Rabbi's Manual*? Are these not guides, are these not Reform halakhah? Few of these decisions make any reference to their theological foundation.

My colleagues, *the so-called absence of a Reform halakhah is fiction, not fact*. Without adding a single resolution, our present halakhah would occupy a good-sized volume. In denying ourselves the full effect of calling it by its proper name we also rob ourselves of the most distinctive element of Jewish existence. Mitzvah is an indigenous part of Judaism; there can be no Judaism without mitzvah. And there can be no Shabbat observance without definable and therefore observable מצוות עשה and מצוות לא תעשה.

To return to a concept of Reform halakhah is not to falsify Reform Judaism but to return to its fountain heads. All the early Conferences and synods were concerned with halakhah. It was never a question of *whether* to have rules, but *what* rules to have. I cannot claim to be the first to advocate a Sabbath guide. Our best tradition advocates it. . . .

Our people are looking for a catalogue of מצוות, and it is our duty to supply it. But it must not be just another circumcised Shulhan Arukh. It must bear the best imaginative qualities of our movement.

We recognize that "rest" in a society which is already surfeited with useless leisure cannot have the meaning which tradition gave to it. . . .

The fragmented metropolis with its proliferating suburbs renders family gatherings more and more difficult and hence infrequent. Sabbath—either Friday night or the day—might be our new family

---

[50] Ed. by Jacob G. Schwarz (UAHC: New York, 1954), mimeographed.

times, as in fact they already are for many. We have something to
build upon and can fill a need which formerly did not exist.

We have, for reasons which must be evident to all, treated
Saturday afternoons as "empty" time. We have here, however, a
splendid opportunity for study, both formal and informal. If it is
true, as the Talmud says, לא נתנו שבתות וימים טובים לישראל אלא
ללמוד בהם תורה, that Sabbaths and festivals were given us only for
the sake of study,[56] then why be satisfied merely to recommend this,
like good deeds and love, to our congregants? Why not provide
opportunities in the synagogue or at study groups in homes? (This
would also help us to revitalize the practice of havdalah, which is
lovely and evocative of much sentiment and which, incidentally,
should be regularly made at Saturday night Bar Mitzvah and wedding parties. It would serve, if nothing else, the purpose of זכור;
even an ex post זכירה is better than none.)

Study and Shabbat—have we not captured this union for many
of our children? They have religious school classes in the morning.
Why not try adult classes as well?

The possibilities are many once we start to think about them
seriously. We might well revive the old rule that activities למען הצבור
are not only permitted but desirable. לא תבערו אש בכל משבתיכם.
said the Bible, but it only said "in *your* habitations," not in God's
habitation. One could and would light fires in the Temple on
Shabbat, for it was for the sake both of God and the people.[57] We
might well focus on the Sabbath as the day on which one serves
the community.[58]

In the very multiplicity of opportunities will lie the attraction of
our new Sabbath guide. It can no longer be an either-or, do-and-
don't; and we must be specific, not vague. We will point out the
mitzvah of having a guest and the mitzvah of abstaining from

---

[57] See commentaries on Ex. 35:3.
[56] *Jer. Shabbat* 15:3.
[58] On the Sabbath as a unifying element for the people and the creation of
loyalty to the community, see Mac. I:30; *Sanh.* 65b; Gen. R. 10; *Pes.* R. 23. See
also M. M. Kaplan, *The Meaning of God in Modern Jewish Religion* (Behrman:
New York, 1937), pp. 34 and 57 ff.

chores and shopping, and even from mourning. And we will, last but not least, speak about the mitzvah of worship.

I have understressed this latter mitzvah up to this point, simply because we have so often tended to identify Shabbat and services. This does not however obviate the obvious. Prayer *is* a mitzvah, public prayer is a mitzvah, and קל וחומר, so is public prayer on the Sabbath. Here too we have ways we have not trod and avenues we have not explored. When we have the authority to demand this mitzvah from people we usually do not hesitate to use it. We apply it to confirmands, not so much מיראת שמים but מיראת רב. Our logic is impeccable: we do not force our children, but if they want to be confirmed they have to comply. We mean well and express it poorly. We mean mitzvah and don't use the word. Why not say what we mean: that a young person who cannot fulfil the mitzvah of worship on a minimal basis cannot be admitted to the privilege of confirmation?

And why make the mitzvah applicable to defenseless confirmands only? Why not tackle your not so defenseless confirmation parents or your boards of trustees? The Union is already on record with a resolution demanding spiritual excellence from the latter. Our boards will be readier than we give them credit for. Why not tell a nominee that standing for election implies the fulfillment of certain mitzvot? It does say לעשות את השבת [59] and R. Ephraim Shlomo ben Aaron comments: כי לא יזכר טוביו כי אם בקום ועשה, one does not begin to know the rewards of Shabbat until one seriously does something about it.[60]

As we multiply the opportunities so will the means for their use be increased. Some of us have experimented with the old-new concept of חבורה and found it appealing to both adults and young people. The saying from Proverbs, ראשית חכמה קנה חכמה, applies here too: to make a beginning we have to begin. The revitalization of the Sabbath for Reform Jews starts with us; *we* have to take it seriously.

---

[59] Ex. 31:16.
[60] עוללות אפרים, #266.

Our battling predecessors were fond of quoting the Talmudic Sabbath dictum: היא מסורה בידכם ולא אתם מסורים בידה "Not you are given into the hands of the Sabbath, but the Sabbath is given into your hands."[61] We have stressed the second half of R. Jonathan's saying, now let us stress the first: *the Sabbath is given into our hands.* The time will never be more propitious. Earlier Reformers challenged us to similar tasks, but neither we nor our people were ready to listen. I think that today we are more inclined to listen *and to do.*

I close with an exhortation from one of the founders of Reform. Leopold Stein, in his guide תורת חיים , wrote almost a hundred years ago:[62]

Therefore, all of you dearest comrades in faith, brothers and sisters of the house of Israel, who are so fortunate still to possess this holy day—maintain it, save it; and thereby you will assist, more than by anything else, to erect anew and to strengthen anew religious life and law in Israel.

[61] *Yoma* 85b. In slightly different form, *Mekhilta, Ki Tissa.*
[62] Stein, *Die Schrift des Lebens* (Strasbourg, 1872–77), vol. II, pp. 463 ff., #17–19. (See Plaut, *The Rise of Reform Judaism,* p. 262.)

Reforming the Prayer Book

From the earliest days of the modern reform movement in Judaism, the prayer book was an object of concern and study to the reformers. Over the centuries its ancient content had been enlarged by the addition of much devotional material that had achieved, for the traditionalist, much of the sanctity of the original collection of testimony, praise and petition. To the mind of the reformers, however, the service had become intolerably long, the Hebrew language of the prayers a barrier to the worshiper's understanding, and the theological content a scandal to the modern mind. Accordingly many nineteenth-century rabbis produced their own personal, occasionally idiosyncratic modernized prayer books, for use in the congregation they served and in those other congregations that were willing to adopt them. Since a high percentage of the most prominent rabbinical revisers of the prayer book had German backgrounds and a limited, inadequate command of English, the early American versions deserve better marks for their earnestness than for their achievement.

One of the first tasks of the Central Conference of American Rabbis was to work together on the production of a version of the prayer book which liberal American Jews could agree to use. The Union Prayer Book, in its first edition, solved the immediate problem by replacing a number of inadequate texts in use with one

255

inadequate text in common use. It did not satisfy anyone completely. It was the product of a committee and necessarily represented the compromises within the committee. From the day of its appearance, the Union Prayer Book has been constantly undergoing intensive study by the Reform rabbis, and each new edition has embodied some of the results of this critical reconsideration.

Moreover, as English rather than German was the mother tongue of the American rabbis, an increasing sensitivity to the nuances of English style is evident in the successive editions of the Union Prayer Book. Each language has its own genius and translation often violates the integrity of the thought in seeking to retain the integrity of the expression. Some beautiful devotional phrases in Hebrew are most impressive when translated into German, but ring with a hollow pomposity in a too-literal English version. Again, modern English, for all its flexibility, is not a particularly good language of prayer. There is a tendency in writing prayers to slip back into the language of the King James version of the Bible, a language that was archaic even in the seventeenth century and is even more so today.

Despite these intellectual and literary perils, the production of prayer books must continue, for the prayer book is, for most people, the chief point of contact with their religion. The two papers reproduced below reveal two sides of the concern of the Central Conference of American Rabbis in this continuing task. Samuel S. Cohon, speaking in 1928, presents a strong and detailed case for a thoroughgoing theological reconsideration. His argument rests chiefly upon the preservation in the traditional texts in the Union Prayer Book of theological ideas that the Reform movement had long rejected. Israel Bettan, replying two years later, argues for a more conservative approach to the traditional texts, leaving to the sermon other functions, such as "to inculcate new doctrines, to impart new truths and facts, or even to make novel applications of old truths." The persistence of both points of view a generation later guarantees that the task of the revisers today is no less complicated and difficult than that of their forerunners.

THE THEOLOGY OF THE UNION
PRAYER BOOK
Samuel S. Cohon
(1928)

The Book of traditional Jewish Prayer is a treasure-trove of devotion. Though non-canonical in character, it bears the stamp of the same creative religious genius which produced the Psalms and the prayers scattered through the historical and prophetic books of the Bible. Uniting the songs and petitions of the Holy Writ with later hymns and supplications, the *Siddur Tefilah* forms the cherished possession of the Jewish people. It furnishes the words with which the Jew praises his Creator at dawn, at the decline of day, and at the appearance of the stars. Its rhythm accompanies his work days, his Sabbaths and his Holy Days. It offers him consolation in sorrow, guidance in perplexity, and a steadying light in prosperity and in joy. As the Bible rendered the Jews a "People of the Book," the daily prayer-book made them a people of piety.

Prayer is essentially the language of faith. It is created by saints and poets in moments of spiritual exaltation and expresses the ardor of their souls and the longing of their hearts for God. In it the mystic, the imaginative and the symbolic elements predominate. There is in it a childlike trust, a simple confidence and an unsophisticated reliance upon God that constitute the pure essence of personal religion. Prayer grows out of the intuitional, emotional or

subjective phases of religion rather than from its intellectual, critical
and objective phases. However, it is of the nature of Judaism that its
faith is inseparable from reason. Its Psalmists in their yearning after
God obtained the richest glimpses of His essence. And its Prophets
comprehended the Divine order best in their intensest moments of
spiritual wrestling with God. As they lifted themselves to the high
Rock of Reality, they caught visions of truth about human life and
duty. Hence, though presenting no systematically defined doctrines
about either God or man, the Psalmists and Prophets are our best
teachers of what religion meant to the noblest of our priest-people.
Similarly, their successors the *Mitpalelim,* like Akiba and Abba
Arika, and the Paitanim, like Ibn Gabirol, Halevi and the Ibn Ezras,
strike the deepest chords in our mental life as they wing themselves
to the heights of religious devotion. Their astronomy may be bad
and their geography faulty, but the stars which they describe radiate hope and the earth upon which they stand is holy ground. They
teach us more of faith than many a rationalistic philosopher, scientist or theologian.

While the God-intoxicated poet and mystic come first in prayer,
the sober philosopher and critical theologian cannot remain away.
The imagination of the inspired poet and mystic may lead them
away from reality and from truth. Unchecked subjectivism has been
ever a danger to religion. Judaism in its purest expressions embodies
its visions in forms of reason as well as of feeling. By the harmonious combination of subjective and objective truth Judaism has
saved its worship from sinking into the morass of emotionalism
and hysteria, on the one hand, and from drying up in arid rationalism on the other.

Consequently the prayers of Israel, while warming the heart,
also enlighten the mind. Through communion with God, the Jew is
led to cast his burden upon the Lord. And at the same time he is
taught to ponder over God's self-manifestation in nature and in
man, over life and destiny, good and evil. The reflective Psalms,
the *Shir Hayihud,* the *Keter Malchut,* the *Adon Olam* and other
favorites of our hymnology embody the loftiest reasoned formula-

tions of Jewish belief. Heine could, therefore, justifiedly say that Jews pray philosophy. And not only the hymns which manifestly belong to the secondary stratum of the *Siddur,* but also its ground-work is cast into a decidedly reasoned form. The *Shema,* with its preceding and accompanying benedictions, holds the center of the morning and evening services because of its affirmation of the Unity of God and its call to citizenship of God's Kingdom. Similarly the *Amidah* sounds like cardinal convictions of Judaism, of God's revelation in the history of Israel (*Abot*), in Nature (*Geburot*) and in holiness (*Kedushat Hashem*) even as it voices the chief needs of the individual and of the Jewish people. The Maimunists displayed no revolutionary tendencies when they added the creed in prose (*Ani Maamin*) and in verse (*Yigdal*) to the daily service. They made explicit what had thitherto been implicit in Jewish worship. Thus the Prayer-book became not only the truest reflection of Jewish piety but also the finest embodiment of Jewish belief. Its appeal and its power are derived not alone from its rich deposit of mysticism and poetry, but also from its theological soundness.

The Union Prayer-book continues the traditions of our classical liturgy. In both structure and thought, it is the lineal descendant of the elements common to both the *Nusaḥ Ashkenaz* and *Nusaḥ Sefarad*. Like them it is the expression of the soul of Israel in its aspiration for the Divine. At the same time no other document manifests more clearly the fundamental departures of Reform from Orthodoxy than the Union Prayer-book. Its omissions as well as its additions—whatever our judgment of their value—grew out of definite theological viewpoints.

I. CONCEPTION OF PRAYER

The Union Prayer-book owes its existence to the desire of en-dowing the services of the Synagog with the sense of reality. The two aspects of reality in worship are, as Dean Sperry has convinc-ingly emphasized, objective truth and personal sincerity. The ideas expressed must be reasonably true and the worshiper must enter into them whole-heartedly, without any mental reservations. As long as a service is real for the worshipers, it possesses the power to affect their lives, but as soon as it raises doubts and suspicions it has lost its usefulness and has become an obstacle to the cause of religion.[1]

It is because of the inability on the part of some spiritually minded Jews to enter sincerely into the old ritual with its emphasis upon the sacrificial cult, the advent of a personal Messiah and the resurrection that the various revisions of the traditional Prayer-book were undertaken by Reformers. From the Hamburg Temple ritual to that of the Liberal Jewish Synagog of London the dominant motive of ritual reforms has been to bring the personal piety of the intelligent worshiper into accord with his convictions of objective truth.[2] The results of philosophy and of science have been applied to the reformation of the services in order to obtain a clearer view of God as the ultimate Reality. Also the methods of art have been employed to invest them with beauty and with joyousness.

Now this very spirit of science and rationalism, which demanded a revision of some of the fundamental ideas of the old service, often crowds out the devotional temper altogether. The critical attitude of the modern man makes prayer both unnecessary and impossible. For the satisfaction of his physical and material needs, he turns to science rather than to prayer. The same science teaches him that he cannot alter the tide, produce rain or stop the raging pestilence through prayer no matter how earnest. It consequently forces him to look for the efficacy of prayer in the sphere of the subjective rather than of the objective. But here another difficulty presents itself. As W. A. Brown observes: "We are living in a world that has lost the habit of prayer, and we tend unconsciously to reflect the conditions of the environment in which we are living. It is not simply that it is hard to pray. It is hard to *want* to pray. And unless we can recover that lost desire, we shall make little headway against

---

[1] Willard L. Sperry, *Reality in Worship*, Ch. XI.
[2] For a brief survey of the leading principles of the Reform Prayer-books see Rall and Cohon, *Christianity and Judaism Compare Notes*, Pt. II, pp. 81-86.

the difficulties of the mind."[3]

The Union Prayer-book unconsciously reflects the present apathy and scepticism toward prayer. Therein lies its chief distinction from the traditional Book of Prayer. It does not present "the prayer of the afflicted when he fainteth, and poureth out his complaint before the Lord." It expresses for the most part only rhetorically the heart's hunger for God and lacks much of the creative character of the historical *Tefilah*. Like most of the older Reform rituals, it is not designed as a book of *daily* devotion for *private* as well as for congregational use. The few meager prayers for the individual are printed as an afterthought. The weekday public services are in reality arranged for public use on Sundays and for houses of mourning. These as well as the Sabbath and Holy Day services are so arranged as to turn the worshiper into an auditor. They are—with but few exceptions—formal in character. In many synagogs they are consciously used as a mere introduction to the rabbi's discourse.

As if to avoid embarrassment the petitionary prayers have been toned down. This is particularly true of the first volume. God is allowed only as much as the current textbooks of science cannot possibly deny Him. Prayer does not function as an expression of deep felt human needs, as a cry for health, for sustenance and for relief from pain, sorrow and distress, but only as a vague meditation on an ethical theme. An examination of the Union Prayer-book leaves the impression that "the intrusion of the scientific mood" into its fabric has done the mischief against which Dean Sperry warns us. Worship appears as "a means to some good other than itself" and "is justified by its reference to the better control of the world and the better conduct of life."[4] Hence the homiletical nature of most of the additions to the traditional prayers, not only in the opening meditations, but also in the body of the services.

This further explains the persistent and often clumsy appeals to the worshiper. For instance in the special prayer for the evening of the fifth Sabbath of the month, we read:

[3] *The Life of Prayer*, p. 34.
[4] *Reality in Worship*, p. 248.

May we so use this gift (of labor) that day by day we may
look back upon our work and declare it good. May the fruit
of our labor be a service acceptable unto Thee. May each
new Sabbath find us going from strength to strength, so that
whatever of good we have done we may do still better; and
wherever we have failed, we may by Thy grace be helped to
worthier work.[5]

Argumentation with oneself is illustrated by the appeal:

May all of us realize more and more the value and the necessity of the observance of the Sabbath day.[6]

Compare this sentence with the rugged petition:

O help us to preserve the Sabbath.[7]

One is personal exhortation, the other is genuine prayer. Particularly disturbing is the dissertation on selfish and unselfish prayer
which marks the opening of the evening service at the house of
mourning.[8] The purpose of this type of prayer is, as the opening

---

[5] Vol. I, p. 35. The Union Prayer-book conveys the impression that it was especially written for a people composed of retired philanthropists and amateur social
workers. The aged are provided with this prayer on Yom Kippur: "Give me the
sweetness of that joy which is reserved for those who serve others through the
counsel and guidance learned in the school of life's experience." (Vol. II, p. 184).
Compare it with the traditional plea: "*Al tashlichenu l'es ziknoh, kichlos kohenu
al ta'azvenu*—Cast us not away in old age, when our strength shall be spent do not
forsake us." In the grace after meals, we have the sentence: "While we enjoy Thy
gifts, may we never forget the needy, nor allow those who want, to be forsaken."
(Vol. I, 344). How strangely this self-satisfied sentiment appears in the light of the
humble petition of the old *Birkat Hamozon*: "We beseech Thee, O Lord our God,
cause us not to become dependent upon the bounty of men or of their loans, but
only upon Thy hand."
This sentiment occurs in numerous places: "Aid us to do what in us lies to
lead into the right path the erring and the wayward." (Vol. I, 25) "May our
hands be outstretched to those who suffer, and our hearts be opened to those who
are in need; may we sympathize with those whose hopes have been disappointed
and whose labors have been unfruitful." (Vol. I, 99).
[6] Vol. I, p. 4.
[7] Vol. I, p. 16.
[8] Vol. I, p. 298.

meditation for the morning service of the three festivals suggests, turning away "from the things of earth *to contemplate the mysterious nature of our inner being.*"[9]

For the religious minded Jew, prayer can be neither a soliloquy nor a dialogue with his own soul. It can have value only if he knows before whom he stands. For him prayer is not a form of auto-suggestion but a communion between finite man and the infinite God, an uplifting of mind and heart on the part of the child of dust toward the heavenly Father.

This conception of prayer, as a means of moral improvement, explains the reduction of Hebrew in the Union Prayer-book to a bare minimum and its virtual elimination from the service of some congregations. In this regard we share the experience of Protestantism, which likewise casts "the whole service in the vernacular. The test of the service is to be its intelligibility and its practicality. The plain man must be able to understand all that takes place, and what takes place must concern his life. Mystery yields place to sound common sense, and wonder is superseded by edification."[10] Dean Sperry refers to Prof. Spratt's observation of the psychological paradox in the circumstance that "the most considerable changes in character are wrought, not by a direct subjective appeal, but by the indirect objective method."[11] If the pragmatic test is applied to the type of service which is conducted exclusively in the vernacular and one conducted either wholly or partially in Latin—as among the Catholics—or in Hebrew, it will be hardly possible to maintain that the more readily intelligible service yields finer fruits of character than the other. The accents of the ancient and hallowed tongue carry a stronger appeal to many minds than the prosy vernacular. They more effectively fill the emptiness of the heart with the consciousness of the Divine and more potently link the worshiper with the *Kenesset Yisroel.*

The attitude of the Union Prayer-book toward tradition is quite

---

[9] Vol. I, p. 203.
[10] Sperry. *op cit.*, p. 258.
[11] *Ibid.*, 259.

naturally eclectic. When feasible it follows the standards of the
historical liturgy. It recognizes that inasmuch as tradition is a potent
channel of Jewish religious life, departure from it is a dangerous
process and may be ventured only in the interest of truth and sincerity. However the Union Prayer-book breaks with established forms
and expressions when these are found to be out of tune with the intellectual atmosphere of the present. Antiquarian exactness is freely
sacrificed for the sake of increased spirituality. It cannot be claimed,
however, that this principle is carried out with any degree of consistency and that the Union Prayer-book has always struck the
right balance between tradition and the modern outlook.

Needless disregard of tradition may be noticed in the arrangement of ancient material. Thus Psalm XIX is removed from the
Sabbath morning service and is placed in the evening service for
week days.[12] The *Pesuke d'zimra* are transferred from the beginning of the morning service for weekdays to the place historically
assigned to the profession of faith, following the Shema. The Hebrew text of the 'Amidah is eliminated from the morning service
and is presented in mutilated form in the evening service.[13] In the
Sabbath service the *Nishmat* does not appear, and in the services
for the three festivals is supplied with a paraphrase that does not
improve the original.[14] Similar unnecessary deviations from the
original appear in the profession of faith in the Sabbath and Holy
Day morning services.[15] Classic prayers that have won their place
into the heart of the Jewish people and that are wholly in keeping
with the outlook of Reform have been omitted. We refer to the
Hebrew texts of the Kiddush, the middle prayers of the Amidah
in the Rosh Hashanah and of Yom Kippur Eve services, *Vyeesoyn
Kol l'ovdecho, Shofet Kol Ho'orets,* etc. These liberties with the
traditional liturgy do not tend to enhance the value of the Union
Prayer-book as preserver of ancient landmarks.

---

[12] Vol. I, p. 281. *Ibid.,* pp. 318 ff.
[13] *Ibid.,* pp. 295-7.
[14] *Ibid.,* pp. 208-9. The version in the second volume differs from that of the first.
[15] *Ibid.,* pp. 72-73, 214-215 and Vol. II, pp. 50-51, 166-167.

II. God, Revelation, and Retribution

Prayer occupies a literary position midway between poetry and prose. As in poetry so in prayer the wording is colored by emotional associations; the appeal is to the heart; the imagination enjoys free range; the soul makes holiday. And as in prose, prayers are bent on reality, on exact meanings attached to words, on definite conceptions of spiritual truths and on clear formulation of human needs. Obviously to balance both aspects—the subjective and the objective—and to avoid mushy sentimentalism and dry formalism, is a task of uncommon difficulty in which only few liturgists have succeeded. An unusual degree of religious fervor, bordering on self-effacement and absorption in God, graced with the Holy Spirit, is necessary to produce prayers that actually live. Otherwise we only compose history, ethical appeals, or sociological disquisitions and offer them as prayers. Whether such offerings are acceptable to God is, of course, beyond our ken. But that they are not acceptable to souls that hunger for the bread of life, who even in an age of scepticism and materialism, occasionally turn "to inquire of the Lord," we can well surmise.

Some of the intellectual difficulties which we experience with our liturgy grow out of the use of language in prayer. Certain words and phrases have become hallowed by ages of usage, but in the course of time, much of their original spirit has evaporated and they have come to convey totally different meanings to men and women of the present. This applies not only to the Hebrew portion of the Union Prayer-book, but also to its English part. Regarded as figures of speech, these expressions heighten our feeling, but when taken—as they usually are—in their literal meaning, they seriously embarrass our faith. We refer to such phrases as "angel choir,"[16] "the book of life"[17] and other simple, almost childlike, expressions of piety, which have been retained through the Psalms and later liturgic creations of the synagog. Similarly the directness of divine

[16] Vol. II, pp. 95, 222, 332.
[17] *Ibid.*, pp. 20, etc.

response to our requests is somewhat difficult for men who have bled and suffered in a hard world. "Thou openest Thy hand and satisfiest every living thing with favor"—is a bit too simple for the searching mind.

We are here on the horns of a dilemma of either qualifying our thoughts in accordance with the canons of rationalism or of frankly accepting the difficulties inherent in personal piety, realizing that without it all religion becomes an empty soap-bubble. Love of God and confidence in Him may be hard to attain in an age of doubt, but without them the religious heart can have no peace. For the religious person God cannot be a mere "by-product of man's changing emotional moods," or a dream-picture screened on nothingness. He can be neither the deliberate projection of Israel's aspirations into the void nor a mere sentiment or ideal of human perfection. Not even the philosophical Absolute can satisfy the heart that hungers and thirsts for the living God. Though His greatness transcends our knowledge, we seek communion with Him. The eternal Lord of the universe must be also the Creative Will, the Wise Omniscience, the All-pervading Presence, the All-sustaining Providence. In the external nature we behold Him as power and as Intelligence, but in the history of humanity we see Him manifested in righteousness and in the life of man as moral power, conscience, justice, compassion and holiness. It has been well said: "Creation is God's transcendent reality introducing itself into the world and becoming immanent in it. And this act of creation is the act of the divine love by which God is eternally pledged to His world, by which His world, becoming self-conscious in man, needs and can receive his grace." God as understood in religion is indeed "nigh unto all who call upon Him, who call upon Him in truth." Religion conceives of God not only *sub specie aeternitatis,* but also *sub specie temporis.* As a modernist puts it: "God condescends to weave the texture of His vast designs with human hands."[18] Consequently the religious person does not hesitate to say: "Not unto

[18] A. L. Lilley, paraphrasing Laberthonnière, art. "Modernism," *Hastings' Encyclopedia of Religion and Ethics,* Vol. VIII, 767.

us, O Lord, not unto us, but unto Thee give glory." "From Thy
hand come all, and but of Thine own have we given unto Thee."
What God is to the myriads of spheres that circle in space not even
the boldest imagination may venture to guess. But to the heart that
seeks His presence, He is a living Father who heareth prayer.

While in the main the conception of God in the Union Prayer-
book is presented with dignity and with soundness, it is not free
from occasional infelicities, which tax the thinking mind and im-
pede its progress in prayer. We might point to expressions which
betray a naive type of teleology, such as:

"Thou dost clothe the earth in radiant beauty and bid it bring
forth its bounteous blessings for the life and welfare of Thy
children."[19]

"He has given us dear ones that we may rejoice in their love."[20]

"What would the earth be with all its abundance and beauty
. . . hadst Thou not placed man at the very summit of creation, to proclaim Thy grandeur?"[21]

However, these sentiments are not as disturbing as the concepts
which piety has created and which now directly contradict the reasoned belief of Reform Judaism.

If Reform Judaism has any scientific and philosophical foundation, it is the application of the theory of evolution to the beliefs,
institutions and sacred writings of Judaism. Here we have the Great
Divide between Orthodoxy and Reform. Belief in the descent of
God on Mt. Sinai and His personal delivery of the Torah constitutes the rock of Orthodoxy. In the Torah—in its double aspect of
Written and Oral Law—traditional Judaism has its magnificent
charter. It conceives of its authority as God-derived. The laws and

---

[19] Vol. I, p. 190.
[20] *Ibid.*, p. 273.
[21] Vol. II, 367.

ordinances, the duties and obligations are all Divine commands.
Even the latest addition to the Law by a modern authority secures
its sanction from its connection with the body of Torah. It too becomes as a *Halacha l'moshe misinai.* On this ground the Shulḥan
Aruch becomes the unassailable authority in Jewish life.

Many of us heartily admire the consistency and beauty of a system of life governed by a "divinely revealed legislation," but, to
our sorrow, we cannot subscribe to its fundamental assumptions.
The concept of revelation as a process whereby the Creator's activity, thought and purpose are disclosed to and apprehended by
some of the pure-souled and spiritually-gifted creatures, of course,
remains pivotal in modern as in ancient Judaism. The very idea of
God implies that despite the unfathomability of His nature, at least
something about Him or His ways may be grasped by man and
turned into a source of influence in human life. It is quite other
to hold on to the older view of revelation as "the final and im-
perfectible deposit" of truth as embodied in a particular literary
document. The historical sciences have taught us that religion
does not descend suddenly amid thunder and lightning from a
physical heaven to a single people, but that in various forms it
grows slowly, gradually, but steadily from the hearts and minds of
all races of men as they lift themselves from brute existence to the
higher realms of the spirit. Biblical scholarship has further demonstrated that our Pentateuch, far from having been delivered by God
to Moses on the 6th of Sivan in the year 2448 after Creation, is the
product of the developing religious idealism of our people in the
course of many centuries, and that only in post-exilic times did it
assume its present form. It has become a truism for students of
Judaism, who have come under the influence of the historical
sciences, that the living stream of Jewish religious creativity was
not exhausted in Prophecy, Pentateuch, Talmud or Shulḥan Aruch,
but that it has run unchecked down to our own day.

This progressive view of revelation, or of a larger Torah as including everything called to life by the religious genius of Israel,
accounts for the many-sided history of Judaism and at the same

time justifies the departures of Reform. It is voiced by the foremost thinkers in the camp of Reform and is embodied in the Pittsburgh Platform. It is nobly expressed in the prayer for the evening service of the fourth Sabbath of the month:

> O Lord, open our eyes that we may see and welcome all truth, whether shining from the annals of ancient revelation or reaching us through the seers of our own time; for Thou hidest not Thy light from any generation of Thy children that feel after Thee and seek Thy guidance."[22]

In view of these considerations, references in the Union Prayer-book to the Torah as *the* Law divinely revealed at Sinai come as a surprise. In conscious deviation from the new English translation,[23] which is generally used in the Union Prayer-book, the minister, upon taking the Scroll from the ark, is instructed to refer to it as "the Torah which God gave through Moses," and thus to condemn the basic position of Reform Judaism with regard to revelation. The Yigdal in both Hebrew text and in translation retains the entire section of the Maimonidean Creed on revelation, including the polemic of a vanished age against Christian and Islamic dogma.[24] It is stated:

> "We remember . . . *when* Thou didst reveal Thy law unto Israel."[25]

Though 'law' is written with a little 'l', the implication is unmistakable. The occasional introduction to Bible citations as God's promise sound confusing to those who have learned to value the Bible as a precious product of the Jewish people rather than the record of supernatural dictation.[26]

[22] Vol. I, p. 32. See also the benediction before reading the Haphtarah, Vol. I, p. 117, cf. pp. 204, 329, etc.
[23] Deuteronomy XXXIII, 4.
[24] Vol. I, pp. 200-1.
[25] Vol. I, p. 190.
[26] Vol. I, p. 269; vol. II, p. 114, etc.

The Union Prayer-book attitude toward the Bible and especially toward the Pentateuch goes back to the ideology of the early Reformers, who, in negation of the authority of Rabbinism, called for a return to Mosaism. The survival of this outworn conception accounts for the almost exclusive use of Bible material for responsive readings. With the exception of a few passages in the Yom Kippur afternoon services, the post-Biblical poems are replaced with Psalms and passages from the prophets. This imitation of Karaism robs the Union Prayer-book of both variety and beauty.

No less confusing is the Union Prayer-book treatment of the belief in retribution. The conviction that there is some kind of reward and punishment for man's actions is rooted in his moral sense and is basic to ethical theism. The Creator and Guide of the world, whose eye is upon His creatures, must care for the way they order and conduct their lives. It must make some difference to Him whether they act in harmony or in disharmony with His cosmic plan. The righteous God thus appears to the religious minded as Judge. Our relation to God, i.e., our religion, becomes "the inmost nerve of obligation, which knits us to responsibility." And duty appears as the "Stern Daughter of the voice of God."

Valuable as this consciousness is for both morality and religion, it is not free from dangerous misinterpretations which threaten to undermine the whole structure of faith. In the attempt to discover the plan of divine retribution, all too human judgments are frequently set up as the dictates of God. The justice of God is often established on the primitive foundation of the *lex talionis*. God gives unto man "according to his ways, and according to the fruit of his doings."[27] Recommended by prudence, sanctioned by piety, and championed by the prophets, this conception of retribution has nevertheless been wrecked again and again on the rock of human experience.

"Will you speak unrighteously for God, and talk deceitfully for Him?"—demands the suffering patriarch.[28] A lie even for the sake

[27] Jer. XXXII, 19; see also Is. II, 10-11 and especially Ezek. XVIII.
[28] Job XIII, 8.

of religion does not turn into truth. It is not true that piety and goodness always yield material benefits and that sin and evil inevitably lead to material punishments. Vigorous health and prosperity are not the infallible signs of saintliness; nor do pain, suffering and poverty betoken wickedness. The author of the great drama of human suffering makes God rebuke the upholders of the orthodox view of retribution: "My wrath is kindled against thee, and against thy two friends; for ye have not spoken of Me the thing that is right, as My servant Job hath."[29]

To solve the baffling enigma of divine retribution the leaders of Judaism, under the influence of Parsee and Greek ideas, resorted to an elaborate system of eschatology, whereby the ills in this life are corrected in the next, where Gehenna awaits the sinner and Gan Eden the righteous. That leading Jewish minds were not in entire accord with this solution is well known. Antigonus of Soko warned against the slave morality which is based on promises of rewards and punishment.[30] Abba Arika emphatically denied all sensual enjoyment and play of passion in the Hereafter, where only spiritual bliss comes from communion with the Shechina.[31] R. Johanan declared that the destiny of the soul after death remains veiled in mystery 'No eye hath seen it, O God, beside Thee.'[32] Maimonides proceeds to state that all considerations of reward and punishment can at best be considered as mere pedagogical devices, but are unworthy of the true lover of God.[33] Man must pursue truth and follow virtue not because of any worldly or other-worldly emoluments but because of their intrinsic value. As a child of God, man attains his full self-realization by leading a godly life. Without demand of clear tariffs of merits and demerits, man must offer his deeds, his strivings and his ideals at the altar of God and live in the hope that he may be worthy of divine approval.

[29] Job XLII, 7.
[30] Aboth 1, 2.
[31] Ber. 17a.
[32] Ber. 34b.
[33] Introduction to Perek Helek and Hilchot Teshubah VII-X. See also K. Kohler, op. cit., pp. 307 ff.

Reform Judaism has generally accepted the higher scale of religious values. It is therefore strange to find in a prayer-book which gives the view of Maimonides[34] so many expressions of both worldly and other-worldly compensations as incentives to goodness. It is significant that of the passages from Job dealing with retribution, only the utterances of Job's disputants are utilized.[35] The same antiquated viewpoint is retained not only in the Psalms, Yigdal and other traditional material, but also in new compositions. Thus we read:

> It is our duty to walk in Thy ways . . . so that when Thou callest us hence, *we may enjoy the reward* which Thou hast prepared for those who have earnestly striven to live in accordance with Thy will.[36]

Another prayer reads:

> Give me strength, O Lord, so to live that we may be worthy . . . to stand before Thee in the presence of the good and righteous who have gone before us.[37]

The worshiper is taught to think of death as "the day of retribution approaching."[38]

> Surely there will be compensation for those who suffer innocently, reward for virtue thwarted, and punishment for wickedness which triumphs but for a day,[39]

---

[34] Vol. II, pp. 297-8.

[35] Job VIII and XI (speeches of Bildad and Zophar), Vol. II, 226-7; XXII and XX (speeches of Eliphaz and Zophar), *Ibid.*, 344-5. The only speech of Job given in the Union Prayer-book is Chs. XXVI; XXVIII, which do not deal with retribution.

[36] Vol. I, p. 309.

[37] Vol. I, p. 333; also Vol. II, p. 334 (in memory of a father).

[38] Vol. II, p. 221.

[39] Vol. II, p. 239. Similar statements are found in the various introductions to the Kaddish and in other meditations and prayers of both volumes. Oblivious of the difficulties involved, retribution is offered as a source of comfort:

announces another prayer. A poetic passage urges the worshiper:

But call to mind affliction's weight and dread
The judgment day;[40]

while another verse assures him:

Then will His angels come and lead thee in
To paradise.[41]

Then let Thine angels of peace receive it (the soul), singing
in joyful chorus: Peace be thy coming. There may it find its
habitation in the blissful light of the spiritual world and its
portion in unmeasured eternity and unending happiness.[42]

On the basis of the statement: "Thou renderest every creature its
due," an artificial argument for immortality is advanced which pro-
motes scepticism rather than greater faith.[43]

How this attitude affects the character that we give to Judaism
may be illustrated with the Kaddish. This glorious exaltation of God
and the jubilation of the soul in the buoyant hope of the establishment of His Kingdom has been placed in the Union Prayer-book in
a funereal setting. It appears no longer as a doxology but only as an

---

But why should man murmur at his lot? Though he be called to toil and to
trouble, his faithfulness shall not fail of reward. Vol. II, p. 180.

For all things stand revealed at last, and all men will be called to render account
for their doings. Then truth will be made manifest, and deception will be ended
for ever. He who worketh righteousness and showeth mercy will find everlasting
peace. His reward surpasses all earthly treasures and honors. A good name is
his here below, and the crown of life eternal beyond. For him the day of death is
better than the day of birth. Vol. II, p. 180.

In the fulness of time *we shall know why we are tried*, and why our love brings us
sorrow as well as happiness. Vol. I, p. 125.

Wait patiently all ye that mourn—for *surely* your longing souls shall be satisfied.
Vol. I, p. 125. Death is not the end, but a beginning. Vol. II, p. 33.

Without the faith that our loved ones . . . are safe with Thee, despair would
envelop us and hopelessness would be our portion. Vol. II, p. 85.

[40] Vol. II, p. 331.
[41] Vol. II, p. 332.
[42] Vol. II. p. 222.
[43] Vol. II, p 329.

orphan's prayer—*kaddish yatom,* with the additional paragraph, first penned for the Hamburg Prayer-book, in which bliss and joy are asked for the departed in "that ineffable good which God has laid up for those who fear Him."[44] The *huloko tovo*—good portion —for the righteous implies a bad lot for the wicked. But this is of course unmentionable! The fire and brimstone theology of an older day at least possessed the double merit of poetic justice and picturesqueness. Of what good is a Paradise for the just if no Hell is provided to which to commit the unjust?

Accordingly the confused view of retribution directly leads to other-worldliness. The funereal note is sounded in many keys:

> Let each day be to us a day of repentance, and every hour as the hour of death, which calls us to appear before Thy throne of judgment.[45]

Echoes of this view appear at the end of the special prayer for the evening of the second Sabbath of the month,[46] in the prayer for the morning of the first Sabbath,[47] and the conclusion of the Shemini Azeret prayer.[48] And Yom Kippur is said to have been appointed "that we may sanctify our life on earth, and prepare ourselves for death and life to come."[49]

That a sturdier ideal actuated the minds of some of the contributors to the Union Prayer-book is evident from this excerpt:

> And when at last the time shall come in which Thou wilt take us hence to be with Thee, may our life not have been in vain; may we leave the world better and richer for our service and our toil. And may we close our earthly career with cheerful trust in Thine eternal love and wisdom.[50]

[44] Several Reform Prayer-books like Geiger's and that of the Liberal Jewish Synagogue omit this paragraph.
[45] Vol. II, p. 193.
[46] Vol. I, p. 25.
[47] Vol. I, p. 82.
[48] Vol. I, p. 237.
[49] Vol. II, p. 324.
[50] Vol. I, p. 237.

As to the settlement of moral accounts the words of the old piyyut ring so much truer than those to which we have referred:

Thy way, O God, is patience and compassion, alike to the wicked and to the good; this is Thy Glory. Instil Thy healing balm into sorrowing hearts; have pity on those who are but dust and ashes.[51]

This too, we believe, is the more truly religious view of life with God.

III. ISRAEL

The Kingdom of God for which Jewish Prophets, Psalmists and saints yearned is not eschatological but ethical. The Kaddish, translated literally, reads: "May He establish His Kingdom during your lifetime, and during the life of all the house of Israel."[52] As Dr. Kohler observes: "It is not the hope of bliss in a future life (which is the leading motive of Christianity), but the building up of the divine Kingdom of truth, justice and peace among men by Israel's teaching and practice."[53] This is the burden of numerous passages in the Union Prayer-book. In the light of this conception, the life and destiny of Israel is consistently and sometimes impressively interpreted in both volumes.[54]

Following the traditional theology of the Synagog, the Union Prayer-book presents the story of God's revelation at Mt. Sinai as the first act in the drama of world history.

Israel was chosen to be the standard bearer of truth and the champion of righteousness, a light to the nations and a covenant to the peoples.[55]

[51] Vol. II, pp. 264-265.
[52] The paraphrase of the Kaddish in the U. P. B. fails to do justice to the original. The inclusion of the sentence: "Just is He in all His ways, and wise are all His decrees" mistakes the Kaddish for the *Zidduk Haddin.*
[53] K. Kohler, *Jewish Theology*, p. 332.
[54] Sometimes the conception of the mission of Israel is forced, as for example: May they (the lulov and Esrog) suggest thoughts of the sublime mission upon which Thou hast sent Thy servant Israel—Vol. I, p. 233.
[55] Vol. 1, pp. 229-230; II, pp. 79-80; 255.

As in the teachings of Deutero-Isaiah, Israel figures as the servant of God, in whose heart is the Law, and as a priest and prophet unto the nation:

> Thou hast sanctified us through Thy commandments, that through Israel Thy great and holy name may become known in all the earth.[56]

Not as a sin-laden exile from the Father's table, as in traditional Jewish theology, nor as a curse-laden wanderer of medieval Christian legend, but as witness to divine truth did Israel go forth from Palestine.

> By Thy grace, O God, it has also been given us to see in our dispersion over the earth, not a means of punishment, but a sign of blessed privilege. Scattered among the nations of the world, Israel is to bear witness to Thy power and Thy truth and to endeavor to unite all peoples in a covenant of brotherhood and peace.[57]

Israel's mission is to "keep aglow the pure faith" in God,[58] and "to be a messenger of peace unto the peoples of the earth."[59]

Rejecting further the ancient belief in the restoration of the theocratic state in Palestine under a Davidic Messiah, the Union Prayerbook wages a needless polemic against both religious and political Zionism:

> Not backward do we turn our eyes, O Lord, but forward to the promised and certain future . . . and though we cherish and revere the place where stood the cradle of our people, the land where Israel grew up like a tender plant, and the knowledge of Thee rose like the morning-dawn, our longings and as-

[56] Vol. I. p. 182.
[57] Vol. II, p. 254.
[58] *Ibid.*, pp. 255, 236, etc.
[59] Vol. I, p. 110.

pirations reach out toward a higher goal. The morning-dawn shall yet brighten into a radiant noonday; the tender sprout shall yet become a heaven-aspiring tree beneath which all the families of the earth will find shelter.[60]

The temper of the Union Prayer-book on Israel's place in the world is reflected in the petition:

Be Thou with the whole house of Israel, so that we may live in freedom everywhere and unite with all men in singing a new song of salvation and deliverance.[61]

This reference to the "whole house of Israel" is rather exceptional, for the unity of Israel is not sufficiently stressed in the Union Prayer-book.[62] Remembering the mission of Israel, the welfare of the missionary in various parts of the world is all too often overlooked.

Neither is Israel's adherence to the ideals which constitute his mission sufficiently emphasized. All too little is said about Israel as a people of Torah, who must learn before it can teach and who must practice before it can serve as an example to others.

Despite the sermonic self-castigation of vol. II, pp. 242-4 and similar self-accusations elsewhere, the Union Prayer-book leaves the impression that all is well with Israel and with the world. Indeed references abound to injustice, poverty, oppression and war—but these only furnish opportunities for melioration. The lecture on the *Klassenkampf* in the Minha service of Yom Kippur[63] which denounces the inequitable distribution of wealth and the pride of possession, which lead men to forget that labor is the true source of wealth, concludes with the modest call: "Let us resolve to be helpful to the men and women who earnestly and sincerely strive to make a

[60] Vol. II, p. 255.
[61] Vol. I, p. 227.
[62] Cf. Vol. I, pp. 96-97, where the reference to the restriction of the dry bones naturally calls for the ideal of Jewish unity, also pp. 108-109.
[63] Vol. II, pp. 314-317.

better world and let us on our own part seek to establish this world by such *justice as shall be stimulated by generous sympathies* and by such righteousness as shall be based upon genuine sacrifice."[64] Whether or not philanthropy is the right solution of the problems arising from the conflict between capital and labor might be better judged from the standpoint of political economy than from that of theology.[65]

IV. THE HOLY SEASONS

The various conceptions of prayer, God, revelation, retribution and Israel, which we have reviewed are, for the most part, embodied in the services for the Sabbath and the Holy Days. Let us, therefore, conclude our inquiry with a brief survey of the meanings attached to the sacred seasons in the pages of the Union Prayer-book. True to enlightened theological opinion, these days are viewed as signs and memorials of religious truths and ideals. They are the creations of Israel's genius as affected by the stern realities of historic experience. And, inasmuch as they help to sanctify the life of Israel, of the family and of the individual, they are conceived as divine.

The full significance of the Sabbath is impressively set forth in the prayer for the evening of the third Sabbath.[66] And despite the unreality of the petition: *Reze vimnuhosenu*—accept our rest—for a Sabbathless age, the traditional prayer in which it occurs still expresses all that the day has meant to our people: "Sanctify us by Thy commandments and grant us our portion in Thy law. Satisfy us with Thy goodness and gladden us with Thy salvation. Purify our hearts that we may serve Thee in truth."[67]

---

[64] Vol. II, p. 317.

[65] The political economist might also ponder the profundity of this declaration: "Whether we will or no, human life is a cooperative venture and the business of life is carried on whenever and wherever two persons transact any enterprise whatsoever." Vol. II, p. 316. Vol. I, pp. 27-9, see also p. 93.

[66] Though couched in classic English, the deviations of the Union Prayer-book version from the original text cannot be regarded as improvements. The same may be said of the little used *Atto Ehod* in the afternoon service for the Sabbath. (Vol. I, p. 140).

[67] Vol. I, p. 3.

The emphasis is laid not on the Sabbath as Israel's mate—*Bas Zug* —or as Queen Sabbath—*Shabbos hamalka*—as in the mystical poem *Lecho Dodi,* but rather on the Sabbath as a day of personal rest. It is referred to as "the heart's own hour of holy gladness, which takes the burden from our shoulders," and "restores our soul and instils new vigor into our tired frame."[68] The stress on the recreational value of the Sabbath cannot have the same significance as the emphasis on the Sabbath as a fundamental institution of Judaism in an age like ours, when the eight-hour labor day is spreading in order to secure for the worker a fair amount of leisure every day and when the upper classes have more leisure than they know what to do with. The old liturgy announced:

They that keep the Sabbath and call it a day of delight shall rejoice in Thy kingdom.[69]

This is the religious aspect of the Sabbath. The Union Prayer-book offers a high ethical idea:

He who has worked faithfully during the week and, according to his strength, has contributed to the larger work of mankind will enjoy the delight of the Sabbath.[70]

One assigns the Sabbath joy to Israel, the people of God; the other limits it to useful workers. The ideal combination of the two is what is needed.

The meanings of the few special Sabbaths for which particular services have been provided are not sufficiently accentuated. The one delightful exception is the evening service for Shabbos Hanukkah. The occasion is made vivid and dramatically stirring by the appropriate selection from the Apocrypha, by the kindling of the lights and by the great hymn, Rock of Ages. The same cannot be claimed for either Shabbos Zochor, or Shuvo, or the Shabbos of

---

[68] Singer, Prayer-book, p. 163.
[69] Union P. B., Vol. I, p. 85.
[70] Vol. II, p. 76.

Hol Hamoed Pesah and Sukkos. They seem perfunctory and do not sound the spiritual depths of the occasions.

The three Pilgrim Festivals are the least satisfactorily treated in the Union Prayer-book. The peculiar historical and poetical character with which each is endowed is but feebly disclosed in the course of these services. They are remote from present day life and are centered too much in past events. They appear principally as reminders of God's kindness to our forefathers and do not bring out with sufficient force their eternal appeal to the hearts of living men. The prayers for Sukkos and Shemini Azeret are especially poverty-stricken. In most favorable contrast stand out the services for Rosh Hashanah and Yom Kippur. The Shofar, Abodah, Memorial and Neilah services—despite valuable omissions and occasional infelicities—reach sublime heights.

These solemn days are presented as occasions for self-searching and for the renewal of heart. They stir us to envisage life as a whole and to realize its divine erdowment. The Rosh Hashanah liturgy fosters the consciousness that our lives are sustained by "the King of Eternity, the immovable rock amidst the ebb and flow of the ages."[71] The confessions and supplications of Yom Kippur awaken us to the sense of sin, to our moral and spiritual weakness and to our need of Divine grace and forgiveness. Attuned to the spirit of Hosea, Jeremiah, Ezekiel, Trito-Isaiah and the penitential Psalms, the Yom Kippur devotions manifest deep religious inwardness.

> Hear me on this solemn day when contemplation of Thy greatness and goodness alone, can soften the bitter memory of sin. Thou hast prepared a healing balm for my betterment, O God, the sacred hour of atonement, which crowns us with Thy mercy.[72]

A considerable portion of the confession is impressive by virtue of its earnestness.[73] The "prayer for young men" is a singularly fine

[71] *Ibid.*, pp. 229-230.
[72] Vol. II, pp. 114-122.
[73] *Ibid.*, p. 93.

addition to our devotional literature. The Atonement services suffer somewhat from the wearisome repetition of Psalms and disconnected selections from the Bible and other Jewish literature, and from an excess of prosy homilies and stereotyped phrases. It is doubtful whether statements like these carry any conviction:

Out of the depth of mine abasement, I cry unto Thee.[74]
Thy people are prostrate before Thee.[75]
Let Thy grace appear, and make an end of mine agony.[76]
The sting of guilt, the sinner's rod,
    Dejects my heart to nameless woe;
I know Thou art my righteous God,
    And I am passion's hunted roe.[77]

The note of self-accusation reaches the point of discord when the worshiper is asked to confess:

Day after day I have sought my own pleasure and gain *without a thought of the higher purpose of life.*[78]

A striking example of intellectual confusion created by an ancient metaphor is the retention of the picturesque reference to "the book of life." The Rosh Hashanah and Yom Kippur prayer runs: *"inscribe us* in the book of life." and the Neilah prayer: *"seal us* in the book of life." These metaphors are most attractive but their danger lies in the fact that they are survivals of the old viewpoint that Rosh Hashanah is the day when God's judgment of men is recorded and

---

[74] *Ibid.*, p. 94.
[75] *Ibid.*, p. 222.
[76] *Ibid.*, p. 219
[77] *Ibid.*, p. 181. The "individual" for whom a special confession is provided on pp. 191-193 is quite enigmatic. It cannot be an aged person, a woman, a young man, a child or a member of a congregation for those are all provided for. By process of elimination and by examining the contents we may infer that an unattached middle aged bachelor is meant. The argument for the single standard of sex morals advanced for his meditation assumes that the male of the species alone breaks the moral standard.
[78] Vol. II, pp. 238-9.

Yom Kippur is the day when it is finally sealed. The sublime prayer *"Unesane tokeph,"* which, with poetic sweep, rivaled only by the Shepherd Psalm, pictures the workings of Providence, is followed by the declaration

> *Berosh hashonoh yikosvun uvyom Zom Kippur yehosemum—*
> On the first day of the year it is inscribed and on the day of Atonement it is sealed: How many shall pass away and how many shall be born, etc.[79]

What to us seem accidents are here presented as inscrutable decrees of the wise Ruler of men. Though subscribing to the belief in Providence, it is hard for us to regard the two Days of Awe as the special occasions of God's notary activities. In the Talmud itself this view was contested. Thus R. Jose maintained that man is judged daily rather than at special seasons.[80]

Coupled with this archaic thought is the declaration that "Penitence, Prayer and Charity avert the evil decree."[81] The thinking person cannot but ascribe great worth to penitence, prayer and charity, but he values them as the manifestation of divine sonship rather than as means of buying off Providence.

---

[79] R. H. 16a.

[80] Vol. II, pp. 238-9.

[81] Those who occasionally suggest the substitution of free prayer for the established liturgy as a means of improving our synagog services might profit from the experience of Protestantism. Dean Sperry testifies that free prayer lies open to the play of the minister's idiosyncracies and private hobbies. Unless rigidly censored, it tends to become either informational or "an exercise in self-analysis." Its ideas are often random and irrelevant. Its informality robs the service of beauty and impressiveness, which is not compensated even by its directness and freshness. Its language generally becomes either stereotyped or haphazard and commonplace. "The present fact is that the original truth of the free service has become in practice a rather uninspired and uninspiring platitude . . . Every minister who has conducted free worship for a period of years has unconsciously developed and in the end has consciously adopted certain forms of speech and action which have become habitual with him. Simply because his prayers have not been printed in a book or his usages dignified by rubrics, he is not necessarily a 'non-liturgical' minister"—(*Reality in Worship*, Chapter XV). Furthermore such worship is divorced from the past and lacks the dignity and the authority which ancient usage bestows.

V. Conclusion

The Union Prayer-book, like the other publications of the Central Conference of American Rabbis, is the product of committee endeavor. Committees are, as a rule, composed of men who are not necessarily saints or poets, men of different minds and of varying viewpoints, which clash on matters which are usually of deep moment. They can, therefore, make progress only through compromise. To this condition we may trace most of the inconsistencies in the Union Prayer-book. Advanced positions in theology sounded in one prayer are not uniformly applied in others. Outworn conceptions occasionally appear beneath modern phrasing, while vital traditional forms and usages are sacrificed for no compelling reason.

While there is much to be desired for the Union Prayer-book from the standpoint of both systematic thought and artistic expression, it contains many noble passages that can answer the spiritual needs of our people. If despite its riches, it is deemed inadequate, the reason must be sought not only in its contents, but also in the manner in which it is used by our congregations. Jewish people, it seems, cannot get accustomed to the Protestant manner of worship in which the minister prays for the congregation, whether extempore or from a printed page.[82] Jews have been accustomed to pray for themselves. They are furthermore left untouched by the routine way in which prayers are read from many pulpits. They have been accustomed to hear their prayers intoned lovingly and feelingly. Greater participation in the service on the part of the congregation and unison song of at least the essential responses and some hymns may endow even the present Union Prayer-book with power.

The greatest desideratum is a new attitude toward prayer. We must strive to recover the lost desire to pray. The critical temper which we bring with us into the pulpit as into the pew must give

---

[82] See M. Friedlander, art. "Devotion," *Jewish Encyclopedia*, Vol. IV, p. 549 and H. Steinthal's stimulating essay on "Andacht" in his *Bibel und Religionsphilosophie*, also H. G. Enelow's essay in Kohler's *Festschrift*.

way to the spirit of appreciation and devotion. As suggested by the *Ma tovu,* with which we begin our morning services, we must enter the house of worship in the consciousness of its goodliness, touched with the sense of reverence for and love of God. Prayer must be an *Abodah shebalev,* a service of the heart, in which the whole inner life is directed toward and centered in the one idea of God's greatness and goodness. A divine service without such religious concentration or *Kavvanah* is indeed "like unto a body without a soul."[83] The stern rationalist, Maimonides, is at one with the mystic in admonishing us that prayer draws its vitality from *Kavvanah.* "How shall *Kavvanah* be practiced? Man must free his mind from all other thoughts and imagine himself standing in the presence of all the Shechinah."[84] A conscious effort must be made to direct the feelings, thought and will upon the inner content of worship. The heart must be laid open to the influence of the Divine. While earnestness in worship may be induced by certain crises in our lives produced by external causes, in its noblest forms it is generated from within. The legalist Joseph Caro opens the Orah Hayyim with the monition: "Let man show himself mighty as a lion in rising early to serve his Creator, and appear as if he were waking the dawn."[85] We must strive to imbue the words of our mouth and the meditations of our hearts with the breath of life and with the spirit of reality.[86]

---

[83] H. Tefilah, IV, 15-16.
[84] Shulhan Aruch, Orah Hayyim, I, 1. See also the Tur, Orah Hayyim.
[85] "Religion," observes Auguste Sabatier, "is nothing if it is not the vital act by which the whole spirit seeks to save itself by attaching itself to its principle. This act is prayer, by which I mean, not an empty utterance of words, not the repetition of sacred formulas, but the movement of the soul putting itself into personal relation and contact with the mysterious power whose presence it feels even before it is able to give it a name. Where this inward prayer is wanting there is no religion; on the other hand, wherever this prayer springs up in the soul and moves it, even in the absence of all form and doctrine clearly defined, there is true religion, living piety" (*Outlines of a Philosophy of Religion,* p. 28).
[86] B. B. 123a referring to Gen. XLVIII:22.

THE FUNCTION OF THE PRAYER BOOK
Israel Bettan
(1930)

I

Religious liberals of the day, to set at naught the disturbing implications of scientific theory, have been at great pains to dissociate spiritual values from material facts, to draw a definite line of demarcation between the realm of religion and the sphere of science. Religion, they tell us, deals with the inner realities of the spirit; science with the outer phenomena of the natural world. Religion lifts the veil of the visible and peers into the unfathomed mysteries of the Unseen; science explores the remotest regions of the known, the perceptible, and restrains its fancy from straying among things beyond its ken.

But no sooner have our liberals thoroughly persuaded themselves of the validity of their claims, the reasonableness of their position, than they proceed forthwith to confound the very fields they would fain keep separate. While eager, when assailed in open court, to refute the testimony of science as irrelevant and unauthoritative, they nonetheless seldom fail to invoke its aid in matters transcending its scope. With utter disregard of their public protestations, they demand unhesitatingly that the standards of measurement employed by science in the world of matter be applied with equal precision to the intangible realities in the world of human hope and aspiration.

In so far as the prevailing discontent with our prayer book springs from a dwindling faith in the efficacy of all prayer, or from a loss of the prayerful mood induced by the sudden intrusion of the methods of science into the domain of religion, no revision, however radical and thoroughgoing, can prove anything more than a palliative, superficial and fleeting. For no prayer can be so worded as to stir hearts unattuned to the spiritual breathings of the best in our liturgy. Souls that can no longer be quickened by the spirit of our worship, by the fullness and manifoldness of our devotion, are too dead to be revived by revised prayers. Those who have forsaken the God of Israel, the fountain of living waters, to worship at the shrine of mechanical force may well be forgiven if in their spiritual isolation they view the prayers of our fathers as broken cisterns that can hold no water. But not for them did the master-builders of the Synagog forge into permanent and symmetrical form the profoundest experiences and loftiest aspirations of the Jewish soul.

II

The function of a new institution or project can be described solely in terms of its future accomplishments; an ancestral creation like our prayer book, whose history is coeval with the history of Judaism itself, affords a more dependable basis for the determination of its function. Its aims are clearly written in its results, which still abide with us. What it has done is an earnest of what it will continue to do. Its design reflects its age-long purpose. Its development in the past bespeaks its destiny in the future.

The first thing that strikes our attention when we carefully examine the structure and content of our liturgy is the familiar fact, so rarely stressed, that our prayer book is not a book of prayers but a manual of divine worship. It comprises many prayers of adoration, of thanksgiving and petition, but it abounds likewise in vital religious instruction. Impressive recitals of the salient facts of our sacred history and solemn reiterations of the fundamental principles of our faith find their place, alongside of the purely devotional elements, in the service. The Shema, with its accompanying paragraphs, occupies as central a position in the liturgy as do the Eighteen Benedictions; and the reading from the Scroll, with the subsequent interpretation of the passage read, is as much a part of our worship as are the prayers and meditations. The oft-repeated witticism that the Jew prays philosophy owes its origin to an unconscious confusion in terms. Prayer, though an essential element of worship, forms but one of its component parts. Instruction in the Law, knowledge of the faith, complement prayer in the order of the service. Worship, Jewishly conceived, is the service of the heart, which is prayer (Taan. 2a) supplemented by the joy of the heart, which is Torah (Can. R. 3). The Jew does not pray philosophy; he worships his God in a prayerful spirit and in a philosophic temper. He worships with his mind as well as with his heart, intellectually as well as emotionally.

This function of the prayer book, to enlighten as well as to renew and sanctify, the molders of our liturgy controlled with admirable skill and foresight. It was a comparatively easy matter to define the attitude in which the worshipper should make known the needs of his soul. For the primary needs of man are more or less static and universal, varying only in the degree of their urgency at any given moment. We all want life and health, clearness of vision and strength of will, faith, courage, peace, happiness. It is quite otherwise with that attitude in which the soul reaches out for a larger truth. For truth is broad, many-sided, and ever-changing. Knowledge is subject to numerous classifications and widely-varying estimates. To determine the nature of the instruction that might best be crystallized in a manual of common worship called for sureness of insight and soundness of judgment. Above all, it called for the wise and careful formulation of some guiding principle by which the process of selection might be conducted with the utmost objectivity. And as we scan the non-intercessory parts of our daily ritual we cannot fail to discern the principle that must have governed the choice of material. For whether the lesson taught is theological, historical, or ethical in character, it is always the cardinal doctrine, the memorable event, the simplest of moral guidance, that claims the attention. There is nothing in these selections derived from Biblical or rabbinic sources, that attempts to do anything more than to confirm the people in a faith that is already theirs, to recall providential acts with which they have been familiar, to rehearse religious or moral precepts from which no believing, right-thinking Jew could well dissent. Take, for example, the passage dealing with the things the fruits of which a man enjoys in this world and whose stock is reserved for him in the world to come, in which are enumerated such rudimentary practices as honoring father and mother, dispensing charity, attending the house of study promptly and regularly, extending hospitality to wayfarers, visiting the sick, dowering the bride, attending the dead to the grave, exercising devotion in prayer, making peace between man and his fellow. Or, take the brief prelude to one of our most beautiful and moving liturgical utterances: "At all times, let a man fear God, secretly or openly; let him acknowledge the truth, and speak the truth in his heart; and let him rise early and say: Lord of all worlds!" and so forth. These, and others too numerous to mention, are all simple and well-known rules of conduct that require no special demonstration to win popular assent. It is quite evident that those who first organized the material of our services held to the view that it was not the function of a manual of common worship to inculcate new doctrines, to impart new truths and facts, or even to make novel applications of old truths. They must have felt, and felt rightly, that instruction of a more minute and complex nature, subtler analyses of the truth, broader and more far-reaching applications of fundamental principles, should come from the teachers and preachers in Israel. In short, the character of the selections made points to a definitely fixed policy, not to allow the prayer book to usurp the place of the pulpit in Synagogal worship.

It is because the Union Prayer Book, in some notable instances, has chosen to deviate from this earlier and saner method that the agitation for revision has assumed in our day such ludicrous expressions. There are not a few who, accustomed to the new style in ritual-building, would presume to advocate the speedy inclusion in our prayer book of the latest pronouncements of a theoretical philosophy, the shrewd surmises of a dubious criticism, the untested nostrums of an experimental sociology. They have learned to regard their ritual as a treatise, a tract, a pamphlet for wholesale propaganda. And, indeed, the Union Prayer Book, as it stands today, gives much comfort and encouragement to such a fantastic notion. What, for example, is the purport of that series of lessons, disguised as prayers, which center around the service of the High Priest in the Temple on the Day of Atonement? (U. P. B. pp. 242-255.) Is it not to impress upon the worshipper the truth, by no means generally accepted among Liberals, that "By Thy grace, O God, it has also been given us to see in our dispersion over the earth, not a means of punishment, but a sign of blessed privilege," and that "though we cherish and revere the place where stood the cradle of our people . . . our longings and aspirations reach out toward a higher goal"? Now, no one will deny us the right so to interpret our Judaism as to dispense with the hope of a renewed national autonomy. We need not be wedded to the vision of a restored Zion. We may well ignore it in our liturgy, and discourse from the pulpit on the reasonableness of our stand. But, surely, we are not ready to deny religious fellowship to those who join us in worship but still cling to a hope that was also their fathers'! When the early champions of Reform turned a negative attitude toward an issue of the day into a positive religious tenet, they may or may not have acted wisely, but when in their excessive zeal they chose to incorporate this dogma of denial in their ritual, they unquestionably helped to becloud the true function of instruction in a manual of worship.

And the same may be said of the sociological discourses which of late have made their sensational appearance in our ritual. The social note is no stranger in our Atonement worship. The creators of our liturgy evidenced deep concern for our shortcomings as members of the social group. When the Jew approached the throne of mercy, he was taught to catalog all his sins and failings, and to lay special emphasis on such malpractices as taking advantage of his neighbor in business transactions, exacting high rates of interest from him, breaking trust with him, deceiving him, wronging him, hating him, hardening his heart toward him. And he was also directed to say: "Thou hast taught us, O Lord our God, to make confession unto Thee of all our sins in order that we may cease from the violence of our hands." To be sure, those who originally fashioned our liturgy refrained from offering solutions to the problems that troubled the business world. In their sermons, our early preachers grappled with the question of economic inequality. Some of them seemed to think that the unequal distribution of wealth served a beneficent purpose (Pesikta, Buber, p. 191; Gen. R. ch. 75). And it may still be regarded as an open question. Nor are we all agreed that "whatever troubles us in the world of business and industry has issued from personal covetousness, arrogance and cold indifference to the welfare of others" (U.P.B., Vol. II, p. 316). At least one of these troubles, the displacement of man by the machine, which has greatly intensified the problem of unemployment, issues from a force that is neither covetous, nor arrogant, nor coldly indifferent to human welfare.

In our comprehensive idea of worship the expression of all those truths by which the religious emotions are sustained must naturally be included. But the liturgy should employ only essential and fundamental truths. It should exclude any interpretation of the truth that voices a mere private opinion and must depend for its acceptance on the further evidences of our reason. Liturgical instruction, unlike the instruction that goes forth from the pulpit, is not designed to demonstrate the truth, to settle difficult points in controversial questions, or to expound new solutions to old problems. It is solely designed to help us actualize the faith we have long espoused, to kindle in us the desire, the passion, to live true to the ideals we proclaim, to stir us to devise such plans of action as will carry into effect the religion we profess. Amid the tempestuous winds of new doctrine, amid the buffeting billows of drifting currents, we look to our liturgy to help us anchor our lives to the sure and everlasting foundations of our faith.

III

But while instruction forms an indispensable element in our worship, it is the emotional side of our nature, rather than the intellectual, that the prayer book, in the main, seeks to stimulate. For worship is essentially a mystical experience, the outreaching of the spirit for God, the overleaping of the boundary line between the world of sense and the world of vision. And the material barriers that interpose between the child and the Father, our rabbis tell us, can be leveled by prayer alone (Sota, 38b). When we pray, in the mood appropriate for such lofty exercise, that is, מתוך שמחה של מצוה (Ber. 31a), buoyed up by a sense of privilege, we find ourselves face to face with the Shekinah (Sanh. 22a), we are in close communion with the divine, or, better still, we are taking earnest counsel with our Maker (Ber. 29b). For God is passionately fond of our prayers (Yalkut, Psalms, 116), when they are not barren prayers, unfruitful of good deeds (Deut. R. 3), or mere routine prayers, devoid of Kawana (Ber. 31a). No prayer is acceptable unless, when we extend our hands in prayer, our very souls are in the palm of our hands (Taan. 8a). And what is the pith of our prayers? It is nothing else but this: "Do Thy will, O God, in heaven above and bestow tranquility of spirit on those who fear Thee below, and what is good in Thine own sight do" (Ber. 29b). It is because of this, its aspirational character, that prayer is regarded by our teachers not only as the profession of the fathers (Mekil. בשלח), but also as the natural mode of God's own expression. For does He not pray: "May it be my will that my mercy shall conquer my anger and my compassion prevail over my justice" (Ber. 7a)?

The term "aspiration," however, must not be too narrowly defined. It embraces, of course, all the higher needs of the soul, but it does not exclude the so-called physical or material wants essential to the complete unfoldment of the personality. The Jew who prayed: "Subdue our inclination so that it may submit itself unto Thee," also prayed: "Heal us, O Lord, and we shall be healed," and "Give dew and rain for a blessing upon the face of the earth."

And no amount of rationalization can successfully displace the firm trust, implicit in all our prayers, that God is near us in all our yearnings and strivings and is ever eager to answer the worthy petitions of our hearts.

But prayer, to reach the height of its possible effectiveness, should be offered at an acceptable time, that is, when the whole congregation engages in worship (Ber. 7a). The monition: "But thou, when thou prayest, enter into thy closet, and when thou hast shut thy door, pray to thy Father which is in secret" (Matthew 6:6), emanates neither from Jewish doctrine nor practice. To the contrary, our teachers insisted that where song is, there should also prayer be, in the Synagog (Ber. 6a). It is in the midst of a congregation at prayer that God's presence will ever be found (*ibid.*). To be sure, prayer is not exclusively restricted to the Synagog. One may pray in the field, in the privacy of his home, and even while reclining on his couch. Yea, he may even pray in the pure meditations of his heart. Yet, the Synagog alone is the true home of prayer (שו״ח ch. 2). God's name is best sanctified through public worship (Ber. 21b). God's anger is aroused when a Synagog fails to muster the necessary quorum for divine worship (*ibid.* 6a). Even when only two enter the Synagog to pray and the one proceeds to recite his prayers without waiting for the other to join him, טורפין לתפלתו , his prayers, as it were, are snatched from his grasp (*ibid.* 8a). There is a special potency in public prayer. God never spurns the prayers of the multitude (*ibid.* 8a). Therefore, a man in distress ought to make his condition known to others, that they may all join in prayer for his relief (Hulin, 78a). Even the feeble, faltering accents of the sinner's heart rise to great worth and favor when they mingle with the strains of a worshipping congregation. For what king will disdain his crown because some humble person helped furnish the purchase price (Lament. R. 3:3)? Every congregation worships as a unit; and it is out of the devout worship of individual Synagogs, blended into one diapason of devotion, that diadems of glory are fashioned for the Holy One, praised be He (Ex. R. 21).

Our prayer book is thus more than a manual of worship; it is a manual of public worship. It speaks to the hearts of all the assembled worshippers. It voices the beliefs, the hopes and aspirations of the entire congregation. It keeps in view the needs of the whole community. In a word, it is a manual designed for the corporate devotion of a compact group, unified in desire, in thought, in spirit. In such a prayer book, what more natural to expect than that only the general, the ordinary emotions of the group, only those emotions which the individual worshipper shares in common with the larger congregation, will find expression? It is for a book of private devotions to stress individual peculiarities and propensities. A public liturgy, the chief aim of which is to unite all worshippers in a service of prayer, should embrace only those special needs of the few that can easily be made the spontaneous sense of all, and only those emotional experiences of the many that can easily be made to flow into the channels of all individual hearts. We cannot make it comprehend the wants and yearnings of the soul in all its individual relations to God without destroying thereby its usefulness and potency as an instrument of public worship.

Viewed from this angle, and as far as this essential quality of a public ritual is concerned, the Union Prayer Book seems to meet adequately the present needs of our American congregations. None but a captious critic will insist on attributing to an instrument the flaws and weaknesses that inhere in the agent who wields it; and none but a hasty theorist will harbor the delusion that one's capacity for thought and feeling can be truly deepened by the frequent repetition of fixed formulas. It may well be that a richer vein of mysticism will improve the quality of our prayers, but not until our worshippers have been spiritually prepared for such a fresh accession of religious insight will the mystic note strike a sensitive chord in their heart. The cry for more mysticism, issuing from the pulpit, must first be answered by the pulpit. Surely, the prayer book cannot be expected to revive what, for these many decades, the ultra-rationalism of the pulpit has been so busily engaged in crushing out? Even when on occasion the worshipper feels impelled

to merge his identity with the adoring hosts of the universe, to join
the invisible choir of Isaiah's mystic vision, and proclaim mightily
the holiness of the Lord of hosts, he is chilled to numbness by the
frigid rationalist in the pulpit blaring forth the stunning assurance
that there is no heaven and that there are no heavenly hosts. And
when the bereaved worshippers, out of the anguish of their bruised
souls, rise to the perception that they are more than an aggregation
of men and women composing a particular group of local worshippers, that they are only a small fragment of a great worshipping
host, both living and dead, and that the latter, though no longer
visible members of the social circle, are still real elements of their
life and love and sorrow, they are forthwith informed by the sober
theologian that such notions are the stuff out of which perilous
superstitions are made. We seem to want more mysticism, but it
must be a mysticism that accords well with the latest approved
specifications of a thoroughgoing rationalism.

It may also be that the older ritual, with its strong sense of the
dramatic and symbolic, with its copious use of religious pageantry,
excels the Union Prayer Book in imaginative appeal and emotional
effectiveness. For nothing will so visualize a service of public worship as the free exercise of the representative faculty. Literalism,
the workshop of the critic, is the scaffold of the artist. And worship
is essentially an art, contemplative, poetic, expressive. It demands,
therefore, an elaborate technique, when groups instead of rare individuals share in its execution. But here, too, the hypercriticism
of the pulpit has blunted the poetic sensibilities of the people, and
one may well wonder if congregations trained to mount heavenward
on a monotonous tower of Babel will trust themselves to the fiery
chariot of Elijah, when piloted by men not quite sure of its magic
power. For, strange to say, the cry for more pageantry in our
worship issues from the same voices that deprecate whatever of an
imaginative and symbolic quality the Union Prayer Book may possess. Let the reader, for example, in a truly impressive bit of traditional pageantry, proclaim before the assembled worshippers while
he raises aloft the sacred Scroll, that the Torah which God gave

through Moses is the heritage of the congregation of Jacob, and the
dull literalist speedily demurs, because, forsooth, Moses was not the
sole author of Israel's Torah. That Moses, as already suggested by
the rabbis, in having preserved Israel, who was destined to perpetuate God's law in the world, thus virtually became the father and
savior of the Torah (Tanna debe Eliyahu, ch. 6), and that his
name, therefore, symbolizes for us the endless stream of divine
inspiration as it flows through the teachings of our prophets and
sages—all this counts for naught with the unimaginative. They
would revel in a pageantry that is prosaically true and of commonplace significance.

But there is another important phase of public worship, which
concerns the conduct rather than the content of the service. In
the usage of the Synagog, the primary function of the Reader was
to prompt the worshipping assembly in the offering of the fixed
prayers. He recited or chanted the opening and closing phrases
of a liturgical passage. He bore the designation of "master of
prayer," "messenger of the congregation," "overseer," but none of
these official titles carried with it the sense of substitution or the
power of communication. He could not pray in place of the congregation; he could not pray for the sole edification of the congregation;
he had to pray with the congregation. Even when, as in the case
of the Eighteen Benedictions, he recited sections of the daily devotions while the worshippers turned listeners, it was only after the
entire congregation, individually and collectively, had given devout
utterance to those very prayers. If the Reader was a "messenger
of the congregation," it was the congregation, not the messenger,
who dictated the message.

Our liturgy, therefore, designed as it is for public use, not only
addresses itself to the common, most fundamental needs of the
whole congregation, but it also requires the active participation
of every one of its members. Public worship, thus conceived, is
nothing but the worship of individuals, intensified by a sense of
contiguity and cooperation and ennobled by a spirit of sympathy
and glad surrender. The Union Prayer Book, in its eagerness

to occidentalize our worship, has all but abandoned this older concept and practice of the Synagog, and many of us justly feel that, in consequence, our services have been immeasurably weakened. For, surely, if there be some among those affiliated with the Synagog who yet protest that they find it difficult to enter into the spirit of our worship, it must be because the prayer book affords them scant opportunity to take active part in the service. The prayers and songs that should be the vehicle of their soul's expression, have been relegated to the Reader and the Choir, leaving them the rôle of interested spectators. Listening to, instead of joining in, the service, they soon weary of the sameness of the liturgy. Were they trained to use the prayer book, they would learn to love it, and the book we really love we never weary of. It becomes more precious the older it grows. We cannot, of course, nor would we if we could, retrace our steps back to the old Synagog. Sound as its theory of public worship may appear to us today, it is well to recall, for our own encouragement, that the practical application of the theory left much to be desired. The cure effected by early Reform may have given rise to a new malady, but the old disorder was real and grave enough. We still feel, as did the pioneers of Reform, that disorganized and undignified devotion cannot be indigenous to true piety. But while consolidating our gains, we can do much to minimize our losses. We can increase the number of collects and responses, or, better still, we can recast existing prayers so as to permit fuller participation of the entire congregation. We can strive, by using the best means at our disposal, to convert weary auditors into joyful participants, languid spectators into ardent worshippers. When our people have learned to use the prayer book, their emotions will again become intertwined with their prayers, and their affections will cluster once more around their liturgy.

IV

But our prayer book is more than a manual of public worship; it is a manual of Jewish public worship. It is designed exclusively

for the use of the devotees and custodians of Judaism, that ancient
faith whose doctrines we cherish and joyfully proclaim, and by
whose teachings we would fain live our lives. For worship is not
the result of a sudden, solitary impulse; it is the steady, comprehensive utterance of the entire personality, engaging all our powers
and interests and experiences. The multicolored strands of Jewish
life and thought are therefore woven into the very texture of our
ritual. When we assemble in the Synagog to pray, we are bidden
to pray as Jews, to voice the deepest needs of our souls in terms
of our common beliefs and hopes and experiences. In fact, it is
the function of the prayer book, among others, to strengthen in
us the consciousness that we are a separate and unique group;
that we are a religious people, held together by the ties of a
common history and faith and destiny; that we are the direct
descendants of the patriarchs, and the rightful heirs to the noble
legacy of prophet and psalmist. To be sure, it teaches us to pray
to the Master of all the worlds, the Creator of all men; but it
insists that the Lord of the universe is none other than the God
of the fathers, and the Father of all men is none other than the
Shepherd of Israel.

It is worthy of note, as evidence of the irreconcilable character
of the conflict in opinion among us, that while some find fault with
the Union Prayer Book because it deviates in too large a measure
from the older ritual to afford adequate stimulus to the Jewish
heart, others seem to object to it on the ground that it adheres
too closely to the ancient model, in its appeal to the God of the
fathers and the Redeemer of Israel, to satisfy the modern mind.
Thus, on the one hand, the plea for a more extensive use of
Hebrew in our worship is put forth by men who yearn for closer
union with the house of Israel. "The accents of the ancient and
hallowed tongue," we are reminded, "carry a stronger appeal to
many minds than the prosy vernacular. They more effectively
fill the emptiness of the heart with the consciousness of the divine
and more potently link the worshipper with the Kenesset Yisroel"
("Theology of Union Prayer-book," Samuel Cohon—*Conference*

Yearbook, Vol. 38, p. 252). One, of course, may wonder why prayers in English must be devoid of poetic thought and imaginative language, seeing that some excellent poetry has been written in this prosy vernacular. One, too, may hesitate to accept the implication that the prayers in "The Book of Common Prayer," or the prayers of a Beecher, a Rauschenbusch, a McComb, because couched in the vernacular and not in Hebrew, do not quite as "effectively fill the emptiness of the heart with the consciousness of the divine." But, then, there is the contention, which none will gainsay, that, as an instrument of worship in the Synagog, Hebrew will "more potently link the worshipper with the Kenesset Yisroel." On the other hand, we are urged, in the name of a broad cosmopolitanism, to loosen the chain that binds us to the larger community of Israel, to delete from the prayers of the Synagog such antiquated provincialisms as the "God of Israel" and the "Shield of Abraham," to stress the God of humanity rather than the God of the fathers (*ibid.,* p. 278–279; Vol. 39, p. 124). And we have on record the case of "five fairly representative rabbis" who, when invited to conduct a Jewish service in the presence of their non-Jewish colleagues, during a good-will conference, sought to conceal the JEWISH character of the service by withholding copies of the Union Prayer Book from general distribution, leaving it to the Reader, presumably, to improvise such changes in the phraseology of the prayers as would best comport with the delicate religious sensibilities of these ambassadors to the Hebrews (*ibid.,* Vol. 38, p. 283).

Confronted as we are by views so diametrically opposed, we can gain steadiness and certainty only when we contemplate the prayer book in the light of its historic rôle and achievements. For the liturgy of the Synagog, be it ever remembered, is not the product of our own wisdom or choice. We have not created it; we have inherited it from the past. The rituals used in the Synagog since the Gaonic period, whatever their differences in arrangement and phraseology, have all sprung from one liturgical type, to which in their essential features they have adhered with singular fidelity.

They represent, with all their numerous modifications, only slightly varied forms of one liturgy. And why have the leaders of the Synagog been so zealous in preserving this universal type? Is it not because of a deep-seated conviction on their part that unity on a liturgical basis must be achieved in Israel if Judaism is to survive? And, indeed, this has been the chief glory of our liturgy, that it has united the scattered congregations of Israel into one spiritual brotherhood. To be sure, it has ever been sufficiently flexible to accommodate itself to the varying changes and conditions of a steadily growing Synagog. Subjected, all through its history, to many formative influences, and molded by the vast and varied experiences of a people dispersed among the nations of the earth, it registers, naturally enough, every important change in our faith, in our outlook, in our hope. But, despite these changes and modifications, in the fundamentals of its worship it has remained so fixed that any Israelite, wherever his place of birth and whatever his medium of expression, can find in it the epitome of his past, the exponent of his faith, and thus feel himself at one with his people in all lands and in all ages. And we cannot tamper with the main elements of our liturgy without weakening this common bond of Jewish union, without impairing this most vital function of our great liturgic heritage.

Those, on the other hand, who advocate the restoration of the older text in the original tongue, as a means of re-enforcing Jewish unity, seem to take no cognizance of the new temper of the age and the changed mood of the modern worshipper. In days past, when the Jew lived under the complete domination of rabbinic law, when the sense of life as an obligation was thus deeply embedded in his consciousness, it was sheer devotion to duty that impelled him to repair to the Synagog for divine worship. His religion, he knew, definitely demanded that he recite the set prayers of his ritual at stated intervals, and what reason or plea, other than the one specified in the Law, could release him from the imperious obligation? Kindled by such intense loyalty to duty, his heart glowed with a religious fervor the sense of the prayers could scarcely impart and the baffling idiom little diminish. But today, with our changed outlook, when the sense of life as an opportunity is widely encouraged, when religious obligations, to win obedience, must first be accepted as privileges, what greater deterrent to voluntary devotion than an obscure vehicle could we possibly devise? If the liturgy of the Synagog is to be wedded once again to the ancient tongue of our sacred literature, not the prayer book, but the religious school, will have to consummate the union. When our people have cultivated familiarity with the language of the Psalmists, the prayer book, even the Union Prayer Book, will gladly teach them to pray as the Psalmists, in Hebrew. In the meantime the number of Hebrew prayers in the existing manual, which in few, if in any, of the congregations of the country are fully utilized, should prove quite adequate for the proposed experimentation in artificial stimulation.

V

The Union Prayer Book, a product of human effort, could not but be strengthened by judicious revision. And if by thoroughgoing we mean without compromise of principle, we shall pursue the contemplated task with equal deference to the principles that must guide us in the making of a fit manual of Jewish public worship. Eager as we are to foster a spirit of genuine Jewish piety in the hearts of our people, we will employ the aids the past has tested and sanctified, rather than engage in the endless experiments of a novelty-craving age. True piety, we know, thrives on thought and principle and not on whims and thrills. Our prayer book, like all fixed rituals, possesses the inevitable quality of sameness, but it is neither flat nor old-fashioned. Multitudes of our people who habitually draw comfort and strength from its pages still find it quite spirited and satisfying. To volatile minds, bitten with the fever of variety, any ritual, even one prepared for pseudo-scientists by tired theologians, will sooner or later grow tame, monotonous, antiquated. Our worship, composed of prayer and instruction, depends for its permanency and effectiveness on the harmonious blending of two disparate elements, sameness and variety. If the prayers provide the one, let the sermon supply the other. Unless we resolve to recede from our traditional position and embrace the view that free prayer, and not a fixed liturgy, makes for effective and satisfying public worship, we cannot escape the dilemma induced by our love of excitement. We shall have to rest content with the unavoidable sameness of our time-honored liturgy, comforted by the assurance that the old will endure and continue to bless when the glamour of the new has long ceased to lure and proffer delight.

ON LAW AND AUTHORITY

The Authority to Reform

Even if we grant, as a theoretical proposition, that a reform of Judaism is necessary and desirable to maintain its relevance to the needs of people living under modern, Western conditions, the question can legitimately be raised whether there is any individual or body of individuals who have the authority to design the reform and thereby to restructure Judaism. In Germany in the 1840s, and again in the United States in the early twentieth century, Reform leaders had argued that such an authority was traditionally vested in a Synod. Some then concluded that it would be desirable to call together such a Synod; others argued, more realistically, that rabbinical conferences such as those at which the question was being debated were, in fact, a modern equivalent of a Synod. Neither party was able to record a significant victory. No Synod was established, and the Central Conference of American Rabbis never claimed for its decisions more than advisory status.

Dr. Ellis Rivkin, at a time in 1951 when the question of authority was revived, effectively cut through all the earlier arguments by demonstrating that there was never any one authorized form of authority in Judaism. At different times and under differing historical and cultural conditions, various types of authority held sway. Some of these authorities were established by powers completely outside of the Jewish community; others reflect the need felt by the Jews themselves for the governance of their internal affairs. Moreover, he showed that these many authorities and forms of authority were not absolute. They underwent many forms of opposition and challenge, so that Jewish life, to the view of the sophisticated historian, appears far less monolithic, far more pluralistic, than the received account admits.

Rivkin's conclusion suggests that the only authority tolerable in the modern Jewish world is one based upon the principle of voluntarism. Leadership must be expressed in the form of persuasive guidance rather than coercive direction. The soundness of the guidance will carry its own inner and spiritual sanction. "A delicate sensitivity to the changing problems of our day is the only real assurance that our message will be heard."

303

SOME HISTORICAL ASPECTS OF AUTHORITY IN JUDAISM
Ellis Rivkin
(1951)

I

This paper is a study of some historical aspects of authority in Judaism. I am not concerned with the normative, legal, juridical, and theoretical arguments that have been, and are being, advanced, in dealing with the question of authority in Judaism. Such aspects of authority must and should be dealt with by those in whose domain these problems fall. As an historian, I am interested in considering with you the effects of historical forces upon the forms that authority in Judaism has taken in the past. What were the historical conditions that now favored one form of authority, now another? Why did the forms of authority change? What were the practical consequences in real life of differing concepts of authority in Judaism? What, in a word, did authority mean in the context of historical development, and what, in a practical sense, does it mean for us today?

In seeking to answer these questions, a very sharp distinction must be drawn at the outset, between social structures in ancient and medieval times, and those which are characteristic of the modern world. One cannot speak meaningfully of authority in Judaism if one uses the term indiscriminately to apply, in the same sense, to both the world of our forefathers, and that of our own day. The realm in which the question of authority is vital in Judaism today is a restricted one in contrast to the all-embracing character of authority in Judaism in ancient and medieval times. In those epochs, Jews were faced with the problems of organizing and regulating highly complex social structures; and they were perforce involved directly in dealing with matters that in our day are the concern of the state or are the private concern of the individual. This involvement could not be avoided, for in ancient and medieval times Jewish society was self-governing, and self-regulating, and consequently there was no choice but to assume the responsibilities of governing, commanding, compelling in all matters affecting Jews. This all-encompassing character of medieval and ancient Jewish authority stemmed from the very texture of society itself. All law was bound up with religious sanctions and concepts; hence professing Jews, once tolerated, could not be made subject to Pagan, Moslem, or Christian law. Pagan emperors, Moslem caliphs, and Christian princes—all granted to the Jews virtually complete autonomy in their internal affairs, which included not only religious matters, but also those which, in our day, would be termed secular.

In a world, then, which looked upon all relationships as aspects of religion and which assumed that all systems of law were underwritten by divine command, it is not surprising that Jews too shared these views and insisted that all relationships were to be regulated by law which ultimately went back to God himself. Problems involving inheritance were of no less religious significance than the laying of *Tefillin* or the proper order of prayer. Authority, therefore, was a crucial matter since it involved the regulation of individuals, groups, and classes, and since it reached into every nook and cranny of Jewish society. It was not something that could be dodged or avoided; for it was functional, vital, and inescapable.

The multiplicity of forms which authority took in ancient and medieval Jewish history can largely be accounted for by the fact that authority in Jewish life was all-inclusive and was by no means confined to the strictly religious sphere. Every clash of interest in

Jewish society was bound to find expression in conflicting views over the question of authority. Thus, all struggles, no matter how secular in nature, involved religious ideologies, for all aspects of life were regulated by religiously sanctioned law.

The problem of authority in these epochs was most crucial when profound historical changes so altered the structure of society that large numbers of Jews challenged the very structure of authority then prevailing. For them, these institutions represented either obstacles in the way of their own needs and interests, or else the incarnation of those forces which were responsible for their own misery and degradation. Only the removal of the existing expressions of authority, and their replacement by other institutions more in keeping with the needs and aspirations of these groups, would satisfy them. They therefore counterposed new concepts of authority to the old.

Such a challenge is clearly seen in the Hellenist movement against the Theocracy which was based on the authority of the Pentateuch. The simple, agricultural life of the restored Judea was rudely transformed by the urbanization process which followed in the wake of Alexander's victories. Expanded trade and commerce created a new wealthy class among the Jews who saw in the Pentateuch an obstacle to their ambitions to become full-fledged Hellenistic citizens and they therefore were not only willing, but insisted upon the suppression of the Pentateuch and its institutions. A system of authority which ran counter to the need and interests of certain elements in the population was thus opposed.

The expansion of the Moslem world was accompanied by vast changes in the lives of the people who were brought under its sway. These tumultuous events were productive of radical changes in both the Gentile and Jewish worlds. New structures were imposed upon the population. The Jews in the Moslem world were ruled by the exilarchs and the *geonim* who derived their authority from the caliphs and from the Talmud. In addition to supervising religious life, the exilarchs and the *geonim* collected taxes, appointed judges, and decided cases affecting every phase of human life.

Many Jews resented the authority of the Exilarchate and the Gaonate: they chafed under the heavy taxes; they disliked the close ties between the exilarchs, *geonim,* and the caliphate; they opposed the abandonment of messianic hopes; they disapproved of the luxurious living of these dignitaries; they complained of having no voice in the governing bodies; they took exception to the oligarchic structure.

Finding their needs, interests, and aspirations thwarted by the existing structure of authority, these elements flocked to the banner of Anan ben David and organized the Karaitic movement. Since the institutions which they opposed were based on the Talmud, the Karaites turned to the Bible as the source of authority and denounced the authority of the exilarchs and *geonim* as a subversion of the meaning and import of biblical writ. Divine biblical law was counterposed to divine rabbinic law.

That the Karaitic movement was basically an attempt to undermine the entire structure of rabbinic authority is indicated by the fact that it was not a return to the Bible pure and simple. Karaism in practice was as far removed from the literal commands of the Pentateuch as talmudic legislation. The return to the Bible was necessary, so as to have a divine sanction for breaking with that which they opposed. The austerity, the longing for Zion, the asceticism, the rejection of offices and titles, the strict laws of consanguinity—all testify to the fact that Karaism was appealing to the needs, interests, and aspirations of those Jews in the Moslem world who were dissatisfied with the way the implementation of rabbinic authority affected them.

This appeal of Karaism cannot be minimized, for it did attract thousands of Jews, despite the fact that it involved, not less, but more restriction in the religious realm and offered only harsh persecution in the secular. The movement and the enthusiasm that it evoked can thus be understood only as the expression of basic conflicts which could not be resolved within the existing pattern of authority.

Another illuminating example of a challenge to the entire structure of authority is to be seen in the rise of Hassidism in the sixteenth century. Vast changes had transformed Eastern Europe from the haven of refuge that it had once been to an area of persecution, and the once flourishing center of learning had undergone serious decline. The seventeenth century witnessed the agonizing collapse of Poland and, along with it, the even more agonizing collapse of the very foundations which had made for a rich and creative spiritual life among the Jews. The *Kahal* structure became more and more oligarchic, and its control became more and more centered in the hands of small cliques which usurped for themselves all authority. Even rabbis were chosen not so much for their learning as for their family connections and the decline in the integrity of the rabbinate became scandalous.

This sad state of affairs was accompanied by the growing poverty of the masses of people not only in the material sense, but in the spiritual sense as well. This disastrous situation made for disillusionment, pessimism, and despair; and once again messianic dreams were the substitute for coming to grips, or at least, coming to understand, the forces which were responsible for the degradation. Betrayed in these dreams by Sabbatai Zevi, many Jews were so sunk in despair that they abandoned themselves to such bizarre sects as the Frankists. For most Jews, however, such a solution was impossible, even though the causes for their unhappiness were as much in evidence as before.

The structure of authority as it existed at this time in Poland not only made no effort to cope with this deterioration but even contributed to its continuance. Nevertheless, authority was vested in the *Kahal* system, and this authority was recognized and protected by whatever powers happened to be ruling in Poland. Furthermore, this authority was given religious sanction and was underwritten by rabbinical law. Any attempt to question the legitimacy of this structure was denounced as heretical.

The Hassidic movement, which arose in response to the spiritual needs and yearnings of the masses of people who daily experienced despair, and who had little hope that their situation would change, was thus basically a challenge to the existing *Kahal* structure and an attack against its concepts of legitimate authority. Implicit in its early teachings was the rejection of the concept that learning alone was deserving of special privilege in both this world and the world to come. God as the loving father who cared for the poor and ignorant, but pious, soul was emphasized. The rich and the arrogant, though learned, rulers of the *Kahal* were contrasted to the kindly, saintly, warmhearted *Zaddik,* who felt and commiserated with the poor victims of the cruel age.

In place of the *Kahal* structure of authority, the Hassidim established the absolute rule of the *Zaddik.* Secular and religious authority within the Hassidic communities were concentrated in his hands and the power and influence of the older families were eliminated. An effective change was introduced and new concepts of authority replaced the old.

Thus in the rise of Hassidism is seen the crystallization of those forces in Jewish society which sought new forms of authority because the old forms were found to be burdensome, restrictive, and oppressive. Precisely because Hassidism undermined the very basis of the existing structure within the Jewish world was it opposed so bitterly. Every effort was made to crush the movement. Its followers were banned as heretics, intermarriages between *mitnagdim* and *hassidim* were forbidden, Hassidic adherents were even deprived of their homes and property, and the government itself was called in to help in its suppression. Such burning hatred is conceivable only when a life and death struggle between opposing systems is involved. The concept of authority of Rabbinism was incompatible with the concept of authority of Hassidism, because the needs and interests of diverse groups could not be resolved within the existing structure.

One set of forces making for decline and decay had set off a series of struggles over authority in Eastern Europe; another set of forces which were creating the modern world was at the very same time undermining the entire medieval structure of authority in Judaism. First in Western Europe, then gradually in Central

Europe, new ideas and concepts were capturing the imagination of men. Science, rationalism, freedom of thought, representative government were the intellectual weapons that were being used to overthrow the basic ideas and concepts of the Middle Ages.

Not the least significant of these new ideas was that which insisted on the separation between Church and State and which sought to eliminate all autonomous structures. The right of a man to choose his religious affiliations was a revolutionary doctrine which gained ever more currency in the eighteenth and nineteenth centuries.

Jews were no less affected by these new changes than their Gentile neighbors, and attempts were made as early as the seventeenth century to apply such ideas in the Jewish world. In doing so however, the fundamental presuppositions of authority current within Jewish communities, such as Italy and Holland, were brought under attack. Uriel da Costa and others lashed out against rabbinical law, asserting that it had been created so as to give rabbis authority to rule the people for their own selfish ends. Da Costa called first for a return to the Bible as the only genuine divine authority, and later he claimed that the only revelation of God is to be found in Nature and in man's reason.

The first glimmerings of new concepts were opposed by the leaders of the Jewish communities and every attempt was made to suppress such heretical thoughts. Clearly these ideas, if accepted, would eliminate completely the entire communal structure. Indeed, wherever the banner of reason was raised, it met with intolerant opposition. Mendelssohn's scrupulous adherence to rabbinical law did not permit him to escape the heretic's label, nor did it protect his works from the attacks of the Orthodox. The mild rationalism of a Rappaport and of a Krochmal met with a storm of protest from the Hassidim of Galicia who saw in such thinking the overthrow of their whole structure of authority. The history of the Haskalah and Reform movement is really nothing more than that of a clash between incompatible concepts of authority, and for this reason the struggle was so acrimonious and so long-lived. Once more profound changes in society affected some groups among Jews in such a way as to make them impatient of prevailing structures of authority which hampered their development. The transition from medieval to modern concepts of authority in religion was a slow and painful one.

II

The ancient and medieval worlds witnessed not only such major conflicts over authority in Judaism as described above, but also differences in the structure of authority which stemmed from the widespread character of the Diaspora and from the contacts with diverse civilizations. These differences were no less real than those which tore communities asunder, but since these communities were usually composed of Jews who were geographically separated from their fellow-Jews, and since in the main they accepted the same religious sources of authority, the Written and the Oral Laws, head-on collisions were generally avoided.

The extent, however, to which geographical dispersion and contact with different civilizations affected the structure of authority was considerable. Although both Palestinian and Babylonian Jews accepted the Mishnah as legally binding, the Mishnah itself came to be understood quite differently in these two countries. Professor Louis Ginzberg, in his monumental commentary on the Palestinian Talmud, points to any number of important differences in the interpretation of and the development of the Halakah, which stem from the contrasting environments of Palestine and Babylonia. In the doctrinal realm too, there was much that divided the two regions, and it is therefore not surprising that the Babylonian and Palestinian Talmuds reflect these differences. Indeed, the struggle of the *geonim* against the authority of the Palestinian Talmud proves conclusively, if such proof were even necessary, that mere agreement on the sanctity of the Oral and Written Laws did not assure unanimity in interpretation.

Friction of this sort involving the claims to ultimate authority between Babylonia and Palestine has had a long history. The attempts of Babylonian Jewry to gain control of calendation were defeated in the second century because the Palestinian authorities were still exerting too much influence to permit the usurpation of their prerogatives. The decline of Palestinian hegemony, however, soon brought with it the loss of control over the calendar which was tantamount to the loss of authority over the vast majority of Jews. Ben Meir's attempt to regain this authority for Palestine in the tenth century, was met with a storm of opposition and the threat to Babylonian authority implicit in his action was so great that, for a moment at least, the *geonim* and exilarchs composed their differences.

The relationship of geographical dispersion to problems of authority is vividly illustrated by the decline of the power of the *geonim* over the Jews throughout the Moslem world. The close alliance between the Jews of Spain and the Ummayad house led to a break with the Babylonian leadership at the very moment when Abdul al-Rahman III declared himself independent, even in religious matters, of the Abassid Caliph. Authority in Spain was now concentrated in the hands of a court favorite, Hasdai ibn Shaprut, who appointed not only the judges throughout the Cordovan caliphate, but also the head of the academy. The structure of authority in Spain was therefore quite different from that which prevailed in Babylonia. In the latter country the exilarch claimed to be of Davidic descent, and exercised full control over the areas allotted to his rule. The *geonim* of Sura and Pumbeditha also exercised similar centralized authority in the territories under their control. Both the Exilarchate and the Geonate derived revenues from the people.

In Spain, on the other hand, Hasdai did not claim Davidic descent; he received no emoluments from the people; he was responsible to the Caliph alone; he kept the academies under his control. This pattern was duplicated in the ensuing period of the emirates. In each territory, such as Granada and Saragossa, a Jewish court favorite was invested with authority by the ruler and he was responsible for directing all aspects of Jewish life within the territory. An especially noteworthy characteristic of the structure of authority in Moslem Spain was the subordinate role played by the scholars.

The structure of Jewish authority in Christian France and Germany of this period stands in sharp contrast to that of Babylonia and of Spain. Feudal decentralization precluded the centralized type of authority that existed in Spain and Babylonia. Each community came to be quite independent of every other, and carefully guarded its sovereignty. Since there was no effective centralized state apparatus, the grant of authority to a single Jew was quite out of the question. From time to time synods would be convoked to deal with problems affecting all the communities, but these synods represented independent communities and their enactments were limited to those measures which secured general approval. Leadership within the communities arose from the communities themselves and was not imposed from without; and from an early date, the rabbis enjoyed many prerogatives and privileges and had an important voice in the councils of the communities.

Such differences in structure—reflecting as they did the contrasting cultural milieus—naturally involved contrasting attitudes with respect to authority. As long as geographical separation kept these disparate groups from merging, the differences were academic. When, however, as a consequence of emigrations, Jews from different areas—with different concepts of Judaism and authority—came together, sharp and often extremely bitter conflicts arose. The Maimunist-anti-Maimunist controversies, with their bans and counter-bans, with their resort to physical violence, with the burning of books, with their denunciation of heresy, are surely to be explained, in part, at least, by the fact that Jews tutored in very different cultural climes had difficulty in peacefully compromising on issues of authority which they considered so vital.

Examples of this sort, although less vivid, are sprinkled throughout the pages of Jewish history. Italo-German and Spanish Jews were at odds in Italy; German and Polish Jews had their troubles with Iberian Jews in Holland; Spanish and native Jews clashed in

Salonica—indeed, wherever one turns, the fruit of dispersion was controversy.

III

Still one other historical aspect of authority in Jewish history remains to be considered, namely that of differences with respect to authority which manifested themselves within the self-same structures. Here the fundamental principles are not in question, but only their implementation. The problem is a jurisdictional one which concerns itself with the division of authority and not its validity.

Examples of such jurisdictional disputes fill the pages of Jewish history. Both the exilarchs and the *geonim* accepted the Talmud as the basic source of authority and both fought the Karaite schism tenaciously. Yet the struggles between the *geonim* and exilarchs for supreme authority were characteristic phenomena of this period. And not only did exilarchs and *geonim* clash, but the *geonim* themselves were constantly at odds with one another, each insisting that his academy be recognized as supreme.

Differences such as these are met with wherever we turn in Jewish history. Maimonides was an ardent supporter of the rights of the exilarchs to supreme authority in the Diaspora, and he insisted that the exilarch must be obeyed whether his decrees were pleasing or not. Indeed, Maimonides was most active in aiding the exilarch against the claims of Samuel ben Ali of Baghdad who asserted that the religious spokesman is to have the final say on all matters touching on authority. In Venice, the rabbis at the turn of the seventeenth century fought long and hard to maintain their former prerogatives and privileges against the encroachments of lay control. The Oral Law was not in question, but merely its proper implementation; yet so severe was the struggle that the rabbis, at one point, banded together and swore to act in unison against the claims of the laity.

Of some interest too is the sixteenth century attempt to restore the process of ordination. Jacob Berab's assertion of authority for himself and the scholars of Safed, met with the heated opposition of Levi ibn Habib in Jerusalem, not only on legal grounds, but also because it would subordinate Jerusalem to Safed. Both Berab and Ibn Habib turn to the same sources for their arguments, yet they disagree sharply over the issues.

Struggles, such as these, involving the implementation of authority, should occasion no surprise. As long as Jewish law regulated the lives of Jews in all their activities, conflicts between disparate interests were inevitable and differing interpretations of authority were bound to emerge. A glance at the Responsa literature should convince even the most skeptical student, of the complex economic, social, and political problems that the rabbis grappled with; they could no more be unanimous in their opinions than our own justices of the Supreme Court.

One final point must be made before concluding this analysis of authority in ancient and medieval times. Authority, once officially recognized, could appeal to force and compulsion to maintain its position. This could not be otherwise as long as religiously sanctioned law regulated relationships between individuals, groups and classes with diverse and often conflicting interests. Force and the threat of punishment had to be resorted to in order to make certain that the law was effectively obeyed. The whole problem of religious authority thus became so enmeshed in the social complexities of the day that frequently the religious message was lost in the constant bickerings between contending interests. The ability to use compulsion inevitably led to forceful repression of all those who questioned authority, no matter how justified their complaints.

IV

The vast changes that have transformed the medieval into the modern world necessitate an entirely different approach to the practical aspects of authority in Judaism. The separation of church and state, the recognition of the dignity of the individual, representative forms of government, freedom of speech and thought, have been achieved with too much hardship and sacrifice, and are too threatened by totalitarian systems today, that we should long for those aspects of authority in Judaism which served the Jews in a qualitatively different world. Every individual, and every group must be free to choose his religious or irreligious affiliations. Liberal Judaism's interpretation of authority cannot involve the imposition, by compulsion, upon others of its doctrines and its beliefs. Surely, Reform rabbis are not interested in having religious institutions regulate such matters as business competition, prices, rents, and wages—matters which in the past were as much the function of religious leaders and of religious authority as the ordering of the prayers or the regulation of ritual. No Reform Jewish leader is interested in having the state burn the writings of Jewish heretics, nor are they desirous of compelling Orthodox or Conservative Jews to install organs in their synagogs, or to abolish the *tallit*. When we speak of authority in Judaism, we do not think of physical sanctions and compulsion. Our concern is not with forcing Jews to go our way, but to give enlightened guidance to those who have accepted our leadership. We can establish norms, we can give direction, we can urge, persuade and dissuade, but we cannot compel.

Indeed, in view of the strength of ecclesiastical parties in Israel today, and the possibility of their utilization of the state apparatus to force other Jews to bend to their conception of authority in Judaism, Reform must, more strongly than ever, break with those aspects of authority in Judaism which belong to the ancient and medieval worlds, and must insist on the right of all religiously-minded Jews to choose whatever brand of Judaism is in keeping with their spiritual needs.

Ultimately, history has shown, the test of a system of religion is its ability to evoke voluntary loyalty and sacrifice on the part of its adherents. The generation of enthusiasm is never attained by force or compulsion. The various movements in Jewish history, such as Pharisaism, Hassidism, Reform, even Karaism, won adherents by virtue of their program, their message, their dynamic answers to the problems besetting the Jews of their time. Only when the original élan was lost did compulsion take the place of persuasion. Surely, if the changing needs and interests of the Jews in the past were responsible, time and time again, for revolts against authority, armed though the latter was with very real power, we today stand very little chance of legislating for those who are to follow. Plastic, supple, intelligent guidance is the only approach that gives promise of long life. The very fact that we are unable to compel and coerce must impress upon us the need to persuade, to convince, and to frame such programs that will serve the spiritual needs of our people. A delicate sensitivity to the changing problems of our day is the only real assurance that our message will be heard and that our leadership and guidance will be sound.

Toward a Reform Interpretation of Halacha

Judaism, throughout its history, formulated the requirements for its adherents in terms of codes of practice that incorporated ritual, ceremonial, and moral law, and at times civil, criminal and family law into an organized code, often referred to as *Halacha* (literally, "the way," and therefore equivalent to the Chinese conception of *tao* or the Indic *dharma*). *Halacha* should be considered as a divine law rather than a canon law. Though admittedly set forth by human agency, its content was considered as derived by established principles of inference from the original Sinaitic revelation. Even its novelties were pronounced to be *Torah* given to Moses on Sinai.

Early Reform Judaism, in its need for a free hand in the re-shaping of an old religion to the conditions of modern life, sweepingly dismissed the entire traditional *Halacha* and the apparatus of rabbinic authority that supported it. By the mid 1920s, however, there are clear indications that many of the American Reform rabbis thought that their predecessors had gone too far. They (and, we may presume, their congregants) sought for a way to reestablish an organic relationship with the past without yielding in their philosophical rejection of the principle of continuity on which the thought of the past was formulated. Their problem was the universal problem of modernization: to make room for innovation without cutting oneself completely adrift from tradition. It was complicated further by the strongly marked trend in American Jewry to the decentralization of authority.

Solomon B. Freehof, in 1946, presented a case for the creative reconstruction of *Halacha* in the Reform movement, crystallized out of the actual practices of Reform Jews and codified, but not petrified. His emphasis was placed upon the establishment of legal norms for religious practice and for morality. More than ten years later, Alexander Guttmann argued that although moral law had often been the concern of Jewish leaders, it could not be considered as *Halacha,* because moral laws are universal, while *Halacha* is particularistic, referring to specifically Jewish laws and practices. His rather conservative recommendation was for a careful reconsideration of historic practices and their reintroduction by Reform Jews whenever possible, combined with a very cautious development of novelties, to be accepted only after long study.

These two papers suggest that, at least on the theoretical level, the question of the development of a Reform *Halacha* has not yet been resolved within the rabbinical leadership of the Reform movement.

REFORM JUDAISM AND THE HALACHA
Solomon B. Freehof
(1946)

The early history of Christianity was a story of chaos. Rival literatures struggled for authenticity. Warring sects and doctrines fought for dominance in the widespread and still shapeless Christian community. There was an urgent need for authority and order. This was achieved when the right to speak for the Christian community was gradually restricted to certain selected individuals who were granted special grace by virtue of their ordination. Bishops were ordained by older bishops whose own right to ordain came down from their teachers, and thus ultimately from the twelve apostles and Paul. This was the historic Christian principle of apostolic succession. Those who were in this unbroken chain of tradition were possessed "of special divine grace enabling them to transmit and interpret without error the teachings of the apostles committed to them." The Greek church and the Roman church both claim this "special divine grace" of unbroken apostolic succession. To them and their adherents this means that not only were the teachings of their church authentic but that the church itself was more than merely human but was an institution ordained by God.

The confidence and assurance which the doctrine of apostolic succession has given to the two ancient Christian churches has created in certain Protestant quarters, especially among High-Church Anglicans, a sense of inferiority, a fear that the Protestant church is not, strictly speaking, a divine institution. That is why certain branches of the Anglican church seek fellowship with the Greek Catholic church so that, without needing to go to Rome, they can obtain the authenticity for their ordinations and their sacraments by an unbroken tradition of apostolic succession back to the founders of Christianity.

The doctrine of apostolic succession with its transmission of a divine grace is, of course, of Jewish origin. The Semicha, the laying on of hand on Joshua by Moses and by Joshua on the elders, involved the transmission of the *spirit* of Moses to Joshua and through Joshua to those whom he ordained. (Numbers 27:23; Deuteronomy 34:9: "And Joshua the son of Nun was filled with the spirit of wisdom for Moses had laid his hands upon him.") This ordination by the laying on of hands and the concomitant transmission of a special spirit of wisdom continued in Judaism to the close of the Judean academies in the fourth century of the present era. The attempt to revive it by the Spanish immigrants to Palestine in the sixteenth century failed. It was never successfully restored.

Although the concept of what the Christians came to call apostolic succession ceased in Jewry fifteen centuries ago, something analogous to it has remained in Jewish life. If there is no longer a succession of men of special grace appointed by the laying on of hands, there is a succession of special books claimed to be of divine origin. The written and the oral law, together with the implications found in them by later teachers, is considered to be of an unbroken tradition and authenticity going back to the revelation of Mt. Sinai. In the words of the Talmud (J. Peah 17a) everything which a conscientious disciple will teach is as if it were given by Moses on Mt. Sinai. Thus Christianity claims a divinely appointed succession of bishops still existent, and Orthodox Judaism claims a divinely given law still authentic in all its present amplifications.

Thus, Orthodoxy has the same imposing advantage in Judaism as the Greek and the Roman churches have in Christianity. The

Orthodox legal system was considered to be more than a mere human achievement based upon secular decisions by conventions or parliaments. It was divinely ordained and has been transmitted through ordination and with authentic interpretation by all the generations. How then could any one generation presume to declare that God's law is no longer binding upon it? We can easily see how, in the eyes of Orthodoxy, Reform Judaism was simply illegal, a wilful rebellion. A Protestant church may ask, have we apostolic succession; is our church divine? Reform Judaism may well ask, is our practice justified by the God-given Jewish law; is our practice legal?

Reform Judaism cannot long refrain from adjusting itself to the fact that the Orthodox wing of Judaism claims a unique authenticity, a divine ordained legality which Reform Judaism is said to lack. Judaism is a religion which was formed by law and has lived by law. It is clear that Reform Judaism must come to an understanding with the law or at least must define clearly its own relationship to it.

With regard to this problem the early reformers were men of surpassing courage. They were confronted with a Jewish rabbinical tradition whose religious authority had never yet been successfully shaken. They had the fortitude to say: we disavow the right of the older rabbis to control our religious life. We ignore their excommunications. We scorn their bans. We will develop Judaism according to the spirit and needs of the age. They were violent combatants. How else could one hope to resist a hitherto unquestioned authority? Only revolutionists could overthrow an ancient regime. They were, of course, right; but by now, a century later, the mood of Reform on this matter has changed.

We have a different attitude towards Orthodoxy than they did. Our greater friendliness towards Orthodoxy has been misunderstood in some quarters. It is not that we undervalue the rights and the liberties won for us by the early reformers, but that we are confronted with an Orthodoxy which is different from theirs. Their Orthodoxy was all-powerful. It had absolute Jewish authority and was frequently supported by state authority. The reformers had to fight for freedom of conscience against dominant rabbinical authority. We no longer have such a battle, first because the rights which they, the pioneers, have won for us have been largely accepted as a fact in Jewish life in the Western world; and secondly, because the authority of Orthodoxy itself has faded. There is no powerful Orthodoxy anywhere in the world whose rabbinical decisions have any widespread force. Its courts exert almost no authority and excommunications by Orthodox rabbis seem curious relics of a vanished age. We are safe from any Orthodox dominance. We can now safely restudy Orthodoxy and see whether in its doctrines there may not be some strength that can be borrowed for Reform Judaism. It is not that we are penitents as some would believe; it is simply that our revolution is now well established and we can afford to be generous, tolerant and friendly.

Besides the negative fact that Orthodoxy is no longer dangerous to our liberty, we have a positive reason for restudying our relationships to traditional Jewish law. There is a growing interest amongst us for greater uniformity in practice and observance in our Reform movement. How long shall each congregation or each rabbi determine what shall be Reform practice with regard to marriage or burial or ritual observances? Must we not revive the concept of *Mitzva,* of *Torah,* and thus attain orderliness and consistency and authority in our Reform Jewish life? All these considerations make it pertinent in our day to restudy the relationship of Reform Judaism to the Halacha.

We cannot discuss Halacha, or Torah, or Mitzva, without evaluating the environment in which these concepts flourished. These words are essential in the Orthodox religio-legal system. If we restudy them we must reappraise the Orthodoxy of which they are an inherent part. All must acknowledge that traditional Judaism has, in the past, been tremendously successful. It developed a theory of Jewish law whereby the life of the individual in almost all its phases was conscious of the will of God. This system successfully maintained Jewish life through many dangerous centuries. In times when travel and intercommunication were immensely difficult and Jews lived in tiny, scattered communities all over the world, traditional Judaism kept Israel a united world body strongly conscious of its group personality and creative in its intellectual and spiritual life. Traditional Judaism was an immense success. Why then was it necessary, a century and a half ago, to rebel against it; and why now, in these more friendly days, should we not come to some agreement with its historic legal system? Why should we look around for new definitions of *Torah* and *Mitzva?* What is wrong with the great Halachic tradition which has served Israel so well?

There is no question that there is something tragically wrong with Jewish Orthodoxy. The breakdown of Jewish observance which so greatly concerned the founders of the Reform movement has accelerated. There is chaos in Orthodox Jewish life. An ever increasing percentage of Jews no longer observe Orthodox law. . . . While it may be asked whether or not Reform is legal, it is an equally valid question whether Orthodoxy itself will long endure. How do we, those of us who admire the magnificent consistency of Jewish law and the deep learning which sustains it, explain the fact that this unbroken succession of authority and culture has finally lost its hold upon the people of Israel?

The usual explanation given for the failure of Orthodoxy is that the rapid social changes of modern life have left it confused and bewildered. This explanation is fairly sound but insufficient. It does not go deep enough into history. Jewish life had frequently undergone radical change, and Judaism was able to cope with every change. . . . Traditional Judaism had great dynamic power. It could create and change and recreate to fit changing circumstances. But somehow and mysteriously, the change over into the modern era proved suddenly too much for it and Orthodoxy began rapidly to fade. . . .

This retreat from creativity manifest all through Orthodox Halachic writings at the beginning of the modern age has brought about a cumulative deterioration in Orthodox thought. Among the

Orthodox leaders of a hundred and fifty years ago this conservatism was still accompanied by a certain stubborn strength. They were confident that their attitude could be successfully maintained. They were sure that if they continued to resist the presumption of the innovators, the innovators would cease to trouble and Israel would return to its traditional life.

But as the years passed this stubborn confidence began to seep out of Orthodoxy. The reader of modern Halachic literature detects in it a note of despair. Increasingly in the successive responsa there is revealed a mood of hopelessness. Orthodox leaders are no longer confident that they can win back the erring house of Israel. . . .

In an essential respect Orthodox Judaism has ceased to be traditional Judaism. Traditional Judaism was creative and confident. It could always adjust itself to change. It could absorb new customs. But now this creativeness has disappeared. Traditional Judaism has become petrified into changeless, despairing Orthodoxy. That is why it has lost control of Jewish life. Its more learned rabbis are admirable as students. Their life is devoted to the Torah. But it is inconceivable that the innovating courage of Rabbenu Gershon or of Maharil could reappear among them. Some so-called modern Orthodox congregations have adopted Oneg Shabbas gatherings and the custom of regular sermons but beyond these no new minhagim have in the last century been embodied in Jewish Orthodox law.

It may sound strange to say so, but surely it is a fact that with regard to creativity and confidence, Reform Judaism is more traditional than modern Orthodoxy. We feel assured that Judaism can be successfully adjusted to the changing world and we are manifesting increasing creativity in devising of new observances and embodying them into our practice. This creativity is our precious inheritance from all the centuries of the past. We must be careful not to discourage it or to petrify it into a fixed system. Whenever we contemplate codifying our customs we must remember the experience of Orthodoxy and do our work in such a way that codification should not discourage creativity. Life will continue to change. Judaism will continue to change. Reform Judaism must not be congealed by premature systematizing, but must develop the dynamism by which alone Judaism can live in this unpredictable world.

We are not the only branch of Judaism which is concerned with the problem of adjusting its relationship to the legal system which we have inherited. The task is just as great in Conservative Judaism. It is not to the discredit of Conservatism that it has not clearly described its underlying legal doctrines. After all, it is normally Jewish to develop a mode of practice before elucidating a philosophy. We have always put deed before doctrine. Conservatism is obviously a different collocation of practice from ours but it is gradually arriving at a doctrine. . . . What the Conservative doctrine amounts to is that it accepts the authority of the legal tradition, but seeks the more lenient decisions found in it. Thus, by using the lenient interpretations, often that of the earlier authorities against that of the later authorities, one may adjust Judaism to life without breaking, as the reformers did, the allegiance to the chain of Halacha.

This is an attractive doctrine but it has basic faults. Its essential fault is that it is impossible to accept the authority of the traditional Halacha without accepting the authority of the Orthodox rabbinate. The Orthodox rabbinate, the legitimate dynasty of the legal system, will consent to no alleviation of the rigors of the law. . . . It is clear that if the Conservative rabbinate accepts the validity of the traditional system of Jewish law, it must accept the authority of the Orthodox leaders and these leaders are inflexible and afraid of change. The founders of Reform were much wiser when they renounced the authority of Orthodox leadership and thus were free to rearrange Judaism according to the needs of the time. There can be no creative legal cooperation with an inflexible Orthodox leadership. They will not move and they will not cooperate.

There is an even more basic difficulty. Beyond the inflexible mood of Orthodox leadership there is the inflexible nature of the law itself in its present state. Jewish law is no longer a normal legal system. It lacks one of the prime essentials of such a system. A normal system contains two sources of law, legislation and interpretation. The interpretive method, the judge-made law, works out the implications of legislative (or inherited) law. These judge-made interpretations multiply and, as far as they can, they adjust the law to life. But when life had changed so much that the law can no longer be stretched far enough by interpretation, then legislation steps in again and creates entirely new laws, often completely changing the old; and on the basis of the new legislative law the process of interpretation begins anew.

Jewish law in the time of our Sanhedrins in the old days of ordination could make new and clear-cut legal remedies by legislation. Even after the days of ordination, great rabbis, courageous and pioneering like Rabbenu Gershon, could convene a synod and achieve, when necessary, radical change. But nowadays Jewish law has no longer any instrument for clear-cut change. There is no legislative remedy, there is only judge-made or interpretive law, and none of the judges, the rabbinical courts, have the courage any more to act as legislature and make vital changes. It is precisely because of the lack of legislative remedy that the exiles from Spain in the sixteenth century tried to revive the Sanhedrin. And it may well be that in Palestine a Sanhedrin may be revived, or, lacking that, it may be that in the future the Orthodox rabbinate of the Yishuv may rediscover the old-time courage of legal enactment without a formal legislature. But for the present the law, lacking legislative remedy, is unchangeable and unusable. . . .

It is simply clear that the legal theory implicit in Conservatism, while attractive, is unworkable. The attempt to maintain the authority of the old legal tradition but to interpret it leniently cannot succeed because the legal tradition itself has become unchangeable and its living authorities inflexible. It is impossible to compromise with Orthodox law. It must be either accepted or its authority rejected. Conservatism therefore presents a disharmony between legal theory and religious practice. In theory it accepts what has grown to be a changeless legalism. In practice it adopts many of the ritual changes developed by Reform. Conservatism is Orthodox theory and Reform practice.

What *we* seek is a legal philosophy which shall be in harmony with our actual practice, and simultaneously, we aim to develop a religious practice consistent with an acceptable theory. We were started in the right direction by the earlier reformers. Their stand was radical and revolutionary. As the American Revolution, or any revolution for that matter, is an abolition of old authority and the beginning of a new legal system, so the work of the Reform pioneers was to give us a Declaration of Independence. They broke the compulsive authority of the old law; but has not the time come for laying the foundation of a new legal system? We have lived, as did this country for a while, under the Declaration of Independence; it may be that now the time has come for creating a new Constitution. We have liberty. Do we not now need law?

The question is not at all rhetorical. It is far from certain how the majority of us would answer it. Most of our predecessors and many of our colleagues would tend to answer the question in the negative. They would say that we do not need to reestablish a religio-legal system, since ceremonies and ritual are no longer a religious imperative for us. They are merely customs which may be accepted or rejected. They may be helpful or become useless. They are not divine; they are human. The only God-given law is the moral law. All the rest is dubious commentary. Kaufmann Kohler, a revered honorary president of our Conference, declared in his *Jewish Theology* (p. 46): "This view (i.e. that of Orthodoxy) is contradicted by all our own knowledge and our whole mode of thinking, and thus both our historical and religious consciousness constrain us to take the position of the prophets. To them and to us the real Torah is the unwritten moral law which underlies the precepts of both the written law and its oral interpretation."

This primacy of the moral law over all other laws and ob-

servances is not repugnant even to Orthodox Judaism. The Talmud
(b. Maccoth 23b–24a) reduces the 613 commandments to one,
namely, either the verse in Amos (5:4): "Seek Me and live"; or
the verse in Habakkuk (2:4): "The righteous shall live by his
faith." But Orthodox Judaism would add the statement from the
Mishnah on the same page, that "God desiring to add merit to
Israel increased for them laws and commandments." To Orthodoxy,
as to us, the moral law is central but the ceremonial laws are likewise divine.

I doubt whether we could ever accept substantially this Orthodox
viewpoint. Certainly in no foreseeable future would a Reform rabbinical conference declare that certain dietary observances or certain detailed hygienic practices or even certain precise wordings of
prayer texts are, according to its conscience, the will of God. These
various types of observances may become quite important to us
but they will never be literally "mitzvos," divine mandates. To this
extent, therefore, we are in agreement with the earlier reformers;
namely, that the only laws which we in full conscience can say
are God's command are the moral laws. The ceremonial and ritual
laws are in another category altogether. They will never be for us,
as they are for Orthodoxy, divine law. But it is equally true that
they are something more for us than they were to the early Reformers. Just how much more is perhaps the central question involved in this entire discussion. When our Columbus Platform
declared that the concept of Torah was essential for us and in the
general description of Torah included ritual and ceremonial observances as well as ethics, the Platform meant to express our sense
of the increased validity of the ritual practices in Judaism. They
are not quite law but they do have certain authority. To deny the
validity of ritual practice is Paulinian. To accept the validity of all
the inherited practice is Orthodox. To declare that practice has
some religious validity and to seek to establish a suitable foundation and structure for it is our concept of the present duty of
Reform.

Of course, the very fact that we, being Reform, do not accept the compulsive validity of the past system of practice, but presume on our own accord to seek to create one that is suitable for us, that very procedure gives to our practice a different legal status from that of Orthodox practice. Orthodox practice claims to be divine. Even though a certain ritual decision will be arrived at by the most complicated pilpulistic methods and will be abstrusely argued by one rabbi with another, the result of the debate is considered by Orthodoxy Torah and divine. But our decisions are human, confessedly and frankly human. If we would ever draw up a list of what work may be done or ought not to be done on the Sabbath, that list would not in any sense be more than a recommendation. There is no ceremony, there is no observance which we can present to the people and say, this is the will of God. They would not accept it and we would not claim it.

How then, lacking the claim of Divine authority, can we presume to develop ceremonies and practices which in Jewish thought constitute actual Torah? Even the legal literature itself is not authoritative to us. The Talmud, the codes and the responsa, are not important to us as law. Yet they are important as inspiration. The texts as such are not sacred. Hence we will never make careful pilpulistic comparisons of the wording of a law in Maimonides with the wording in the Tur. We know that both are human documents. Maimonides himself wrote like any other human author, scratching out words, inverting phrases, substituting other words. (See Atlas's edition of the Maimonidean fragments, documents "Ketaim.") So with all the documents. These are not sacrosanct, but are repositories of the Jewish spirit. They are divine only to the extent that somewhere in the mazes of these vast materials we find God speaking to the hearts and minds of Israel; and we and our conscience must make the decision of what, in all these materials, we consider binding or meaningful for us.

Without going into the deep and difficult questions involved in the problem of revelation, it is sufficient for our practical purposes to say that those observances which, inspired by the past, are accepted by Israel in the present or become acceptable to Israel, can serve us as a description of the content of Torah. That, in fact, is the way in which the law was creatively developed. Minhagim arose all over the world. They were the creative part of Jewish law. It would be a fascinating study to go through the notes of Isserles to the Shulchan Aruch and the Tur and to list all the instances in which he says: "This is our custom," or, "This is not our custom," or, "It is our custom to do thus and thus." It would be revealed that a large bulk of Jewish law was derived spontaneously, creatively and anonymously from the life of the people of Israel. This minhag was more basic to the development of Jewish law than the law itself has ever acknowledged. At this point I wish to do honor to the memory of our departed colleague, Jacob S. Raisin, who in 1907 in his book *Sect, Creed and Custom,* saw clearly the creative power of this anonymous force in Judaism.

This essentially Jewish procedure is the only practicable one for us and that indeed is what we actually follow. On the basis of material which we find in Jewish literature, we are developing practices which we present before our people. Practices also arise spontaneously. Who, for example, first thought of the late Friday evening service? Who was the first to have the ceremonial lighting of Sabbath candles in the synagog? These things simply arose. We can trace some of them. Some of them are even in our day no longer traceable, as the origin of the Bar Mitzvah is no longer traceable. Thus is Torah being developed in our day.

This is for us the direction of growth. We are grateful to the founders of Reform Judaism who had the courage of revolutionists to break away from the stifling authority of a legal system once flexible and inspiring and which already in their day had become dogmatic and immovable. Had they left us under the authority of Orthodoxy, Judaism today would have been deprived of its freest creative religious force. Our liberty gives us our opportunity and our obligation. The content of Torah must be built up through minhag and we are the ones who are free, creative and confident enough to do it, not only for ourselves but for all of Israel.

Thus Reform Judaism has a special role in Jewish life, a new and creative role. We are the only religious division in Judaism which is completely free from the compulsive power of the now immobile legal system. We are the only ones who can create new minhagim freely, try them out without hindrance, and accept or reject according to our experience. We, therefore, are the only branch of Judaism which can best build new ceremonial forms for all of Jewish life. Many of the forms which we have developed in the past are already widely accepted. Many that we will build in the future will provide for Judaism a more stately mansion.

But this task, if we accept it, involves a definite type of self-restraint. We must give up the easy comfort of early codification. We have a great deal of thinking, debating and selection to do before we can presume to say what is God's command and what is mere experiment. We must take a great deal of time to work out general categories as to which observances, which department of observances are of religious moment. Which types of action are the concern of religion to such an extent that Judaism should regulate them? The ethical life is, of course, first of all and preeminent. Then perhaps the duty of public and private worship must be rebuilt into an intensely felt mitzva. People have lost that sense of personal obligation and individual responsibility to worship God in the midst of the congregation. The duty to study Jewish law and literature must certainly be rebuilt into a mitzva. These are just indications of the general task which confronts us.

It is, of course, not only our own convictions which must be considered but the convictions and moods of the people. The people have often made their own decision on Jewish practice. Sometimes the popular decisions were wrong and the rabbis combatted them. Sometimes the rabbis yielded. Rabbenu Tam in the twelfth century says surprisingly: "Ten years ago in this locality there were no Mezuzahs at all" (quoted from Responsa of Meir of Rothenberg, #118, ed. Cremona; cf. Boaz Cohen, "Kuntres Ha-teshuvos," p. 4 note 2). Rabbenu Tam needed to conduct a great propaganda before this mitzva was accepted. The mere fact that it was recorded as a mitzva was far from sufficient. Isaac b. Sheshet, when he was exiled to North Africa, found many popular customs to combat and many observances which were neglected. At many periods in Jewish history the people had to be won over to certain observances. So it is with us. It is far from sufficient for us to declare that certain rituals and ceremonials are to be used. We must judge the mood of our people. We must change the mood of the people. Otherwise our listing of mitzvoth will seem meaningless and even ludicrous to them.

The task is as delicate as it is complicated. We must analyze the concept of Torah. We must estimate the true mood of our people, and we must ask ourselves, judging by our own conscience which must remain the ultimate test for free men, what types of commandments can justly be regulated by religion? These shall constitute Torah for us.

When we will have arrived at a general agreement as to what categories of action we can in conscience regulate, then we must develop systematically the growth and the encouragement of specific minhagim. This will involve a wider interest on the part of many of us in the whole mass of Halachic literature which, besides being an evidence of the tremendous mental alertness of Jewish scholarship, is also a repository of Jewish ceremonial creativity.

For all this great and enheartening task we must keep our hands and our minds free. We must not yield to the quick and easy solution of establishing prematurely a code of present practice. Our present practice is hopelessly inadequate. It is hardly worth codification. It is just the prelude to a richer and more effective religious practice yet to be created. Furthermore, any code that we publish now will be spiritually premature. We are far from having developed the conviction which will enable us to say with clear heart that these and these specific customs are, in our conviction, Torah, the command of God. A premature code would at present lack a spiritual foundation and would actually hamper us in our creative process. It is psychologically difficult, particularly with modern people, to create a minimum code which will not become a maximum code. Those practices to which we today would say: "This is the least which you must do," they will say: "This is all that we need do." You cannot have the command, thou shalt not subtract, *lo sigra,* without its inevitable companion, thou shalt not add, *lo sosef.*

Of course, there are certain things which we can do already. In a previous paper (CCAR Vol. 51) I had the privilege of indicating before the Conference which of our observances at their present state can be safely, if tentatively systematized. I suggested then that the dietary laws be left alone for we do not wish to raise any dietary observance to the status of law; that our ritual ceremonies be allowed to continue in their present experimental stage; that synagog observances have been regularized through the Union Prayer Book; and that our revision of the Prayer Book, approximately every quarter of a century, gives us an opportunity for including newly developed practices; that for home ceremonies, such as Sabbath lights, Hannukah, visiting the cemeteries, etc., in our Union Home Prayer Book, yet to be written, notes describing our customs precede every liturgical text; that our responsa be regularly collected and indexed; but that our marriage laws, which involve our relations to the laws of the state, be definitely fixed and codified. The Committee on Code and Practice, reporting in the following year, accepted these general principles. Its suggestion for a manual of religious practices seems to refer to the annotated Union Home Prayer Book, or it may mean a separate manual. But in general the report calls for much more discussion of the whole question at successive Conferences.

We must move slowly and carefully. There is in fact no great hurry. Our Reform Jewish life is not chaotic. On the contrary, it is the least chaotic of all the three branches of Judaism. Orthodox life, looked at merely from the books, seems orderly, but the gulf between actual Orthodox practice and Orthodox law is immense. The difference in practice between the growing variety of Orthodox congregations is already considerable. The Conservative congregations vary greatly from each other in their types of observances. I believe that the most consistent orderly segment of Jewish life is Reform Judaism. There is less variety and divergence from the norm of practice in our Reform synagogs and in our Reform Jewish practice than there is, in actual fact, in other branches of Judaism. We have achieved order and have achieved it in liberty.

Now, *L'maan zidko, yagdil Torah;* may God develop Torah through us, that He may be nobly worshipped.

THE MORAL LAW AS HALACHA IN REFORM JUDAISM
Alexander Guttmann
(1958)

... This topic, I am told, was prompted not by academic considerations, but by most practical ones. American Reform Judaism abandoned many laws and customs of Biblical and Rabbinical Judaism within a short period of just a few decades, and this resulted in a vacuum which has to be filled with a meaningful content if Liberal-Reform Judaism is to grow and prosper.

Before discussing the question whether moral law might fill this void, let us survey the state of religious observances in Judaism.

The Bible, Talmud, and *Shulchan Aruch* are the foundations of today's Judaism. This does not mean, however, that any branch of today's Judaism observes, or even tries to observe, all the precepts of these basic books. The difference between the various branches lies, aside from the theological aspect, in the method of selecting certain practices, while rejecting or disregarding others, and in the number of practices actually observed.

The need for changes and adjustments in regard to religious life was felt whenever changes in other areas of life took place. Since one of the fundamentals of religion is loyalty to God and His (revealed) law, changes in this realm have been made, in former times, reluctantly, hesitantly, and only when it was deemed necessary to ease the tension between changing conditions and established religious life.[1]

[1] A. Guttmann, *Hebrew Union College Annual* 1950–51, pp. 453 ff.

The most extensive changes in regard to our religious practices were made by sages of the Talmud. The principal method of those changes was that of interpretation. By this I do not mean text interpretation alone. The sages also interpreted Judaism and its laws in the light of historical events and other changing conditions of their time. For example, with the destruction of the Temple, the sacrificial cult terminated and no attempt was made to continue it outside Jerusalem nor to revive it as was the case in earlier centuries under similar conditions.[2] The sages also suspended a whole category of laws that depend on the land of Israel.[3] Rabbi Yochanan ben Zakkai suspended the Sota procedure claiming that the conditions making this law meaningful exist no longer, and with the original motif gone, the law is to be dispensed with. Similar is the case with the law of the עגלה ערופה, the heifer whose neck is to be broken.[4] The Rabbis also advised against the Yibbum, the Levirate Marriage, claiming that since the reason given in the Torah (Deut. 25:7 "to raise up unto his brother a name . . .") is not heeded today, such marriage must not be performed.[5]

The Biblical law of cancellation of debts in the Sabbatical year was made inoperative by Hillel's institution of the Prozbul, introduced by him because the respective Biblical law lost its original purposefulness.[6] In matters of civil law certain principles were developed which make decisions legally valid though at variance with the law of the Torah, thus giving preference to the need of

---

[2] M. Guttmann, ארץ ישראל במדרש ותלמוד , pp. 71 ff.

[3] Mishna *Kiddushin*, 1.9 ". . . any *mitzva* that depends on the Land (*e.g.* Heave-offering, Tithes, Dough-Offering, Gleanings, Forgotten Sheaf, *Peah*) is to be observed in the Land alone . . ."

[4] Mishna *Sota* IX.9 "When the murderers became many the rite of breaking the heifer's neck ceased . . . When adulterers became many the rite of the bitter water ceased; and R. Jochanan ben Zakkai brought it to an end . . ."

[5] *Yebamoth* 39b; *Shulchan Aruch, Eben Ha-Ezer* 165, 1; Cf. Responsa of D. Hoffman מלמד להועיל III.50.

[6] Mishna *Shebi'ith* X.3 "A loan secured by a *prozbul* is not cancelled by the Sabbatical year. This is one of the things that Hillel the Elder ordained. When he saw that the people refrained from giving loans one to another and transgressed what is written in the Torah 'Beware that there be not a base thought in thine heart' (Deut. 15:9) Hillel ordained the *prozbul*."

the time, or to equity over the law of the Torah.[7] Among principles developed for maintaining good relations with the gentile nations is Samuel's ruling: דינא דמלכותא דינא "The law of the land is valid law,"[8] which originally did not mean that Jewish law (civil law) is to be replaced indiscriminately by the law of the land. Yet it was often understood as a command to accept generally the civil law of the land in place of the civil law of the Torah. No matter what the original intent of this principle was, it helped to promote better integration of the Jewish community into its gentile surroundings.

Whereas the Talmud suspended many old laws, no vacuum was allowed to develop. And herein lies a fundamental difference between Talmudic and Reform Judaism. Even before the sacrificial cult terminated, worship through prayer became widespread and was fully developed, and moved into the limelight immediately after the destruction of the Temple. With the diminishing agricultural significance of the festivals, particularly in the Diaspora, the emphasis was shifted to their religious and historical significance. Purim and Hanukka were added to the festivals of the Torah. Among the rituals introduced in post-Biblical, mainly Talmudic times, are: the lighting of candles, the cup of wine, the requirement of breaking bread, and the recital of the Kiddush on Sabbath and festivals. A shift of emphasis also played an important role in the history of our rituals. For example, the laws of ritual impurity played in earlier times a most important role, but already in later Talmudic times were very much neglected.[9]

In post-Talmudic and especially in post-Gaonic times the pace of changes slowed down considerably, on the one hand because of the absence of a leadership recognized by all the Jewish communities of the spreading Diaspora, on the other hand because the prevailing medieval spirit made major changes unnecessary. Ghettos and ghetto-like conditions were not conducive to changes, either. However, with the conclusion of the Middle Ages, which

---

[7] *Yebamoth* 89b and parallels הפקר בית דין הפקר "The *hefker* of the (Jewish) court is legal *hefker*."

[8] *Gittin* 10b דינא דמלכותא דינא

[9] Cf. Friedmann, *Sifre*, Introduction, note 18.

lasted for the Jews up to the end of the 18th century,[10] adjustments
to new conditions became imperative, just as in Talmudic times.
Unfortunately, there was no select body or academy recognized
as the authoritative interpreters of Judaism that could have directed
the needed adjustments. Yet, the adjustments had to be made and
have been made ever since to a considerable extent by all the
branches of Judaism.

While the *Shulchan Aruch* has been for centuries the recognized
Code of Judaism, if we examine its rulings in the light of their actual
observance, we shall discover a marked discrepancy. A few examples
may illustrate this: Deut. 49:17 commands that the first born male
should receive a double portion as his inheritance. The Talmud
(*Baba Bathra* 122) and Codes, including Maimonides (*Yad, Hilchot Nachalot,* Chapter 2) and Karo in his *Shulchan Aruch* (*Cho-
shen Mishpat,* 277) uphold this law. Yet, it is generally ignored
even by the most scrupulous law-abiding Jew. There is nowhere,
to my knowledge, a "law of the land" that prohibits the observance
of this Jewish law. Formally, one may stretch הפקר בית דין הפקר
or Samuel's דינא דמלכותא דינא and claim that it includes not merely
statutory law, but also the custom, or the unwritten law of the land,
but this was certainly not the intent of the originator of this principle and of the codifiers. The fact is that the fourth part of the
Shulchan Aruch dealing with civil law is almost entirely ignored
due to the integration of the Jewish community into the general
society.

Yet the changes do not concern merely Jewish civil law. A large
number of ritual laws and ceremonies had been modified or dropped
tacitly. For example, *Shulchan Aruch, Orach Chayyim* requires in
accordance with the Talmud the performance of certain acts to
commemorate the destruction of the Temple in Jerusalem.[11] This
is today generally ignored. The same holds true for the Biblical
chadash-law, prohibiting the eating from the new crop before the

---

[10] See J. R. Marcus, *Communal Sick-Care in the German Ghetto,* p. vii.
[11] *Orach Chayyim* 560, Prohibited is, *e.g.,* to listen to music, singing, and to laugh
heartily, unless these are done in connection with a *mitzva,* such as a wedding.

second day of Pesach. The *Shulchan Aruch* (in contradistinction to some other authorities) considers this law as a still operative one (*Orach Chayyim,* 490; *Yoreh De'ah* 293), while in reality it is ignored. On the other hand, the *Shulchan Aruch,* based on Talmudic sources, (Cf. particularly M. *Sota* VII. 1) rules that, among other prayers, the *Shema,* the *Tefilla,* and the Grace after the Meal may be recited in any language (see *Orach Chayyim* 62.2; 101.4 and 186.1), whereas conformity with the *Shulchan Aruch* in these instances is today considered to be most anti-traditional.

If we examine the laws of Torah and *Shulchan Aruch* one by one, we shall find that many, if not most of them are not observed today by any branch of Judaism.

Liberal Judaism of Europe differed in regard to the rituals from Reform in that it moved slower, changes were made gradually over a longer period of time and to a lesser extent, thus allowing no vacuum to generate. As a result, the liberal rabbis of Europe did not have to grapple with the weighty problems the Reform rabbis of America are so much concerned with: how to fill existing void with meaningful content. Liberal Jewry of Europe also grew numerically much faster than do Reform congregations of America. Berlin, the largest Jewish community of Germany (over 200,000) had a liberal majority for over seventy years.

The question whether Moral Law can be regarded as Halacha implies that it is the Halacha that must fill the vacuum which resulted from the speedy abandonment of a large body of religious practices. In order to be able to answer this question, let us first briefly define the concept Halacha.

The word Halacha has been in use from Talmudic times to date to designate a number of concepts, *e.g.,* Traditional or Oral Law; Rabbinic law accepted in conclusion of a controversy[12]; הלכה למשה מסיני , *i.e.,* an old, undisputed traditional law, so well established that no support from the Torah was deemed necessary.[13] It may

---

[12] הלכה מכלל דפליגי *i.e.,* the use of the term Halacha implies that controversy preceded.

[13] Cf. Tchernowitz, תולדות ההלכה I. 67 ff.; W. Bacher, *Tradition und Tradenten,* pp. 33 ff.; Z. Frankel, דרכי המשנה , pp. 20 ff.

denote a Rabbinic law that is independent of a Biblical law, or an implementation of a law of the Torah. Exceptionally, it is used synonymously with Torah.[14]

Since in ancient society religion, morals, and law were not differentiated, this was also the rule for the ancient Jewish society, and Halacha therefore could denote moral law as any other law. It is a fact that statutory law and moral law often have the same source: custom.[15] The Latin *mos* and the Greek $\H{\eta}\theta os$ and $\acute{\epsilon}\theta os$ mean "custom." A number of customs were converted into laws, many other customs found recognition as moral obligations. There are also customs that did not find their way to either of these two categories and remained customs, folkways. Whereas a moral obligation is not a (statutory) law and legally not enforceable, the statutory law is often but a legalized moral obligation, as for example the laws against slander, theft, murder, adultery.

Whatever the origin of a law may be, the Torah prides itself that our laws are *just* laws.[16] This means that morality is a *conditio sine qua non* for a law, including, of course, ritual law. Why are we the chosen people and not one of the other nations? One answer of our sages is: because the other nations refused to accept the Moral Law.[17] A Mitzva (here meaning ritual law) performed while violating a moral law, is not acceptable, thus our sages declare.[18] Well known are the pronouncements of Hillel and Akiba, perhaps the two greatest personalities of the Talmudic period. Hillel: "What is hateful to you do not to your fellow creature— this is the entire Torah, the rest is commentary. Go and learn!" (*Shabat* 31a.) Akiba: "Love thy fellow-man as thyself" is the great principle of the Torah (P. *Nedarim* X. 4; 41c). According to

---

[14] M. Guttmann, *Zur Einleitung in die Halacha*, pp. 16 ff.

[15] Cf. B. Cohen, *Law and Ethics in the Light of the Jewish Tradition*, N.Y., 1957; Ch. W. Reines, תורה ומוסר Jerusalem, 1954; M. Silberg, חוק ומוסר במשפט העברי Jerusalem, 1952.

[16] Deut. IV. 8 "And what great nation is there, that has statutes and ordinances so righteous as all this law, which I set before you all this day?"

[17] *Mekilta, Bachodesh*, ed. Lauterbach vol. II. pp. 234 f., and parallels, cf. L. Ginzberg, *The Legends of the Jews* VI. p. 30. Note 181.

[18] Mishna *Sukka* II.1 ff. "If a *lulav* was obtained by robbery . . . it is not valid" etc.

these and many other pronouncements, the ultimate purpose of the Torah is the establishment of the Moral Law. All the other laws are merely means toward this goal. Quite significant in this regard is also R. Simlai's account: Moses received 613 commandments . . . David came and reduced them to eleven (Psalms, 15, 1–5): ". . . He that walketh uprightly, and worketh righteousness, and speaketh truth in his heart . . . He that doeth these things shall never be moved" (all ethical tenets). Then Isaiah came and reduced them to six (Isa. 33:15): "He that walketh righteously, and speaketh uprightly; he that despiseth the gain of oppressions, that shaketh his hands from holding of bribes, that stoppeth his ears from hearing of blood, and shutteth his eyes from looking upon evil" (again, moral precepts). Micah reduced them to three (Mic. 6:8): "It hath been told thee, O man, what is good, and what the Lord doth require of thee: only to do justly and to love mercy, and to walk humbly with thy God" (moral precepts). Isaiah reduced the number again, this time to two (Isa. 56:1): "Thus saith the Lord: Keep ye justice, and do righteousness." Amos reduced them to one (Amos 5:4): "For thus saith the Lord unto the house of Israel: Seek ye Me, and live." Habakkuk also reduced them to one (Hab. 2:4): "But the righteous shall live by his faith"[19] (*Makkot* 23b–24a).

These and other passages show that the Rabbis were well aware of the ultimate purpose of the commandments: to lead us to a life governed by the Moral Law, the prerequisite (according to predominant Talmudic view) for the coming of the Messiah. Therefore, having served their purpose, the *mitzvot* (rituals) will be voided in the Messianic Age,[20] our sages declare.

Jewish ethics is God-centered. The sages believed that without a belief in God there was no ethical behavior possible. *Tosefta Shebuot* III. 6 (449–450) relates: Hananya son of Hakhinai said

---

[19] העמידן does not mean "reduced them" in the sense of eliminating the other commandments, but its meaning is that he comprised them, giving the essence of the *mitzva*.

[20] *Nidda* 61b מצוות בטילות לעתיד לבוא. Cf. M. Guttmann בחינת קיום המצוות ,Breslau, 1931, pp. 75 ff.; J. Z. Lauterbach, *Essays*, pp. 267 ff.

"And if one sin, and commit a trespass against the Lord, and deal falsely with his neighbour" (Lev. 5:21) No man deals falsely with his neighbour until he has denied the Root (God). Once R. Reuben was in Tiberias on a Sabbath and he met there a philosopher who asked him: "Who is the most despicable man on earth?" He replied, "He who denies his Creator." "How so?" He replied to him, "Honor thy father and thy mother, thou shalt not murder, thou shalt not commit adultery, thou shalt not steal, thou shalt not bear false witness against thy neighbour, thou shalt not covet" (Exod. 20:12, 13). No man violates these things until he has previously denied God and no man commits any other sin unless he has denied Him who prohibited it.

The major part of the moral obligations that were developed into laws has a negative character. Their purpose is to protect the society and the individual, primarily the weak, thus preventing anarchy and chaos. The positive moral obligations, while often emphasized in most lofty pronouncements, were less frequently transformed into laws. There are two obvious reasons for this: their infraction would not lead to chaos—the primary concern of society, and, in some instances, the moral precept, if converted into a law, would lose its original value or would be unenforceable by its nature. How, for example, could love, love of fellow men, of God, of the Torah, etc., be enforced?

However, some of the positive moral obligations actually had been converted into laws. The Bible has numerous noble pronouncements demanding support of the poor. On the whole, however, helping the poor particularly in the Diaspora remained a moral obligation. The Rabbis developed the mitzva—here meaning moral obligation—of helping the poor into a full system of legal (halachic) obligations, that are enforceable as any other legal obligation.

Gemiluth Chasadim גמילות חסדים "deeds of lovingkindness" is another moral obligation, considered even more important than charity that found its way, to some extent, into the realm of the Halacha. Our Rabbis taught that in three respects is *Gemiluth*

Chasadim superior to charity: charity can be done only with one's money, but *Gemiluth Chasadim* can be done with one's person *and* one's money. Charity can be given only to the poor, *Gemiluth Chasadim* both to the rich *and* the poor. Charity can be given to the living only, *Gemiluth Chasadim* can be done both to the living *and* to the dead.[21]

Occasionally Halacha is used synonymously with Mitzva which often denotes a moral obligation,[22] but more often Halacha designates the details of a mitzva. From among the many uses of the term Halacha in Talmudic literature it most often denotes a Rabbinic law, excluding not merely Biblical law, but also *minhag* (custom), Midrash and Aggada.[23]

In post-Talmudic times, the use of the term Halacha became even more popular. Many outstanding codifiers use *Halacha* or *Halachot* as a title for their law codes, or for subdivision—headings of their codes. Alfassi's code is named *Halachot,* and it includes both Biblical and Rabbinical law. Maimonides also includes both under the sub-titles *Hilchot* of his *Mishneh Torah.* The subdivisions of the *Shulchan Aruch* are likewise called *Hilchot,* no matter whether the laws listed are Biblical, Rabbinical, or both. Yet, we have to keep in mind that captions are no definitions and do not have to be precise. Their function is merely to indicate in a few words *pars pro toto* the main content of the respective section.

If we want to use today the word Halacha in its broadest sense, we could designate Moral Law as Halacha. However, in using an expression in a given time, the contemporary usage of the term should be considered. Today, the word Halacha is used as a term designating distinctly Jewish (post-Biblical) laws and practices that are rooted in the past and are particularistic. Moral Law, however, is basically universalistic (though it may be particularistic in some

[21] *Tosefta Peah,* IV.19 and parallels. Codified examples of *Gemiluth Chasadim* s. Maimonides, *Mishneh Torah,* Evel 14.

[22] A Biblical term, used there, among others, to designate positive and negative commandments; in post-Biblical times its meaning was broadened and could denote Rabbinical precepts, moral obligations, etc. Cf. M. Guttmann, בחינת המצוות Breslau 1928.

[23] M. Guttmann, *Zur Einleitung in die Halacha.*

details), as is the case with the Talmudic-Rabbinic charity regulations. The mitzva of helping the needy is universalistic, a moral obligation which the Rabbis converted into a legal obligation with particularistic details, such as *Shulchan Aruch, Yoreh De'ah* 249, 1: If a man is unable to give all the poor need, he should (preferably) give them the first year one fifth of his property and in subsequent years one fifth of his income. Par. 15 rules that charity funds should be used primarily for marrying off poor virgins. And 256, 3: The collection should be done by at least two men, etc.

In this and in other areas of moral law the tendency of all the branches of today's Judaism is to steer away from the particularistic details of the Halacha and to adjust to the prevailing standards. This is a natural development as ghettos and quasi-ghettos disappear from the scene of history and adjustments to the new circumstances become inevitable.

I do not believe that we can or should reverse this trend and build up the Moral Law as an area of particularistic Halacha.

If the question were only whether Moral Law can be designated as Halacha, I could rest the case right here. Halacha is today a term designating distinctly Jewish laws and practices, but moral law is universalistic. Yet our problem here is not to indulge in semantics. The answer to the original question (my topic) leads directly to another question: If moral law cannot fill the vacuum caused by the discarded Halacha, what else might remedy the situation?

Although this is not my topic, a few remarks may be in order. There are two possible ways of filling the existing void: first, by introducing new practices, and second, by reconsidering some of the old, neglected or discarded practices.

An arbitrary introduction of new practices, just to fill the vacuum, could do more harm than good. It would widen the gap between Reform and the other branches of Judaism, and restrict its growth. Whatever new practices were to be introduced next should not be done hastily, but only after a thorough investigation of all the aspects and should be well motivated. *Tosefta Sanhedrin* IV. 5 (see also Talmud *ibid.* 20b) relates: Israel, upon entering the Land, was commanded to fulfill three commandments: To install a king, to destroy Amalek, and to build a sanctuary. If this is so, why were they punished in the days of Samuel (for asking him to install a king)? One answer is, because they hastened the matter. Another answer, R. Elazar says, is that the sages asked in the proper manner "Give us a king, to judge us" (I Sam. 8:6), yet, the common people (*amme haaretz*) corrupted the matter by saying, "that we also may be ככל הגוים, like all the nations etc." (I Sam. 8:20).

This is a good illustration that haste and wrong motivation may turn an otherwise good thing into the opposite. The reverse is true, too. Secular or foreign customs or institutions may become good Jewish practices, if adapted with circumspection and reinterpreted in the spirit of our faith. Examples: Sabbath and festival candles, cup of wine, part of the Seder ritual. Originality in the realm of religion and ethics is of no real importance. Herein lies a basic difference between religion and scholarship. To illustrate: A professor, reviewing the book of his colleague, started out with this statement: "The book of Dr. X . . . contains many good and new ideas. However," he continued, "the good ideas in this book are not new, and the new ideas are not good." What we as Jews and religionists have to look for is that which is good, no matter whether it is new or old.

Should we return to Prophetic Judaism? This we could not do for two reasons: first, because Prophetic Judaism never existed, just as Plato's Republic never existed. Prophetic Judaism is a goal which we may reach באחרית הימים "in the end of days" opening for us the doors of the Messianic Age. True, the Prophets sought the realization of their great ideas in their own day, but were unsuccessful. They were bound to be a failure, because the people were not ready for their ideals. And secondly, even if Prophetic Judaism had existed, we could not return to it, as we could or would not return to (non-Prophetic) Biblical, Pharisaic, or Talmudic Judaism. We can learn quite a good deal from our past history, but we cannot revive it.

The Rabbis, successors to the Prophets, worked toward the same goal as did the Prophets, but with considerably more success because they were standing with both feet on solid ground. They were, so to speak, pedagogues. They knew that the road leading to the goal is long, thorny and difficult, and we have to proceed step by step, as well expressed by our sages. "Heedfulness leads to cleanliness, and cleanliness leads to purity, and purity leads to abstinence, and abstinence leads to holiness, and holiness leads to humility, and humility leads to shunning of sin, and shunning of sin leads to saintliness, and saintliness leads to (the gift of) the Holy Spirit, and the Holy Spirit leads to the resurrection of the dead" (M. *Sota* IX. 15).

A way of giving our religious life more meaningful content would be to reconsider some neglected areas of the Halacha, strengthening the common denominator of Jewish life, replacing the concept of convenience with the idea of sacrifice in the fulfillment of religious duties. Significant in this respect is the observation of the Talmud, that only those *mitzvot* are still faithfully observed for which our fathers accepted martyrdom; those, however, for which they would not do this, are weak (*Shabbat* 130a). Let us not be frightened by the word *tradition,* when considering our way for the future. Dr. Baeck, in one of his last lectures before his deportation to the concentration camp, discussed the importance of tradition for *K'lal Yisrael,* including, of course, liberal Judaism. Without tradition, he pointed out, we would be gypsies. Of course, there is quite a difference between tradition and tradition.

One of the most difficult tasks before us is making the right selection, which cannot be done haphazardly but requires in each instance thorough investigation of all the aspects involved, coupled with the love of the Torah and Israel. "Study is greater for it leads to practice" (*Kiddushin* 40b and parallels). Thus our sages decide.

Whereas the laws are given to live by, and not to die by (*Yoma,* 85b; Lev. 18:5), sacrifices for our faith have been the great ideal of our forefathers, as demonstrated so often throughout our history. Let us keep this in mind, as we proceed to our task.

A Major Reform Responsum

Although the theoretical status of traditional *Halacha* in Reform Judaism was a subject of discussion among members of the Central Conference of American Rabbis, members of their congregations occasionally followed the traditional Jewish practice of addressing technical questions on Jewish law to their rabbis. In the early days of the American movement, the individual rabbis replied to these queries without consulting with their rabbinical colleagues. Some, however, began to present their responses at the annual meetings, largely to inform their fellows. Later it was decided that this method was too anarchic; the Central Conference set up a committee on responsa so that queries, either from the laity or from rabbis, might be answered with authority on the basis of consensus. Thus for many years the committee on responsa has acted as the equivalent of a rabbinical court. Each year, the committee presents a report of the queries received and the precise text of the responsa agreed upon by the members of the committee.

For the most part, these responsa are brief and deal with very specific questions and are, therefore, not appropriate for presentation in this volume. In a few cases, however, a longer responsum on a more general issue was given full treatment in the pages of the *Yearbook*. The responsum below, written by Professor Jacob Z. Lauterbach of the Hebrew Union College in 1927, is an excellent example of this type. It rests on very broad scholarship, handled with care and sensitivity, in the interest of the most humane and generous interpretation of traditional law. The high quality of Dr. Lauterbach's presentation is attested by the fact that this responsum is still the foundation of the position of the Central Conference of American Rabbis on birth control.

348

TALMUDIC-RABBINIC VIEW ON
BIRTH CONTROL
Jacob Z. Lauterbach
(1927)

In considering the question of the Talmudic-Rabbinic attitude towards birth-control we must seek to clear up the confusion that prevails in the discussion of the subject and define the principles involved in the whole question.

Some rabbis are inclined to regard all forms of birth-conrtol, excepting self control or continence, as הוצאת שכבת זרע לבטלה and therefore put them in a class with masturbation or self-abuse. Hence, they believe that, with the citing of agadic sayings from the Talmud and Midrashim against the evil practice of self-abuse, they have also proved the opposition of rabbinic law to the various forms of birth-control. Such a method, however, is unscientific and not justified in the discussion of such a serious and important question.

In the first place, the method of adjudging questions of religious practice on the basis of agadic utterances is altogether unwarranted. The talmudic rule is אין מורין מן ההגדות that "we cannot decide the questions ,of practice by citing agadic sayings" (P. *Hagigah* I, 8 76d). The Agadah may set up an exalted ideal óf the highest ethical living. It may teach the lofty precept קדש עצמך במותר לך to aspire to a holy life and to avoid even such actions or practices which, though permitted by the law, do not measure up with its high standard. But it does not rest with the Agadah to decide what is forbidden or

349

permitted by the law. "The Agadist cannot declare anything
forbidden or . permitted, unclean or clean," says the Talmud
בעל אגדה שאינו לא אוסר ולא מתיר לא מטמא ולא מטהר
(P.*Horayot* III, 7 48c). The answer to questions of practice, that
is, as to what is permitted by Jewish law and what is not, can be
given only on the basis of the teachings of the Halakah.

Secondly, it is absolutely wrong to consider cohabitation with
one's wife under conditions which might not result in procreation,
an act of הוצאתשכבת זרע לבטלה and to class it with sexual perversions such as self-abuse.

In the following, therefore, we must consider only what the Halakah teaches about the various forms of birth-control and ignore
what the Agadah has to say in condemnation of the evil practices
of self-abuse and sexual perversions.

In order to avoid confusion and for the sake of a clearer understanding and a systematic presentation of the rabbinic teachings
bearing upon our subject, it is necessary to formulate the question
properly. It seems to me that the correct formulation of our question is as follows: Does the talmudic-rabbinic law permit cohabitation between husband and wife in such a manner or under such
conditions as would make conception impossible; and if so, what
are the conditions under which such cohabitation is permitted?

As to the first and main part of the question, there is no doubt
that it must be answered in the affirmative. To begin with, the
rabbinic law not only permits but even commands the husband to
fulfill his conjugal duties to his wife, even after she has experienced
the change of life and has become incapable of having children.
Likewise, the husband is permitted to have sexual intercourse with
his wife even if she is congenitally incapable of conception, as, for
instance, when she is an עקרה sterile, or an אילונית that is a womb-
less woman (Tossafot and Mordecai, quoted by Isserles in Shulhan
Aruk *Eben Ha-Ezer* XXIII, 2). The later rabbinic law goes even
further and permits even a man who has never had children and
thus has not fulfilled the duty of propagation of the race מצות פו״ר
to marry a woman incapable of bearing children, that is, a sterile

woman עקרה or an old woman זקנה (Isaac b. Sheshet quoted by Isserles *op. cit.* I. 3). From all this it is evident that the act of cohabitation, even when it cannot possibly result in conception, is in itself not only not immoral or forbidden, but in some cases even mandatory. Hence we may conclude that the discharge of sperm through sexual intercourse even though it does not effect impregnation of the woman, is not considered an act of "wasteful discharge of semen", הוצאת שכבת זרע לבטלהwhich is so strongly condemned by the agadic sayings of the Talmud. For while, as regards procreation, such a discharge is without results and purposeless, yet since it results from legitimate gratification of a normal desire, it has fulfilled a legitimate function and is not to be considered as in vain.

Now it may be argued that only in such cases where the parties through no fault of their own are incapable of procreation does the law consider the mere gratification of their natural desire a legitimate act and hence does not condemn it as הוצאת שכבת זרע לבטלה. We have, therefore, to further inquire whether the gratification of their legitimate desire by sexual intercourse in a manner not resulting in procreation would be permissible even to young and normally healthy husband and wife who are capable of having children.

To my knowledge, the Halakah, aside from recommending decency and consideration for the feelings of the wife in these matters, does not put any restrictions upon the husband's gratification of his sexual desire for his wife and certainly does not forbid him any manner of sexual intercourse with her. This is evident from the following passage in the Talmud (Nedarim 20b) where R. Johanan b. Nappaha, commenting upon a saying of R. Johanan b. Dahabai in disapproval of certain practices indulged in by some husbands, says: "These are but the words (i.e. the individual opinion) of Johanan b. Dahabai; the sages, however, have said that the decision of the law, i.e. the הלכה , is not according to Johanan b. Dahabai, but a husband may indulge with his wife in whatever manner of sexual gratification he desires.

אמר רבי יוחנן זו דברי יוחנן בן דהבאי אבל אמרו חכמים אין הלכה כיוחנן
בן דהבאי אלא כל מה שאדם רוצה לעשות באשתו עושה

This Halakah of R. Johanan b. Nappaha, supported by the decisions of Judah ha-Nasi and Abba Areka, reported in the Talmud (*ibidem* l. c.) has been accepted as law by all medieval rabbinic authorities, and they accordingly permit intercourse with one's wife in any manner כדרכה ושלא כדרכה (Maimonides Yad, Issure Biah XXI, 9; Tur Eben ha-Ezer 25 and Isserles in Shulhan Aruk, *Eben ha-Ezer* 25, 2). Maimonides (l.c.) would limit the permission of sexual indulgence שלא כדרכה only to such forms of שלא כדרכה which do not result in הוצאת שכבת זרע לבטלה for he says: ובלבד שלא יוצא שכבת זרע לבטלה . But other medieval authorities permit intercourse שלא כדרכה even when resulting in הוצאת ש"ז לבטלה . The only restriction they would put on this permission is that a man should not habituate himself always to do it only in such a manner.

דלא חשוב כמעשה ער ואונן אלא כשמתכוין להשחית זרע ורגיל לעשות תמיד אבל באקראי בעלמא ומתאוה לבא על אשתו שלא כדרכו שרי כן (Tossafot, Yebamot 34b s.v. ולא כמעשה ער ואונן ; Tur and Isserles l.c.)

From the fact that they permit שלא כדרכה even when it necessarily results in הוצאת ש"ז לבטלה we need not, however, necessarily conclude that these authorities would also permit such practices of שלא כדרכה as are performed שלא במקום זרע or ממקום אחר (See Rashi to Yebamot 34b s. v. שלא כדרכה and Rashi to Genesis XXIV, 16, compared with Genesis R. XL, 5), which are really sexual perversions and not sexual intercourse. See R. Isaiah Horowitz in his *Sh'ne Luhot ha-Brith* שער האותיות (Josefow, 1878, pp. 132–133). It seems rather that the Rabbis were of the opinion that when intercourse is had by what they euphemistically term הפיכת השולחן whether פנים כנגד עורף or היא למעלה והוא למטה the very position of the woman is such as to prevent conception. Compare their saying אשה מזנה מתהפכת כדי שלא תתעבר (Yebamot 35a); also Tur Eben ha-Ezer 76 end. Hence according to their theory, though not sustained by modern medicine, there are forms of sexual intercourse שלא כדרכה which cannot result in conception. These alone, not sexual perversions, do they permit. The statement of Raba (Sanhedrin 58b) taking for granted that an Israelite is permitted (read דלישראל שרי see Tossafot and מהרש"א *ad loc.*) to have intercourse with his wife שלא כדרכה is also to be understood in this sense, though from the phrase ודבק ולא שלא כדרכה: used in the amended saying of Raba it would appear that the term שלא כדרכה means ביאה ממקום אחר. From a Baraita in *Yebamot*, 34b we learn that during the period of lactation the husband is allowed, if not commanded, to practice coitus abruptus when having intercourse with his wife. The Baraita reads as follows: כל עשרים וארבעה חדש דש מבפנים וזורה מבחוץ דברי רבי אליעזר אמרו לו הללו אינו אלא כמעשה ער ואונן, כמעשה ער ואונן ולא כמעשה ער ואונן

"During the 24 months in which his wife nurses, or should nurse, the child, the husband when having intercourse with her should, or may practice coitus abruptus (to avoid her becoming pregnant again. For in the latter eventuality she will not be able to continue nursing the child and the child might die as a result of an early weaning Rashi *ad loc.*) כדי שלא תתעבר ותגמול את בנה וימות The other teachers, however, said to R. Eliezer that such intercourse would be almost like the acts of Er and Onan." One may argue that this permission or recommendation of practicing coitus abruptus represents only the opinion of R. Eliezer and we should decide against him, according to the principle יחיד ורבים הלכה כרבים. But such an argument does not hold good in our case. In the first place, when the individual opinion has a good reason in its support דמסתבר טעמיה as, according to Rashi, R. Eliezer's opinion in our case has, the decision may follow the individual against the many (see Alfasi and Asheri to B. B. Chapter 1, end, and comp. Maleachi Cohn, Yad Maleachi 296). Secondly, we cannot here decide against R. Eliezer since the other teachers do not express a definite opinion contrary to his. For we notice that the other teachers do not say "It is forbidden to do so." They do not even say that it is Onanism. They merely say: "It is almost like the conduct of Er and Onan." This certainly is not a strong and definite opposition to R. Eliezer's opinion. It seems to me that even the other teachers did not forbid the practice under the circumstances. They merely refused to recommend it as R. Eliezer did, because they hesitated to recommend a practice which is so much like the acts of Er and Onan, even under circumstances which make it imperative that conception be prevented. And we have to understand R. Eliezer's opinion as making it obligatory for the husband to perform coitus abruptus during the period of lactation.

That this interpretation of the respective positions of R. Eliezer and the other teachers in our Baraita is correct will be confirmed by our consideration of another Baraita dealing with the question of using contraceptives. This other Baraita is found in Yebamot 12b, 100b, Ketubot 39a, Nedarim 35b and Niddah 45b. It reads as follows:

תני רב ביבי קמיה דרב נחמן שלש נשים משמשות במוך קטנה מעוברת
ומניקה, קטנה שמא תתעבר ושמא תמות מעוברת שמא תעשה עוברה סנדל
מניקה שמא תגמול בנה וימות. ואיזו היא קטנה מבת י"א שנים ויום אחד עד
י"ב שנים ויום אחד פחות מכאן ויתר על כן משמשת כדרכה והולכת דברי
רבי מאיר וחכמים אומרים אחת זו ואחת זו משמשת כדרכה והולכת ומן
השמים ירחמו משום שנאמר שומר פתאים ה'

Before we proceed to interpret this Baraita, we must ascertain the correct meaning of the phrase משמשות במוך as there are different interpretations given to it. According to Rashi, (Yebamot, 12b) it means putting cotton or another absorbent into the vagina before the cohabitation, so that the semen discharged during cohabitation will fall upon the cotton and be absorbed by it and conception will not take place. According to R. Jacob Tam (Tossafot, ibidem s. v. שלש נשים) however, it means using cotton or the absorbent after the act of cohabitation in order to remove the semen and thus prevent conception. Whether the latter is according to modern medical science an effective contraceptive or not is not our concern; the rabbis believed it to be such.

It is evident that according to R. Tam the use of a douche or any other means of removing or destroying the sperm would be the same as משמשות במוך. Likewise, according to Rashi the use of other contraceptives, on the part of the woman, would be the same as משמשות מוך. Possibly, R. Tam would permit the use of chemical contraceptives even if employed before cohabitation. For his objection to the cotton put in before cohabitation is that then the semen is discharged upon the cotton, it does not touch the mucous membrane of the vagina. This he considers "no real sexual intercourse, but like scattering the semen upon wood and stone." דרך דאין תשמיש בכך והרי הוא כמטיל זרע על העצים ועל האבנים כשמטיל על המוך A practice which, according to the Midrash (Genesis R. XXVI, 6) was indulged in by the "generation of the flood" דור המבול . This objection, then, would not hold good when chemical contraceptives are used.

Again, according to Rashi (*Yebamot,* 100b) the phrase משמשות במוך means מותרות ליתן מוך באותו מקום שלא יתעברו , that is, that in these three conditions women are allowed to use this contraceptive; this would imply that other women who do not expose themselves or their children to danger by another pregnancy are forbidden to do so. According to R. Tam (Tossafot, *Ketubot,* 39a s.v. שלש נשים). Asheri and R. Nissim (on *Nedarim,* 35b) the phrase משמשות במוך means צריכות or as R. Nissim puts it חייבות לשמש במוך משום סכנה וכו׳ that is, that these three women because of the danger of possible harm which might result from pregnancy are obliged to use this precaution. If we interpret the phrase in this sense, it would imply that other women, not threatened by any danger from pregnancy, are merely not obliged to use this precaution against conception but are not forbidden to do so. It would also follow from this interpretation that if the other teachers differ from R. Meier, they differ only in so far as they do not consider it obligatory upon these three women (or to be more correct, upon the קטנה) to take this precaution, but as to permitting these three women or any other woman to use a contraceptive, there is no difference of opinion between R. Meier and the other teachers. R. Solomon Lurya (1510–1573) in his ים של שלמה to Yebamot ch. I, No. 8 (Altona, 1739) p. 4 bc, has indeed so interpreted our Baraita. He points out that from the Talmud, *Niddah,* 3a, it is evident that Rashi's interpretation of משמשות במוך as meaning "putting in the absorbent before cohabitation takes place" is correct. As to R. Tam's objection, Lurya correctly states that such a practice is not to be compared to מטיל על העצים For after all, it is a normal manner of having sexual intercourse, and the two bodies derive pleasure from one another and experience gratification of their desire. It is, therefore, not different from any other normal sexual intercourse with a woman who is incapable of having children אין זה כמטיל על עצים דסוף סוף דרך תשמיש בכך וגוף נהנה מן הגוף ודמי למשמש הקטנה Lurya further points out that since from *Nidda,* 3a, it is also evident that all women are permitted to use this contraceptive, the meaning of the phrase משמשות במוך in our Baraita must therefore be that these three women *must* use this precaution—which implies that all other women may use it. From this, argues Lurya, we must conclude that even if we should decide that the law הלכה follows the חכמים who differ from R. Meier, it would only mean that we would not make it obligatory for these three women to use this precaution. But these three women like all other women are permitted to use it if they so desire. This is in essence the opinion of Lurya.

It seems to me that a correct analysis of the Baraita will show that Lurya did not go far enough in his conclusions, and that there is no difference of opinion between R. Meier and the other teachers on the question whether a pregnant or a nursing woman must take this precaution. For this is what the Baraita says: "There are three women who, when having intercourse with their husbands, must take the precaution of using an absorbent to prevent conception, a minor, a pregnant woman and a woman nursing her baby. In the case of the minor, lest she become pregnant and die when giving birth to the child (it was believed by some of the Rabbis that if a girl became pregnant before having reached the age of puberty, she and her child would both die at the moment of childbirth. (comp. Saying of Rabbah b. Livai, *Yebamot,* 12b and Tossafot *ad loc.* s. v. שמא תתעבר also saying in P. Pesahim, VIII, 1 (35c) עיברה וילדה עד שלא הביאה שתי שערות היא ובנה מתים)

In case of a pregnant woman, this precaution is necessary, lest, if another conception takes place the embryo becomes a foetus papyraceus (com. Julius Preuss, *Biblisch-Talmudische Medizin,* Berlin 1921 p. 486–7).

In the case of a nursing mother, this precaution is necessary, for if she should become pregnant, she will have to wean her child before the proper time (which was considered to extend for twenty-four months) and the child may die as a result of such an early weaning. So far the Baraita apparently represents a unanimous statement. It then proceeds to discuss the age up to which a woman is considered a minor in this respect. R. Meier says that the minor in this case is a girl between the age of eleven years and one day and twelve years and one day, and that during that period only must she take this precaution. Before or after this age she need not take any precaution, but may have natural intercourse משמשת כדרכה והולכת The other teachers, however, say that even during the period when she is a קטנה i.e., between the age of eleven and twelve she may have natural intercourse and is not obliged to take any precaution. For the heavenly powers will have mercy and protect her from all danger as it is said, "The Lord preserveth the simple" (Ps. 116, 6). The other teachers evidently did not consider the danger of a minor dying as a result of childbirth so probable. They must have believed that a girl even before the age of puberty could give birth to a living child and survive (comp. Preuss, *op. cit.,* p. 441). But as regards the nursing or the pregnant woman, even the other teachers do not say that she may dispense with this precaution, for we notice that they do not say כולן משמשות כדרכן והולכות

The rules of law laid down in this Baraita according to our interpretation are, therefore, the following: When there is a danger of harm resulting to the unborn child or the child already born, all teachers agree that it is obligatory to take the precaution of using a contraceptive. According to R. Meier, however, this obligation holds good also in the case when conception might result in danger or harm to the mother. But even if we should understand the Baraita to indicate that the other teachers differed with R. Meier in all three cases, it would still only follow, as Lurya correctly points out, that in all three cases we decide the הלכה according to the חכמים and do not make it obligatory upon these three women to take the precaution of using contraceptives; the rule indicated by the Baraita would still teach us that, according to the opinion of all the teachers, it is not forbidden to use a contraceptive in cases where conception would bring harm either to the mother or the child born or unborn. And I cannot see any difference between the protection of a minor from a conception which might prove fatal to her and the protection of a grown up woman whose health is, according to the opinion of physicians, such that a pregnancy might be fatal to her. Neither can I see any difference between protecting a child from the danger of being deprived of the nourishment of its mother's milk, and protecting the already born children of the family from the harm which might come to them due to the competition of a larger number of sisters and brothers. For the care and the comfort which the parents can give to their children already born, will certainly be less if there be added to the family other children claiming attention, care and comfort.

The Talmudic law also permits a woman even to permanently sterilize herself האשה רשאי לשתות כוס של עיקרין (Tosefta, *Yebamot,* VIII, 4). And the wife of the famous R. Hiyya is reported to have taken such a medicine כסא דעקרתא which made her sterile. Yebamot 65b. Whether there be such a drug according to modern medicine or not, is not our concern. The Rabbis believed that there was such a drug which, if taken internally makes a person sterile (see *Sabbath,* 110ab and Preuss, *op. cit.* p. 439–440 and p. 479–80), and they permitted the woman to take it and become sterile. According to Lurya (*op. cit., Yebamot,* IV, 44) this permission is given to a woman who experiences great pain at child-birth, which she wishes to escape, as was the case of the wife of R. Hiyya. Even more so, says Lurya, is this permitted to a woman whose children are morally corrupt and of bad character, and who fears to bring into the world other moral delinquents

אלא למי שיש לה צער לידה כעין דביתהו דרבי חייא וכל שכן אם בניה
אין הולכין בדרך ישרה ומתייראה שלא תרבה מגידולין כאלה שהרשות בידה

To these I would also add the woman who, because of a heredi-
tary disease with which she or her husband is afflicted, fears to
have children who might be born with these diseases and suffer
and be a burden to their family or to society.

From the passage in the Talmud (*Yebamot,* 65b) we learn, however, that there is an objection which the Jewish law might have
to a man's using contraceptive means, or having intercourse with
his wife in such a manner as to make conception impossible. This
objection is based, not on the view that such an act is in itself
immoral or against the law, but merely on consideration for another
religious duty which could not be fulfilled if such a practice would
be indulged in all the time. The wife of R. Hiyya, so the Talmud
tells us, incapacitated herself only after she had learned that the
duty of propagation of the race was not incumbent upon her,
since, according to the decision of the Rabbis, women were not included in the commandment, "Be fruitful and multiply" (Genesis
I, 28), which was given to men only. Since a man must fulfill the
duty of propagation of the race מצות פו״ר he cannot be allowed the
practice of having intercourse with his wife only in such a manner
as to make conception impossible. For in doing so he fails to fulfill
the law commanding him to have children. It is accordingly a sin
of omission but not of commission; for the practice as such is not
immoral or against the law.

But—and this is peculiar to the Jewish point of view on this
question—the man who practices absolute self-restraint or total
abstinence is also guilty of the same sin of omission, for he likewise
fails to fulfill the duty of propagation of the race. No distinction can
be made, according to Jewish law, between the two ways of avoiding the duty of begetting children, whether by total abstention from
sexual intercourse or by being careful not to have intercourse in
such a manner as would result in conception. For, as has already
been pointed out, the act of having intercourse with one's wife in
a manner not effecting conception is in itself not forbidden by
Jewish law. If, however, a man has fulfilled the duty of propagation
of the race, as when he already has two children (i.e. two boys

according to the school of Shammai or a boy and a girl according to
to the school of Hillel) and is no longer obliged by law to beget
more children (*Yebamot,* 61b and Shulhan Aruk, *Eben ha-Ezer,*
I, 5) there can be no objection at all to the practice of birth control. For while the Rabbis of old, considering children a great
blessing, would advise a man to continue to beget children even
after he has already fulfilled the duty of propagation of the race,
yet they grant that any man has a right to avoid having more
children, when for one reason or another he does not consider it
a blessing to have too many children and deems it advisable in his
particular case not to have more than the two that the law commands him to have.

But even in the case of one who has not yet fulfilled the duty
of propagation of the race מצות פריה ורביה it might, under certain conditions, be permitted to practice birth control, if it is done
not for selfish purposes but for the sake of some higher ideal or
worthy moral purpose. For the rabbinic law permits a man to delay
his marrying and having children, or even to remain all his life unmarried, like Ben Azzai, if he is engaged in study and fears that
having a family to take care of would interfere with his work and
hinder in the pursuit of his studies (*Kiddushin,* 29b, Maimonides,
Yad Ishut, XV, 2–3; Shulhan Aruk, *Eben ha-Ezer,* I, 3–4).

Since, as we have seen, the act of having intercourse with one's
wife in a manner not resulting in conception is in itself not against
the law, there can be no difference between the failure to fulfill the
commandment of propagation of the race by abstaining altogether
from marriage and the failure to fulfill this commandment by practicing birth control. The considerations that permit the one permit
also the other. It would even seem that the other, i.e. the practice
of birth control, should be preferred to the one of total abstention.
For, in granting permission to practice the latter, the Rabbis make
the proviso that the man be so constituted, or so deeply engrossed
in his work, as not to be troubled by his sexual desires, or be
strong enough to withstand temptation (והוא שלא יהא יצרו מתגבר עליו)
(Maimonides and Shulhan Aruk l. c.) Now, if a man is so consti-

tuted that he is troubled by his desires and suffers from the lack of
gratification of them and yet is engaged in some noble and moral
pursuit like the study of the Torah, which pursuit hinders him from
taking on the responsibilities of a family, he may marry and avoid
having children. He may say with Ben Azzai, "I am very much
attached to my work and cannot afford to have a family to take
care of. The propagation of the race can and will be carried on by
others."(אפשר לעולם שיתקיים על ידי אחרים *Yebamot,* 36b, Tosefta,
ibidem, VIII, end). For the Rabbis also teach that "it is better to
marry" even if not for the sake of having children, "than to burn"
with passion and ungratified desires. And, as we have seen above,
the rabbinic law permits marriage even when it must needs result
in failure to fulfill the commandment "be fruitful and multiply,"
as when a young man marries an old or sterile woman. The rabbis
did not teach total abstention. They did not agree with Paul that
"it is good for a man not to touch a woman" (I Corinth. VIII, 1).
While the institution of marriage may have for its main purpose the
propagation of the race, this is not its sole and exclusive purpose.
And the Rabbis urge and recommend marriage as such without
regard to this purpose, or even under conditions when this purpose
cannot be achieved. The companionship or mutual helpfulness in
leading a pure, good and useful life, achieved by a true marriage
is also a noble purpose worthy of this divine institution. In fact,
according to the biblical account, this was the first consideration in
the Divine mind when creating woman for man. He said: "It is not
good that the man should be alone, I will make him a help meet
for him" (Genesis II, 18). He did not say I will make him a wife
that he have children by her. The commandment to have children
God gave to Adam later on. When husband and wife live together
and help each other to lead a good life, whether they have children
or not, God is with them and their home is a place for the שכינה
the Divine presence, says R. Akiba (Sotah 17a). Ben Azzai did not
say like Paul: "I would that all men were even as I myself" (I
Corinth. VII, 7). He did not set up celibacy in itself as an ideal,
nor would he recommend it to others (comp. H. Graetz, *Gnosticis-*

mus und Judenthum, Krotoshin, 1846, p. 73 ff). Ben Azzai considered marriage a Divine institution and recognized the obligation of propagating the race as a religious duty. But he believed that he was exempted from this duty in consideration of the fact that it might interfere with another religious duty like the study of the Torah in which he was engaged. Of course, the same right would, according to Ben Azzai, be given to others in a similar position, i.e., pursuing studies or engaged in any other moral religious activities which might be interfered with by the taking on of the obligation of having children. We have seen that the medieval rabbinic authorities have concurred in the opinion of Ben Azzai and allowed a man engaged in a religious pursuit like the study of the Torah to delay or even altogether neglect fulfilling the commandment of "Be fruitful and multiply." And we have also found that no distinction can be made between neglecting this duty by abstaining from marriage or neglecting it by practicing birth control.

The above represents the logical conclusion which one must draw from a correct understanding and a sound interpretation of the halakic statements in the Talmud touching this question, disregarding the ideas expressed in the agadic literature as to the advisability of having many children.

The later Jewish mystics emphasized these agadic sayings, as well as the agadic condemnations of the evil practices of הוצאת שכבת זרע לבטלה. They came to regard any discharge of semen which might have resulted in conception but did not, almost like הוצאת שכבת זרע לבטלה. Nay, even an unconscious seminal emission is regarded a sin against which one must take all possible precautions and for which one must repent and make atonement. But even the mystics permit intercourse with one's wife even when she is incapable of having children, see Zohar Emor 90b ואי תימא דאפיק ליה באנתו דלא מתעברא הכי נמי? לא. אלא כדאמרן.

Some rabbinic authorities of the eighteenth and nineteenth centuries, under the spell of the agadic sayings of the Talmud and more or less influenced by the mystic literature, are loath to permit birth control. But even these authorities do not altogether prohibit the practice when there is a valid reason for exercising it. The reasons given by some of them for opposing the practice are not justified in the light of the Halakic statements of the Talmud which we discussed above. Their arguments are not based upon correct interpretations of the talmudic passages bearing upon this question, and they utterly ignore or overlook the correct interpretations and the sound reasoning of R. Solomon Lurya quoted above. In the following I will present the opinions of some of the authorities of the eighteenth and nineteenth centuries on this question.

R. Salom Zalman of Posen, Rabbi in Warsaw (died 1839) in his responsa חמדת שלמה (quoted in Piṭḥe Teshubah to Eben ha-Ezer XXIII, 2) in answer to a question about a woman to whom, according to the opinion of physicians, pregnancy might be dangerous, declares that she may use a contraceptive. He permits even the putting into the vagina an absorbent before cohabitation, declaring that since the intercourse takes place in the normal way, the discharge of the semen in such a case cannot be considered השחתת זרע .

R. Joseph Modiano, a Turkish Rabbi of the second half of the eighteenth century in his Responsa collection ראש משביר part II (Salonica 1840) No. 49, discusses the case of a woman who during her pregnancy becomes extremely nervous and almost insane. He quotes the great rabbinical authority R. Michael who declared that the woman *should* use a contraceptive. R. Michael argued that since the woman is exposed to the danger by pregnancy she is in a class with the three women mentioned in the Baraita of R. Bibi and should therefore, like them, use an absorbent, even putting it in before cohabitation שישמש בעלה במוך כדי שלא תתעבר and her husband cannot object to it. Modiano himself does not concur in the opinion of R. Michael; he argues that the use of the absorbent could only be permitted if employed after cohabitation, and the husband who may find the use of this contraceptive inconvenient or may doubt its effectiveness should therefore be permitted to marry another woman. But even Modiano would not forbid the use of this contraceptive if the husband had no objection.

R. Akiba Eger in his Responsa, No. 71 and 72 (Warsaw 1834) p. 51b–53a also permits the use of an absorbent but only if it is employed after cohabitation. The questioner, R. Eleazar Zilz, a rabbinical authority of Posen, however, argued that it should be permitted even when employed before cohabitation.

R. Moses Sofer in his Hatam Sofer, part Yore Deah No. 172 (Pressburg 1860) p. 67d–68a, likewise permits it only when used after cohabitation. R. Abraham Danzig in his Hokmat Adam and Binat Adam, שער בית הנשים No. 36 (Warsaw 1914) p.156 permits the use of an absorbent or a douche or any other method of removing or destroying the semen after cohabitation. He adds, however, that according to Rashi's interpretation, it would be permitted to the woman in question to whom pregnancy was dangerous, to use this contraceptive even before cohabitation.

R. Jacob Etlinger (1798–1871) in his Responsa *Binyan Zion* (No. 137) (Altona 1868) p. 57b–58b and R. Joseph Saul Nathanson (1808–1875) in his Responsa שואל ומשיב מהדורא תנינא part IV (Lemberg 1874) No. 13 are inclined to forbid the use of any contraceptive even when used after cohabitation.

The authorities objecting to the use of an absorbent before cohabitation do so, of course, on the ground that, like R. Tam, they consider such a practice כמטיל על העצים ואל האבנים. On the same ground they would no doubt object to the use of a condom. But as already pointed out above, they could have no objection to the use of chemical contraceptives on the part of the woman.

In summing up the results of our discussion, I would say that while there may be some differences of opinion about one detail or another or about the exact meaning of one talmudic passage or another, we can formulate the following principles in regard to the question of birth control as based upon a correct understanding of the halakic teachings of the Talmud as accepted by the medieval rabbinic authorities, and especially upon the sound interpretation given by R. Solomon Lurya to some of these talmudic passages:

1). The Talmudic-Rabbinic law does not consider the use of

contraceptives as such immoral or against the law. It does not forbid birth control but it forbids birth suppression.

2). The Talmudic-Rabbinic law requires that every Jew have at least two children in fulfillment of the biblical command to propagate the race which is incumbent upon every man.

3). There are, however, conditions under which a man may be exempt from this prime duty: (a) when a man is engaged in religious work like the study of the Torah, and fears that he may be hindered in his work by taking on the responsibilities of a family; (b) when a man because of love or other considerations marries a woman who is incapable of having children, as an old or sterile woman; (c) when a man is married to a woman whose health is in such a condition as to make it dangerous for her to bear children. For, considerations for the saving of human life פקוח נפש or even ספק פקוח נפש set aside the obligation to fulfill a religious duty. In this case, then, the woman is allowed to use any contraceptives or even to permanently sterilize herself in order to escape the dangers that would threaten her at childbirth.

4). In case a man has fulfilled the duty of propagation of the race, as when he has already two children, he is no longer obliged to beget children and the law does not forbid him to have intercourse with his wife even in a manner which would not result in conception. In such a case the woman certainly is allowed to use any kind of contraceptive or preventive.

Of course, in any case, the use of contraceptives or of any device to prevent conception is allowed only when both parties, i.e., husband and wife, consent.

Some rabbinic authorities of the eighteenth and nineteenth centuries would object to one or another of the above rules, and especially put restrictions upon the use of contraceptives. But we need not expect absolute agreement on questions of rabbinic law. We must be content to have good and reliable authority for our decisions, even though other authorities may differ. We have the right to judge for ourselves which view is the sounder and which authorities are more correct. We have found that the arguments of those authorities of the eighteenth and nineteenth centuries who would oppose or restrict the use of contraceptives in cases where we would recommend it, are not convincing. With all our respect for these authorities we may ignore their opinions just as they in turn have ignored the opinions of other authorities, especially those of R. Solomon Lurya, on our question.

ON PEOPLE AND LAND

On People and Land: The Question of Zionism ·

Central to the original conception of Reform Judaism was the abandonment of the traditional dream of a reestablished Jewish nation under the rule of a restored Davidic monarchy. Particularistic political messianism was replaced, under the influence of the cosmopolitan ideals of the Enlightenment, by the universalistic ethical and spiritual notion of a mission of Israel among the nations. The description of the messianic age as a time when truth, justice, and peace would prevail did not change. What changed, in Reform thinkers, was the emphasis. Their stress was placed on the extension of the spiritual values of the messianic age to all mankind, whereas the traditional doctrine accented the return of the Jewish people to power and sovereignty as the consequence of a supernatural transformation of the long continued "underdog" situation of the Jews.

When the new political Zionism of the 1890s began to be bruited about, most of the leaders of Reform Judaism saw the movement to return the Jews to a place as a nation among nations as a repudiation of the goals of the Reform movement and a reversion (without the advantage of supernaturalism) to an earlier narrowness of outlook. The Pittsburgh Platform of 1885 set the major tone of the American Reform movement for nearly fifty years: "We consider ourselves no longer a nation, but a religious community, and therefore expect neither a return to Palestine, nor a sacrificial worship under the sons of Aaron, nor the restoration of any of the laws concerning the Jewish state."

In the early discussions at the annual meetings of the Central Conference of American Rabbis, the characteristic note was that struck by Dr. Henry Berkowitz in 1899. In his address, entitled "Why I am not a Zionist," Berkowitz urged against the nascent Zionist movement the consideration that just treatment for the Jew in the modern world was on the increase, and that, therefore, the misery of the Jews would be lessened, given enough time. Newer techniques of organization had begun to develop "practical, feasible and sensible" methods for working toward the elimination of specific Jewish problems; by contrast, Zionism is "sentimental" and "chimerical." Most important, Zionism represents a turning away from the ultimate religious mission of the Jews, who "have no lasting claims for a separate existence excepting their religious mission." On behalf of this mission, Jews must be prepared to face the prospect of martyrdom.

A rare spokesman for "The Justification of Zionism" in the councils of the Reform rabbis of that time was Professor Caspar Levias, who argued that even if we accept the notion of a Jewish mission, Jews themselves must learn to live out the "prophetic ideal," in a homeland of their own, before they can successfully carry the message to the nations of the world. Moreover, the mission need not require the exposure to martyrdom of all the Jews; since Palestine could not, in any case, accommodate all the Jews of the world, there would be enough left over to carry out the Jewish mission. In addition, Levias rejected the view that nationalism is a totally evil development; to suggest the positive values of the nationalist ideal, he substituted for "nationalism" the term "collective individualism" and argued that only under such collective individualism is it in fact possible for each person to maximize his development, "for the fullness of individuality can be developed only in congenial society." The Ghetto-Jew stands as evidence of what happens to a human being subject to uncongenial influences. In response to the charge that Zionism is impractical,

Levias claimed that inasmuch as Zionist leaders did not expect instantaneous results, but anticipated that the changes to be brought about by the reestablishment of a Jewish homeland might take several generations, their practicality could not be evaluated.

This justification of Zionism by Professor Levias has been called one of the early masterpieces of Zionist apologetic. It had, however, little immediate effect upon the views of the majority of the members of the Central Conference of American Rabbis. Through the early years of the twentieth century there was a slowly increasing Zionist minority in the Conference. Repeated attempts were made to induce the membership to pass resolutions less unfavorable to the Zionist position than the stand based on the Pittsburgh Platform. Not until the 1930s brought with them the Nazi horror were the Reform rabbis sufficiently shaken out of their complacency to vote even a moderately firm pro-Zionist stand. Some individual members of the Reform rabbinate became extremely effective and prominent figures in the Zionist movement long before the organizational stand of the Central Conference was modified.

Evidence of individual opinion is still clearly present in the exchange, in 1935, between two distinguished Reform leaders. Samuel Schulman, one of the most able members of the older generation of Reform rabbis, defended the classical Reform, antinationalist position with great passion and eloquence. His antagonist, Abba Hillel Silver, was a Zionist leader of comparable ability. Their confrontation in 1935 was truly a meeting of giants; regrettably only portions of their addresses can be reproduced here. It is noteworthy, however, that a reversal of momentum took place between the papers of 1899 and those of 1935. Now it is the anti-Zionist case that Dr. Schulman presents as apologetic, even allowing the concession of offering personal support for the Palestinian Jews, while retaining the theoretical principle that the Jews are a people, not a nation. Dr. Silver's pro-Zionist statement now reveals the forthrightness of one who is completely certain not only of the correctness of his stand but also of the sympathies of the majority

of his hearers. These two addresses make the direction of the
Reform leadership clear. Dr. Schulman was fighting a rear-guard
action, Dr. Silver riding the wave of the future.

WHY I AM NOT A ZIONIST
Henry Berkowitz
(1899)

The fundamental principles of Zionism are formulated by Prof. Richard Gottheil, President of the Federation of American Zionists, in these words: "We believe that the Jews are something more than a purely religious body; that they are not only a race, but a nation, though a nation without, as yet, two important requisites— a common home and a common language.

"We believe that if an end is to be made to Jewish misery and to the exceptional position of the Jews a new home must be supplied. We believe that such a regeneration would be the fulfillment of the Jews' greatest hope.

"We believe that the home of their fathers, Palestine, is the only place for such a home, and that a guarantee of such a return must be given by the Great Powers of the world. We further hold that this does not mean that all Jews shall return to Palestine."

Against each one of the doctrines of this creed I respectfully enter my protest and demurrer. In my judgment there is not a sound plank in the platform and the whole platform rests upon unreliable supports.

The basic proposition is that three-fourths of the Jews of the world are living in hopeless misery. Of the ten millions one-half live in the pale of Settlement in Russia under conditions which have been depicted again and again to the horror of civilized mankind. One million are in Galicia, ninety-five per cent of whom are daily subject to the passion of the mob, liable to pillage and torture. Five hundred thousand in Roumania are robbed of the rights of citizenship. In Austria, Germany and alas, now most of all, in France the Jews are the victims of the malicious Anti-Semites, while even in enlightened Great Britain and free America they are not exempt from exclusion and prejudice.

This arraignment against the nations is true in every count. Our hearts bleed with those of the Zionists in doleful grief at the cruelty, injustice and godlessness which disgrace the persecutor and degrade the persecuted.

Paint the picture of suffering as black as you will, you can hardly exaggerate, but do not fail to see that there is also a companion picture of brighter colors. It is an egregious and fatal error of the Zionists that they accept the misery of Israel as permanent, his wretchedness as hopeless. Three-fourths of the Jews of the world in bondage! Yes, but when in these nineteen hundred years were one fourth as free as to-day?

The Zionist portrays with pathos the scene at Basle where five hundred and fifty years ago the Jews were burned by their foes, bu' he sees not that the holding of the congress there and the greetings of the populace in procession who cried aloud, "Hail to the Jews!" constitute a sublime instance of the retributive justice at work in history as well as a tribute to the heroic endurance of Israel, and at once a total subversion of the basic doctrine of Zionism itself, that the position of the Jew is exceptional and hopeless.

Let it not be forgotten that while there is a strong party of Judea-phobists in nearly every European country, yet these noisy agitators are held in check by the fair-minded and moral elements of each land. We do wrong to forget the thousands of friends of justice and right because of the hundreds of foes. In France the best people, the whole intellectual world, the men and women of light and leading, the true Patriots like Scheurer-Kestner, Emile Zola and Reinach are on the side of truth and honor and will, under God, prevail.

The press of all civilized countries is voicing the sentiment of the people with almost perfect accord against the outrageous invasion of human rights in the Dreyfus case. Let us not forget that from Macaulay to Beaconsfield and Gladstone, England has been on our side. Let us not forget that when Alwardt came to America trumpeting his purpose to plant the Anti-Semitic movement here, he was hooted out of the land by the liberty loving press and people.

Let us remember that the era of emancipation is hardly a hundred years old. What is a hundred years in our history! Sad as is still the fate of the myriads of Israel, it is to-day not as hopeless as at any time in the last nineteen hundred years. The pathway of civilization is tortuous, often winding back on its own course, but it is nevertheless progressive. Never before was the evidence so strong that mankind has set its face resolutely towards a future of justice. This is not theory, but history.

In affirming that Israel's misery is hopeless Zionism makes an inference from a partial and not from a full and fair statement of facts. It founds its movement on a basis which under the humanizing influences at work in the world is day by day surely crumbling away. This is one reason why I am not a Zionist.

But in the meantime what is to be done? Are the three-fourths of Israel who neither by their own efforts nor by the progress of the world have yet come to their rights to be permitted to suffer the agonies of their present state until sluggish time shall rouse the torpid consciences of their brutal oppressors? By no means if any effort of the other one-fourth can prevent it.

Such an effort was made by Cerf Beer in France, at the close of the last century and he so roused his co-religionists that they rested not until the civil rights of the Jews of France had been secured.

Such an effort was made in Germany by Gabriel Riesser and he rested not until he commanded the homage which gave the Jew a seat of honor in the German Parliament.

Such an effort was inaugrated in England by Isaac Lyon Goldsmid and it never was permitted to rest until the civil disabilities of the Jews in England were fully removed.

It was through such earnest efforts that Sir Moses Montefiore performed his world embracing work of securing the advancement of his co-religionists in many lands.

Under like inspiration Adolph Cremieux made the *"Alliance Israelite Universelle"* a union of Israelites and bound them by the sense of common responsibility to found schools throughout Europe, Asia and Africa and to effectively plead the cause of the oppressed in many lands.

It was a like motive which called into being the Anglo-Jewish Association of Great Britain, the Israelitische Allianz of Germany and of Austria, the Union of American Hebrew Congregations of America, the unparalleled philanthropies of the Rothschilds, the stupendous projects of Baron and Baroness de Hirsch for colonizing, educating and seeking to uplift the Jews, and to the same motive we owe the great systems of Jewish charitable, educational and religious organizations that now exist throughout the world.

Magnificent work has already been done and is continuously and untiringly being performed through these agencies in behalf of our co-religionists. There seems to be a studied purpose on the part of Zionism to ignore all these noble and generous enterprises in which millions are expended, or to belittle, or deny the results achieved.

Because I believe that these methods are approved by reason and experience as practical and are on the right lines, I favor them and am not a Zionist.

True, the measure of results achieved is meager as compared with the work still to be done. This is partly due to the fact that the Jewish problem is really bound up with the great economic problems of the age, for let it not be forgotten that the "Jew quarter" now exists in the cities of free America as well as of despotic

Russia. But if more has not been directly accomplished it is due largely to the fact that of the one-fourth in Israel upon whom the obligation rests, only a small proportion have actually done the work. Those prominent in Zionism have hitherto been, for the most part, derelict in their duties towards their co-religionists; indeed many of them never wanted to be Jews, some concealed, some even denied their Jewish affinity, and now forsooth, they turn upon those who have been doing valiant service and demand that something be done for the helpless and depressed.

I rejoice in Zionism in so far as it is awakening in thousands a sense of obligation to their fellows and rousing them out of an attitude of shameless indifference. To many who had put on the gaudy garments of modern culture and learned to wear them jauntily, crowding forward into the circles of the snobbish and elect, Anti-Semitism has been a slap in the face, and smarting under the sting they are grown humbly conscious of themselves as Jews. At last they have come to cry out, "The Jew must help himself!"

I set the work actually being done by the Jew to help himself over against the propositions of political Zionism that our only help is securing a legally guaranteed possession of Palestine as a home.

I shall not enter into a consideration of the feasibility of this suggestion. It seems childish to suppose that those powers which do not now give the Jew human rights at home, will magnanimously enrich him with a land. It seems absurd to expect that the jealousies of the Christian and Mohammedan worlds will dissolve in a loving gift to the Jew of that soil which all three hold sacred.

The grave problems of the re-establishment of a Jewish state and a Jewish national church seems to have no terrors for the Zionists. The utter unlikelihood, even with a Jewish state, of the successful attainment of the coveted peace and security for the three-fourths of Israel, makes the whole scheme, to my mind, chimerical and absurd.

But I am free to grant that somehow, beyond my comprehension, all these problems may be solved, and even then should the plans of Zionism be carried out I would oppose the whole project on principle.

Zionism declares that "the Jews are more than a purely religious body, they are not only a race but also a nation." The proposition should be reversed. The Jews are more than a race or a nation, they are primarily a religious body. The difference lies in putting the emphasis where it belongs, and that is on our religion. Leroy-Beaulieu has clarified to the every-day reader what students of ethnology know, viz., that there is no pure Jewish race. To elevate the race tie, such as it is, above the religious, is simply to fall into the trap of those who for political reasons have brought back old race hatreds into the world to set heedless and thoughtless men against their fellow-men, Teutons against Slavs, Huns against Magyars, Aryans against Semites. It is a sad blunder which Zionism here commits to urge upon the Jews to draw apart on racial lines.

Therefore again I am not a Zionist.

The ultimate end and aim of our history is the maintenance of Judaism, not the maintenance of Jews. Judaism has preserved itself thus far because of the power of its ideals, the inspiration of its precepts. These are eternal and superior to race or nationality. As Judaism has persisted despite the passing of its pure racial expression, so has it developed out of and superior to nationalism.

When Abram left Ur of the Chaldees to proclaim the monotheistic truth his first motive was the acquisition of a land in which to maintain that truth. The patriarchal family developed into a nation under Moses and the conquest of the Promised Land was the tangible motive of its history. This was then a matter of course, for in ancient thought every God was a King who ruled over a definite earthly domain. The wars of nations were the wars of their Gods as well. "Who is like thee among the Gods, O Jehovah!" is the most ancient war-cry of Israel. A God without a land was inconceivable.

It was the great discovery of the prophets of the eighth century that the God of Israel is the God of mankind, the God of Judea is the God of the universe. This great thought then for the first time broke through the bonds of nationality and announced the Universal religion. Twice nationality was an episode in the history of our people, necessary purely for the maintenance and development of the religion. Nationalism was not the end and aim of the great Maccabean victory, but the restoration and re-dedication of the Temple which symbolized the triumph of the religion.

For nineteen hundred years we have lived without a land. We have come to read our history in a new light. The fall of Jerusalem and the destruction of our nationality was not the calamity we dreamed it to be. "Centuries have since then passed away," says Zunz, "the Jews have lost their independence and their country; but on the downfall of every institution the Synagogue remained as the sole representative of their nationality. Towards this centre their faith was directed and from it they obtained instruction for their daily conduct, strength to endure unheard of sufferings and hope for a future dawn of freedom."

The Synagogue has supplanted the Temple and the land as the tangible expression of the Jewish religion. Zionism in the face of all our history denied this. It avers that the regeneration of Palestine is the greatest hope of the Jew. It reverts to a lesser ideal, that of government, in which the Jews were never successful. It subverts the philosophical foundations on which the prophets rested our religion and which kept it from being implicated in the fall of the nation. It restores the fantastic dreams of the Middle Ages and values the tinsel of the kingly crown of a David Reubeni or a Sabbathai Zvi higher than the true halo that wreathes the sainted martyrs of the ages.

I do not believe in pious resignation to our fate, nor in a passive martyrdom, but in a vigorous and heroic resistance.

My solution of the Jewish problem is not the Jewish race or the Jewish State but the Jewish Religion.

Its ideals have enabled our forefathers to endure the worst of martyrdoms in behalf of principle. These powers of these ideals and these principles are not exhausted for us. These ideals are slowly but surely becoming the possession of mankind and they have created the best in civilization.

Let us take our religion seriously and we shall be able to do wonders. Let us labor to educate and arouse the lax and cowardly in our midst and infuse them with the conviction that we are indeed the possessors of world-redeeming truths for mankind. Let them love their religion, gladly, openly live it, and under its inspiration, when once we get as we are getting the brains, the means, the ability, the genius of the liberated Jews to work on this Jewish problem we shall, under God, work out its solution along the practical lines that commend themselves to the day and age in which we are living.

These then are the reasons why I am not a Zionist.

First. Because I do not believe that the misery of my people is hopeless. I have not lost faith in the triumph of justice in the world.

Second. Because I believe that the methods of our modern organizations and the efforts made through them for colonization, education and the working out of the great economic problems of the day are practical, feasible and sensible, while Zionism is sentimental and in my judgment chimerical. What is needed in all our people is the awakening of a deeper Jewish consciousness to arouse their slumbering consciences and unite them in heroic moral action.

Third. Because Zionism makes race and nationality, rather than religion ultimate and essential for Jews. Jews have no lasting claims for a separate existence excepting their religious mission. To be faithful to this they must willfully assume the martyrdom and the struggle and not weakly evade it.

Providence has sent us into the world to oppose all forms of Paganism and immorality and work for principles of right, truth and justice among men. Our duty is to stay in the face of all ills and do our work until the final triumph.

THE JUSTIFICATION OF ZIONISM
Caspar Levias
(1899)

. . . The roseate view taken of the future by those who enjoy at this moment comparative ease is due to various delusions. It would lead me too far were I to attempt to expose all of them, since arguments that are not susceptible to logical demonstration are apt to lead to interminable controversies, which I, not being of a polemical disposition, wish to avoid. I confess that I would never have thought of publishing the present paper but for the public challenge I have received; for I take no active interest in theological discussions, my entire interest being wholly absorbed by my scientific studies. . . . I would, therefore, call the attention of the reader to the fact that in the following discussion only such points are taken up as admit of logical argument. Subjective opinions, personal sentiments, declarations and *ipse dixits,* as they do not admit of logical proof, are entirely disregarded. The sole purpose of this paper is to investigate whether the opponents of Zionism within the camp of progressive Judaism have any theoretical ground to stand on.

I wish to state that I am not aware of anybody before me having attempted to solve the problem under discussion from the point of view I have taken here. Knowing that to err is human, I shall be ready to acknowledge my mistake, if convinced of it by the opposite side.

The first move of the anti-Zionists in discussing Zionism is to drag into the arena the mission of Israel. The Zionists cannot help admitting that Israel has a mission; but they differ as to the mode of carrying on that mission; or, if you wish, as to the base of operations. The Zionists claim that we could carry out that mission only after we ourselves shall have realized the prophetic ideal; and this can be consummated only in a home of our own. When we shall have built up an ideal state in the land of our fathers, then will we attract the eyes of all nations; and they will be prompted to go up to Mount Zion and learn the ways of the God of Jacob. The anti-Zionists hold that the Jews in dispersion can best accomplish the desired end. The Zionists quote numerous passages from Scripture, where the gathering of all Israel from the four corners of the earth to Jerusalem is predicted and promised, in support of their view. The antis muster an equal number of scriptural passages to prove their side. The prophets themselves disagreeing, there is no way of proving the correctness of either view, and the argument from these premises becomes irrelevant to the question at issue.

But, for argument's sake, we will admit the correctness of the position taken by the antis. The question then arises, how large a contingent of Jews is there necessary to carry on that mission among the various nations? Happily, the antis themselves have given us an answer to this question. I will not mention the action of the Sephardic Jews in Holland, some centuries since, who endeavored to prevent the German Jews from settling in *their* Palestine—this is old history, but I shall come down to modern times. Some of the Rabbis, not very many years ago, denounced Jewish immigration to *their* Palestine. Many a layman did the same. Similar things happened lately in Memel, Bremen, Frankfurt a. M. and other cities of the fatherland, as well as Hungary. It is not a matter of doubt, that should the German Jews be inclined to emigrate to France, the Frenchmen of the Mosaic religion would not treat them with any more courtesy. Now, I am loth to believe that the representatives of the mission of Israel, both ministers and laymen, should have acted so from sordid motives; and I am rather inclined to assume that they were actuated by the sincere conviction that, in order to carry out their holy mission, there must be in the country as few Jews as possible. The Zionists have pointed out more than once that, should a Jewish state be established, it could never accommodate all the Jews, even if all of them were willing to leave the country of their birth or adoption. Hence, even then, there would remain among the nations a sufficient number of Jews to carry on the mission of Israel in the fashion of the antis.

The next point advanced by one of the speakers against Zionism was that the establishment of a petty Jewish state does not comport with the glorious future predicted for us by the prophetic dreamers. The dream of the prophet that nature shall be transformed, that the lion shall lie down with the lamb, and a small boy shall lead them, is a beautiful dream, an inspiring dream, but an unrealizable dream after all. The Jew that takes this dream into consideration in affairs of practical life is no less a visionary than his Christian neighbor who attempts to realize in human society the New Testament dream of non-resistance to evil.

But, again for argument's sake, I will grant the literal interpretation of messianic prophecy. Even the antis cannot deny that the realization of the messianic ideal lies still in the far distant future. By what logic do they bring themselves to the belief that, in expectation of that distant contingency, it is preferable for us to allow ourselves to be kicked by the Cossack and abused by the Junker, rather than live in the enjoyment of peace and human rights in Palestine? Would the existence of a Jewish state hinder the realization of a common humanity? If the prophetic ideal should prove so powerful as to transform the lion pupils into gentle lambs, would it not prove to be equally potent in keeping the lamb teacher in his lamblike purity?

Nationalism was brought up by one of the speakers as another bugaboo. Pointing to the turbulent state of the Austrian peoples, he showed the evil lurking in such a movement. It is not very many months since, that the Sultan of Turkey, pointing to the riotous scenes in the Austrian Reichstag, proved, to his own satisfaction, that parliamentarianism was impracticable. The trouble in the Austrian empire is that all its component elements have come to the recognition that nationalism is a good thing; but the more powerful element claims that good thing all for itself, and tries to crush out the nationalistic aspirations of the weaker elements. Naturally, the latter raise a disturbance. To argue from this that nationalism in itself is an evil, is as rational as if one should argue that the right of any man to his life and liberty is an evil, because he raised a disturbance in defending himself against a highwayman or a political corruptionist.

Nationalism is one of those big words which speakers and writers bandy about nowadays, frequently without having a clear idea of their meaning. . . . Nationalism is but a synonym of what I should call collective individualism. If the antis believe that every human being has the inalienable right to develop his latent individuality to the fullness of his God-given powers, then they must consistently be nationalists; for the fullness of individuality can be developed only in congenial society. If one have artistic gifts, he could not develop them on a Texas ranch, or in a Nevada mining camp, but would have to go to Paris or Rome, where the surrounding influences tend to further the development of his talents. Just as a plant-germ cannot develop its latent powers to the full when planted in uncongenial soil and under unfavorable conditions, so the human individual remains stunted and crippled when lacking congenial influences. And these congenial influences can be created only by a separate nation.

What uncongenial influences have made of the Ghetto-Jew we all know. Although the walls of the Ghetto have fallen, and brute force has ceased to harass us, the hostile spiritual influences of Christianity are still stunting our spiritual development, without our having any hope of avoiding them. The hostility of Christianity lies in its very essence, and will only cease with the ceasing of Christianity itself; (I hope the reader will not confuse Christianity with Christians;) and this will prove to be too long a time even for an anti-Zionist. The only way, therefore, to develop the peculiar spiritual gifts of the Jew is to take him out of his Christian *milieu*. To those that are tempted to deny the existence of a peculiarly Jewish genius, I would say that the ethical and religious ideals of which we rightly boast are nothing but a product, one of the embodiments of that genius. If you deny this peculiar genius, then what becomes of your mission? If you admit it, then you must admit the justness of Jewish nationalism. There are only two alternatives, either you are a nation, or you have no mission. If you have no mission, you have no reason for wishing to stay in dispersion. Turn as you will, if you are consistent, you must become Zionists.

Nationalism, that is, collective individualism, involves as little hatred towards other nationalities as single individualism does toward another individual. Nor does nationalism imply a shutting oneself up and isolating oneself from the influences of other nations; this just as little as single individualism means isolation from the influence of other individuals. Nationalism is merely the logical development and necessary outcome of individualism; it is only a higher stage of the latter. The friction between the rising nationalities at present is the result of new ideas trying to work themselves out under old forms. The process of adaptation to new conditions always requires fight and sacrifices; but after the adjustment of the warring interests, follow the blessings of peace and of increased happiness for all parties. With the spread of nationalistic feeling throughout the world, and with the recognition of the inalienability of national rights, the present political systems will have to break down. Whether every small nationality will become autonomous, or some new form of political confederation will be worked out, only the future can tell.

Just as the development of single individualism is not equal among all nations—some being belated, others never able to reach it; as, *e.g.,* the believers in fatalism; so the nationalistic development shows abnormalities; as, *e.g.,* in the United States. Here,

elements of various nationalities are in the process of amalgamation. This is due to exceptional conditions, which could never
repeat themselves in history. None of the national elements can
lay claim to any particular stretch of territory, all being scattered
among others. None of them need give up his religion. And even
if this should be necessary, it might perhaps be done, though this
is very unlikely; because, after all, the differences between the
Christian sects amount to tweedlededee and tweedlededum, as witness the changes of denominations taking place almost daily. And,
after all, we shall get, sooner or later, a new nation. Supposing
that some more Americans could be discovered, the process might
repeat itself. But the result would only be the shifting of nationalities, not the elimination of nationalism. Thus, even the United
States is but an apparent anomaly.

The question arises, how about the Jews? Could they not be
assimilated by the surrounding nations? To this question there
can be only one answer—an emphatic no. That such assimilation
is impossible on account of socio-political causes, has been lucidly
demonstrated by the much maligned Dr. Herzl in the introduction to his pamphlet, "The Jewish State." That this is impossible
on account of religious causes, the following will make clear:

I consider this to be the proper place to enter into an examination of the nature of the mission of Israel; or, in other words, to
find out what the messianic ideal of the present generation really is,
when divested of flowery rhetoric and nebulous generalities—the
pathological phenomena of our days—and expressed in plain
words. After considerable trouble in removing the husks, I succeeded in finding a solid kernel—a common humanity. But before swallowing it, I was careful to subject it to an analysis. The
result follows.

A common humanity can be conceived as accomplished in one of
four ways:

1. By the uniformity of the human species achieved through
intermarriage.

2. By the throwing down of political barriers.

3. By the uniformity of ethical and religious ideals within the human species.

4. By a combination of the three preceding means, or of any two of them.

Let us now examine the possibility and efficiency of each means separately.

1. Assuming that there will ever come a time when the Jews and the civilized Christian nations shall intermarry with the Zulus, the Hottentots, the Patagonians, and the cannibals of the South Sea Islands, the question arises, would the resulting mongrel breed prove a higher type of humanity? It does not take much wisdom to see that the answer must be in the negative. Now, if the highest types of humanity in the present cannot get along without our mission, in other words, cannot realize the prophetic ideals, how could we expect that from a lower type?

2. If the tendency to nationalism should disappear, and all peoples should form one government, we should simply get a universal Austria of prenationalistic times. That such a stage would be a realization of the messianic ideal is subject to grave doubts; for, if that were possible, then historic Austria of the past would have already realized that ideal within its limited boundaries—something that nobody has so far claimed.

3. The uniformity of ethical and religious ideals is the only means of achieving a common humanity. But, is a realization of it within the limits, I would not say of the probable, but of the possible? To answer this question, I must quote an abstract from a passage which I treated fully on another occasion:

"If different people employ different means to attain avowedly one and the same ideal, it follows that they contemplate that ideal under different aspects. Whence the difference? The difference arises from the realization of the ideal. The absolute has no existence in reality, it is a mere abstraction. In order to have a definite individuality, to become tangible, it must contain, besides its essence, a multiplicity of qualities and conditions. It is just these conditions which enable it to assume a definite form, to become concrete. Now, if the absolute may, and does, find its embodiment through various mediums, it must necessarily present to us various aspects.

"What is true of other things applies also to religious verities. Two nations, starting from the same premises, are bound to develop their ethical and religious ideals on different lines, because their natural gifts constitute different mediums, and their conditions and experiences must unavoidably differ from one another. A universal religion dreamt of by our visionaries is as impossible as a universal language. The road to messianic times does not lead through an imaginary universality of belief, but lies rather in the development of the various groups of mankind along the innate peculiarities and natural idiosyncrasies to the greatest possible perfection each one of them is capable of attaining." In other words, religious development can only advance along parallel lines.

4. On the principle that a chain cannot be stronger than its weakest link, the fourth means is out of consideration.

From the above it follows that a cosmopolitan religion is an impossibility, that the watchword, "a common humanity," is but a meaningless jingle, and that the mission of Israel is to further the nationalization of all groups of humanity; of course, of their own first of all. If the Jews wanted to assimilate with the nations, a cosmopolitan religion being impossible, they could only do it by adopting Christianity in one form or another, something that no man, even the most visionary, can ever expect to happen. The hope of assimilation, therefore, turns out to be a sad delusion.

One of the speakers remarked that he cared only for Judaism, but not for the Jews. As I have shown above, religion is not transferable, and does not exist in the abstract. Religion is not a bundle of intellectual ideas, but a complex phenomenon of a given nation's soul-life, which must disappear with the disappearance of the people. Without Jews there can be no Judaism; as the ancient rabbis said: "Israel, the Torah, and God form one indivisible whole." Judaism could very well get along without theologians, but we could not have Judaism without Jews.

The fact that some individuals become converted to another religion is not so difficult to explain as seems at first sight. Such individuals are simply natural anomalies. An individual Christian may be near to the soul-life of the Jew, or *vice versa;* just as there are effeminate men and masculine women; and even these anomalies could only be assimilated in negligible quantities; but the mass of the Christians can as little possess the soul-life of the Jew as the mass of men could be effeminate.

I said above that the antis muster a number of passages to prove their side. I wish not to be understood to have admitted that they really can prove their side by the passages in question. It is a matter of fact that to the prophets, even in their most universalistic visions, the separate national existence of the Jews remained the centre of all their thoughts. The opposite of that can be read out of their words only by taking single passages out of their context. I shall not trouble myself to prove that the prophets never for a moment dreamt of giving up Jewish nationalism; should this be necessary, it could be done at short notice. But even if the prophets had committed the folly of declaring the Jews to be no nation, this would as little unmake Jewish nationality as if they had declared the sun to be a lobster, the sun would really be a lobster, as I explain further on.

The well-known Hebrew scholar, Dr. S. Rubin, in an article to which my attention has been drawn by our revered president, Dr. Wise, encouraging the nationalistic movement among the Jews, repeats the common mistake in assuming that we have borrowed this idea from the Christians; and tries to defend it by showing that we have borrowed and assimilated many things from the surrounding nations through all periods of our history. I beg to differ with him. Nationalism is a genuinely Jewish idea, running like a thread through all our history, from its very beginning to our days. If the modern nations succeed in realizing their nationalistic aspirations, they shall have unintentionally realized in full one of the Jewish ideals. If the Jewish nationalistic aspirations have just made an appearance, it is not due to their having borrowed them from the Christians; the Christian aspiration merely gave them the courage to speak out publicly that which they had to hide in their hearts in the face of unfavorable conditions up to the present day.

The present nationalistic movement bears remarkable resemblance to the reform movement, although the two stand in the relation of effect and cause to one another. Both genuinely Jewish, they received their first impulses from the outside. Both have encountered fierce opposition amongst us. The light of both is not without shadows, and both call for prudent handling. As the success of the one is an accomplished fact, the success of the other is beyond the shadow of a doubt. But the striking similarity is not without a difference. Whereas the Reform movement was accompanied by outbursts of wild passion, we have now learned to listen with deference to opinions we do not share, and to discuss them calmly. Years ago a progressive German congregation in Albany dragged Dr. Wise from the pulpit for preaching new-fangled theories; today, a proverbially backward Sephardic congregation in London refuses to make an exhibition of itself by voting down the proposition of a benighted trustee to reduce Dr. Gaster's salary for preaching Zionism. The world moves on, after all.

To understand how the prophets, who were not only eloquent talkers, but also profound thinkers, could, at one and the same time, be so intensely nationalistic and so enthusiastically universalistic, let us examine what is meant by a universalistic religion. When the Christians claim that their religion is universalistic, what do they mean by that? Do they mean to say that it is the same among all nations? Is the Christianity of the Swedes, for instance, really the same as that of the Abyssinians? Of course not. As I have shown above, it could not be. Do they mean to say that all those professing Christianity form one nation? No proof is necessary to show that that is not what is meant by it. Universalistic religion must, therefore, mean something else—namely, that such a religion does not exclude any other nation from professing it. Universalistic religion, as can be seen, does not conflict with nationalism. If, now, we claim, and rightly so, that our religion is just as universalistic as the Christian is, then why should we fight shy of confessing that we are a nation? Do Frenchmen, for instance, deny Italians the right of a separate political existence? Now, if to France and to Italy, being of the same religious belief and of kindred race, the justness of separate political existence is admitted by Jew and Christian, then why should Jews not be able to form a separate nation? Suppose for a moment, that the Japanese and the Bulgarians have adopted our religion, would you not admit that there are three nations professing the Mosaic religion—the Jews, the Japanese, and the Bulgarians? Is it because the latter have not done so, that the Jews lose their nationality? It is evident that the inference drawn from the premises posited by a universalistic religion, that we are not a nation, is just as rational as the inference from the same premises, that we must all have red hair.

There exists a deplorable confusion of thought as to what constitutes a nation. The confusion arises from mixing up the two meanings of the word 'nation'—the ethnological and the political. 'Nation' in an ethnological sense, is a given group of people that possess in common certain natural characteristics and innate peculiarities. Such a group, by virtue of such innate peculiarities, have the inalienable right to form a separate political group, a nation in the political sense, as I have explained above. The voluntary or involuntary suspension of such inalienable right cannot annul the right; much less can it change the ethnological status of any of the groups. One example, for illustration, will suffice. The sexes have the inalienable right to marry and to form separate families. An individual, man or woman, may, for some reason or other, remain unmarried. He or she may even solemnly renounce marriage, as the members of some religious orders actually do; but this does not annul their right to marry whenever they find it possible and desirable to do so. Much less does a nun, by renouncing marriage, become a man, or a monk, a woman.

The word 'family,' like 'nation,' has a double meaning. It means a group of people united by physical kinship, and corresponds to 'nation' in its ethnological sense. Then again, it means a 'household,' and corresponds to 'nation' in its socio-political sense. A number of families may acquire one estate and conduct one household, each family enjoying the same rights and privileges enjoyed by the others. All of them form then one family in the socio-economical sense, and correspond to a nation like that of the Austrians. In course of time, some of the families may intermarry, while others may continue to keep up their physical separateness. Such a family corresponds to a nation like that of the United States. The intermarrying of a part of the families does not impair the right of the others to the common household.

The confusion existing with regard to the meaning of 'nation' is no less great than the one existing with regard to the relations between the latter and 'race.' I shall not enter here upon a lengthy discussion of the subject, but try to make it clear by an example. The French and the English are not pure races; still they are separate not only as nations, but also as races. For in amalgamation of nations or races it is the prevailing element which determines the character of the mixture. Coffee, no matter how sweetened, remains coffee; wine, no matter how spiced, remains wine, and nothing else. In this connection I want to say that, as far as I have a judgment in the matter, the so-called Semitic race is not the antithesis to the Aryan race, but is a subdivision of the latter, like the Celtic, Slavic, or Teutonic. The only difference is that the Semitic races have separated from the parent stock earlier. That we have behind us a longer line of individual development, is certainly no cause for regret or shame.

One of the speakers finished his address with the declaration: "America is our Palestine and Washington is our Zion." As stated in the introductory remark, the discussion of such declarations lies without the scope of this paper. But we may examine into the cause of these patriotic hysterics. It is the fear that our Christian fellow-citizens might deny our patriotism, or impugn our loyalty. That the moral courage of the German protest-rabbis fails them whenever they contemplate such a possibility does not astonish those who know European conditions. But to us Americans this may remain a subject of little concern. Our population consists of various elements. Nobody has ever thought of impugning the patriotism of our Irishmen, or of denying the loyalty of our German citizens, merely because their kinsfolk and co-religionists have a home of their own across the Atlantic. Why should our loyalty be impugned? The best proof that Zionism does not impair our loyalty and patriotism was furnished by the present war. The greatest number of volunteers that have offered their services to the country of their adoption were Russian, Roumanian and Galician immigrants, avowedly all Zionists.

Finally, I must say a word about the practicability of Zionism. I humbly confess that I have no opinion on this subject; but I claim with good right that others do not know a whit more about it. The Zionists have repeatedly declared that their aim is not to be achieved in a year or two; it might take two or more generations. Not only this, but even if we could get Palestine today, we could not take it, because the mass of our people is not yet fit for self-government. The immediate aims of the Zionists are the preparing of the way and the fitting of the people for the future. If our statesmen could not hitherto foretell the outbreak of anti-Semitism in Germany, the Dreyfus case and the anti-Jewish riots in France, the breaking of the constitution and the shooting down of men fighting for their liberty in the United States, how can they know what attitude Russia would assume toward Zionism two or three generations hence?

But even assuming that after all our work in that direction it should be found that the idea must be for the present abandoned as temporarily impossible of realization, what will we have lost by it? The beneficial effects of the preparatory work will remain a permanent gain to the nation. The masses will have been raised to a higher plane of life, and thus brought nearer to ourselves; the religious factions will have been united through a common ideal, and the indifferent who had stayed away will have been regained—all results which are as desirable to the progressive party as to the rest of the people. On the other hand, should the movement succeed, the powers having guaranteed the existence of a Jewish state, the people would be removed from the sphere of international politics and be able to devote themselves to their internal affairs. With the increase of material prosperity and the entrance into the life of modern civilization will come a higher view of life and religion, the obnoxious obscurantism of the ghetto will make room for an enlightened Judaism, and the whole nation reunited will then be able to carry out its mission among the nations of the world. . . .

ISRAEL
Samuel Schulman
(1935)

The time in which we are living is a challenge to Israel, such as
it has more than once received from the world. We are entering,
as I believe, upon a new chapter of its history. We Jews, especially
in the Western world, are called upon once more to take stock of
our spiritual assets and to become clear in our own minds as to what
is the meaning of the wonderful persistence, the will to live of the
Jewish people which very significantly we call, Israel.

The time is one of great sorrow and tribulation for Israel. We
are standing, as it were, in a period of temporary disenchantment.
All over the world there is a reaction against the ideas of liberty
and democracy and humanity by the help of which Israel, after
centuries of matchless suffering was enabled to enter the life of the
Western world with the rights of the individual Israelite recognized
as inalienable. We hear again the cry of a brutal aggressive and
exclusive nationalism in the midst of a nation that was held as
standing in the vanguard of Western culture. The effort is being
made, and sad to say with disheartening success, to undo the
achievement of Jewish emancipation and to force the Jew back into
what was called the ghetto. The hopes that ran high in the beginning
of the nineteenth century, seem to have been turned into delusion
and the Western world, recreant to its own ideals of human progress, is naturally making the Jew the conspicuous victim of its moral

and spiritual retrogression. As always in the course of its history, rich in duty and in glory, Israel becomes the victim of the world's iniquity and is sacrificed for the world's sin. It was therefore natural for the Central Conference of American Rabbis to invite a discussion on the fundamental conception of Judaism, fifty years after the remarkable proclamation was made of the fundamental principles of Reform Judaism as these had been formulated and most fruitfully developed in this, our beloved country. American Judaism, as we have been accustomed to call it, having an individuality of its own and having developed in the midst of a nation which by its constitution and character is most hospitable to Jewish aspiration should become conscious again of the aims and ideals of the great movement in Jewish history during the last one hundred years, of which we, with all that we stand for in this Conference, have been a determining factor.

This movement of Reform, or Liberal, or Progressive Judaism—by whatever name we wish to call it—can be described at large, as an expression of the new hopes which animated Israel as it faced a new world . . .

In the process of adaptation to the new environment, there was a rediscovery of the difference between what is lasting and indestructible in the individuality of Israel as a divine power in history and what is temporary and changing, and therefore changeable, between the spirit of Israel—God's priest in the world—and the form in which the service of that priesthood is expressed. It was a veritable revolution if you will, in the attitude of the Jew which was expressed in the Reform movement. It meant a rejection of the idea that Israel considered itself to be in exile and must therefore everlastingly mourn until it was returned to the land of the fathers in which, under the creative inspiration of the Prophets, it became equipped with the moral and spiritual ideas with which it was ever afterwards to live.

The movement of which we are part profoundly changed the prayers in which Israel expressed its interpretation of its destiny and its aspiration for the future. It eliminated every petition for a return to Palestine, for the rebuilding of the ancient Temple and the restoration of the sacrificial cult that went with it. It rejected the belief in a personal Messiah because it felt that the conception of the "Kingdom of God" was a more comprehensive idea than the peculiar form of the personal Messiah in which, by some of the Prophets, it was expressed. It felt that such a royal personage was part of the conception of a political nationalism of the Jew which it was ready to disavow. It harked back to that other aspect of Messianism expressed by many Prophets and especially by him who is called the second Isaiah. It rededicated itself to that which was always an undying idea: the hunger for union with the nations of the world. It committed itself to the universalism of Israel's message. In a free world where the Jew is accepted as free and equal, what more natural than that the Jew should become conscious again of his distinction as the servant of God, of his destiny to be a light to the nations. And if Israel is to be a light to the nations, it cannot for ever hide itself in a corner and conceal its light but must accept with a sense of enthusiastic consecration all the opportunities offered and live among the nations and be judged by the purity and power of the light it has to offer. The modern movement in Judaism hailed with joy the opportunity. . . .

. . . Judaism has a character. It has from the beginning of its existence as a living organism a definite genius which distinguishes it from other religions; and to that character it really remains true all through its changes as shaped by the new environments with which it comes in contact and by the living parties which express the meaning of that contact. In other words, Judaism has a rich past. . . .

Now Israel, it is acknowledged on all sides, is a distinct group in the world. What is the character of this group today? What differentiates it? It is not a race, although Jews and non-Jews equally use this word *race* loosely. I am not quibbling about words. If anyone wishes to refer to Israel of today as being a race, he is welcome to do so, but as a matter of fact if the word *race* is to be used with some consciousness as meaning a group of people of absolutely pure blood as descended from one ancestor, there is, as far as I can gather from the welter of voices, no such thing as a pure race. Every group of people that exists today is mixed. It is an historical fact that Israel after the exile received many converts, not to speak of the mixed origin of Israel in the flesh. These converts came from many nations. And there has been all through the course of Jewish history, a mixture, an admission of non-Jew to the Jewish faith. There has even been a whole kingdom of the Chazars[68] who accepted the Jewish religion. And Israel today despite popular conception is by no means a physical unity. There is no such thing as a Jewish type always recognizable. Environments play a tremendous rôle as scientists have pointed out. Of course, I cannot go at length into this.

Israel is not a nation in the modern sense of the word. By nation we understand today a people with a common language, with common traditions, which expresses its nationalism in the form of a political organization, the "State."[69] A nation in the accepted sense of the word today, is practically synonymous with the State. The smallest State in the world is called a nation from the point of view of the "League of Nations." And that is absolutely correct. There is no such thing as a "nation" without an organization of the body of people that lives in the land, into a State. . . . But "nation" in the modern age has one distinct connotation. It is a people having a country of its own, a common history and language and has become a recognized State. Modern nations have room for many Churches within them, although they cannot have room for many nations within them.

Is Israel a nationality? Nationality is sometimes defined as a group of people who have a common religion, an historic tradition, common customs and nevertheless have no State of their own. Every nationality, however, is considered *in spe*[70] a nation. Its tendency is to try to become a nation and to organize itself as such.

---

[68] Graetz, *History of the Jews*, Jewish Publication Society, Vol. 3, pp. 138–141.
[69] Bluntschli, quoted by Bernard Lazare, *L'Antisemitisme*.
[70] Laveleye, *Le Gouvernement dans la Democratie*, Paris, 1871.

Now Israel certainly has a common religion. I have been trying to prove that this is the only thing that makes Israel to be what it is and certainly there is an unbroken historic continuity of Israel in the world. But it is begging the question to call such a group as is Israel, a "nationality" which would imply that it is a candidate for nationhood. As a matter of fact the particular character of Israel as a community is to reject ordinary nationality and to be what it is, a religious community. What it wants is freedom to be such a community in any part of the world. The home of a group whose essence is loyalty to the universal God is and ought to be all over the world. It can and does participate with joy and self-sacrifice in the life of all nations. Different sections of Israel belong today to different nations and where freedom reigns, they feel themselves quite at home there. They love their country. The reason people cannot cease calling Israel a nationality or a nation, comes from the fact that in the Bible, Israel is referred to by words that are translated "people" and "nation," but to insist upon this is again to beg the question. Herbert Loewe[71] well points out that these words did not have in the Hebrew language, did not possess in Semitic thought, that connotation which the current translation imports into them. In the Semitic world, human beings were not grouped according to physical origin or blood. They were grouped around their god. There was no such thing as nation in the modern sense of the word. There were communities whose existence centered in their god. A stranger could come from one country to another and if he adopted the god of the new community, he became a member of it. Therefore Israel today, if we are to translate correctly what was intended in the words in Exodus is a "Kingdom of Priests and a Holy Group," that is to say a consecrated people. And if some nationalists tell us that Jeremiah said that: "If these ordinances[72] depart from before me," (referring to the ordinance of the moon and of the stars) "saith the Lord, then the seed of Israel shall cease from being a nation before Me for ever," we answer

[71] Hastings, *Encyclopedia,* Vol. 7, p. 584.
[72] Jer. 31:35.

Jeremiah did not talk of "nation" in the modern secular sense and Jeremiah, if I may be permitted to say without irreverence, would certainly be astonished if he came back to earth and heard the language of our secular nationalists today. What Jeremiah meant was what I believe, and it is simply this. He was so convinced of the indestructibility of Israel, a conviction I share, that he says, can you imagine the laws of nature to pass away, so can you imagine this Israel ceasing to be a group before God and witnessing to Him. Israel is deathless. Now, that is exactly what Israel is today: a religious group witnessing to a particular kind of faith in God and an interpretation of that faith, and nothing else. If we ask ourselves, in all frankness, just what is that all who belong to Israel today have in common, the Falasha Jew of Abyssinia and ourselves; here is Israel, scattered all over the world, made up of people that speak different languages, made up of people observant of different customs, made up of people who are different physical types, even differing in color—just what have all these people in common? There is only one correct and honest answer. What they have in common is the fact that mornings and evenings they say, or ought to say: Hear, O Israel, the Lord our God, the Lord is One. There is nothing else that binds them. And if in love and sincerity any human being today comes to us, no matter what his tribal origin, and says: "I accept the Jewish faith," we receive him cordially although we do not do missionary work in the conventional sense, because we do not believe that anyone can only find salvation by joining us. We receive such a proselyte cordially and he becomes, as Maimonides[73] tells a proselyte of his time, son or daughter of Israel, and is considered as of the seed of Abraham who is called in the Bible, God's friend.

But what of the individual who no longer does say: Hear, O Israel, etc.? Is he to be read out of the community? Is my theology of Israel a theology of exclusion? Even those who assume a purely negative attitude to religion or are aggressively opposed to it, may nevertheless, and that is one of the doctrines of Israel, be considered

[73] *Iggereth.*

as potential Jews, as by their birth consecrated to God. The election of Israel, as I said above, is one of the fundamental teachings
of Judaism. Israel is a family religion. The presumption is that
the child will continue the faith of the fathers. In this connection
it occurs to me that when Amos refers to the election of Israel,
he uses the suggestive phrase "families[74] of the earth." He does not
say "only you I knew of all the *Goyim,* of all nations." Historically
Judaism begins in the family of Abraham and Judaism has been
preserved through the fidelity of child to the heritage of the fathers.
And very lovingly accepted converts became grafted on the family
tree. Therefore one born a Jew, belonging to Israel of the flesh,
is always counted as a Jew and considered as potentially a son or
daughter of spiritual Israel. Only if he deliberately leaves Israel
and joins another religious communion is he considered as excluding himself. . . . Once an Israelite, always an Israelite, provided one
is in profound sympathy with the "consecration" involved in the
very term Israel. And though it may make uncomfortable many
born Jews who sit in high places, political, literary or scientific, in
the modern nations of which we, as Jews in free lands, are part, to
be told that they cannot be of Israel if they reject what Israel stands
for, it nonetheless remains a fact that the character of Israel as a
group is given in nothing else than in its unbroken sense of service
unto God which has endured from Abraham unto our time. Israel
today is what it always was: God's witness on earth. It is the
Keneseth Israel.

From the nationalistic side, naturally inspired by its belief in the
fundamental secular character of Israel as a nation like other
nations in the world, has come a suggestion that what is characteristic of Israel is not its "religion" but "its civilization." Religion may
be an incident of that civilization and no doubt will continue to be,
but it is not the dominant thing since we are all modern and free in
our thoughts. A man can be a good national Jew and not have
any particular religion. The test is no longer loyalty to the religion
in some form, whether it be orthodox, conservative or reform as we

[74] Amos 3:2.

conventionally use these terms of division, the test is loyalty to the Jewish nation and the characteristic thing about this "Jewish nation" is its "civilization." And so we hear, nowadays, talk of Judaism as a civilization." In the first place it is good to become clear as to what the word "civilization" means. The word "civilization" as used in the circles which talk of a "Jewish civilization" is really a translation of the German word *Kultur,* and this German word as used in Germany denotes two things: civilization and culture. But some German[76] writers very correctly make a distinction between the two terms, between "civilization" and "Kultur" which latter they regard as the equivalent of our English word culture; and they say that civilization refers to things, external achievements, and culture refers to spiritual creations or values. I accept this distinction. Now, civilization for me has to do with things external. . . . A civilized person is a person who lives according to the rules of comfort and opportunities of action which have been given by the inventions of science. In short he has the manners and advantages and the sophistications of the city dweller or country dweller if you will. He is no longer a child of nature. If civilization has to do with things, culture is the spiritual aspect of civilization. All cultured people are civilized, but all civilized people are not necessarily cultured. Civilization has to do with the mastery of the environment. Culture is the expression of the spirit and has to do with the interpretation of civilization and what it means for the inner life of the human spirit. . . . Culture is a judgment, an interpretation and creative transformation of civilization through religion, ethical and social ideals. Man begins his progress with civilization and civilization on the whole, amongst all peoples, is a common reaction to environment. The differentiating things with respect to peoples are their culture, less so their civilization which they can easily borrow one from the other. The distinctive things are always of the spirit. . . .

Now, as to civilization, the Jewish people or community was

---

[76] Chamberlain, *Die Grundlagen des Neunzehnten Jahrhunderts,* 4 Auflage, Erste Haelfte, pp. 62, 63.

always like a little island floating on the larger ocean of the civilization to which it belonged. Israel was sometimes a part of Egyptian
civilization, of Canaanite civilization, Philistine civilization, Babylonian civilization, Greek civilization, Roman civilization and jump-
ing to our day, modern civilization, European or American. . . .

The distinctive genius or contribution of Israel is not in inventions or things, although of course individual Jews have proven
themselves magnificent inventors and creators of things that we
value in civilization, when they came in contact with the larger
world. But the record of the classic creative Israel in antiquity,
makes it very clear that its originality as a community consisted
in what it produced of religion, of the ethical ideals of purity,
morality, social justice, as the triumph of human righteousness and
love. Their originality produced the conception of a God who is
One, who created the universe, who is moral in character and was
conceived as hating iniquity so terribly that the whole drama of
history is understood as a bloody tragedy of the life and death of
nations in order to vindicate righteousness. Even the phenomena
of nature were naively conceived as connected with the iniquities
and the moral excellencies of humanity. This God whom Israel
revealed to the world or who revealed glimpses of Himself to
Israel, cares for man. The individual is precious in His eyes whether
he be a native Israelite or a stranger. This God hears the cry of the
poor and the oppressed and defends them. He loves people and
not merely Israelites, also those that come to dwell in Israel and
sojourn with him. He is a God very jealous for His own uniqueness
which is truth. He is the "I am[78] that I am," that is His name; and
He refuses to share His glory[79] with any other being whom He
created. He is a God who is jealous for the Law of righteousness
so that He will not compromise and He will not accept bribes in
the form of material offerings on the altar or ceremonial lip-
service. What He wants is loving kindness[80] in human beings and

[78] Exodus 3:14.
[79] Isaiah 42:8.
[80] Hosea 6:6.

not their gifts of lambs or beautiful temples. And He is a God who, to speak with Lincoln, likes the masses because He made many of them and therefore we are told that He looks to the "poor"[81] and to "the broken in spirit" and cares and concerns Himself about them most. Now, with such a God Israel identified itself. It saw its own essence as a people and a historic community in the expression of His essence as a God, and loyalty to Him. Never in the history of the world was there such a union between people and God. This is all that is meant, humanly speaking, by the phrase "Chosen People." Subjectively the phrase means that Israel, to use the words of Deuteronomy,[82] felt that it "avouched God" before the world. Objectively it meant that God "avouched Israel" in so far as in His mysterious providence He revealed Himself to Israel through its chosen spirits. The human fact is, in the last analysis, the revelation of the divine Will. All peoples found in their gods a sanction of their morality. This is a commonplace of history and proves the natural inevitableness of the connection of religion with the growing and purifying ethical life, but no people felt like Israel that its whole life was bound up with God. And therefore no people produced a literature so uniquely saturated with God. This people could survive loss of land and nationality, so that now it carries the Bible, its only "center" with it, all over the world. The great paradox of Israel's history is that there was in this people a hunger for universalism, for union with humanity that transcends race or nationality. And on the other hand there was the mysterious tenacity of will, in self-conscious persistence in living, in remaining itself—an intense particularism because of the conviction that Israel as a community has something to do in the world but also a readiness to receive those who came within its folds. This universalism in Israel writes large the fact that religion in its essence flees race and nationality, because it is human and is individualistic, and is communion of the soul with God, and is therefore the possible experience and achievement of any human soul. Now if a whole

[81] Isaiah 66:2.
[82] Deut. 26:17, 18.

community or people, using the word "people" in its original connotation, as a group, without any commitment on modern political
theories, one way or another, makes itself one with God, lives for
religion, it ceases to be an ordinary people and reaches out to a
vision of the union of humanity. In the end, after running through
all the stages of human organization, Israel became a Congregation
of God and this is what Israel is today, a religious community and
nothing else. Its Messianic vision is the expression of its two-fold
character. It hopes for the glorious future; it has never recognized
any realization of its hopes. It is interesting to observe that every
Messianic movement in Jewish history which attempted to see the
fulfillment of the hope in any particular person, invariably led out
of Judaism as a religion. Israel says the Kingdom is still to come.
Ten thousand years after today, Israel, if still alive, and I believe
it will be, will still say the perfection is not yet here. God is still
not completely established in human hearts, because, with the
realization of every ideal, Israel will demand more. *A people that
stakes its existence upon the inexhaustible God is an immortal
people. . . .*

Now, while I am very liberal about letting other people use what
words they like, I find that the trouble with the use of a word like
"civilization" to describe what Judaism is, as a substitute for the
ordinary word "religion," is that there peeps through it—very ill-
concealed for a discerning eye—a tremendous heresy which de-
stroys the whole tradition of Israel. This word is a desperate attempt
to grab at the rag of racialism with which to cover the spiritual
nakedness of a timid atheism or, at best, old-fashioned agnosticism.
What it really is, is a flirtation with what we call today Humanism.
It emphasizes man and throws God into the background, if it thinks
of Him at all. As I said some time ago, Jewish nationalism for the
first time in Jewish history enthroned,[83] in the consciousness of the
Jew, Israel in the place of God. It is a distinctive break with the
whole of Jewish history. That is the real motive behind the use
of the new word. It wants to emphasize the fact that what the

[83] *The Outlook,* January 5, 1916, p. 41, lines 35, 36.

Jew has to contribute is a so-called "civilization" which, as I intimated, is a wrong use of the word, or a so-called culture, Israel being a people like other peoples, only one of whose values is religion. For this reason I object to the use of the word. It is not justified by Jewish history and it is an insidious attack on the values of Israel in the present.

Moreover the conception of Judaism as a distinct civilization in our land, is shallow and superficial. It is after all a mere play of words. There is no reality behind it. For, what is the Jewish civilization today in America? Is it Jewish cooking? As far as I know Jew and Jewish life in America, they are steeped up to the neck in American civilization. I am sure that the young ladies who belong to the circles to which has been revealed the new name for our old and beloved Judaism, are quite the products of our American environment. They wear short hair and some of them shorter clothes. They are quite up-to-date in their appreciation of jazz. . . .

I know nothing which can be called Jewish civilization. Why then deal so seriously with the term? My answer is that it is dangerous. We must assume that when a serious thinking man uses such a term with which to describe the heritage of Israel, he must be in earnest, therefore if there is not enough of Jewish civilization in America at present, he will try to create it. That is the only consistent thing to do. But Jewish "civilization" within the American life, means the creation of a new ghetto, and we do not wish a new ghetto. We share American civilization, we learn from it and we contribute to it, and the only difference which distinguishes us from the other elements of American civilization is our religion, and nothing else.

If we live our religion, we will prove ourselves to be very helpful Americans and we can influence the spiritual life of America.

America I consider the greatest opportunity offered to Israel. America, our beloved country, is the noble illustration of what a nation ought to be in the modern sense of the world. It is not based on the conception of blood, it is based on moral ideas, on the conception of the inalienable rights of man. As such, it has organized itself in the broad daylight of history; it is as I like to call it, the clearly conceived humanitarian nation of the world. When I use such a term as "humanitarian" I do not mean self-righteously to claim for America superior charity or virtue as compared with any other nations. What I mean is that, as the genius of our American institutions is to give the right to the individual and to judge him purely as man or woman without any prejudicial concern because of his religious creed or physical origin, his so-called racial blood, America is the nation that rejects, by its very constitution, all that is evil in modern nationalism. It becomes the symbol of the possibility of union of men and women irrespective of the blood in their veins, into a Commonwealth. By "nationalism" I understand that political doctrine of a group, of an actual nation which says that the unity of the nation must rest on what it conceives to be, the unity and the purity of blood of the dwellers of the land which go to make the nation and the State, nation and State being synonymous. This evil is of course most disastrously exemplified in German nationalism which claims that only human beings of so-called Aryan blood (by the way, there is no such a thing as an Aryan race) can be members of the nation's body politic. Now, the very opposite of that kind of nationalism is our American nationalism. American nationality can be shared in by men and women, irrespective of the particular blood in their veins. Therefore, we of Israel whose so-called "nationality," to speak with Saadya, is our Torah, find in America our greatest opportunity and our greatest responsibility. American civilization is good enough for us. American culture has much of the spiritual heritage of Israel which came to it through Christianity directly, and indirectly through the absorption of the spirit of the ancient Hebrew literature. Far from pointedly, talking of any particular Jewish civilization that we have to create in the life of American people, we would say that here, if ever, we have to make ourselves felt a purely spiritual influence as a religious community that is allowed to live in perfect freedom. Of course, back of the use of this phrase

"Jewish civilization" lies the conception of Jewish blood as the creative power in achieving what is called Jewish culture. I deny the whole theory that it is blood that created the Jewish values. It was individual genius as inspired by God that transformed Israel and gave it, and through it, eternal values to western civilization and to the whole world. If it is bad to attempt to define and constitute a nation in the modern world, exclusively on the basis of assumed uniformity of tribal blood in Germany, it is wrong all over the world, in Palestine and anywhere else. We must think clearly and must think through on this subject. Human beings must learn that no corner of the earth is the exclusive monopolistic property of any so-called "race." Not blood, but ideas unite and distinguish human beings and Israel scattered all over the world is to be the living example of the duty of a modern commonwealth to recognize this truth. That is part of our mission; to be the goad unto humanitarianism, even if we become the victim in places where brutal nationalism is dominant and humanitarianism is trodden under foot. Claiming a home for Israel all over the world, we rejoice in our beloved land and we are happy in the thought that many men and women of liberal spirit are with us. Nay more, we are glad to see that not only secularist liberals, but Christians, Protestants and Catholics, are feeling that resurgent, brutal nationalism in the Western world is a denial of the great Judeo-Christian tradition which has taught that world all that is best in its moral and spiritual culture.

Religion is being threatened and it is no accident that those who would excommunicate Israel from the life of a modern nation, feel compelled to deny their Christian heritage, and to revert to pagan gods. For while, if the Jew is to be regarded as free and equal in the Western world, he must be permitted to speak freely what is in his heart with respect to his distinctive religious individuality and not to be merely tolerated in so far as he consents to be only an echo of the creed of the majority, yet we must say that, important as are the differences which divide us religiously from the majority concerning doctrine, they are overshadowed by the threat which pagan nationalism is making to destroy the whole spiritual heritage that came from Sinai and from Jerusalem for the whole world. Therefore, when great representatives of Christianity fight bravely in Germany and outside of Germany for the rights of conscience, they are fighting our battle. And we should not impair the vigor of their contest; we should not as Israel, weaken our position in the world by ourselves bending the knee before the idols of racialism and nationalism, which have been erected anew in the world, as if no instruction or law had ever gone out of Zion. We cannot have it both ways. If we want to revert to outgrown notions of Israel in the flesh, and emphasize race or nationality as our distinguishing feature, we run great danger lest we be taken at our word and be called upon to pay for it and to suffer for the new heresy. And to use a phrase of Ezekiel, the secular nationalists might learn again that sometimes the Eternal says in our history: "I will reign over you with outpoured fury."[84] So we dispose of this secular conception of Israel. And now we ask how is the individuality of Israel to be maintained today? What will Israel be in the future? What ought Israel to be? To answer that question means an attempted definition of the mission of Israel in the world today. You know that the nationalists and the secularists have poked fun at the whole idea of "mission." They say: What have we to teach the world? Monotheism has been accepted, what are we fighting for?

Well, I think we have something to teach the world. We can still give something worthwhile to the modern men and women, many of whom seem to have lost their God. Is this too bold a claim? Does there linger in this assertion the old Adam of national vanity? Well, Israel is not an ordinary community. It is a community that produced a Moses, a Jeremiah, the great Anonymous and a whole brilliant galaxy of Hebrew prophets. It is a community in which arose Jesus,[85] who claimed to be the realization of all Israel's hopes as the longed-for Messiah, and Paul[86] who broke with the concep-

[84] Ezekiel 20:32, 33.
[85] Matthew 16:13–20; Mark 8:27–33.
[86] Romans 3:20, 21, 22.

tion of law as the means of salvation. Thus the one by his claim and the other by his interpretation, became respectively the cornerstone and the builder of a new religion, a religion which, as already emphasized, had a wonderful work to do in the world, and which has carried much of Israel's teaching to the ends of the earth and made it a part of the life of nations. We speak of this with the profoundest reverence. Israel is a community in which arose a man like Spinoza who, a mystic at heart, though a mathematical rationalist in thought, attempted to find God as the inner side of the mechanism of the Universe which modern science has envisaged as an unbroken realm of natural law and thus made possible the sentimental religiosity by which the souls of hundreds of thousands of human beings in the Western world live though they are unchurched, for his influence has been profound on modern poetry and he is the father of modern Pantheism. This born Jew was more in sympathy with Christian values because he never forgot the smart of his experience, and great spirit as he was, was still unjust to Judaism and above all to persecuted Israel. Paradoxical as it may sound, but nevertheless following logically from the intercourse of Israel with the world, taking and giving culture, I think the philosopher Kant, born a Christian, is more sympathetic to me as a Jewish theologian than Spinoza, born a Jew. Little Israel has thus far done very much in ancient and in modern times for the spiritual education of the world. It has been a central sun throwing off planets. I think we ought not to take such a pessimistic view of the dormant spiritual power of Israel. Let us only be true to ourselves and we will create spiritual values in the Western world, and if secular nationalism ceases to be in our midst, perhaps something new may be created in the new spiritual centre that is building in Palestine.

The modern world is hungering for God; but many in it think that the food offered is unappetizing, that it is poisonous to the scientific mentality upon which the modern man prides himself, by means of which he has obtained great power in providing himself with material things, which things, alas! nevertheless, do not seem to satisfy his spiritual hunger. Is it not possible that Israel's uncompromising conception of a spiritual unimaged God may in the end be discovered by the modern man, if he envisages it without prejudice as the God he is hungering for, the idea of whom will satisfy his intellect, and the moral nature of whom, as righteous God and loving Father, will stimulate the conscience and warm the heart? Such a God is unimaged not merely in the sense that He must not plastically be represented, but in the sense that no mortal that walked the earth can be said to have completely and exhaustively represented Him. It is an unimaged God who is not tied to any supernatural event of the past, who is not completely expressed in any historic achievement, whose absoluteness as Perfect Truth transcends not only every formulation in words or dogma, but every historic myth which tries to portray Him to man. Might not such a conception of God, who is constantly to be explored, for whose complete triumph in human life humanity is constantly to yearn while it does not look backward saying "The best was" but rather, that the ideal can only be realized through mankind's progress in the far off event in the "end of days"—might not such a conception of God appeal to the modern man? Such a conception of God means that His teaching cannot be conceived as for ever completed in the promulgation of any book but whose instruction is fructifying the advancing mind and the growing conscience and the opening heart of mankind. And does not Israel whose faith was always turned to the future, who remained upon the scene of history as a living commentary upon its Holy book, and yet looked always beyond it to the Redemption that was still to come, does not Israel with its martyrdom lend itself as a symbol for the unending work which all communities must spiritually perform with themselves until every group in the world is animated by faith in the God of truth and by a social righeousness which will be the visible proof of God's Kingdom on earth? I think in all humility and reverence that this might happen.

The modern man thinks he can find a substitute for the God as Israel taught the world, in humanity itself. Modern humanism is logically the outcome of Western religion, because after all in the consciousness of Christendom, the central fact was a type of manhood which, we say it with reverence, Christian faith regarded as more than man, as both man and God. But man was, in the deeper sense, worshiped and not the Invisible who transcends man though he does speak in every heart. Only modern humanism strips Christianity altogether of its Jewish heritage, namely, of the objective Eternal God. Humanism speaks of a growing God, of a God who is becoming a power in the world through man. In a book by a brilliant Norwegian writer, Bojer, called *The Great Hunger,* we find a passage which sums up the whole Humanist theory. He makes his hero say, "I will go out in my enemy's field and sow seeds and thus make God." For the modern Humanist, God is not an objective reality, a Power, not ourselves, before and after man, and transcending man, but is being made by man. Such a conception can only be temporary, it cannot feed the starving heart of humanity. Man advances in culture by looking beyond himself; he cannot lift himself by his own boot-straps. The voice of God within him has only overwhelming validity, if it is recognized as the voice of God. Judaism says man in his supremest virtue does not make God, he does not create Him, he only discovers Him and knows that he is in the presence of an Eternal Power, who is creating righteousness. And if the modern man is to become religious again, might he not be won by the thought that the ethical life is sufficient for salvation, that the obedience of the law of justice and love to the utmost of our powers, brings bliss to us here on earth and has its own eternal value.

Just what was considered the weakness of Israel's religion, that it did not emphasize too much and concentrate the attention of human beings too much upon celestial regions, might that not be the very thing which would in the end win the modern mind? Do we not need something, on the one hand, of Hebraic immediacy so that the purified heart hears God's presence right here and does not need any postponement to supernatural worlds, of the joy of meeting Divinity, and, on the other hand, do we need that urge to transform *this world* by social justice and make it a Heaven on earth, an urge not to be impaired by weakening the will through promises of happiness for the oppressed in a celestial world? Judaism, too, as a minor note in its symphony, makes the promise but the dominant note of Judaism is "the kingdom of God is built in this world." In the process of right living and in the process of right dreaming of humanity's future, might not the modern man find, as Judaism gives it, a sufficient ethical and social program as the content of religion? And above all, must not the daily duty, the civic virtue, the sanctity of the process of life itself, at last come to be seen as the wherewithal to serve God? Does not the education of the Western world show a deficiency in so far as the Decalog, not to speak of the crowning commandment of "Love thy neighbor as thyself," has not as yet entered into the life blood of the masses?

I think Israel has much to teach the world, but Israel must first teach itself. If we have a mission we also have a method of our own, and our method has been the method of example. As Law, the Moral Law is the essence of Judaism, we cannot and Israel never did, make salvation for a human being dependent upon joining the community of Israel. All human beings according to our teaching will be saved if they obey the law of righteousness and live according to the best light of their conscience. "The righteous[87] of all nations will inherit the everlasting life." Our method has been to draw by the virtue of the Jewish hearth, by the sanctification of our lives. At least history tells us that is the way converts came to us and they were very welcome. We always recognized that humanity has been well provided for by its Creator and Father so that our ambition has not been to make of humanity one church. And if we go our own way and seek to perform our mission as a spiritual influence in the world, we must so live our religion, that, to use the old precious phrase "It will prove itself to be our wisdom[88] and understanding in the eyes of the peoples." I think the time for reforming Judaism is over for the present. Our main work is to reform

[87] T. B., Sanhedrin, 105a.
[88] Deut. 4:6.

the Jew, to make again Israel of the flesh to be an Israel of the spirit. And therefore, we who have emphasized the mission idea must ask, whether in our justified approach to the world, we have not, swung by the impetus of our movement, been carried too far from Jewish individuality. And I revert to the idea that we must rediscover and apply to our lives the fruitful power of the ceremonial law as a discipline and a hallowing and purifying influence in our lives. Living in the midst of the nations, loving the countries of the peoples of which we are part, we shall, while being an influence for social righteousness and for peace, take pains to restore the conception of holiness in the personal experience of the individual son and daughter of Israel.

Israel is a spiritual power because, if true to its tradition and prophetic vision, it must be an influence in the life of any nation of which any section of Israel is a part, on behalf of more justice and more loving kindness. But it is a great fallacy to attempt to commit Israel to any particular "ism." Individual Jews may in freedom of spirit and urged by conscience be in the vanguard of this or that party in the political and social life of any nation. But Israel is above all temporary "isms" which come and go—for Israel knows that salvation is not found in any political or social program but rather in the moralization of the individual and through him, in the transformation of society. The Prophets were very concrete indeed, but we know of no political or social program that they had. I do not feel that Israel will not have too much to do in the world. On the contrary the task is great. Let us not lose heart. The sun will shine again. Western culture will be destroyed if the Western world should, God forbid, destroy what it has achieved, all the rights of man, all humanitarian idealism. I think that the Jew will see better times in the Western world. Let him prepare himself well.

And now I come to what I call the new synthesis. The nationalists and the religionists, in so far as we, the party of Reform Judaism in Israel represent the latter, are above all thoroughly modern. The future belongs to them and not to any kind of petrified worship of the letter of the past. Both these modern movements have their strength and their weakness.

The strength of our movement has been the rediscovery of the universal element in Judaism, the emphasis of the ethical life as the content of the prophetic Torah, the Divine revelation. The strength of our movement has been to prove to the modern mind that forms may change because forms must change in the course of life's demands. The spirit is indestructible. If we are not to become a sect like Karaism, then what will happen is, that like all great movements in Israel's history, we will pour our spirit into (to use the great phrase of Solomon Schechter) "Catholic Israel." We have already influenced Israel, we will influence it more. Our weakness has been that because, as the Midrash says, the same messenger[89] cannot perform two different errands, we, by the very work of our universalism, may not have kept a sufficiently strong hold on the thought of Israel as a distinct community.

The strength of the nationalist party consists in the fact that it has emphasized the importance of Israel. It called it a nation. Indirectly thus it strengthened the backbone of Jewish consciousness although it braced it artificially. It too borrowed too much from the Western environment. It talks like a Western nationalist. The great man who founded this Conference, Isaac Mayer Wise, who was the "unifier[90] and organizer" of American Judaism, was so absorbed in the building of the edifice we love, that he said, referring to the Zionist movement, that "it was an unpleasant[91] episode in our history." He felt disturbed by it and naturally so. But this movement has proved to be a tremendous power. Its weakness is just this very thing that, while it wants to strengthen the backbone of Jewish consciousness, it has assimilated away the Jewish soul by making Israel a *goy* like other *goyim,* a nation like other nations.

This is a time for union and not for bitter controversy amongst Jews. Let us recognize that good is to be found in every earnest soul that feels the woe of Jacob. And so let us work together, we the religionists and those who differ with us. Palestine will lead to the new synthesis. Reform Judaism has the grandest opportunity

[89] Ber. Rabbah, 50, 2.
[90] Philipson, p. 342.
[91] Philipson, p. 361.

in its history; it has the opportunity of martyrdom. Let it send half a dozen young men or more to Palestine to bring the message of Progressive Judaism. That name is the best and avoids controversy. What Palestine needs today, in my humble opinion, is a message that will teach the rising generation the religious and ethical content of the heritage of Israel. What exists today in Palestine is, on the one hand, an immovable orthodoxy which has very little appeal to the young, and, on the other hand, there exists a bare secular nationalism which is not good for the mentality of the growing youth. We have already pledged ourselves in this Conference to help build up a Jewish Palestine. We are cooperating with our brethren who differ with us in their philosophy of Jewish life. Let us also feel that Palestine is a field for us. Perhaps just as the Babylonian Hillel taught something worthwhile to the Palestinians of his time, so we may have something worthwhile to teach to the self-sufficient nationalists in Palestine of our time. Not to stand aloof is our aim, but recognizing the value of Palestine for hundreds of thousands of our brethren in Israel, let us help increase the settlement and, at the same time, let us bravely uphold the truth that Israel is not a *Goy* like other *Goyim,* but it always was, it is now, and if it is to live at all, will always be, a witness to God . . .

ISRAEL
Abba Hillel Silver
(1935)

I shall devote myself principally to a discussion of paragraph 5 of the Declaration of Principles adopted by the Pittsburgh Rabbinical Conference in 1885 which reads as follows: "We recognize, in the modern era of universal culture of heart and intellect, the approaching of the realization of Israel's great Messianic hope for the establishment of the kingdom of truth, justice, and peace among all men. We consider ourselves no longer a nation, but a religious community, and therefore expect neither a return to Palestine, nor a sacrificial worship under the sons of Aaron, nor the restoration of any of the laws concerning the Jewish state."

This declaration is noteworthy in that it was the first of its kind ever made by an assembly of Jewish religious leaders, lay or cleric. No similarly constituted conference anywhere in the whole history of Israel up to that time declared categorically: "We consider ourselves no longer a nation, but a religious community." Individual Reform Rabbis, like Geiger and Holdheim and many others, did of course, prior to 1885, proclaim this thesis time and again. But it is significant that even the Frankfurt Conference of 1845 which was dominated by the extreme left wing of the German Reform movement contented itself with a resolution that: "The Messianic idea should receive prominent mention in the prayers, but all petitions for our return to the land of our fathers, and for the restoration of a Jewish state should be eliminated from the prayers."

It is, of course, one thing to say that it is desirable, for one reason or another, for the Jewish people to remain where they are and not to strive after national restoration in Palestine; Galut nationalists of the Dubnow School, the proletarian Yiddishists of Soviet Russia and many others besides anti-Zionist Reform Rabbis would subscribe to such a doctrine. It is quite another thing to announce that: "We consider ourselves no longer a nation but a religious community."

Rabbi Wechsler, for example, clearly grasped this difference which seems to have escaped the notice of so many of his Reform colleagues of that day. He, too, was opposed to the Restoration idea but he nevertheless maintained that we were a people united not merely by religious ties but also by racial and national ties and by historical experiences commonly shared. (See S. Bernfeld,— תולדות הרפורמציון הדתית Cracow, 1900, p. 49, note.)

It is quite possible that if a set of principles had been adopted by the Frankfurt Conference, or by its predecessor, the Brunswick Conference of 1844, a declaration similar to the one of the Pittsburgh Conference would have been adopted. But their very reluctance to adopt such a declaration of principles is itself significant.

The Philadelphia Conference of 1869 was the first to formulate a platform of Reform Judaism. This declaration likewise does not contain the creed of national abjuration found in the Pittsburgh platform. The theologic cosmopolitanism of the framers of the Philadelphia constitution of Reform Judaism found sufficient peace of mind in the avowal that: "The Messianic aim of Israel is not the restoration of the old Jewish state under a descendant of David, involving a second separation from the nations of the earth. . . . We look upon the destruction of the second Jewish commonwealth not as a punishment for the sinfulness of Israel, but as a result of the divine purpose revealed to Abraham, which, as has become ever clearer in the course of the world's history, consists in the dispersion of the Jews to all parts of the earth, for the realization of their high priestly mission, to lead the nations to the true knowledge and worship of God."

The early Reform Rabbis of America were certainly more eager to formulate Principles and Declarations than were their confreres in Germany. They did not shrink from dogmatic pronouncements, nor did the old adage of Erasmus—*omnis definitio periculosa est*—discourage them. The fact that they had to reckon with far fewer restraints in the New World, traditional or institutional, and with an inchoate Jewish community and a minimum of local Jewish history, undoubtedly gave wing to their spacious and care-free theologic depositions. What impresses one, however, is the fact that it was in the United States, of all countries, where such a declaration on the subject of Jewish nationalism as one finds in the Pittsburgh platform was made. One cannot account for it except on the basis of its being an importation, an exotic plant brought to these shores by immigrant Rabbis from Germany and transplanted here without any particular reference to soil or climate. For there was nothing in the American Jewish scene in the eighties that made such a declaration urgent or significant. There was no political pressure from without, no need to placate organized anti-Semitic forces, no necessity to purchase political equality through any public renunciation of earlier ways of life and thought. Nor was there visible any strong nationalist movement among the American Jews of those days. One can readily understand the political motives behind such formal surrender of Jewish nationalism made by some Jews who lived in Germany during the period of struggle for emancipation and equality in the nineteenth century, and by some groups of Jews in Russia in the eager, hopeful years of the early reign of Alexander II. But why in America?

The Reform movement in Germany did not originate in any great outpouring of spirit, or in any outburst of religious fervor or revivalism. Hence, while producing a vigorous polemic and *Wissen-*

schaft literature, it produced no great theologic or mystic literature. It was part of a comprehensive purpose to adjust Jewish life pragmatically to its new environment. It was a conscious expedient, not to reinstate prophetic universalism in Jewish religious thought—that was rationalization—but to gain for the Jew full rights of citizenship by producing the proper effect upon the civil authorities. It was assumed, albeit erroneously, that Jewish separatism, manifested in speech, dress, folkways, rituals and ceremonies and in the Messianic expectation of a return to Palestine, was responsible for the non-Jews' suspicion and hostility and for their reluctance to concede to Jews full political equality. The accusations of the cruder and less sophisticated anti-Semites of that day lent credence to that assumption. The solution, accordingly, lay in a thoroughgoing eradication of all evidences of separatism. For some Jews this meant total assimilation, apostasy not excluded. For others assimilation stopped short of religious surrender but religion purged of all nationalistic elements.

The process began in the *Aufklaerung* era whose symbol is Moses Mendelssohn. Mendelssohn was, of course, neither a reformer nor an anti-nationalist. He was a humanist who sought to find a place for the religiously observant Jew in the political and intellectual milieu of Western European civilization. But under the influence of the rationalism and cosmopolitanism of his day and in his eagerness to persuade the German people of the Jew's qualifications for citizenship, he "neutralized" Judaism theologically by denying its unique and challenging character as a system of beliefs and restricted it to the status of a revealed law or divine legislation which was in no way in conflict with the law of the land. He, furthermore, passed over in silence, though perhaps not intentionally, the *national* character of the Jewish people. Nationalism, be it remembered, was in Mendelssohn's day not a fully developed concept and the idea of separate nationalities within a state was not quite as repugnant and sinister as it became later. Nevertheless Mendelssohn's thesis that theology is a private matter and that Judaism is nothing more than a revealed code of laws, largely ceremonial,

and his reticence touching the *national* destiny of Israel was seized
upon by contemporaries as justification for assimilation. It was but
one step, regardless of its logical *non-sequitur,* from the position
taken by Mendelssohn to that of his friend and admirer, David
Friedländer, who in the *Epistle of Several Jewish Fathers to
Councillor Teller* offered to accept Christianity if certain doctrines
such as the Trinity were eliminated. Dorothea Mendelssohn, after
her conversion to Christianity, felt justified in saying that her father,
if he had been alive, would not have been saddened by her act.
This first generation of *enlightened* Berlin, Frankfurt and Viennese
Jews were convinced that their political and social salvation lay in
deorientalizing and Germanizing themselves, in making themselves
like other people in order to be accepted as equals *by* other people.
Of course they were naive. In the land of the poll-tax where Jew-
hatred had always been the most vulgar, violent, and sustained in
all Europe, they permitted themselves to indulge in wishful thinking. They might have been cautioned by the cool admonitions of
some of their Christian contemporaries who advised them, as Teller
deftly advised Friedländer, not to confound Jewish efforts at
religious modernization with the hope of political equality. Schleiermacher, the non-Jew, grasped the Jewish problem far more realistically and fundamentally than did the German Jews of his day. He
warned them that the important difference between them and the
non-Jewish world was not religious but national. It took the German Jews a century and a half to reconcile themselves finally to this
unyielding fact.

The *national* character of the Jewish problem became evident
within a few years after the French Revolution. In the superb exultation of the Revolution the rights of citizenship were granted to
the Jews of France. But when the revolutionary ardor had abated,
grumblings and mutterings were soon heard against them. An
anti-Semitic literature made its appearance. A particularly violent
outburst of Jew-hatred made itself manifest in the German-speak-
ing French province of Alsace. The attitude of Napoleon was anything but friendly to the Jews. He was considering the revocation

or curtailment of their civil rights. The real motive which prompted the convocation of the Assembly of Jewish notables in Paris in 1806 —the forerunner of the Sanhedrin—was to cross-examine the Jews of France, to discover whether they were one hundred percent patriotic and deserving of the citizenship which the Revolution had bestowed upon them. The questionnaire submitted to the Assembly was to ferret out some possible excuse for the abrogation of their rights. Thus the sixth question read: "Do the Jews who are natives of France and are treated as French citizens by the law look upon France as their Fatherland?" The fourth question read: "Do the Jews consider the French their brethren or do they look upon them as aliens?"

The Assembly, of course, affirmed that the Jews of France regarded France as their Fatherland, and all Frenchmen as their brothers. They loudly proclaimed their loyalty to France and their readiness to defend her at all costs. They did not feel called upon, however, as did the Rabbis of the Pittsburgh Conference who were neither solicited for an opinion, nor were hard-pressed politically, to declare that the Jews were not a nation, only a religious community. Nor did they deny the hope of national restoration as did the all-too-zealous German reformers a few decades later.

But it was clear from the very fact that such an assembly had been convoked, and such questions asked that *nationalism* would from then on be the central fact of Jewish experience not only in France, but everywhere as soon as the Jews left their ghettos and reached out for civil and political rights. As in Germany, so also in France, there were Jews who met the increasing nationalist sentiments in their environment with a corresponding modulation of their own, although there did not transpire any such thoroughgoing religious reform movement among the French as among the German Jews. France was Catholic, religiously orthodox. There was no popular Protestant movement for the Jews of France to model themselves after.

Most marked, however, were the anti-nationalist tendencies among German Jews because German anti-Semitism was far more

virulent and uncompromising, and German nationalism, following
the War of Liberation, far more intense and jaundiced. The opposition to the political emancipation of the Jews in Germany was
bitter and relentless throughout the nineteenth century, continuing
into the twentieth and achieving a complete victory under the Nazi
regime in our day. Rising like a miasma from the poisoned soil of
the Dark Ages, Jew-hatred has swept uninterruptedly like a pesti-
lential plague through German life and literature, infesting masses
and classes alike, poisoning the hearts and minds of liberals as well
as reactionaries, of poets, philosophers, statesmen, historians, mu-
sicians and churchmen. The venomous anti-Jewish Nazi propaganda literature of the last fifteen years drew its inspiration,
program and slogans from the prolific school of Jew-baiting preachers, pundits and pamphleteers of the Bismarckian era, and they, in
turn, derived their leading ideas from their precursors in post-
Napoleonic era, whose mentor and model was the liberal, anti-
clerical philosopher Fichte whose attitude is summed up in his
statement: "The only way I see by which civil rights can be
conceded to them [Jews] is to cut off all their heads in one night
and set new ones on their shoulders, which shall contain not a
single Jewish idea. The only means of protecting ourselves against
them is to conquer their promised land and send them there." The
Nazi cry, *Juda Verrecke,* is the authentic echo of the *Hep, Hep,*
cry shouted by frenzied mobs in the streets of Frankfurt and
Hamburg a century and more before. There is an unbroken line
of ideologically formulated, metaphysically sanctioned and ar-
tistically embellished Judeophobia in Germany, centuries old,
unmatched anywhere else in the world. It was in such a milieu
that the Jews of Germany lived and struggled for their civil and
political rights. If, therefore, Jewish lay and religious leaders of
the reform group, and also of some of the Germanized orthodox
and conservative groups attempted to throw overboard all the racial
and national baggage of Israel in the fond hope of calming this sea
of hate, if they believed that they could exorcise anti-Semitism by
professions of patriotism, and in an age of *crescendo* nationalism,

could solve the Jewish problem by a corresponding *diminuendo* in *Jewish* nationalism, one can understand their plight and forgive their blindness, whereas one finds it difficult to account for the action of American reformers except on the grounds suggested above.

The Russian Jewish intelligentsia of the sixties and seventies resorted to the self-same unavailing tactics in a land in which there was far less literary anti-Semitism than in Germany, and in which the educated classes of society were definitely pro-Jewish. The anti-national incantation which Holdheim chanted in Germany to appease the intolerant spirits of German nationalism, Pinsker, for example, chanted in Russia for many years before tragic, disillusioning events forced him upon the long hard road which leads from assimilation to auto-emancipation. Many others among the best minds of Russian Jewry believed that in thorough Russification and assimilation lay the hope of ultimate salvation. They advocated the use of the Russian language and the abandonment both of Yiddish and Hebrew. At most they conceded a minimal religious distinctiveness. The idea of a Jewish national renaissance, or the reconstruction of a Jewish homeland in Palestine was to them both fantastic and unwelcome. It was too reactionary an idea to entertain in an age of enlightenment when a favoring breeze filled their sails and they felt themselves carried along to the delectable harbor of liberty and equality. It was too reactionary an idea and too illogical. But history has a logic of her own. A sharp reaction set in under the same Liberator Czar Alexander II, and in 1871, the Jews of Russia sampled the gall and bitterness of a pogrom. The pogrom of 1871 and the more extensive and brutal pogroms of 1881 broke the back of assimilation in Russia. The solution clearly did not lie in the formula, "Russians of the Mosaic Persuasian." In 1882 the *Chovevei Zion* appear on the scene. In the same year the converted Pinsker publishes his *Auto-Emancipation*. Russian Jewry sets about solving its problems through self-help, through mass emigration to other lands, through the upbuilding of a Jewish homeland in Palestine, through national concentration and cultural revival, and through revolutionary economico-political agitation and action in an effort to break the power of the hostile reactionary regime

German Jewry might have learned the same lesson in the seventies when the great reaction set in and anti-Semitism flared up again. Treitschke, Bernhardi, Stöcker, Dürer, Marr, Mole,—all the forerunners of the present-day Nazis—told them exactly how the German people felt about the Jews and why and what the German people would do to them when the hour of decision arrived. But the German Jews continued in their ineluctable optative mood, confident as was Rabbi Auerbach at the Rabbinical Conference of Frankfurt, that: "In our day the ideals of justice and the brotherhood of men have been so strengthened through the laws and institutions of modern states, *that they can never again be shattered.* We are witnessing an ever nearer approach of the establishment of the Kingdom of God on earth through the strivings of mankind" (quoted from Philipson's *The Reform Movement in Judaism,* p. 178). This was uttered in Frankfurt in 1845. Frankfurt of 1935 is of course a sad and discouraging refutation of all this apocalyptic romancing in which German Jewry immersed itself in those days. The catastrophe of 1933 broke the back of assimilation in Germany. The whole improvised philosophy of Jewish history which is expressed in the doctrine that we are not a nation but a religious community has proved bankrupt and has been liquidated in the very home of its origin.

While the leaders of German Jewry, with the exception of course of the small but distinguished group of nationally-minded thinkers of the type of Moses Hess, Bodenheimer, Franz Oppenheimer, Wolffsohn, Ruppin, Hantke, Otto Warburg and Martin Buber, talked to unheeding Gentile ears about the unoffending status of the Jews as only another religious sect who in all other regards were *Echt-und-Nur-Deutschen,* the Germans were reading and absorbing the nationalistic theses and the Aryan race mythologies of Chamberlain, Friedrich Delitzsch, Günther and Rosenberg and the relentless processes of history, made *race* and *nation* the order of the day in Germany. In their name and at their behest the Jews of

Germany have been disfranchised, stripped of all their hard-won gains of a century and a half, and degraded as few Jewish communities have ever been degraded in the last two thousand years. And now the Jews of Germany, except those of the small and pathologically chauvinistic Naumannite group, are meeting the crisis of their inner and outer lives in the same way as their Russian brethren a half century before—a strong national revival, the rediscovery of the cultural heritage of their own people, Palestine, emigration and presumably also, such underground political action as their stoutest spirits dare to resort to. . . .

How confidently Ludwig Geiger of Berlin proclaimed thirty years ago: "Any desire to form, together with his coreligionists, a people outside of Germany is, not to speak of its impracticability, downright thanklessness toward the nation in whose midst he lives —a chimera; for the German Jew is a German in his *national peculiarities* (*sic!*) and Zion is for him the land only of the past, *not of the future*" (Quoted in *J.E.* Vol. XII, p. 673). Thirty years later, Germans whose *national peculiarities* were all German (in the eyes of Jews, of course, but not of Germans) were fleeing from Germany and finding refuge by the thousands in the land which was never really the land of their past but which must very definitely now become the land of their future. The Munich community which forced the transfer of the first Zionist Congress, scheduled to be held there, to Basel, is now grateful that some of its sons and daughters are finding a haven and a new hope in the land which those ungrateful and *unpatriotic* Zionists had built. . . .

Human history is replete with the clash and conflict of nations, races, peoples, religions and classes. The Jewish nation had its full quota of these conflicts when it was a political nation in Palestine. It certainly could not escape them as a non-political and scattered nation in the diaspora. Those who could not stand the strain of Jewish existence disappeared. Myriads of such Jews were lost to us. Many others were forcibly assimilated. Those who cannot endure the pressures of Jewish life today, their סבל הירושה will also disappear—if they can. The newer racial anti-Semitism of the Nazi

type is making such desertion extremely difficult. It is impossible
to propound any formula for Jewish survival in the diaspora—if
we really mean *survival*—free from a measure of stress and conflict.

In our long history we never had a uniform plan or formula for
survival. Such a formula, if it is to be something more than academic, must take into account not only the shifting interests and
needs of the Jews themselves but also the varied and changing
political and economic milieu in which Jewish groups find themselves. A formula which would be valid for Jewish communities
living in an empire like that of ancient Persia, Greece or Rome
which embraced numerous nationalities and allowed them full
national autonomy short of political independence, would not meet
the situation of a Jewish community living in a closely-knit, uni-
cultural national state like modern France, Germany, or Italy; and
a formula valid for these countries would not be adequate for a
multi-national state like Poland, Czechoslovakia, or Russia. A Jewish community living in the midst of a people whose cultural *niveau*
was far inferior to its own, would face altogether different problems
of adjustment than one living in the midst of a superior culture.

But there was always the will to survive! Not in all sections of
our people, to be sure, nor at all times, but certainly in sufficiently
large sections of our people at all times to have enabled Israel to
survive to this day. . . .

So great was this desire not to die as a people, that when it found
its life besieged and threatened, it threw additional bulwarks around
its security and raised stronger walls of defense. It did not hesitate
to impose upon itself in the centuries following the second Destruction, a code of discipline, a regimen מצוות מעשיות which was
far more rigorous than any military discipline, and which effectively safeguarded the individuality of the people and secured it
against disintegration. The people, as a whole, never relaxed its
vigilance. It never whittled down its requirements or its survival
program to appease enemies or detractors. It never countenanced a
minimal program to satisfy others. It always insisted upon a maximum program to protect its own life. . . .

The source of the Mission Idea must . . . be looked for in the fact of the Dispersion and not in any automatic spiritual development of prophetic Judaism. It was evolved, consciously or unconsciously, in response to a desperate national emergency, out of the indomitable *will to live* of the race, as a means of strengthening the morale of the scattered hosts of Israel and of giving meaning and dignity to their exile and their vast tribulations. It was a noble compensatory ideal, warranted by the fact that Israel *did* possess a religious outlook which far transcended that of the heathen, and a moral code of superior excellence. Israel knew itself to be a great people because of the spiritual heights to which it had attained in its religious and ethical development. This achievement made it contemptuous of the superstitions and idolatries of the world about it. But politically it was a small, scattered and defeated people— a *worm* among the nations, despised and condemned. Wherein shall this proud but defeated people, of which only a miserable remnant now remained in the waste and desolate places of Judea, whilst its hosts were captives and exiles in foreign lands, now find that indemnifying conception of destiny which would take the edge off their defeat, sweeten the bitterness of exile, and restore confidence to those utterly cast down? The answer was soon forthcoming—the cup of comfort to the parched lips. . . . Light and salvation will come to the whole world through Israel, who is God's servant, suffering in the present but destined to ultimate triumph and vindication. This is the חדשות אני מגיד —the wonderfully new gospel which the Second Isaiah now proclaims. This is the new vision and hope which the spiritual guides of Israel projected for their people in order to save them from death in defeat and exile.

Note that this ideal of mission is not a denial, a revision or a substitution for any other concept heretofore held basic in Jewish thought but only a supplement, an addition, another bulwark for national security. It does not supplant nationalism. It re-enforces it. It does not look upon the Dispersion as a blessing. It confronts it as a tragic fact which, however, must not be permitted to endanger the survival of Israel. It does not assume that the Jew must remain in exile in order that Yahweh may become the God of all the nations. It does not proclaim that Israel is no longer a nation but only a religious community, whose sole *raison d'être* is the conversion of the Gentiles. It does not divorce religion from nationalism. . . . And when the prophets speak of Restoration they are not thinking of "the colonization of Palestine as a philanthropic effort deserving of general support" (a concession made to Palestine even by anti-Zionist Reform Rabbis), but of the rebuilding of the political life and home of the Jewish nation.

Zion rebuilt and Israel ingathered are the passionate themes of the prophets following the exile, and they did not regard them as being in any way irreconcilable with the hope of converting the whole world to Yahweh. The nations will come to *Zion*. Zion will become the religious center of mankind. "Thus saith the Lord of hosts: I am *jealous* for Zion with great jealousy, and I am jealous for her with great fury! . . . I shall return to Zion, and will dwell in the midst of Jerusalem . . . Behold, I will have My people from the east country and from the west country and I will bring them and they shall dwell in the midst of Jerusalem" (Zech. 8.2.) . . .

Anyone, therefore, who attempts to exploit the historic Mission Idea of Israel as an argument against Jewish nationalism or against the rebuilding of Palestine or in justification of the *Galut* is guilty of gross distortion of an idea which is very clearly and unambiguously defined in its original sources. The prophets did not believe that the Jews should continue to live in exile, nor that they should welcome the Dispersion as a blessing for the sake of their mission. They did not say that the Jews were exiled *in order* that they might become God's witnesses to the Gentiles. They exhorted the Jews in exile to find strength in defeat. They sought to sustain them by the thought that though they had been driven into exile their significance in the economy of the world was not at an end. On the contrary, they now had the opportunity, through the examples of their steadfastness to Yahweh, and through the moral tone of their lives, to acquaint the whole heathen world with their great spiritual heritage—the true knowledge of God, and the nobility of His worship.

The Jews, during the chaotic centuries which followed the Destruction, employed *every* means to preserve their national life. We have seen how the prophets sought to restore the morale of the people by giving those living inside and outside of Palestine an inspiriting and sustaining sense of destiny. The people, themselves, in exile, once the first shock of terror and dismay was over, recovered their ancient faith and loyalties. By the rivers of Babylon they vowed eternal loyalty to Zion, their national home . . .

Nation, race, land, language were always vital and indispensable concepts in Jewish life, indissolubly associated of course with religion. It was never a case of one or the other. They were all one, organically united. There were times when one or the other had to be stressed. Whenever one of these factors of survival was threatened, the strong instinct of the people rallied to its defense. Hence in our history we find eras of accentuation of one or another of these several concepts and eras of attenuation. But never was any one of them abandoned—until the time of the Reform Rabbis of Germany which is, of course, a very recent and seemingly a rapidly vanishing phenomenon.

The sound, practical sense of Israel and its experience through many centuries of partial or total dispersion over the earth, saved it from being dogmatic or fanatic concerning any of these concepts. On one subject only was Israel fanatically dogmatic—the monotheistic article of its faith. Jewish life could never stomach the type of doctrinaire, arrogant and militant racialism and nationalism which is devastating the life of the Western World today. Israel reconciled in life and practice ideas theoretically irreconcilable . . .

Doctrinaires of the white-black, either-or variety, who like to have life and history simplified to fit in neatly in some theoretic framework which they arbitrarily construct to serve their tastes or their times, are impatient with these seeming incongruities and contradictions in Jewish life. They lightly reject whatever they find, practically or ideologically, inconvenient. They are unaware of, or they consciously ignore the strong life-sense, the survival-wisdom, the adjustment-genius of the people which produced them. A religious creed, once you grant its premises, may well be logically consistent and undeviating. But a people is not a creed and a people's life and culture are determined by historic forces which are not logical. Israel, confronted through most of its history with an ever changing and theatening environment, and wishing to survive, had to take into account all the economic, political, sociologic and psychologic facts in its environment and make proper adjustments to them. . . .

But in the case of Christianity, it was the Pauline insistence upon religious creed entirely divorced from nation, race, land or language and from the disciplines of Jewish law, that finally placed the movement outside the sphere of Jewish life. . . .

The mastering idea of Paul was that, in as much as the millennium was fast approaching when the purging and winnowing of mankind would take place, the whole human race should be rapidly converted to the one true faith. This one true faith consisted in the abjuration of polytheism and idolatry and in leading a pure life—in other words—ethical monotheism. Such a faith has been in the keeping of Israel since the days of Abraham. But because of the Law of Moses—the ceremonial and ritual law, e.g., circumcision, the observance of Sabbaths and Holy Days and the dietary laws,— this pure faith has been obscured, veiled even to Israel (II Cor. 3.5) and made difficult of acceptance by non-Jews. The coming of the Messiah in the person of Jesus put an end to the reign of this Law. Now conversion to the true faith is accessible to every man merely through faith—faith in the One, Universal Lord and in the atoning power of the death of Jesus. This latter idea is essential to the doctrine of Paul. . . .

But what then was the purpose of giving the Law by God to Israel, and what is the significance of the election of Israel—a doctrine which Paul accepts (Rom. 11.29). In Paul's reply one finds the clue to the reason why the Jewish people had finally to reject him and his religious teachings. The giving of the Laws of the Torah to the Jews carried with it the possibility and the opportunity of transgressing them. It is the Law that gives sin its power. . . .

As far as Paul's new message of glad tidings is concerned, the

Jews are treated as enemies of God (Rom. 11.28.). But because
they had been chosen by God and are beloved by Him for their
fathers' sakes, they, too, will be saved from sin through the grace
of God ultimately, after all the heathen have been redeemed. Thus
Israel, in the hands of this fervid, mystical theologian, is no longer
a nation but a theologic pawn. The national character of the Jewish
Messianic ideal is ignored, as it was ignored centuries later by
Reform Rabbis. It is dissolved in a universal salvationism, quite
like the denationalized "Messianic Age" of the Reform Rabbis.
There is, however, one exception: With Paul *all* nations vanish
into the spiritual anonymity of Kingdom Come. With the Reform
Rabbis, only the Jewish nation. *Their* theology took zealous toll of
Jewish nationalism but stopped short at German, Austrian, French
or American nationalism. . . . With Paul the age-old hope of the
ingathering of the dispersion and the deliverance of Israel from the
yoke of Rome gives way to an apocalyptic conversionism in which
Israel is only incidentally significant because in olden days God
had announced in advance the good news to Abraham. . . .

This is the sole role ascribed by Paul to Israel in the economy of
world-salvation. With the nationalist prophets of Israel, a reborn
and politically rehabilitated people, strong and secure in its own
land, was to become a light unto the world. The nations of the
earth would flow unto Zion redeemed, "for out of Zion would go
forth the Torah." With Paul, Torah was a form of slavery, and
Zion had no significance as the capital of a nation but only as the
locale of a Temple of whose ritual he scarcely approved. No wonder that this new program of proselytism which demanded the
sacrifice of so many of the essential survival-values of Israel, met
with stubborn resistance not alone from Jews who had not accepted Jesus as the Messiah but even from the early-Judaeo-
Christians.

In classic Judaism there were always two elements, one universal,
i.e., pure religion intended for all men, the other local, i.e., the
laws of the Hebrew polity, intended for Jews only. Paul, the
Roman citizen and the product of the Mediterranean cultural melt-

ing-pot, accepted the first. The second he regarded principally as a
stumbling block in the way of the first. Therefore, nothing but
faith mattered. The Jewish nation, land, language and law were
of small consequence, particularly in view of the approaching
millennial denouement. . . .

There is a striking similarity to be seen between the theoretic
position taken by Paul and that taken by the extreme leaders of
Reform Judaism; and had these men been as consistent as Paul,
and had they translated their loquacity about the mission of Israel
into a real missionary propaganda as did Paul and his followers,
the logic of events would have brought about the secession of their
group also from Jewish life. But with Paul, the mission was a race
to save the world. With the Reform Rabbis it was a rocking-horse
race. These reformist Rabbis, too, were denationalized Jews. They,
too, conceived of Israel as "a candle which lights others and con-
sumes itself." They, too, tried to erect Jewish life upon the slender,
sagging stilts of a few theologic abstractions. They, too, felt the
Law to be a burden. They focused *their* anti-nomist odium on the
Talmud and the Shulchan Aruch. The Bible they spared, for after
all the Bible was sacred also to Christians. . . . But those laws of
the Bible, against which Paul inveighed—circumcision, Sabbath observance and dietary laws—came under their obloquy also. The
use of the Hebrew language in public worship, they maintained, was
not only unnecessary from a legal point of view but from any other
point of view (Frankfurt Conference). And while Jewish Rabbis
were thus practically consigning the Hebrew language to oblivion,
Dohm of Breslau, a Christian, rose to its defense, urged its retention by Jews as the language of the prayers and as a bond of unity,
and reminded them that if many Jews no longer understand the
language, the solution lies, not in abandoning the language but
rather in teaching it more energetically than before. They, too, believed that the world was on the threshold of great, new beginnings.
They, too, were bewitched by the hope of *Maranatha*. To them, too,
as to the apocalyptic visionaries of the first century, the Kingdom
of God was just around the corner. . . . Listen to the words of

Article 5 of the Pittsburgh Declaration which echoed similar sentiments among Reformers everywhere: "We recognize, in the modern era of universal culture of heart and intellect, *the approaching of the realization* of Israel's great Messianic hope for the establishment of truth, justice, and peace among all men. . . ." They, too, converted the national Messianic hope of Israel into something like a Pauline apocalypse.

A Messianic hope not bound up with the restoration of Israel to Palestine is simply not found in Jewish religious literature anywhere from the time of the Second Isaiah to our own day, except, of course, in the writings of these Reformers and some of the Hellenistic apocalyptic writers, who through allegory and other devices attempted to universalize the teachings of the Torah, so as to impress the non-Jewish world with the excellency of the Jewish faith, and who converted the Jewish national Messiah into an "incarnation of a divine power who should judge men at the end of days." National restoration was the very heart of the Messianic ideal from its very inception. To substitute for this national ideal an antinational, purely transcendental, nebulous *Messianic Age,* on the plea of religious evolution, is to be guilty not of revision but of distortion. It is both new and counterfeit.

Fortunately the views of these men did not prevail. They were quickly challenged. The masses of Jewry recoiled from them. The facts of life soon dissipated the fumes of their universalistic romancing. They have now been discredited in the very land of their nativity. The United States, because of its peculiar political and social configuration, for a time gave scope to these ideas and they were received with considerable favor among certain classes of our people, particularly among our German-Jewish immigrants. But they are being rapidly abandoned. The very men who framed the Pittsburgh Declaration felt the inadequacy of their definition. Twice in the Declaration they speak of the "Jewish people." They do not define the term "people," but the very fact that they resorted to the term indicates that they felt that the term "religious community" somehow failed to cover the full canvass of Jewish realities.

Dr. Kohler, who convoked the Pittsburgh Conference, and helped to draft its Declaration, found it necessary in his *Theology* to supplement this definition of Israel as a religious community, with the concept of race. "The Jew is born into it [Judaism] and cannot extricate himself from it even by the renunciation of his faith, which would but render him an apostate Jew. This condition exists, because the racial community formed, and still forms, the basis of the religious community. It is birth, not confession, that imposes on the Jew the obligation to work and strive for the eternal verities of Israel, for the preservation and propagation of which he has been chosen by the God of history" (p. 6).

But why is the concept of "race" any more exalted than "nation"? Why should racial fatalism commit one irrevocably to religious beliefs which should be voluntary? If one, not of the race, can become a Jew by accepting Judaism, why cannot one "extricate" himself from Judaism by rejecting it? Identifying Judaism with race is no more logical, and in our day, far more provocative than identifying it with "nation."

Dr. Cyrus Adler, though belonging to the conservative wing, also believes that the Jews are only a religious community, but he is quite as vigorous in *denying* that the Jews are a race. In his recent address before the Seminary National Council, he declared: "Sometimes people say that they are Jews by race and sometimes that they are Jews by nationality. No people is suffering today more from this race or national theory than the Jewish people, and to the extent that these doctrines have been preached, we have given a weapon into the hands of our enemies. . . . The German State does not close synagogs, it does not forbid religious teachings. The State outlaws the Jew on the race theory. . . . Why then should we fall into this trap? Why should we declare ourselves a race or *kultur?* . . . Let us get into our minds definitely once for all that even before the destruction of the Temple, even before the destruction of our nation in Palestine, we became a religious community, and *that* we are or we are nothing."

Dr. Adler labors under that fond illusion which we discussed above—that if our enemies would only realize that we are a religious community and not a race or a nationality, they would automatically cease to hate us. But this highly adjustable *diplomatic* philosophy of Jewish history deceives no one. Instead of centering his attacks upon the whole false race-theory of the State which, in Germany, had its origin in the Hegelian thesis that the State must be a national unit based on race homogeneity, Dr. Adler counsels the Jews to abandon entirely the very concept of race as a factor in Jewish survival. This is in keeping with those sad and futile tactics of so many Jews in the last one hundred years who tried to whittle down the content of Jewish life in order to meet a temporary political emergency.

It is idle, of course, to talk of our people as no longer a nation but a religious community, in the face of the fact that millions of Jews are today recognized by the law of nations as national minorities in Poland, Lithuania, Czechoslovakia, millions more as a distinct nationality in Soviet Russia, where an autonomous Jewish region is actually being built, and hundreds of thousands in Palestine where a Jewish homeland is being created under the terms of a mandate of the League of Nations which recognizes not only the national existence of the Jewish people but its historic claim to a national home. It is not only idle today to repeat the "religious-community" shibboleth of the early Reformers but also quite fantastic.

It should be borne in mind, also, that nationalism is sometimes *forced* upon the Jew, even when he does not particularly crave it. In the struggle, for example, between the numerous nationalities in Eastern and Central Europe, each clamoring for self-determination, the Jews, living in their midst, have had to take sides or to declare themselves to be an independent nationality. It was a case of accepting the cultures of Ruthenians, Croatians, Slovaks and of other nationality groups which were far inferior to their own or of asserting their own. No Jewish group was as completely denationalized as were the Jewish communists of Russia. They were anti-religious, anti-Zionist, anti-Hebraist. They were Internationalists. Their sole allegiance was to the proletarian class. And yet, with the triumph of communism, these very Jewish communists have been forced by the logic of events not only to carry on as members of a distinct Jewish nationality in Soviet Russia but to undertake the building of a separate Jewish Republic in Siberia. One cannot, therefore, in the face of these political realities in Jewish life, maintain the theologic fiction that the Jews are only a religious community. . . .

Should we not rather regard it as providential that in these days when formal religion is losing its hold upon great numbers of our people and when this loss threatens to undermine our existence as a people, that the national and racial sentiment has been rekindled among many of them so that they wish to remain Jews and to link up their destiny with the destiny of Israel in some if not in all of the spheres of its creative life?

The Jewish people produced the Jewish religion, but people and religion are not synonymous terms. The Jewish religion—and I use the term in its customary sense, for I do not believe that a clever neology—the use of a word in a new and unsanctioned sense—is equivalent to a new theology—is a colossal and world-revolutionizing concourse of spiritual ideas unfolding itself in the life of a people of a particular character and temperament, but the Jewish religion does not exhaust the full content of the Jewish people. In relation to its religion, Israel is both immanent and transcendent as is every great artist in relation to the creation of his genius. . . .

The Jewish religion is the crowning achievement of our people and our supreme gift to civilization. It possessed such vast reservoirs of spiritual truth that it has been able to sustain and inspire generations upon generations of our people and to retain their sacrificial loyalty under all circumstances and upon all levels of culture. It thus became the strongest factor in the survival of our people, the קשר של קיימא , the enduring tie. It is doubtful whether the Jewish people can long survive in the diaspora without it— unless the other survival factors are reinforced to a degree which will compensate such a major loss. Jewish secular cultural autonomy may be possible in countries where the Jewish groups achieve minority rights. In such countries the Jewish group may survive even if divorced from religious loyalties. This is possible, though not probable. But in countries where minority rights are not possible, where there exists no active anti-Semitism which forces the Jew back upon himself, the task of Jewish survival will become increasingly difficult as religion uses its influence upon Jews and therewith also its power of national conservation. Those religious leaders, therefore, who are, today, teaching the religion of Israel to their people are not only leading them to fountains of living truth which can sweeten and refresh their individual lives, but are also conserving the most potent force which, throughout the ages, has sheltered and preserved the Jewish people.

But such religious leaders should not attempt to substitute a part for the whole—even if it is the major part. Havelock Ellis, in his introduction to J. K. Huysman's *A Rebours,* makes the interesting observation that the essential distinction between the classic and the decadent in art and literature is to be found in the fact that in the classic the parts are subordinated to the whole, whereas in the decadent, the whole is subordinated to the parts. . . .

Jewish life also possessed in its great epochs this classic balance, and the aim of religious leaders today should be to restore it. Many tributaries flow into the historic channel of Jewish life. In recent years some zealous and mostly uninformed partisans have attempted to reduce Jewish life to what is only a fraction of itself—to race or nationalism or folkways or theologic abstractions. Quite unconsciously they are all falsifying Jewish life. It is a mark of decadence in the diaspora that so many of our people have lost the sense of the classic harmony in Jewish life and are attempting to substitute a part for the whole.

It is the *total* program of Jewish life and destiny which the religious leaders of our people should stress today—the religious and moral values, the universal concepts, the mandate of mission, as well as the *Jewish people itself,* and all of its national aspirations. Thus the strength and security of our life will be retrieved, and, whether in Palestine or in the diaspora, we shall move forward unafraid upon the road of our destiny.

SOME UNUSUAL THEMES

God and the World Crisis

The problem of evil, always a nagging undercurrent in western religious thought, rises to the surface of sensitive minds in ages of crisis. The twentieth century has been such an age throughout the west, but the problem has loomed particularly large and ominous in the thinking of Jews because the Jewish experience of moral evil in our times includes the Holocaust. For many Jews, the witless and insane butchering of six million of their fellow-Jews in Central Europe was taken as evidence that divine Providence is an unfounded myth. If God were indeed the beneficent and providential Ruler of heaven and earth, He could not have permitted this slaughter of the innocent.

Joshua Loth Liebman, whose untimely death robbed American Reform Judaism of one of its most original and profound leaders, suggested in this essay on the problem of evil an alternative interpretation. His view of Providence, based upon the biblical and rabbinic literature, as well as upon theologians and philosophers, both Jewish and non-Jewish, emphasized man's co-responsibility with God in the creation of a moral and social world. Liebman stressed also the time factor implied in the Jewish messianic faith, anticipating in this discussion the more-recently fashionable 'theology of hope.' "Two things helped above all else to save Israel from despair and atheism: the futurity and the sociality of our thinking."

GOD AND THE WORLD CRISIS—CAN WE
STILL BELIEVE IN PROVIDENCE?
Joshua Loth Liebman
(1941)

From the day of our birth, we are all subjects of a universal monarch—Crisis. We anticipate love that is not always forthcoming. We need security that is often denied. Every frustration provides an occasion for that spiritual tension, which is Crisis. The decisive moments of our individual lives are written large also in the history of society. Wars, revolutions, mass persecutions, are the social equivalents of love rejected, hunger frustrated, security denied, in the soul of the individual personality.

Today, living in a parched and weary age, when Capitalism and Nationalism have been harnessed to the chariot of demonic forces, humanity experiences tensions and resistances which strain the fabric of life to the breaking point. The havoc and the ruin which the mechanized armies of tyranny bring to the earth, awaken the slumbering theologian in us all.

Men today find it difficult to believe in God and Providence because of the tragic evil in experience. The problem of Providence is inescapably bound up with the problem of evil. The greatest religious geniuses have wrestled with this issue, have sought to find

438

some coherent explanation for the evil in the world—in that world which we assume contains the revelation of the Divine Power greater than man. It is true that western culture has produced some writers with extremely facile solutions of this spiritual dilemma. We recall Leibnitz, with his unctuous phrase, "This is the best of all possible worlds"; Alexander Pope, with his consoling, "Whatever is, is right"; Hegel, with his rationalization that all evil is a part of the larger good. The truly profound spiritual personalities of the race from the time of the Psalmist and the prophet to our own day, have not been so complacent. One remembers the savage irony of a Voltaire using the Lisbon earthquake to deflate Leibnitz's "perfect" universe.

One can sympathize with the mood of a Pierre Bayle who could find no solace for his searching spirit in the saccharine sanctimoniousness of previous Christian theologians and who pricked with the rapier of his skeptical intelligence the sacred balloons of many thinkers who acted as though they were privileged palace politicians at the heavenly court. One can hear, echoing down the centuries, the poignant cry of a Pascal, restless seeker after God, who could not find Him except at the gaming table of cosmic chance. One recalls his immortal wager, his advice to men to bet on God as the safest of two tremendous alternatives—Heads, Heaven; Tails, Hell. All of these ghosts of genius and others also: Hume, Tolstoy, Dostoievsky, come before us to remind us that we are not the first nor shall we be the last in the long line of men striving to find some satisfying answer to the question of God's way with the world.

Before we can come to any conclusions of our own as to the meaning of Providence today, we should examine several of the classic efforts of the past to reconcile God and evil and to trace the relationship between the human and the Divine. We shall turn first to the one mind in the pagan world whose spiritual idiom is closest to our own universe of thought: to Plato. How did he explain the existence of evil in a world created by God? He gave an interpretation of the universe in which God is not the only factor. In the *Timaeus,* you remember, we are told why God created the world.

"He desired that all things should be good and nothing bad, *so far as this was attainable.*" Professor Demos in his brilliant work *The Philosophy of Plato* reminds us that God, however, is limited by the fact that existing eternally there is what he calls "The Receptacle"; that which might be called primal matter or chaos. God works upon this "Receptacle" in accordance with the Pattern, which also exists eternally. God, in other words, in Plato, is not Omnipotent. He is an artist working upon materials which He finds at hand. He labors to transform "The Receptacle," the original material chaos, into harmonious cosmic order.

Evil originates because there is refractory, intractable Matter which wages everlasting war against the imposition of order. Plato, it is true, is not altogether consistent in his explanation of evil. At times it frightens him and he bends every effort to treat it as a mere illusion of our finite minds. In other places, he interprets evil as negation, the mere absence of good, uncreated and uncaused. In one of his little known myths, in *The Politicus,* the philosopher explains the suffering and tragedy of earth as the result of God's temporary withdrawal from the active control of the universe. The pilot has left the bridge and the ship of existence flounders in uncharted seas.

Why Plato came to this picture of reality, we do not definitely know. Perhaps he too had to find justification and explanation for a world in which a beloved teacher, Socrates, could be put to death by the passionate superstitions of the Athenians; a world where the tyrant of Syracuse could callously spurn the advice of a philosopher-king while pursuing his dictatorial path of injustice. The age in which he lived and the frustrations he experienced no doubt helped to fashion Plato's view of Providence and of evil—his theory that God struggles against obstacles not of His own making and encounters resistances not of His own willing.

We may say parenthetically that while a basic trend in Judaism is to regard God as both the source of good and of evil, nevertheless this Platonic conception of God as the source only of the good and of the co-existence of an eternal matter which is the source of all evil in the world, is reflected in some of our greatest Jewish thinkers: in a Philo, a Gersonides, an Halevi.

Now the philosopher, seeking an all-inclusive system, makes God responsible only for the good and matter the matrix of evil. What, however, was the approach of the Rabbis to this question of God and theodicy? They began with the assumption of the reality of the Divine. God, for them, as for Plato, was their First Premise. The following unusual parable illustrates the Rabbis' conviction on this point. When Hadrian, the Roman Emperor, conquered the world, he said to his courtiers, "I desire that you should make of me a God since I have conquered the entire world." Rabbi Berachiah said Hadrian had three philosophers around him. The first said to him, "A man does not rebel against the King while he is still within the King's palace. He leads the revolution outside of the palace. Therefore, go thou, Hadrian, outside of the palace of the Lord and then thou shalt be made a god. The Heavens and the Earth He created. Remove thyself beyond the Heavens and the Earth and then thou shalt be made a god. . . ."

There is no more striking or unforgettable portrayal of man's inescapable reliance upon Divinity than in this conversation between Hadrian and the wise philosopher. Man's physical survival is conditioned by the forces of nature upon which he relies with every breath he takes. Man's moral Prometheanism is itself created, sustained and made possible by the greater moral nature of the world whose child he is.

Yet, believing in God and the inescapability of the Divine, the Rabbis too could not avoid wrestling with the problem of evil. They saw iniquitous peoples rise in power, men of bribery and corruption gleam with the diadem of dominion. There are many passages which might be cited to show how deeply theodicy concerned the Rabbis. In Berachot 7a, we read, "And Moses asked that the Holy One, blessed be He, make known His ways. He said: Sovereign of the universe, why is there a righteous man who prospers while another righteous person suffers? Some wicked person prospers while another wicked person suffers."

An even more audacious dialogue between Moses and God is the following: When Moses saw the tragic suffering of his people, he proclaimed, "I have read the book of Genesis through and found the doom in it pronounced upon the generation of the Deluge. It was a just judgment. I found also, the punishments decreed against the generation of Sodom: these also were just. *But what has this nation of Israel done unto Thee that it is oppressed more than any other nation in history? . . .*"

Rabbi Akiba said that Moses argued thus:

יודע אני שאתה עתיד להצילם אלה מה איכפת לך באותן הנתונים תחת הבנין

"I know that Thou wilt one day deliver them, but what about those that have been immured in the buildings?" (Exodus Rabbah, V 22).

Certainly this indicates that the Rabbis wrestled with the nature of God in as profound and daring a way as Plato ever did. Moses is depicted neither as dogmatist nor as pietist. He will not rest content until he understands why Israel suffers. Even though confident of the future salvation of Israel, he is not satisfied to accept that as a compensation for the suffering of his contemporaries.

Now what did the Rabbis finally do with the problem of evil? How did they preserve their faith in Providence? No student of Judaism can fail to sense the stress and strain, the heartache and the concern that this problem caused the Rabbis. At times it seems as though they were prepared to abandon evil in the *Olam Ha Tohu,* as if it lived an independent existence outside of the realm and dominion of God.

א״ר אלעזר לעולם אין הקב״ה מיחד שמו על הרעה אלא על הטובה

"The Holy One does not link His name with evil but only with good."

אין דבר רע יורד מן השמים "Nothing evil descends from above."

At times the Rabbis went to the other extreme and almost made God a participant in the consequences of evil. He becomes the partner of man or of Israel in suffering. "In all of their afflictions, He was afflicted" (Isaiah 63:9). "He was with Israel in Egypt; He went into exile with them to Babylonia and was delivered with them."

The problem remains, however, why there has to be any suffering at all in the world. The woes from which mankind suffers are the effects of human willfulness and blindness. Man lives in a moral universe and himself is the source of the evil as well as of the good. As the Rabbis say, "Piety and wickedness alone are left to the determination of man himself."

Man, in other words, is a vital factor in the cosmic process. In a certain sense, the fate of the universe proceeds from him. Man has the power of bringing God nearer to the world or of driving him farther from the world. The responsibility placed upon man in rabbinic thought is the source of his dignity and his worth. He is no marionette. He is a master. He is not only the clay; he is the potter.

Judaism in its classic mood never thinks of man as an utterly sinful and worthless creature and of God as Absentee Perfection. There is, rather, eternal interaction between humanity and Divinity, and God, so to speak, is almost as dependent for His unity and His sanctification upon man's will as man is dependent for his life and future upon the Divine undergirding.

Professor Schechter tells us that "to a certain Jewish mystic of the last century, Rabbi Moses Loeb of Sasow, the question was put by one of his disciples to the effect, 'Why did God in whom everything originates create the quality of skepticism?' The Master's answer was, 'That thou mayest not let the poor starve, putting them off with the joys of the next world, or simply tell them to trust in God who will help them, instead of supplying them with food.' " Here is rabbinic thought in its purest form. The Rabbi said in effect to his disciple, "We are not to make Providence a reed to lean on or an alibi to excuse our moral indolence. Rather are we to use the force and powers in the universe, which are perhaps God's Providence in action, in order to liberate and redeem mankind."

The rabbinic point of view on God and Providence, which was not expressed in any systematic manner, was crystallized in philosophic form in Maimonides. In his mood as worshiper, he may have closed his mind to gnawing doubts, but in his role as philosopher, Maimonides grappled with the deepest issues of God and of man, and did not hesitate to enunciate new, subtle and unfamiliar doctrines, even though retaining, of course, many traditional views. The great Jewish thinker, for example, in the original aspect of his discussion of Providence was not primarily interested in justifying the view that God looks down upon earth, directs and guides the fluctuating fortunes of man and beast and intervenes miraculously and capriciously in the affairs of nations. Maimonides concerned himself with an entirely different interpretation. Providence means no more than that there is a cosmic, rational influence permeating the world—what he calls *shepha*—with which man can identify himself by realizing his own intellectual possibilities. Each man possesses more or less of Providence in the degree to which he develops Reason.

The Providence of God is thus made conditional upon man's intellectual self-fulfillment. In Maimonides, Providence is not *given* but *taken;* it originates in man's actions or, it is perhaps more correct to say, is made available through man's actions. Providence in Jewish Philosophy is mainly man-conditioned or man-initiated and is not mere Divine grace—the Unconditioned breaking in upon the Conditioned, as Brunner and Barth today maintain.

Maimonides not only presented a highly rationalistic interpretation of Providence, but also gave some original explanations of the meaning of the Book of Job, which he insisted is a kind of Platonic Dialogue, a Symposium on Providence. The participants in this dialogue on suffering were Job and his friends. They expressed divergent views about God's relation to the world. One friend followed the Ashariya and asserted that everything is the result of God's Will, and that therefore there is no cause nor explanation of anything that happens. Another friend belonged to the school of the Mutazilites and attributed everything to God's Wisdom.

Job at first believed that there was no Providence at work in the world, that man was abandoned to chance and chaos. Then after his cosmic vision, Job came to a new comprehension of God, His majesty and His glory. The Book of Job, I believe Maimonides felt, is not a study primarily in the causes of human suffering, but rather a study in the effects of suffering on the human soul. At no place does Job declare that he understands why he suffers or that he comprehends the providential cause of his misery. There is no causal answer. There is, however, the achievement of a new level of understanding as a result of the suffering. Job is presented, then, as the prototype of the "twice-born man" who arrives ultimately at the true measuring-rod of life, namely, the knowledge of God.

The Book of Job then is a work not primarily of theodicy, but of teleology, not of the explanation of human suffering, but of the ways in which that suffering can be transmuted into creative nobility and spiritual sensitivity.

With these conclusions of Plato, the Rabbis, and Maimonides in mind, what can we moderns say about the eternal problem of God and His relation to the world? This, of course, is a metaphysical issue and there are some contemporary thinkers who on principle will have nothing to do with metaphysics. The followers of Dewey on the one hand and of Carnap on the other, are avowedly disinterested in ultimates. Pragmatists and logical positivists both believe that we should concern ourselves primarily with facts. Religion, like poetry, belongs, so they imply, to the realm of fantasy, not truth.

Now the contemporary deflation of metaphysics may have profound justification. Yet the human mind for a long time to come will not only be interested in the 'What' and the 'How' of things, but also in the 'Why' of things. We are inveterate adventurers in the realm of ideas and most of us are not satisfied until we can find some deeper connection between our thoughts and our visions and the larger universe which is their matrix and their context. It is just in such an age of crisis as this that men need cosmic reassurance in order to increase the tenacity of their devotion to human purpose. And where shall we find that reassurance? Many of us to whom religion is neither fantasy nor illusion have nevertheless been profoundly influenced by the pragmatic, scientific traditions of our century. We just do not possess the oriental mystic's technique of absorption in God. By practice or by temperament we are empiricists, unable to achieve the sublime certitude of the mystic; we are always subject to tentativeness and quest.

We see no All, but only flashing intimations of a Power greater than man, shaping an unfinished masterpiece. Beginning as empirical theologians we admit initially that we cannot prove God in any absolute way. His reality, the reality of the Divine in the world, is a matter of probability, not of certainty. Modern science, however, should have taught us to understand that in all areas of experience we can hope to achieve only probability, not proof. This does not mean that we are condemned to the cosmic agnosticism of the dogmatic humanist. Rather is it my conviction that, even on the empirical basis, it is possible to find striking evidence for the divine in the world, to discover a rational explanation for the evil in human experience and, when properly interpreted, to retain deep faith in Providence and Divine Immanence.

In the first place there are many factors in human experience which would at least suggest, though they would never prove, the reality of a world Designer. The world of nature is a persuasive argument for a purposive universe. The starry heavens, the irridescent gems, the patterned snow-flakes, and the infinite blanket of flowers, warming the brown, naked body of the earth, a blanket richly brushed with the colors from Nature's palette—all this saturation of the earth with beauty seems, in spite of the exceptions, to point a finger to some Divine artist.

The scientists today agree that nature exhibits organic pattern. The physicist speaks of "fields of force," the biologist of "organismic wholes," the psychologist of *"gestalt* configurations." Everywhere there appears to be striking testimony to design, inter-relationship; organization. If all this is blind chance and sheer accident, then we have, indeed, coincidences more miraculous than Creation.

Man, too, at his best, is one of the clues, the footprints of the Divine. It is rather incredible to imagine a moral being arising out of an utterly amoral world. If we say that truth, beauty, and goodness are cosmic orphans, without a universal Source, then indeed are we lost in magic and in mystery. He who maintains that moral values are irrelevant to the universe, is the true follower of the doctrine *Creatio ex nihilo*.

This is the most naive and magical of all ideas, perhaps—to assert that moral values are real in a totally accidental world, that they have miraculously sprung up like trees in a waterless, seedless, sunless wasteland and at the same time to maintain that there can be no God at work in the world. The ethical atheists do not realize their own inconsistencies. They find it impossible to believe in God creating the world out of nothing, but, strangely enough, find it easy to believe that values emerge out of nothing.

God, in fact, is indicated both by order in the physical universe and by morality in the human world. The resolute atheist will, however, be unconvinced by this empirical approach to the universe. He may admit the existence of a certain amount of order, design and purpose in the universe, but he might well say to the religionist, "You ignore the bloody and brutal disharmonies of the world. Before me, however, stretches the landscape of bombed cities and blighted fields. In a world of earthquake and flood, strife and war, disease and death, can you still speak of a Providential Divinity?"

This problem of evil is for us, as it was for our ancestors, the crux of the matter. We have to arrive at some understanding of its presence in the world before we can come to any conclusions about Providence. Parenthetically it may be said that there is not only the difficult question of how God and evil can co-exist, but the equally difficult question, 'How can God and good not co-exist?' For good is as much a problem as is evil.

At the very outset, we should clearly state that if God's reality is to be called into question by evil, then it is logically irrelevant whether the quantity of that evil is great or small, for any drop of evil in the sea of Being constitutes a mystery.

If man could ever believe in God, he may still believe in Him,

for if God is disproved today because of the amount of evil in the
world, then by the same token He should never have been believed
in in previous ages, when the evil, though perhaps less in quantity,
differed not in the slightest in quality from that which we now
confront.

If we wish, however, to achieve a coherent rational explanation
of reality, we have to find a place for physical evils and for moral
evils in the economy of the world. All of our experience seems to
point to the nature of this world as an ordered cosmos, in which
rational and moral life is possible. In order for the earth to be
what Tennant calls in his *Philosophical Theology* "a theatre of
moral possibility," there must be "a physical order characterized by
'law or regularity.' "

"To illustrate what is here meant: if water is to have the various
properties in virtue of which it plays its beneficial part in the
economy of the physical world and the life of mankind, it cannot
at the same time lack its obnoxious capacity to drown us. The
specific gravity of water is as much a necessary outcome of its
ultimate constitution as its freezing-point, or its thirst-quenching
and cleansing functions."

This view places emphasis on the autonomous nature of our
world. It does not regard God as the immediate cause of every
event in natural or inhuman life. Physical suffering and evil are
the accompaniments of a calculable cosmos. There can be no
realization of goodliness unless there be first of all a world with
autonomy, uniformity and predictability.

There are, however, not only physical evils in the world but
moral evils. These have their source in man's free choice. Appalled
at the colossal iniquity for which some men are responsible, there
are moments when sensitive spirits in despair dream of a world in
which the human race would be ethically sterilized, made impotent
as far as decisive action is concerned. "Why," we ask "did not
God fashion man incapable of doing wrong?" Speaking symbolically, we may say that God was logically faced with two alternatives.
He could make man either all-good—therefore a replica of Him-

self and therefore superfluous—or He could make man not God but man and therefore partly good and partly evil. Man is not a duplicate of God. If he were he would be redundant. We may take from Plato the idea of limitation, but instead of considering this limitation, namely, the possibility of evil in the world, as a defeat, we would rather ascribe it to the generosity of God. He tolerates the possibility of evil in order to give man the opportunity of building a moral world.

Morality, then, cannot be created by God. It is never a Divine gift. It is a human achievement. It is not the child of grace but of effort. Now as a matter of fact, even though moral evil originates in the very fact of human freedom, we would not cast our ballot for an ethically neutral world, a world without tasks, without challenge. We would not desire a petrified moral forest of a world. We could not enjoy the sun, love friends, write books, fashion governments, pursue justice—were we but emotionless puppets.

We resent coercion and force. We wish to be responsible agents, compelled neither by man nor by God, but persuaded to action by our own insight and counsel. We have to pay the price of pain and sorrow if we wish to achieve worth and dignity. No personality is possible in a tyranny, whether it be man-built or God-ruled. Man is a thing, an It, in a dictatorship, whether human or divine. The deepest yearning of man, however, is always to be a subject, not an object; a person, not a thing.

The evil that there is in the world is a by-product, therefore, of a determinate universe in which physical laws have to be obeyed and moral personalities have to be given room to breathe and grow.

Today we tend to lose sight of the truth that evil is unstable and that "that instability," as Whitehead declared, "is the moral order of the world." We tend to forget the residual gains made by humanity in its long struggle upwards, to forget also that evil has within it the seeds of its own destruction. Tyranny, for example, being the very denial of man's essential nature, namely, his freedom to choose, can only be a temporary and never a permanent pattern of human society. Tyranny appeals to the death-wish in man, the de-

sire for non-being, for anonymity, for absorption in the All. Dictatorship may well be thought of as a secular version of the mystic's
surrender and submission to a Will greater than his own. Occidental
man, however, cannot permanently deny himself and his individual-
ist, freedom-seeking, life-affirming desires. Tyranny therefore becomes an ever more unstable and impossible form of social
organization. Democracy, in this sense, has the future on its side in
that it appeals to the life-wish of man rather than to the death-wish.

When we speak of the instability of evil, we mean that transitory
wickedness cannot negate the beauty, order and morality which
have already been manifest in the human adventure and which
have issued in their highest reaches in the ethical genius of a Moses,
the saintliness of an Akiba, the beauty of a Beethoven and the
humanitarianism of a Lincoln. These, we maintain, are cosmic
products and cosmic mirrors, and no man should be so arrogant
as to believe that his wickedness is powerful enough ultimately to
defeat the universe in its slow march toward the Messianic
Kingdom.

Speaking of the Messianic Kingdom, it occurs to us that it has
been too little recognized that Messianism is a basic solution of
theodicy in Judaism. Time is God's most precious substance. It
is the very stuff of hope. Messianism is postponed Providence. It
meant that our sages were too honest and too realistic ever to believe that happiness and righteousness were achieveable early in the
story of the human race. They felt intuitively that this is an unfinished world, a very young world, and that the future will redeem
the present. If the Jew had ever said, "I demand vindication and
explanation in my own lifetime and in terms of my own egocentric
values," he would have been lost.

Two things helped above all else to save Israel from despair and
atheism: the futurity and the sociality of our thinking. Time and
the social process give us the possibility of an answer to theodicy.
Today always may be redeemed by tomorrow and the individual
always may be explained, justified, protected, or caught up in the
group and the group has continuity and eternity. God uses infinite

time in order to work out His purpose for man. No temporal limits are to be placed upon the divine-human struggle in the world.

Can we still believe in Providence? Much depends upon how we interpret that term. If to believe in Providence would require us to maintain the view that "no man hurts his finger below but that they immediately announce it on high," then there are many of us who do not believe in that kind of Providence. To assert that the Jews dying in concentration camps, the liberals standing before the firing squad, the adolescent soldiers perishing upon the blood-stained battlefield; to assert that every tragic loss of each individual is directly willed by the personal Providence of God, may well be a glowing testimony to a faith which not even the mountains of sorrow can shake. Those who are able to achieve such unshaken confidence are among the blessed of the earth. Yet there is room in the religion of Israel for those who have a different interpretation of Providence.

Our interpretation today must be close to the Maimonidean view—the belief that we are not alone, that our powers for goodness and for intelligence are cosmically grounded and rooted, that we are dependent upon Divinity for the achievement of a noble, worthy, human society, but that we in our time cannot be absolved of the primary responsibility of utilizing and cooperating with the Divine force in the universe.

God, so Judaism has taught, manifests Himself in human history. Divinity is immanent in our world, primarily in the conscience of man. Now if the pessimists are correct and man is essentially cruel and evil, then it would appear as though God's immanence would be denied and His Providence negated. And there are influential thinkers today who maintain that man himself is the best argument for atheism and humanity the strongest disproof of Providential Divinity.

Now Judaism has been able to avoid ultimate skepticism and the denial of God because Judaism has always been truly realistic in its estimate of human nature. It has never glossed over the evils that man can commit. On the other hand, it has maintained an unshakable faith that the good of human nature outweighs the evil and that if humanity could only learn wisdom, be freed of its self-imposed shackles, social and intellectual, then surely a creative joyous society of men would not be impossible.

Modern psychology substantiates and corroborates the Jewish religious view of man. The discoveries of Freud and his co-workers have long been subject to popular misunderstanding. The time has come when we should grasp the true implications of these revolutionary insights into human nature.

The neurotic struggles of our day, leading to war, injustice and social oppression, are not inevitable. In fact, man is born into the world seeking love and capable of giving love. Fundamentally we are cooperative rather than competitive personalities. A distinguished psychologist recently has said that it is the inherent goodness of human nature which continually amazes him, that man begins with an infinite capacity for decency, fellowship and response to high and creative goals. Education and society carrying with them the vestiges of an undiscarded past, fanning into abnormal flame the normal desires for power, prestige or possession, conspire to maim and distort this creative human nature with which we all begin our adventure on earth.

We are just at the beginning of an age when we shall learn how to penetrate into the recesses of the human spirit, clean out the Augean stables; if the new discoveries of psychology will be properly utilized, then mankind will be able to avoid many of the catastrophes from which we now suffer and a new world of social and individual happiness and righteousness may indeed be born.

Pessimism is therefore not justified by modern psychology. Freud, even in his *The Future of an Illusion,* does not imply a hopeless outlook for man. Quite the contrary. Psychiatry has taken some of the most tangled personalities, apparently hopelessly enmeshed in criminality, brutishness and evil and has succeeded in unravelling the knotted skein of personality and bringing integration, adjustment and light into the soul's dark and shadowy room. This is just a symbol of what might yet be accomplished with humanity as a whole.

And there are deep spiritual implications in this strange, good news from the psychologists' laboratory—that man in substance is good and that the evils in society are remedial, contingent, and glimpsed in the long range view of history—transitory. I say that there are deep spiritual implications for this reason:

In recent years theists have tended to rely upon the conclusions of physical science for their God-centered interpretation of the world. Eddington and Jeans have found evidences for the Divine Mathematician in the discoveries of modern physics and astronomy. Yet, physical science has not yielded a morally inspiring view of God and there has been a basic disagreement among physicists themselves as to whether the quantum theory or the theory of indeterminacy or Relativity in any way justifies the religious hypothesis. And what kind of God is it that could be suggested by the physicists' laboratory? A God of power—whereas we seek primarily a God of goodness.

In fact Judaism, from its inception, sought God not primarily in the order of nature, namely as Power, but in the order of human nature, namely as Goodness. This is the meaning of the prophetic doctrine that God is manifest in the moral law, in the conscience of the human personality. Man would never know of God if He did not first speak to him in the still, small voice. Divinity would have remained forever a mystery to the human race if it were not already implicit within our strivings for peace, nobility, compassion, holiness.

It is understandable of course that we should be impatient with the episodic character of God's working on the human scene. Life seems to be so much a matter of fitful flashes. Yet beneath the seeming discontinuity of things, there is the slowly maturing process which manifests itself from time to time in some dramatic revelation, some intellectual, moral or spiritual climax.

The present era with its new discoveries of the topology of the human mind and the beginning of the cultivation of the continent of the subconscious which has been throughout all these centuries an undiscovered jungle contains, even though hidden from our immediate gaze, the seeds of a happier, more harmonious, better controlled and therefore more Divine human society. It is in the slow, imperceptible evolution of human genius that God's Providence is immanent in our world.

In the very fact that modern depth psychology, on the basis of its objective scientific experiments, can proclaim human nature to be essentially good, we have scientific witness to the truth of our religious intuition. Freud and his disciples may have come like Balaam to curse, but their works remain to bless, for psychological science even more than physical science can tend to negate our contemporary atheism and can help us to proclaim that man may indeed be proved to be the child of the Divine, the Creator of goodness.

It is to be regretted that the wholesomeness and the positiveness of Judaism, its belief in the goodness of man, its Messianic dream of a better world, its insistence on the tentativeness of evil, are not sufficiently emphasized even by many teachers of Judaism.

For at this particular time in history, we Jews are especially challenged. We have become so naturally obsessed with the problem of physical survival that we have not yet sufficiently appreciated the menace to our spiritual philosophy of life. I do not refer primarily to the menace of the pagan totalitarian forces. The challenge is much subtler and is not even consciously directed to us. Yet it is here. It is here in the form of that new, dark theology which, if victorious, would nullify the Jewish view of man and of God quite as much as the forces of dictatorship intend, if victorious, to destroy the people of Israel.

The time has come when we rabbis must have the courage to enunciate the truth that Judaism as a religion has something of value to say to a bewildered world. . . . Judaism has an important message to give at this critical juncture of history. I know full well that the idea of mission has become suspect, as though it were proof of a leprous chauvinism. Yet Judaism does have a vital function to perform in aiding mankind to retain sanity and perspective. . . .

Judaism does have a unique view of God and of man. There is a Jewish cosmology and a Jewish anthropology. The time has come when we should emphasize our view of God as a Power greater than man, who needs man, however, as his co-worker. God too, obeys laws and uses Time in which to achieve His Messianic purposes.

We believe, in other words, in a God of process and we are confident that Divinity is manifest not only in the magnificence of nature but also in the sublime, intangible qualities of human nature. Judaism teaches fundamentally that man is not the victim of original sin. He is often the beneficiary of Original Virtue. He receives much from the great and good men who have been the moral pioneers of civilization. And although there is the evil *Yezer* in everyman's makeup, Judaism teaches no fatalism and no pessimism but is ever confident that the human being can become victorious over lust and passion and can become the master over all temptation.

There is an essential optimism about our Jewish anthropology; an optimism achieved, let it be noted, in the midst of continual world crises, when human nature certainly did not seem to merit high compliments. The world that has produced us has also given us the capacity to learn more and more about the stars and about our souls. This is Providence in history—this very ability of man to learn new secrets about himself, his temperament, his desires and emotions that, left undirected, create crises. We Jews believe that mankind will learn more and more how to control, guide and channel the impulses of the human spirit.

Judaism can inspire men, walking through this dark and scowling valley, to believe that there is a source of goodness in the world; that the evils we experience are real and must be resisted; that they emerge both from the fact that this is a law-abiding universe and that man is a creature of freedom. We human beings are children of an evolving universe and there are creative forces both within us and outside of us which we can use to build a better world.

True, we are not privileged to penetrate the ultimate secrets of eternity. Our minds are fragmentary beams of light like the flashes of glow-worms in a summer's night. The fleeting illumination they

provide, enables us to see in the midst of the darkness many wonderful summits of social achievement still attainable by the restless
feet of this youthful race of men. Divinity is here; both on the earth
that provides the possibility of life, order, intelligence, and also
in the insatiable moral hunger of man; man never quite ready to
accept tyranny as natural, defeat as inevitable, society as irre-
mediable. . . .

The Limits of Rationalism

The intellectual formulation and development of Reform Judaism began and has been carried on in the climate of modern rationalism. Modern rationalism must be distinguished from its medieval antecedents by its insistence that in the world of fact, our failure to discover uniformity results from our ignorance, not from the presence of exceptions to uniformity. Apparent exceptions become, when such a principle is operative, stimuli to further inquiry, not terminal points. The Reform Jew, a rationalist bred under the influence of this principle, cannot accept the reported miracles of the Bible as accounts of empirical fact, for they are reported as exceptions to uniformity. If he accepts the factual character of the biblical stories, he must reject their miraculousness. Thus he can no longer reconcile faith and reason after the manner of Maimonides and the medievals. Dr. Emil L. Fackenheim regards the full and ready embracing of this principle of Reform Jewish thought as highly creditable.

Yet he is deeply disturbed by what the over-ardent application of this principle, in the interest of consistency, does to the concept of God in the Reform movement. For, he argues, the idea of a transcendent God who is nevertheless concerned about the here and now, is essential to a living Judaism. Fackenheim suggests a resolution of the difficulty by referring to a "second" type of Reform, based upon insights of the Hassidic movement, especially as interpreted by Martin Buber. These insights involve a recognition of the "stubborn" particularity of the individual human person, whose meaning can be found only with "the God of Israel," not with "the God of the Greeks." If modern rationalism leads to any God, it is to God as Cosmic Process, the God of Greek philosophic speculation. Only by the introduction of a critical dimension to our rationalism (a dimension that Fackenheim traces to Kant among modern philosophers) is it possible to reinstate the God of Israel, a God who is actively engaged in an intersubjective, "I-Thou" relationship with human persons.

TWO TYPES OF REFORM:
REFLECTIONS OCCASIONED BY HASIDISM
Emil L. Fackenheim
(1961)

I

In 1870 Heinrich Graetz denounced the Hasidic movement as the radical antithesis of the reform required by Judaism in the modern age.[1] In 1907 Martin Buber described Hasidism as itself a reform movement, indeed, as the greatest in all of Diaspora history; and he was bold enough to assert that to find new life in our time Judaism had to assimilate Hasidic elements.[2]

These conflicting judgments illustrate the problem of this paper. Two reforms, we shall argue, are required by modern Judaism; the one if it is to be modern, the other if it is to remain Judaism. But how to reconcile them is our problem, dramatically illustrated by Graetz' and Buber's conflicting views on Hasidism.

In the light of present-day scholarship, no one could still take seriously Graetz' actual judgment on Hasidism, made almost a hundred years ago. On that subject, the great historian was prey to the prejudices of his age, to which all myth, symbol and mysticism were mere superstition.[3] But it would be a romantic blunder simply to dismiss, along with Graetz' judgments, the standards in the light

[1] *Geschichte der Juden*, vol. xi, Leipzig, 1870, pp. 102 ff.
[2] *Die Chassidischen Buecher*, Berlin, 1927, p. 130.
[3] On this subject, cf. e.g. S. Minkin, *The Romance of Hasidism*, New York 1955, pp. 281 ff., and S. Dresner, *The Zaddik*, New York, 1960, pp. 15 ff.

of which they were made. If Graetz repudiated miracles and magic; if he took a low view of the authoritarianism of the Zaddik; if he suspected ecstatic experiences of being at worst a fraud and at best mere self-deception—all this was at least in part because he saw the need to reform Judaism in the light of modern scientific rationalism. And this reform, called for and carried out by men such as Graetz, has remained permanent and irrevocable.

And yet, with the passage of time it has become increasingly clear that the rationalist kind of criticism would fail to dispose of Hasidism even if it were suitably brought up to date. This is less because of developments in Hasidic scholarship than because of a shift in liberal Jewish life and outlook. At one time, the great question may have been how to make Judaism modern. Today, the great question is how to save it as Judaism. The rationalistic kind of reform, it is now very plain, is largely negative in character; and an additional positive reform is needed if Judaism is not to be dissipated into generalities and irrelevancies. But those who seek such a reform have learned to look on Hasidism, not as a quaint and superseded phenomenon, but rather as a source of inspiration and hope.

II

We begin with the first of the two reforms, and with the modern, scientific rationalism by which it is inspired. For our present purpose, this rationalism is sufficiently distinguished from its pre-modern, mediaeval predecessor in terms of its methodological principle of inquiry. Rational inquiry, in the modern view, is the search of uniformities; and it seeks these throughout the whole world of empirical fact. To come upon the non-uniform, in this view, is not to discover an exception to uniformity but merely one's ignorance; it is, therefore, not an occasion for ceasing to inquire, but rather a spur to further inquiry.

This seemingly simple and innocuous methodological principle has proved to be a source of extraordinary power. If modern science has advanced with unprecedented swiftness; if it has tossed aside ancient authorities and scientific systems, however reasonable on the surface; if it has achieved an unheard-of measure of control over nature—all this has been far less because of specific scientific discoveries than because of the principle referred to, by which all modern science is inspired. This principle is the true source of the revolution in modern scientific thought.

But this principle caused a revolution in the sphere of religious thought as well. If modern thought had merely advanced new world-views instead of the old it would have called for only minor revisions in religious thought. Because the new world-views sprang from a new principle of inquiry the required change was revolutionary. For whereas pre-modern religious thinkers could confine themselves to the task of reconciling the facts of science with other facts, accepted on Scriptural authority, their modern successors were faced with a rationalism rejecting this authority, by claiming for itself the whole sphere of empirical fact.

Thus Maimonides, for example, was a rationalist in search of uniformities. But his rationalism being pre-modern in kind, he was prepared to accept exceptions to uniformity, even in the domain of empirical fact; and for that reason he could accept the Torah as an authoritative source of empirical facts.[4] Modern rationalists, in contrast, were bound to regard such acceptance as an arbitrary limitation of rational inquiry. Whatever their views on revelation and authority, they could not, at any rate, accept empirical facts on revealed authority. For their methodological principle allowed no exceptions to uniformity but merely the appearance of such exceptions, due to ignorance. But ignorance is not an occasion for

---

[4] For the Maimonides interpretation given in this paper, cf. מורה נבוכים II, 35 and 39, and הלכות יסודי התורה, VII, 6, VIII, IX. Cf. also my article "The Possibility of the Universe in Al-Farabi, Ibn Sina and Maimonides" (*Proceedings of the American Academy for Jewish Research*, XVI, 1947, pp. 39–70), which seeks to show that for the Rambam, creation is the *ratio essendi* of revealed authority, and revealed authority, the *ratio cognoscendi* of creation. The crucial difference between the "created" world of Maimonides and the "emanated" world of the Islamic Aristotelians is that the laws of the former may be interrupted by a free act of God.

submitting to authority. It is, as we have said, a spur to further inquiry.[5]

III

It is to their credit that liberal Jewish spokesmen should have been quick to embrace the spirit of modern scientific rationalism; and that, in contrast with many other religious spokesmen, they should have embraced it, not as a matter of mere pious proclamation, but in full readiness to accept the consequences. True, there are in our midst, even today, apologists on the right, who busy themselves reconciling archaeology with the Biblical story of the flood; and apologists on the left extolling the Bible for anticipating Einstein and Freud. But on the whole it is clearly seen that the time for reconciliations in the mediaeval style is long past; and that this is because, whatever our views on religious authority, we can no longer regard the Torah as an authoritative source of empirical facts.

Thus a modern Jew might believe in the splitting of the Red Sea, like his pre-modern ancestor. But unlike that ancestor he would believe it as an hypothetical result of historical reconstruction, not on the categorical authority of the Torah. Or he might share Jehuda Halevi's conviction that Israel once stood at Mount Sinai, hearing not only thunder but also the voice of God. But whereas Halevi's conviction could rest on the authority of 600,000 witnesses, and on an unbroken tradition reporting their testimony,[6] its modern counterpart had to spring from an inquiry recognizing no factual authorities. Most important of all, the reconstructed

---

[5] For the effect of the modern view on historiography — a branch of knowledge of special concern for the religious thinker in the Jewish tradition — cf. R. G. Collingwood, *The Idea of History,* Oxford, 1946. Collingwood brilliantly expounds the difference between the pre-modern historian, who is prepared to accept documents as authoritative statements of what happened, and the modern historian, who regards all documents as mere sources aiding in the reconstruction of what happened. One of the earliest statements of the modern view is contained in David Hume's famous essay on miracles (*An Enquiry Concerning Human Understanding,* section X).

[6] ספר הכוזרי I, 84 ff.

events of modern rational inquiry were instances of uniformity, not exceptions to it.

Thus however modern inquiry might explain the splitting of the Red Sea, it would not seek refuge in suspensions of natural law. And whatever the terms in which it might interpret the hearing of the voice of God on Mt. Sinai, they would not include an actual voice of God. In short, modern scientific rationalism demanded that all empirical aspects of the Jewish past should become the legitimate object of modern rational inquiry—of an unlimited quest for uniformity. And the moment this demand was accepted modern Jewish scholarship was born.

This was also the birth-moment of the intellectual reform of Judaism presently under discussion. It used to be said that modern liberal differs from pre-modern orthodox Judaism in being open to change. But it has long been recognized that this is no adequate mark of distinction, since orthodoxy—except in its most ossified forms—is itself open to change. The new factor is not openness to change but rather an altered basis for openness. And at least one cause of this alteration was the modern principle of rational inquiry.

A pre-modern rationalist such as Maimonides was forced to alter Jewish belief, as well as seek new טעמי המצות, so as to make them rationally acceptable. At the same time he could draw sharp limits to alterations of belief; and while allowing changes in the meaning of the הלכה he could rule out all changes of consequence in the הלכה itself. For his rationalism allowed acceptance of the Torah as containing authoritative disclosures of empirical fact. Maimonides, in short, could be a rationalist and yet an orthodox Jew.

But no modern rationalist could remain an orthodox Jew. For unlike its pre-modern counterparts, modern rationalism claimed all empirical fact as its legitimate domain. And acceptance of this claim, and of its religious implications, is one thing all liberal Jews have in common. They may disagree among themselves as to the degree and direction of change necessary or desirable. They may disagree on the positive basis of such change, battling over revelation and authority. The one point agreed on is a negative principle.

This is that no empirical facts, however sacred, may be exempted from the modern search for rational uniformity; that therefore, whatever the place of revelation and authority in liberal Judaism, revelation cannot be verbal revelation; and authority cannot include the authoritative disclosure of empirical facts.[7]

IV

But ever since Mendelssohn, there has been no lack of liberal spokesmen demanding, in the name of scientific rationalism, a far more radical reform of Judaism than that thus far described. The one reform is mainly negative in character; the other would make modern rationalism the positive basis of a transformed Judaism. The one is a matter of common agreement; the other could not be more controversial. For whereas some regard this latter, radical reform of Judaism as necessary if Judaism is to be modern, others regard it as impossible if Judaism is to remain Judaism; and they deny that it is rationally necessary. The proposed reform would transform the God of Israel into a timeless universal principle—a First Cause transcending the universe, or a Process identical with it.

Earlier reformers of this radical kind believed in a Deistic First Cause beyond the universe. Their contemporary successors prefer a Process immanent in the universe and animating it as a whole. What unites both groups is common opposition to the God of Israel who, while transcending Nature and History, was yet capable of entering into both. Both groups dismiss such a God, as incompatible with modern rationalism. A God beyond the universe is in no conflict with the search for rational uniformity; nor is this true of a

---

[7] It must be emphasized at this point that to rule out *verbal* revelation and *factual* authority is by no means to rule out revelation and authority as a whole. And the view that even to pre-modern believers revelation was nothing *more* than supernaturally handed-down information of empirical facts is a mere modern legend. On the writer's views on revelation and authority, cf, his "Can there be Judaism without Revelation?" (*Commentary*, December 1951); "An Outline of a Modern Jewish Theology" (*Judaism*, Summer 1954); and "The Dilemma of Liberal Judaism" (*Commentary*, October 1960). Cf. also J. J. Petuchowski's thorough and thoughtful "The Concept of Revelation in Reform Judaism" (CCAR *Yearbook*, vol. LXIX,1960), as well as J. H. Gumbiner, "Revelation and Liberal Jewish Faith" (*Judaism*, Spring, 1961).

God somehow identical with the universe as a whole. If the radical rationalist reformers are right, however, such a conflict does exist in the case of a God who, while beyond the universe, yet enters into it. For does not every such entry shatter the system of uniformities? If these reformers are right, then the enlightened modern Jew may believe in a First Cause beyond the universe, or in a Divine Process immanent in it. But he must let go of the God of Israel, as a mere myth of bygone ages. Such, in brief, is the reform which radical rationalists have called for, ever since Mendelssohn.[8] And if accepted, it would be of profound consequence.

The God of Jewish tradition could be present, in the here and now. He could single out persons and peoples, and be sought out by them according to the need of time and place. A transcendent First Cause or immanent Cosmic Process, in contrast, is a timeless principle; and it can inspire to action, not by acts of singling out, but only as an eternal ideal. For a First Cause is indifferent to the particular; and while a Process contains all particulars, it embraces them as a homogenizing Whole. Moreover, neither God can be sought out by men in the here and now. He is accessible, if at all, only by thought rising to timelessness. In short, if the radical rationalist reformers are right, then the here and now, once of the essence of Jewish religious belief and life, reduces itself to a mere unessential accident.

V

The proponents of the radical reform under discussion are prepared to accept this implication. They may even regard it as a purification of a formerly impure Jewish essence. Yet one must say with all bluntness at one's command that this is no purification but rather a distortion. No doubt there is need for eternal verities in Judaism. But the reduction of the God of Israel to such a verity, if it

---

[8] However, Mendelssohn (who, after all, remained an orthodox Jew) retained misgivings about a radical rationalist reform of Judaism — misgivings which, as we say below, are characteristic of most modern Jews retaining a positive Jewish identification. As is well known, while reducing Jewish *belief* to universal verities, Mendelssohn left room for revealed *law*. This left the theoretical basis of revealed law — of necessity itself belief — in a state of obscurity.

were ever carried out through the length and breadth of Jewish life, would be the end of Judaism.

The very first commandment ever addressed to the first Jew—that Abraham leave his country—is an act of singling out, not an application of a universal ideal, unless a universal peoples' migration were the will of God. The very exodus which constitutes Israel is not an acceptance of timeless verities, but a response to a unique historic challenge. Whatever the facts of early Jewish history, they lived on in Jewish memory as disclosing a God of the here and now.

Moreover, He remained such a God in Jewish experience. The God of Jewish prayer is universal Creator, but He can also be present to each worshipper. His הלכה is law valid in all situations. But it is also commandment, which discloses the Giver along with the commandment; and the Giver wants *this* man to act, not someone else, and now, not at some other time.

Nor is the God of Israel present only to Israel. For in contrast with the God of the Greeks, He is a God of history, and a God caring for personality. But this is the nature of history, that each of its moments differs from every other; and this is the characteristic of persons, that every one of them is unique. Throughout their history, Jews have stubbornly clung to this God, against all doubts and all critics. Even mediaeval rationalists, enamoured though they were with Greek thought, did not forsake Him.[9] If indeed modern rationalism requires, after all, the transformation of this God into a timeless principle, then the change required is no minor loss, let alone a purifying gain. It is nothing less than unconditional surrender to the Greeks. It is little wonder that liberal spokesmen always had their misgivings about this kind of reform. The outstanding fact—indeed, one of the most astounding facts of

[9] Thus while the Aristotelian God can know only Himself, and the God of the Islamic Aristotelians only the species of things in the world, Maimonides, ardent Aristotelian though he is, insists that God can know at least *human* individuals — thus defending a Jewish view of providence (מורה נבוכים III 20). We may refer, in this connection, to a point astutely made by Steven Schwarzchild. This is that, despite the Rambam's debt to the contemplative ideals of the *Nicomachean Ethics*, the last major statement in the *Guide* exalts the speculative knowledge of God, not for its own sake, but for the sake of a life of mercy and justice (*Judaism*, Winter 1961, p. 73).

modern Jewish history—is that their misgivings were so rarely flaming protests. And nothing could testify more eloquently to the power of modern rationalism over the Jewish mind.

VI

Still, liberal spokesmen always *did* have misgivings. Thus they were never quite prepared to reduce historical revelation to a set of timeless verities, or הלכה to a set of universal values. Nor, though inclined to view history as a universal upward movement, did they ever wholly abandon the particular—Israel and the individual human person. And while in philosophizing moments they may have thought of God as universal First Cause or Cosmic Process they were apt, in moments of worship, to pray to the God of Israel. In short, throughout its history liberal Judaism has never wholly forsaken the ancient Jewish belief in the ultimate significance of the here and now in the sight of God.

Moreover, as the nineteenth passed into the twentieth century, and as the latter unfolded its grim and unpredicted aspects, this belief assumed new and unprecedented importance, not only for the modern Jew but for all modern men. Once, perhaps, it could seem that the Jew's Jewishness was a mere accident of his humanity, and his Judaism a set of universal verities. But this time is long gone. Today as always, the Jew must hold fast to his humanity—and hence to any man's humanity—as to a religious ultimate. But if, in an age which has singled the Jew out with unprecedented grimness, this holding-fast sheds no light or meaning on his Jewishness, then it must degenerate into a hollow irrelevancy, if not into a dishonest device for escape.[10]

Again, once, perhaps, it could seem that the human person could live by universal verities alone, such as a Deistic First Cause or a Divine Cosmic Process. But this time too is long gone. For in the present age, the human individual is called into question to a degree which has rarely been equalled and never surpassed. Nature

---

[10] Cf. further on this point, my article "Jewish Existence and the Living God" (*Commentary*, August 1959, especially p. 136).

seems ever larger to human consciousness, and the individual person, ever less significant in it. History seems prey, more and more, to anonymous forces, over which even individuals favored by history have little control; hence even those still believing in necessary progress in history tend to regard the individual as a mere means to its impersonal or superpersonal ends.[11] Depersonalization has insinuated itself even into the individual's most intimate relations. For here at least each man is meant to be a unique person; but the impersonal instruments of an industrial mass society threaten to reduce him to a mere instance of the species man. Such a time needs timeless verities and values, which are needed at any time. Its great specific need, however, is for what will give meaning, not to universals such as nature or mankind or history as a whole, but to that most stubborn of all particulars—the individual human person. But such meaning, if ultimate, can be found only with God; and not with the God of the Greeks but only with the God of Israel. Rarely in human history have men—non-Jews as well as Jews—stood in so great a need of the God of Israel. It is not without irony that this need should coincide with a time of widespread surrender, on the part of Jews, to the God of the Greeks.[12]

[11] The traditional belief in the Messiah does not entail the reduction of the individual to a mere means to the ends of history, especially if coupled with the belief in the world-to-come. In contrast, such a reduction always *was* entailed by the modernistic belief in necessary progress, at least when this belief is the sum total of eschatological expectation. This was clearly recognized, for example, by Kant (who for that reason refused to abandon belief in immortality for belief in necessary progress). Kant writes: "Befremdend bleibt es immer hierbei: dass die älteren Generationen nur scheinen um der späteren willen ihr mühseliges Geschäfte zu treiben, um nämlich diesen eine Stufe zu bereiten, von der diese das Bauwerk, welches die Natur zur Absicht hat, höher bringen könnten; und dass doch nur die spätesten das Glück haben sollen in dem Gebäude zu wohnen. . . ." (*Werke*, Prussian Academy edition, VIII 20).

[12] The expression "God of the Greeks" is more aptly applied to current "Process" concepts than to the First-Cause concept of earlier Deism. For contemporary philosophers who, under the influence of contemporary science, adopt that concept — as well as those among us who follow their lead — hark back to Greek philosophy. In abandoning the inert matter of atomists and Newtonians for creative energy, contemporary science returns to the Greeks, who thought of nature as alive. And in identifying this energy with a divine Process immanent in the universe, modern thinkers take up ideas going back to the very first Greek philosophers. Further, they are often quite fully aware of this fact. Thus Bergson recognized his debt to Heraclitus, and Whitehead regarded all philosophy as a series of footnotes to Plato.

VII

But recent events have not been without effect on liberal Judaism. They have led to a growing stress on the here and now—the Jewish people, the human person, the particular in its stubborn concreteness. This stress, however, has not always, or even for the most part, coincided with a return to the God of Israel. For while today there is widespread stress on the here and now, the belief remains no less widespread that a God of the here and now is no longer acceptable. And those among us who stress the one, and believe the other, have resorted to a new escape from a new dilemma. They have surrendered objective truth to universal verities—the First Cause or Cosmic Process—and have withdrawn the here and now into a sphere of mere human subjectivity.

In consequence of this withdrawal, Jewish prayer, once *between* a "subjective" self and an "objective" God, is viewed as the self's disport with its own feelings, conducive to aesthetic or therapeutic benefit. הלכה once a way walked on *before* God, is reduced to "custom and ceremony," performed for the sake of warm emotions within or wholesome relations without. Judaism, once a covenant involving a singling-out God and a singled-out Israel, is seen as a man-made civilization, created by Jewish genius in its human solitariness. And the human person, who once believed that he *actually* mattered to God, is now engineered into the mere *feeling* that he matters, on the ground that such feeling banishes anxiety and alienation. All too rarely has our new emphasis on the here and now amounted to a challenge to the God of the Greeks, on behalf of the God of Israel. For the most part, it has been a new form of surrender.

But if this surrender is a rational necessity, then all our attempts to give religious re-assertion to the here and now are foredoomed to failure. For Judaism can be a creative religious civilization only if we forget creativity and civilization, and turn to God. Prayer can bring its benefit only to those directing their heart, away from benefit and toward Heaven. Custom and ceremony can acquire true religious life only if transmuted into מצוה —deed done before God.

And the individual can conquer anxiety and alienation, not through mere *feelings* that he matters, no matter how skillfully they are aroused and maintained, but only through the *belief* that he matters. But belief is not belief at all unless it lays claim to objective truth.

The events of our age, then, together with the stress on the here and now with which we have tried to meet them, raise one problem surpassing all others in religious significance. This is whether it is possible for the liberal Jew, in the here and now of mid-twentieth century America, to return to the God of Israel.

VIII

It is this question which confronts the liberal Jew, heir to the modern rationalist reform, with that other great reform in modern Judaism, the Hasidic movement.[13] Though worlds apart in space if not in time, the two reforms have much in common, notably the wish to liberate life from forces stifling it. Yet even as regards this aim there is at least one crucial difference. Whereas the Western rationalist reform seeks to free the life of the human intellect, the Eastern Hasidic reform seeks to free the life between man and God. While the one creates something new, the other restores what has always been. And whereas the former reform must break with orthodox authority, the latter must rebel only against orthodox decadence. Orthodoxy, in the decadent form in which Hasidism found it, had clogged up the channels of communication between God and the human here and now. It was the fundamental aim of Hasidism to reopen these channels, so that the interrupted life

[13] The interpretation of Hasidism here offered is indebted to many writers, such as Scholem, Minkin, Dresner. It owes its decisive debt, however, to Martin Buber. The writer is not unaware of the many criticisms which have been directed against Buber's interpretation of Hasidism. But he has found most of these unimpressive. The most common criticism is that Buber, instead of writing the kind of history which separates sources in painstaking analysis, has given the kind which is a creative synthesis. But the prejudices of positivistic scholarship to the contrary notwithstanding, there is always need for the latter as well as the former type of history, unless one is to be left, not with the spirit of the age or movement one seeks to understand, but merely with its dead bones. Moreover, while Buber's kind of history has great dangers of subjectivity and distortion—which, incidentally, Buber himself has been the first to admit—Buber would seem to have coped with these with extraordinary success. His treatment of Hasidism shows him to be a thinker capable of practicing the empathetic openness which he preaches.

between God and Israel might be resumed. It is, therefore, not this aim which makes Hasidism unique. Its uniqueness lies, rather, in the passion with which it pursued the ancient aim, seeking, as it were, to storm the Heavens.[14]

No doubt the above is an oversimplification, for Hasidism is a phenomenon with many facets. Yet at least in the view of this writer—admittedly no specialist in Hasidic studies—the oversimplification is not a distortion. For it would seem that most of the facets of Hasidism subserve the fundamental aim just stated, and that few if any conflict with it.

Thus while Hasidism is a kind of mysticism it is not the kind which dissolves the human here and now into a conflux with Infinity. Hasidic mysticism is a practical mysticism, one of human action. But action asserts the human here and now, and the mysticism gives this action ultimate significance, by placing it into reciprocal contact with God. For this reason, Hasidic mysticism is a truly Jewish mysticism. And the Baal Shem Tov uttered good Jewish doctrine when he claimed that there is no place in which God may not be found; and that all true actions, performed in the here and now, leave permanent traces beyond the here and now—in the "upper world."[15]

Again, Hasidism may seem to speak on behalf of the heart against the intellect, and on behalf of the common man against the scholarly aristocrat. It speaks, however, not on behalf of one half of a dichotomy against the other but on the contrary against all dichotomies, in the name of a relation between God and the whole

---

[14] Cf. the following characteristic statement: "He who serves God in the 'great way' assembles all his inner power and rises upwards in his thoughts, and *breaks through all skies in one act,* and rises higher than the angels and seraphs and thrones, and that is perfect worship." (Quoted by G. Scholem, *Major Trends in Jewish Mysticism,* New York, 1961, p. 335; our italics).

[15] The fact that neither the first (the Baal Shem) nor the last great Hasidic master (Nahman of Bratzlav) wrote books would seem symbolic of this faith. One must admit the existence in Hasidism of the kind of mysticism which dissolves the self into the אַיִן סוֹף —a tendency no doubt inherited from the Kabbala. But one may question that this is a major trend in a movement placing so much stress on human action. For the concept of a mysticism of action, cf. Scholem, *op. cit.,* pp. 341 ff. and Buber, *The Origin and Meaning of Hasidism,* New York, 1960, pp. 198 ff.

man. Hence Hasidism is, in essence, neither anti-intellectual nor
anti-Halachist. An ignorant boy's playing of a whistle may be a
gift acceptable to God; but so may the prayer of a learned man.
The Zaddik's life includes far more than orthodox הלכה ; it includes
הלכה as well.

Hasidism, further, asserts rungs or degrees of human perfection.
But this is not to set up ideals beyond ordinary life, surpassing
ordinary capacities, and indifferent to the here and now of realization. It is, on the contrary, to lead into ordinary life, and to challenge capacities which are unique and irreplaceable. Said the Baal
Shem: "Every man should know that since creation no other man
ever was like him. Had there been such another, there would be no
need for him to be. Each is called on to perfect his unique qualities.
And it is his failure to heed this call which delays the Messiah."[16]

Finally, Hasidism contains elements of pantheistic metaphysics.
But metaphysics is only a by-product of its central endeavor, which
is not to explain mystery but to live with it. And what metaphysics
it has is not pantheism of the Eastern kind, which dissolves the here
and now in Infinity; nor of the Spinozistic kind, which makes it an
accident of Nature; nor of the Bergsonian kind, which sweeps it
along in a cosmic Onward Push. Hasidism asserts divine sparks
in nature in order to teach that there is no here and now in which
God cannot be met. It asserts such sparks in man in order to teach
that man must do the meeting; that the divine sparks in nature are
not actualities overwhelming man into passive surrender but potentialities to be redeemed by human action. But such action—
whether it be overt action or the inward act of prayer—is מצוה
performed in the here and now. The pantheistic elements in Hasidism, then, are so reorganized as to focus on the meeting, in the here
and now, between man and God. And this raises doubt as to
whether they remain pantheistic in any sense at all.

Considered as a whole, then, Hasidism may be viewed as a passionate attempt to reopen, in the here and now, communication
between Israel and the God of Israel. When viewed in this light, it

[16] Buber, *Die Chassidischen Buecher*, p. 157.

confronts the liberal Jew of today with a direct challenge. For while much in Hasidism may be time-bound, alien to us and even odd in itself,[17] its essential aim makes as strong a claim today as it did when Judaism was born. This aim is the search for the God of the here and now—the God of Israel.

IX

But can the Jew of today accept the validity of this search? What of the view of radical rationalist reformers, stated earlier, that the God of Israel is a mere myth of the past? It is now time to show that this view follows not from science but from scientism; not from a critical rationalism which knows what it is doing, but from a rationalism expanded into uncritical dogma. To show this, one requires neither originality nor insights peculiar to believers and theologians. One need but borrow from a philosophical tradition of nearly two centuries' duration, begun by that great rationalist, Immanuel Kant. Kant, it is true, was not essentially concerned with the God of the here and now. But he *was* essentially concerned with the here and now of the human person.[18] And from this concern of his has sprung the greatest tradition in modern philosophy.

As the rational search for uniformity conquered the modern West one implication became quickly obvious. The terms of this search leave no room for human freedom and personal uniqueness. For if explanation is in terms of laws it is without reference to

[17] No doubt the aspect in Hasidism most alien to us (and also, perhaps, most responsible for the decline of Hasidism — cf. Minkin, *op. cit.,* pp. 335 ff.) is the exaltation of the Zaddik. Yet Rabbi Dresner's excellent study shows that even Zaddikism originally springs, if not from what we have called the basic aim of Hasidism, so at least from the Heaven-storming passion with which it seeks to reach it. For where passion seeks to "break through all skies in one act," and yet honesty discovers obstruction and failure, there the need springs up for a human mediator who might bridge that gap. And the Zaddik, finding himself placed into this mediating role, may respond with a rise to saintliness — or with a lapse into arrogance or even charlatanism.

[18] While the Kant-interpretation here offered is simplified and even controversial (as regards personal uniqueness, not as regards human freedom), we obviously cannot pause to defend it. It may be mentioned, however, that although Kant denies the possibility of experience of God in the here and now, he refuses to follow contemporary Deism which reduces God to a universal verity indifferent to the here and now. Religion, for Kant, is hope; and this hope remains essentially related to the individual.

human freedom; and if it seeks uniformity it must aim at explaining personal uniqueness away. For this reason, some thinkers have denied the reality of both freedom and personal uniqueness; and lesser thinkers—notably social scientists—do so even today.

But Kant saw the dogmatism inherent in this denial. He admitted that rational inquiry must *treat* man as an instance of law and uniformity, as much as any natural object. But he denied that this proves that man *is* an object among objects. What if all explanation of man as an object presupposes prior abstraction from man as a subject? What if human freedom and personal uniqueness, instead of being non-existent, merely escape the reach of rational inquiry? A critical rationalism, Kant perceived, must admit this as at least a theoretical possibility.

Kant further perceived that this theoretical possibility is a moral and practical necessity. For while *qua* observer man may view himself as a mere instance of law, *qua* responsible agent he must act as if he were free and unique. Nor can this belief be a mere illusion. If it were, all responsibility would lie in shambles. According to Kant, our freedom and uniqueness is as certain as any scientific knowledge.

It is, however, a certainty of a different kind. Explanation is of objects, in terms of laws. The certainty now referred to is of at least one subject—oneself; and it is not in terms of laws but rather in its unique here and now. And while certainty of the former kind is by a detached observer, who views the world *sub specie aeternitatis,* certainty of the free and unique self is found only *by* the free and unique self, and only in the moment of action and involvement. This is Kant's great philosophical discovery, destined to make history.[19]

Kant's discovery gave rise to the problem of interpersonal certainty. If one follows Kant, one cannot assert one's own freedom and uniqueness and yet deny the freedom and uniqueness of others. But can we know others *qua* free and unique persons? Are they

---

[19] Kant distinguishes between scientific truths which take the form "it is certain," and moral and religious truths which take the form "I am certain."

accessible to our experience? This has been a grave problem for modern philosophy, from Kant down to Buber's *I and Thou.*

The problem is grave because one cannot reject I-Thou experience, while to admit it is to run the risk of scientific obscurantism. One runs this risk because I-Thou experience forsakes objective detachment for inter-active participation; and because both the self and the other appear in it, not as objects manifesting uniformity, but as subjects shattering it like a miracle. And yet, whatever the limits and dangers of I-Thou experience, it cannot be rejected as in principle vain and illusory. For human action does not take place in solipsistic isolation. It is inter-action with others. Action, therefore, cannot disclose our own freedom and uniqueness without also disclosing that of others; and if the latter disclosure is in principle impossible so is the former. There is a direct line from Kant to Buber's *I and Thou.*[20]

This is not the place for coping with this problem. It is the place, however, for raising the religious question to which it in turn gives rise. If it is necessary to admit inter-human involvement as an authentic form of experience side by side with objective cognition, is it possible to admit human-divine involvement as an experience no less authentic? And if it is necessary to admit the free human other, as a quasi-miraculous break-through of the fixed world of objects governed by laws, is it possible to admit a miracle of miracles—a break-through of a free Divine Other into that world?[21]

---

[20] Cf. my forthcoming "Buber's Concept of Revelation," to be published, in 1961, in the Buber volume of the Library of Living Philosophers. One of the problems which has arisen in the Kantian tradition is whether human free actions can, *qua* free, be explained; and the conclusion which has emerged is that, if such explanation is possible, it cannot be in terms of laws. Cf. Collingwood, *op. cit.,* and W. Dray, *Laws and Explanation in History,* Oxford, 1957.

[21] Cf. Buber, *Moses,* Oxford and London, 1946, p. 77: "The real miracle means that in the astounding experience of the event the current system of cause and effect becomes, as it were, transparent, and permits a glimpse of the sphere in which the sole power, not restricted by any other, is at work." Buber's doctrine of miracle — which makes it, not an exception to the natural, but a manifestation of God to the believer in the natural — is anticipated by the Baal Shem: "the first time a thing occurs in nature it is called a miracle; later it becomes natural, and no attention is paid to it. Let your worship and your service be a fresh miracle every day to you. Only such worship, performed from the heart with enthusiasm, is acceptable." (Newman and Spitz, *Hasidic Anthology,* New York, 1944, pp. 336 ff.)

In the terms of Kantian and post-Kantian philosophy, the implications of the denial of this possibility achieve unprecedented clarity.[22] Such a denial implies that God must remain an object for us while even another human being can become a subject; that religion must remain confined by the conditions of a spectator-relation whereas even inter-human relations can become forms of participation. But can God be God and yet a mere object? And can religion be religion and yet a mere spectator-relation? Religion is life with mystery. But the denial of the possibility of a divine break through law and uniformity would reduce religion to a mere theory seeking to explain mystery.

But while such a denial follows from a dogmatic rationalism, it does not follow from a critical rationalism of the Kantian kind. For while the former asserts that the world is a fixed system of laws and uniformities, the latter confines itself to the assertion that it must be treated as such a system by the observer who seeks to explain it. And it further recognizes that both the system and the observing attitude are superseded in moments of human interaction. Such a rationalism does not rule out the possibility of a divine break-through into the fixed world of laws and uniformities—provided it is asserted to take place, not by and for the metaphysical observer who seeks to explain mystery, but by and for the religious participant who lives with it.

But while critical rationalism suffices to validate the possibility of inter-human I-Thou experience, it does not suffice to validate the possibility of such experience between the human and the divine. For while the possibility of the former is implied in all responsible action, this is not true of the latter, which presupposes an additional dimension: the faith that man can seek out God in the here and now, and that God can be found in it. At its culminating point, therefore, critical rationalism raises the momentous question

---

[22] Most great post-Kantian philosophers who are concerned with God at all are concerned, not with an abstract Deity but with a God capable of being *present*. Cf. e.g. Hegel's attempt to synthesize eternity with history, Nietzsche's insistence that God is dead, and Heidegger's that He is absent. (The important question to Nietzsche and Heidegger is not God's existence but His presence).

whether the world is open to the incursion of God, or a fixed system of laws and uniformities closed to it. But this question it can only raise, not answer.

For this reason, the liberal Jew who faces the Hasidic challenge must at this point turn from a problem of modern thought to a problem of modern life. Philosophical analysis shows that a religious effort to reopen communication with God is no offense to modern critical reason. The question still remains—and it is the vastly more complex and more difficult one—whether such an effort is a concrete possibility of modern life, as well as compatible with the requirements of modern thought.

X

If we wish to face up to this question in all its gravity we must begin with a realistic acceptance of the gulf which separates the modern world from that of the Hasidim. Modern industrial society differs from the society of the *Shtetl;* and, unlike the nature the Hasidim knew, modern nature is subject to unheard-of technological control. In their world, the Hasidim could seek to arouse divine sparks in nature and society, with an enthusiastic directness storming the Heavens. But if there are divine sparks capable of being aroused in modern nature and society, they are more elusive and ambiguous than ever before.

Even more elusive and ambiguous are divine sparks in the inner world of modern man. Living in a world of pre-reflexive immediacy, the Hasidim were capable of direct trust in the self-authenticating power of religious intensity. Modern man, in contrast, if capable of such trust at all, is no longer capable of direct and simple trust. For the inner world of today is dominated by a spirit of reflection and self-consciousness. Moments of religious immediacy are inevitably followed by moments of reflection, in which what immediacy may have taken for the presence of God is suspected of being the self's own production—the projection of wish or fear. Whatever the Hasidic claim on us, therefore, we cannot share the Hasidic style of storming the Heavens. Social conditions without, and a spirit of self-consciousness and reflection within, have ruled this out. And imitation, on our part, of that style would not only be a flight from our own here and now. It might also be to lapse into idolatry. For to know that projections of hope and fear may masquerade as the voice of God, and yet to seek escape from this knowledge in pre-reflexive immediacy, is to run the risk of worshipping false gods.

Aware of this danger, the liberal Jew may seek to avoid it by abandoning, along with Hasidic-style storming of Heavens, the whole search for God in the here and now. For it is all-too-true that if God is made to dwell in safe and infinite distance—as First Cause or Cosmic Process—then there can be no mistaking of a merely human here and now for His presence. And yet, this escape from one form of idolatry is bound to lead to another. For even though God be remote, the human here and now continues to make its religious demands; and, if cut off from God, these turn it into a pseudo-god. Man comes to worship feeling instead of God; the symbol, not what it stands for; Jewish genius, not Him whose presence stimulates it. There is, to be sure, an idolatrous emotionalism which, born of impatient need, mistakes projected desire for God. But there is also an idolatry of pseudo-sophistication which, denying man's actual need of the present God, treats the human as if it were divine. Between these two abysses the liberal Jew of today must walk, in sophisticated simplicity, on a narrow ridge.

Can he walk on this ridge? And can the ridge in due course expand itself, if not into a royal road, at least into a safe pathway? This question will find its answer, not in grand prognostications but only in simple moments of actual walking. Those who walk on the ridge, open to the future, will find strength in the Hasidic example. But they will not attempt to imitate it. For they will walk as the Hasidim walked—not in a world of others but in their own.

Imitation would not only be the wrong way of seeking strength in Hasidism. It would also be a misunderstanding of Hasidism itself. A great Zaddik was asked why he did not follow the example of his teacher in his own way of life. The Zaddik replied: "On the contrary, I do follow his example. For just as he left his teacher, so I leave mine."[23]

[23] Scholem, *op. cit.*, p. 348.

Moses Maimonides and Reform Today

Many of the papers collected here attempt to come to grips with aspects of Jewish tradition or of Western tradition and to explore the meaning these traditions can have for a modern, liberal Judaism. Omitted thus far, however, has been any attempt to assess the relevance of earlier Jewish philosophers for the Reform movement. In part, we may explain the small attention paid to Jewish philosophy as the result of the relative lack of centrality of philosophy to the enterprise of formulating Judaism. Only at those times and in those places where the wandering Jew has confronted a philosophically sophisticated culture has philosophical formulation of Judaism become an apologetic necessity.

One such confrontation occurred in the Middle Ages and, by common consent, its greatest consequence in Jewish thought was the philosophy of Maimonides. Professor Samuel Atlas, in the memorable essay reprinted below, made a striking and stimulating investigation and assessment of "The Contemporary Relevance of the Philosophy of Maimonides." Dr. Atlas assumed, at the outset, that there would be such relevance because the questions Maimonides dealt with were those of philosophy, which are perennial questions. Maimonides, Atlas claims, was neither a pure rationalist nor an anti-rationalist, but rather a "critical" rationalist, and in that sense, though not in all senses, anticipated the strain of modern philosophic thought deriving from Immanuel Kant.

Since, in Atlas's view, "we live in a time in which all sorts of philosophies of unreason are in vogue," the rationalist emphases in Maimonides are of great value as a corrective to such philosophies as the overly subjectivistic existentialism popular among theologians and the overly relativistic pragmatism on which many current socio-ethical positions are based. The self-critical limitations of the Maimonidean view serve to restrain him from regarding human reason as capable of solving all the problems that human reason can propound. Man's mind is inexorably finite; this is the heart of Maimonidean criticism. Yet man does have a mind which it is his moral obligation to use to its utmost; this is the heart of Maimonidean rationalism.

Atlas finds in the consequences of this critical-rationalist position "the very fruitful idea that the essence of Judaism is grounded in philosophy and not in the revelation of a dogmatic law." The conception of revealed law leads to a static view of the nature of Judaism, where as the notion ascribed to Maimonides of Judaism as a philosophy never in contradiction with rationality "opens up new vistas for the possibility of a development of Jewish thought in the light of the further growth of philosophic thought in general." Maimonides is thus, in a sense, co-opted, or at least adopted, as the ancestor of a re-forming of Judaism. Of course this adoption requires the adoptive descendant to go far beyond his adopted ancestor. But, concludes Dr. Atlas, "the most significant lesson which the understanding of Maimonides' philosophy teaches is that with Maimonides we can supersede Maimonides."

THE CONTEMPORARY RELEVANCE OF THE PHILOSOPHY OF MAIMONIDES

Samuel Atlas

(1954)

I

Moses Maimonides occupies a central place in the history of Jewish thought as well as in the history of the philosophy of the Middle Ages in general. The philosophical works which preceded that of Maimonides were eclipsed by the sun of Maimonides. The Jewish philosophers who came after Maimonides were concerned mainly with the examination and the interpretation of Maimonides' thought and with an investigation of his doctrines. Such original thinkers as Gersonides (Levi ben Gershon) and Hasdai Crescas developed their own philosophical systems in connection with their investigation of the fundamental doctrines of Maimonides.

And, in modern times, Spinoza, Moses Mendelssohn, Solomon Maimon, and Hermann Cohen considered *The Guide to the Perplexed* of Maimonides as a thesaurus of philosophical thought, from which some fundamental ideas entered into the web of their own philosophical constructions to form an integral part thereof. This is especially true with regard to Spinoza and Maimon. Moreover, the philosophical *eros* of Spinoza and Maimon was awakened by their study of the work of Maimonides.

In view of the fact that Maimonides' thought fruitfully influenced various thinkers of the past, the question naturally arises: What has Maimonides' philosophy to offer to the perplexed of our own time? Is the thought of Maimonides a thing of the past? We have thus to recognize it as possessing only a historical value, a sort of historical curiosity. Or can we, perhaps, find in it teachings which are of a perennial nature, thus recognizing some of its doctrines as possessing vital interest for us? The *Guide* could perhaps show us the way out of the labyrinth of the perplexities of contemporary thought.

Considering the vast impact of Maimonides' thought on various thinkers belonging to different periods and to divergent climates of ideas, we are surely entitled to assume, even before entering into a detailed examination of his thought, that Maimonides' philosophy would contain ideas which are of supreme importance for us. We have a right to expect that Maimonides' work would be of contemporary relevance, a "Guide to the Perplexed" of our time.

All great thinkers of the past, though belonging to, and rooted in, the historical period in which they lived, in dealing with the perennial problems of philosophy, transcended their own time. They are, therefore, of relevance to all times, if not in all the aspects of their thought, at least in their main trends and tendencies. Such a thinker was Maimonides.

Maimonides is generally known as an Aristotelian. The fundamental concepts with which he operates, such as matter and form, potentiality and actuality, the idea of God as a prime mover, the impossibility of an infinite reality, whether in the form of an infinite body or in that of an infinite number of finite bodies, are all Aristotelian. But the individuality of Maimonides, the characteristic features of his creative thought, consist in those doctrines in which he deviates from Aristotle. Of course, Maimonides, so to say, went to school to the Aristotelians of his time. Al Farabi and Ibn Sina were his masters. Aristotelianism, in the light of the great Arabic interpreters, constitutes the fundamental concepts and principles with which he operates. But the basic core of his thought resides not in those teachings which constitute the common ground of all

Aristotelians, but rather in those doctrines which he originally developed and which differ fundamentally from Aristotelianism.

As a matter of fact, many aspects of Maimonides' thought do have contemporary significance. Maimonides' rationalism, which we will define as a critical rationalism, his concept of the unity of truth which is the basis of his doctrine of the harmony of philosophy and revelation, his concept of God, of the world and of man, are all of vital importance for us today. In the struggle of ideas, the voice of Maimonides should be loudly heard on the battleground of ideas in favor of reason versus unreason.

We live in a time in which all sorts of philosophies of unreason are in vogue. All kinds of mysticism are flourishing. The overemphasis on the idea of God as the "wholly other," the transcendent, and the ineffable, is loudly heard from different quarters, and is gaining adepts and followers. Such an approach may lead to obscurantism, to dogmatism, and to the elevation of all sorts of personal, imaginary, subjective experiences to the level of a divine oracle. In such a situation it is healthy and salutary to be reminded of a simple but wise word of a contemporary thinker, Ludwig Wittgenstein: Of what we do not know, it is better to keep silent.

In connection with the task before us, it is particularly proper to call to mind the sound and sober rationalism of Maimonides which implies a belief in the human capacity of reason, making the belief in the idea of progress possible. The feasibility of progress is dependent on the belief in man's capacities to master the problems with which he has to cope.

The specific characteristic of man consists, according to Maimonides, in his rational capacity. Man is capable of attaining an intellectual comprehension of the logical forms of thought and of the forms of being, and by developing, i.e., bringing forth from a potential state into an actual state, his rational faculty, man is capable of achieving a clear idea of God and the world. Herein consists the uniqueness of man as distinct from all other biological species. The belief in the existence, the absolute unity, and the incorporeality of God can be rationally deduced; and it is the moral task of man to strive for an intellectual comprehension of these principles. Maimonides counted among the positive commandments the striving for the cognition of the existence, unity, and incorporeality of God. These ideas constitute the minimum of rational cognition which is an indispensable requirement for any Jew.

Maimonides is fully aware of the difficulties in attaining metaphysical knowledge; he is conscious also of the causes and obstacles hindering the attainment of such cognition. Therefore, the purpose of his Creed is to teach the people articles of faith which can and should be attained as knowledge by rational means. The meaning of faith is to show the way and direction towards the ideal goal which is cognition. The concept of faith is in the sense of *credo ut intelligam.*

The *Moreh* is a work intended not for the masses, but for a special type of man, namely, a man who is troubled by the problem of the reconciliation of philosophic thought and revelation. But the *Yad Hachazakah* is a work of *Halachah,* a guide for action and conduct, written for the people as a whole. It encompasses the totality of law, binding upon every Jew.

In one of the paragraphs (*Halachoth*) of this work, Maimonides defines a person who ascribes corporeal qualities to God as a heretic (*Min*). That is to say, a person believing in God's possessing corporeal attributes is excluded from the fold of Israel, which is a community of believers in monotheism with all its implications, as demanded by a rational definition of this term. Now, Rabbi Abraham ben David (RABaD), in his critical note to this passage, raises objection to Maimonides' definition by pointing out that a view of God as a being possessing corporeal attributes may be the result of a literal interpretation of some Biblical expressions and rabbinic utterances. Since a person holding such a view may have been misled by the understanding of some Biblical terms and expressions in their literal sense, he should not be classified as a heretic. Maimonides' intention, however, was to point out that ignorance and misunderstanding are no excuses for holding a view contrary to the very essence of monotheism.

As a matter of fact, Maimonides explicitly states that the belief in God's having corporeal form is just as destructive to the belief in the unity of God as the belief in idol-worship (*Moreh,* I, 36). Just as the latter cannot be excused by referring to ignorance or to habit as its cause, so in relation to the former, ignorance and habit, and for that matter also the misunderstanding of certain Biblical terms and expressions because of their literal interpretation, cannot be invoked as an excuse for the holding of such a view.

In order fully to grasp the implications of Maimonides' view in this matter as bearing upon the very essence of his rationalism, it is proper to consider the difference existing between an error and a lie. It is obvious that the distinction between them consists in that an error is an unintentional and unconscious falsehood, whereas a lie is an intentional and conscious falsehood. Such a definition, however, takes into account merely the state of the subject giving utterance to a false statement; it is thus only a psychological distinction. An essential and logical distinction between them could, however, be defined thus: while an error is an offense against logic, a lie is an offense against ethics. In view of this logical definition of the essential difference obtaining between an error and a lie, it can be recognized that there is a kind of error which attains the rank of a lie. This is the case when the error is not merely an offense against logic, but is, by implication, also an offense against ethics. This happens to be the case when it is incumbent upon man to strive for a true, clear concept and to avoid errors and mistakes. Here an error will be an offense against logic by commission, but at the same time it will imply an offense against ethics by omission.

Now since man is, according to Maimonides, morally bound to strive for a true concept of monotheism which is incompatible with corporeality in any shape or form, an error in this respect is an offense not only against logic but also against ethics. This seems to be the motive of Maimonides' view of a person's believing in corporeal attributes, even when this belief may be the result of an error in the interpretation of Biblical passages in their literal meaning.

The Biblical commandment, "Know thy God," is, according to

Maimonides, an imperative intellectually to comprehend the essence of monotheism. Man possesses the intellectual capacity for the achievement of a pure concept of God. And since man can achieve it, he is morally bound to strive for its attainment.

The Kantian derivation of the reality of freedom of the will from the human consciousness of the categorical imperative: "Thou shalt, therefore thou canst," can be reversed with reference to Maimonides' derivation of the moral obligation of the striving for metaphysical cognition from the rational capacity of man and formulated thus: "Thou canst, therefore thou shalt."

Maimonides' rationalism determining the relation obtaining between philosophy and theology, between rational thought and revelation, can best be expressed by a picture which Kant used for an illustration of this same relationship. In view of the well-known saying that "Philosophy is the handmaid of Theology," Kant said: "It can be admitted, but we have to put the question for consideration whether she is a handmaid who follows, bearing the train of her mistress, or whether she goes before, bearing a torch to illumine her path." By raising knowledge to the position of the sublime, ethical task of man and by subordinating faith to knowledge, Maimonides thus declared philosophy to be the handmaid which bears the torchlight of reason to illumine the way of faith.

For the proper understanding of the significance and the relevance of the idea of the unity and incorporeality of God, the following consideration is of paramount importance.

In the conception of the idea of the unity of God is implied the idea of the unity of man. Then, the conception of unity in its ultimate abstraction is the result of a pure act of thought. The idea of the unity of the supreme being possessing no corporeal quality can be attained only by a process of thought not infected by sensuous perceptions.

Hence, in the demand of such a concept of unity is implied the idea of the prevalence of thought over sensuous perceptions. Through the medium of the senses, by which various aspects of reality are perceived, unity cannot be attained. Only clear and pure thought, abstracted from the sensuous perceptions, can conceive an idea of an absolute unity underlying the manifoldness of the appearances of reality. What is "given" to the senses is always a multiplicity of impressions and sensations, not a unity. Consequently, the conception of an abstract unity of God is grounded in an idealistic epistemology. This epistemology tries to show that the senses could not be relied upon in the determination of the ultimate ground of reality or in the definition of God as the source of all reality. There is, thus, a close connection between pure monotheism demanding the removal of all corporeality from the idea of God, as required by Maimonides, and the epistemology of idealism with its central idea that the basic principles of cognition are not to be found in the senses but in the pure ideas and concepts of thought which are not contaminated by the senses. Thus, the overcoming of the senses as a basis of cognition is common to both, to epistemological idealism and to pure monotheism.

Furthermore, there is a relationship between the idealism of the pure concept and the idealism of action, that is to say, ethical idealism. The idealism implied in Maimonides' demand of an absolute unity of God, abstract from all corporeality, is bound up with his ethical idealism as manifested in Maimonides' conception of the ethical attributes as the only positive attributes which we are allowed to ascribe to God.

The deep meaning of the second Biblical commandment, not to make any image of God, must be understood in this sense, namely, that the spiritual principle of thought must prevail over the sensuous perceptions. And in this spirit the second commandment was understood by Maimonides, who elevated it to a principle of faith in the form of a demand not to ascribe to God any corporeal quality.

For the understanding of the significance of the idea of incorporeality, as demanded by Maimonides, it is appropriate to quote an eminent passage in the *Critique of Judgment* (*Kritik der Urteilskraft,* Cassirer edition, Vol. 5, p. 347), in which Kant writes: "In the Book of Laws of the Jews there is perhaps no passage more sublime than the prohibition: Thou shalt not make unto thee any graven image, or any likeness of anything that is in the heaven above, or that is in the earth beneath, or that is in the water under the earth. This commandment alone can explain the enthusiasm which the Jewish people had shown for its religion in the period of its highest civilization, when it compared itself with other nations."

Herein lies the significance of the historical role of monotheism as a universal mission. Polytheism deifies the natural forces which are perceived by the senses. Pantheism acknowledges in the unity of the world the unity of God. Only monotheism conceived the unity of God as the unity of personality, as the unity of self-consciousness. By penetrating to the depth of the human ego and to the human self-consciousness in which the fundamental principle of unity is discovered, monotheism posits the idea of an absolute Ego, an absolute self-consciousness which is the creator of all being. God as infinite personality is conceived as the counterpart of man the finite personality.

The idea of the unity of God is thus closely bound up with the realization of human self-consciousness as the source of all unity. The prophets discovered a new concept of God and a new concept of the world, a new heaven and a new earth, because a new concept of man was disclosed to them, that is to say, a new concept of man in an individual, social, ethical, and religious sense.

Maimonides' concept of the absolute character of truth derived by logical methods and of the unity of philosophy and revelation has contemporary relevance with reference to the various concepts of truth prevalent in our time. In the main, two concepts of truth are competing with one another, and both are dangerous and pernicious, undermining the very foundations of our culture. One is the existentialist concept of truth, and the other is the pragmatic concept of truth. The concept of truth as evolved by existentialism is grounded entirely in the personal commitment to an idea. Truth is subjective, for it is solely determined by the existential attitude towards an idea, belief, or doctrine. Any idea can be designated as true if it has existential reality, that is to say, if it is attended by the total commitment of the whole existence of a person.

Such a concept actually involves the denial of the very idea of truth as an objective reality, as a value in itself independent of the subjective and personal attitude towards it. It opens the door to all kinds of mysticism, obscurantism, and subjectivism. Any superstition, any personal, mystical experience, may claim to be true, provided that it is accompanied by the existential commitment. It may even lead to a conscious falsification of reality and history. The justification of such falsification lies in the proposition basic to this school of thought, that the existential commitment to an idea is the sole and exclusive factor in determining its truth.

Pragmatism, in some of its trends, maintains that the sole validation of the truth of a concept is its usefulness for human life. There is no objective realm of truth as such. Any idea which is purposeful and useful for human life and existence is true. Such a pragmatist must consistently consider his own doctrine of truth to be true because of its usefulness, since it asserts that all truths are true becaue of their usefulness. But pragmatism claims absolute validity for its own epistemology, i.e., for its own doctrine of truth. Thus pragmatism involves itself in a contradiction. However, the pragmatist is not afraid of a contradiction so long as it is useful.

Moreover, pragmatism leads necessarily to relativism. Since there is no form of criterion for truth except its usefulness, any idea may be declared to be true as long as it is thought to be useful for a society or a people. To realize that such a concept of truth may lead to disastrous consequences, it is sufficient to recall some political movements of our own time which were bound up with a conscious falsification of reality and history. Relativism, which is the outgrowth of pragmatism, may lead to the justification of a lie because of its supposed usefulness.

The question therefore arises: Is relativism useful? Is not relativism rather the greatest danger to what is best in our culture? The consideration of the danger implied in the pragmatic concept of truth is its best refutation. The terms "usefulness" and "uselessness" belong to the realm of biology. Man, however, is more than a mere biological species. Man, by the rational faculty with which he is endowed, constitutes a form of being *sui generis*. Man transcends the biological realm by his capacity of transcending himself. Maimonides acknowledges the uniqueness of man by recognizing his rational faculty as a spark of the infinite divine reason. He expressed it in theological terms by interpreting in this sense the Biblical passage, "in the image of God created He him." Correspondingly, his epistemology is grounded in the recognition of the absolute validity of rational, logical thinking.

II

Maimonides, however, was aware of the cognitive limitations of reason. Maimonides recognizes that there are metaphysical problems which cannot be solved by rational methods. In relation to those problems, Maimonides emphasizes the essential and absolute difference between the human, finite mind and the divine, infinite mind. This is manifest in Maimonides' treatment of the problem of freedom of the will and of some aspects of the problem of creation. The problem of freedom of the will, as it was formulated in medieval philosophy, consists of the question: How could man be free to choose a line of action in face of the omniscience of God? Since God's foreknowledge encompasses what man will do, how could man still be free? Maimonides resolves this problem by pointing out the essential, not merely gradual, difference between the human, finite mind and the divine, infinite mind. Since the divine foreknowledge is the result of a totally different kind of knowledge, the assumption of man's freedom of choice is not contradictory to the idea of God's omniscience.

Also with regard to the problem of the creation of the world out of nothing, the idea of the cognitive limitations of the human mind is expressed. The Aristotelians proved the impossibility of creation from the very idea of God as an absolute and all-perfect being. Every agent who acts at a certain time is determined by causes motivating his action. It is unthinkable of God to say that He is determined by outside causes. Then, every agent who acts at a certain time does so to attain a certain goal and purpose beyond itself. God is unthinkable in such terms. This is one of the decisive proofs for non-creation as promulgated by the Aristotelians. Now Maimonides refutes these proofs by bringing to bear the concept of homonymous terms. These are words which mean one thing within the realm of human experience and something totally different with respect to God. God as an agent is a metaphysical concept; it is totally different from agents in the realm of human experience. The human mind can only comprehend God as an agent in a negative sense, namely, God is not an agent. Here, too, Maimonides emphasizes the limitations of the human reason with regard to the comprehension of the essence of God.

Likewise, the acknowledgment of man's limitations with references to the solution of metaphysical problems is manifest in Maimonides' treatment of the problem of divine providence and that of the relation obtaining between suffering and evil in the world. Maimonides is against the Mohammedan school of thought (*Ashariyah*) whose adherents maintain that all reality is completely dependent on the divine will. There is no freedom of the will. There is no law in nature and there is no law governing the affairs of man and the relation between sin and suffering. The inscrutable will of God may cause suffering to the righteous and happiness and bliss to the wicked. The emphasis on the unfathomable divine will as the only source and root of all being removes God completely from the domain of man. It is, therefore, impossible for man to form any positive idea of the essence of God and of the relation of man to God. God is the absolutely transcendent and the "wholly other," to use a modern theological term. According to this school of thought, there is no problem of theodicy. The metaphysical problem of theodicy, which consists in the search for a vindication of divine justice in the face of the suffering of the righteous and the prosperity of the wicked, is possible only on the assumption of the reality of the moral law, i.e., that there obtains a relation between sin and suffering and between the conduct of man and his well-being. For those theologians, however, who emphasize the absolute transcendence of God and recognize the divine will as the only source of all being, thus denying both the existence of law in nature and the reality of a moral order in the destiny of man, the problem of theodicy is non-existent.

Maimonides dedicated a great part of his work to the struggle against this school of thought. With regard to nature, Maimonides seeks to vindicate a concept of the world as an ordered cosmos governed by necessary, natural laws established by God at the moment of creation. The act of creation itself is due to the divine will. But the world is an ordered cosmos governed by laws which can be comprehended by the human mind. And, correspondingly, in the ethical realm, Maimonides tries to show that there are law and order governing the affairs of man. Man has the capacity of comprehending the moral law and of forming ideas of right and wrong, of good and evil, of justice and righteousness. As a matter of fact, the ethical attributes of God are the only positive attributes concerning the essence of God which man is capable of comprehending, according to Maimonides. We can thus translate this central idea of Maimonides into the following terms: The very essence of the religious experience consists in the experience of the absolute character of the ethical law. That is to say, the conception of the ethical commandments as absolute and divine commandments constitutes the very essence of the concept of God. Such a concept of God is diametrically opposed to some contemporary schools of thought with their emphasis on the "theological suspension of the ethical" as the very essence of the religious experience.

The ethical concept of God as evolved by Maimonides demands the reality of freedom of the will, for without freedom there is no place for man as an ethical being. In consequence of Maimonides' concept of nature as an ordered cosmos and of man as being governed by a moral law, it follows that there must be a relation between sin and suffering. Suffering and individual providence must also be subject to law and order. Suffering must therefore be the result of sin and evil, and divine providence and protection must be the result of the attainment of ethical and intellectual perfection. This is the demand of the moral law.

Just as Maimonides was opposed to the school of thought which stressed the will of God as the transcendent and the "wholly other," he equally resisted the other school of thought (*Mutazila*) which maintains that an absolute law of justice governs the affairs of man and the world and that all phenomena of suffering must be explained by the principle of the absolute justice of God. Evil and suffering stand in relation of cause and effect to one another. Those phenomena of suffering which cannot be explained as resulting from evil and sin must be compensated by the award of greater bliss in the world to come, according to this school of thought. The absolute vindication of divine justice led the protagonists of this school of thought to demand even the rewarding of animals for their suffering.

Now, Maimonides accepts the principle of a law of justice determining the relation of sin and suffering; they generally stand to one another in a relation of cause and effect. Maimonides, however, is well aware of the fact that there are phenomena of suffering which cannot be explained as consequences of sin and evil, as, for instance, the suffering of children or the suffering resulting from natural catastrophes. Here Maimonides has as his last recourse the recognition of the limitations of the human mind. It is impossible for man fully to account for the totality of being. We have to recognize that there are metaphysical problems which are insoluble by man due to the limitations of the human mind. Just as man is morally bound to strive for an intellectual comprehension of the essence of reality, of man and of God, so it is incumbent upon man to recognize his creaturehood and the essential difference between the finite and the infinite; the infinite cannot be fully comprehended by the finite.

Maimonides' rationalism can thus be defined as a critical rationalism. As a rationalist, Maimonides is opposed to the doctrine that God cannot be approached by reason altogether, for the essence of

God is the transcendent and absolute will. But Maimonides equally resisted dogmatic rationalism, which maintained that all phenomena of reality must and can be explained by the absolute principle of justice. Maimonides is the critical rationalist, for he recognizes the limitations of the human mind and admits that there are metaphysical problems which cannot be fully solved by man. He was thus equally opposed to the dogmatic antirationalism of the *Ashariyas,* who deprecated reason altogether, as well as to the dogmatic absolute rationalism of the *Mutazila.*

The question concerning man's capacity of comprehending the essence of God was formulated in medieval times thus: *Finitum est capax infiniti* versus *Finitum non est capax infiniti.* In our own time there is a revived overemphasis on the second position: man cannot attain a rational comprehension of the Infinite; he should not attempt to approach rationally the idea of God, for God is the "wholly other." God can only be believed in, but not rationally approached. For the essence of God cannot be approximated by rational methods. In short: *Finitum non est capax infiniti.* Now, Maimonides is against the dogmatism of both schools. Our approach to God can be only through reason; man is *capable* of approximating the Infinite by rational means. In this sense we say: *Finitum est capax infiniti.* But it is wrong to conclude that we can fully comprehend the metaphysical realm. We should recognize that the totality of being and the absolute essence of God cannot be fully comprehended by man due to his limitations. In relation to an absolute solution of such metaphysical problems as the adversity of the righteous and the prosperity of the wicked (צדיק ורע לו, רשע וטוב לו), the comprehension of the reality of freedom of the will in the face of the omniscience of God, and the essence of God's positive attributes, other than the ethical, we should recognize that *finitum non est capax infiniti.* Maimonides recognized a tension between these two principles. The tension between man's desire and capacity to embrace and comprehend the Infinite, on the one hand, and man's admission of his incapacity fully to recognize the Infinite, on the other hand, constitutes the very essence of man.

It seems to me that Maimonides has here expressed a central idea, a fundamental principle of Judaism, the tradition of which can be traced back to the earliest sources. In pleading with God for the sake of Sodom, Abraham gave utterance to two ideas which seem to contradict each other. On the one hand, he demands of God not to destroy the righteous alongside of the wicked, by asking: "Shall not the Judge of all the earth do justice?" (Gen. 18:25). But on the other hand, he says: "I . . . who am but dust and ashes" (Gen. 18:27). In the first instance, Abraham challenges God, demanding the fulfillment of the law of justice by which even God is bound. Here he assumes the capacity of man to comprehend the Absolute. He claims to know God's essence as "the righteous Judge of all the earth"; he knows the laws by which God is bound; God is not the transcendent and the "wholly other." But when Abraham says: "I . . . who am but dust and ashes," he recognizes the unfathomable abyss dividing man from God, the finite from the Infiinite. Both ideas expressed by Abraham are absolutely necessary for the understanding of the religious consciousness as promulgated by the prophets of Israel as well as by the authorities of rabbinic Judaism; they are both constitutive elements of the very essence of ethical monotheism; they are both necessary ideas, supplementing and fulfilling each other. The latter without the former would be an empty idea. The overemphasis on the nothingness of man, resulting in a concept of man as a finite being incapable of attaining any positive idea of the Infinite, would remove God entirely from the affairs of man. The idea of God as the absolutely transcendent and the "wholly other," with the corollary, crushing concept of man as "dust and ashes," would threaten to render the idea of God an empty idea. For there is no way for man, recognizing himself as "dust and ashes," to enter into any relationship with the absolutely transcendent and infinite being.

On the other hand, the overemphasis on man's capacity to comprehend fully the absolute, and the stressing of the nearness of God to man, the "I-Thou" relationship, without recognizing the limitations of man, would render man dogmatically blind. An overbearing dogmatism concerning the human capacity for comprehending the Infinite would blind man to the realization of the magnitude of the problems to which no solution can be found; it would deprive man of the comprehension of the nature of the metaphysical problems as being beyond the reach of a solution by rational methods.

To sum up: dogmatic anti-rationalism (the Kalam in Maimonides' time and some contemporary theological schools of thought) is empty and lame; dogmatic rationalism (some aspects of Aristotelianism and of the *Mutazila* in Maimonides' time, and some metaphysical trends of thought in our own time) is blind. Maimonides tries to avoid both dogmatic rationalism as well as dogmatic anti-rationalism. He steers a middle road, which we are inclined to characterize as "critical rationalism."

"Critical" implies self-criticism, and the import of the critical method is the recognition of the limitations of the cognitive capacity of man. The subject-matter of this method is thought itself; it is a process of thought about the possibility and the limitations of thought.

Thus Maimonides recognized that the world is a rationally ordered cosmos and man is essentially a rational being capable of attaining pure knowledge of the forms of being and of God, but the human mind has its limitations, owing to which man is incapable of comprehending fully the totality of being; there are metaphysical problems which are in principle insoluble by the human mind.

The problem of the suffering of the elect (צדיק ורע לו) engaged the minds of the Prophets and of the psalmists, reaching its climax in Job, who finally recognized the transcendence of God and the impossibility of man's fully comprehending the totality of being and of solving the problem of theodicy. The problem of theodicy, to which no solution can be found, is, however, a necessary religious problem, for it is based upon a necessary religious assumption of ethical monotheism, that there is a relation obtaining between sin and suffering, between evil and adversity, as well as between righteousness and prosperity. Therefore Job's struggle with the problem was in itself a religious act. This is, to my mind, the reason for the finale of the Book of Job, where it is related that God's anger was aroused against Job's friends, with God saying to them: "For you have not spoken rightly of me, as my friend Job hath" (42:7).

Maimonides also recognized that there are cases of suffering which cannot be vindicated. But this does not mean that the principle of a relation obtaining between evil and suffering is subject to doubt. Thus, for the dogmatic anti-rationalists who stress the transcendence and the absolute will of God (the *Ashariyah,* and contemporary schools of thought, such as the "crisis theology"), there is no problem of theodicy, since they deny that there is a relation obtaining between evil and suffering. This problem arises only on the assumption of the reality of a moral order. On the other hand, for those schools of thought whose adherents dogmatically maintain that all metaphysical problems are in principle soluble by the human mind, the dogmatic rationalists, the solution of the problem of theodicy lies in the conception of a future world in which all will be righted (the *Mutazila*).

For Maimonides, who belongs neither to the former nor to the latter, there is a problem of theodicy which belongs to those metaphysical problems for which there is no solution.

Thus the dilemma expressed by Abraham in the form of two deeply rooted religious sentiments, seemingly contradictory, but nonetheless constituting the very essence of his religious experience, reached, in Maimonides, the level of a philosophic consciousness in the formulation of a logical tension.

In Abraham we have, on the one hand, a daring, almost Promethean challenge, demanding of God justice for the righteous, thus implying a conviction of the possession of an absolutely true idea concerning the essence of God. But, on the other hand, there is a recognition by Abraham of the infinite chasm dividing man the creature from God the Creator.

This corresponds to the doctrine of Maimonides that there are law and order in the world as well as in the ethical realm, that suffering and adversity must, on the whole, be understood as a result of sin and evil. But, at the same time, one must recognize the incapacity of man fully to comprehend the infinite. Man should realize that the problem of suffering in its totality is beyond the reach of human comprehension.

III

Maimonides' concept of the world as a cosmos in which law prevails makes the striving for progress towards a greater comprehension of reality possible, while in a world in which every point of reality is due to an immediate act of creation by the divine will, as the Kalam taught, the striving for progress towards a greater unity is impossible. It is quite irrelevant whether progress is conceived as a reality or as a mere functional idea; the idea of progress as such is absolutely indispensable for ethical life. The belief in the final triumph of the good and the idea of a state of justice and righteousness for which man strives—the basic ethical ideas—are unthinkable without the idea of progress.

Also, the work of science searching for greater unity and order in the phenomena of the world, which is one of the noblest tasks of the ethical life, is impossible without the idea of progress. Behind the work of the creative scientist striving for the establishment of law and order and for a solution of the problems in which he is engaged, there is either present a belief that the world in itself is an ordered cosmos created by an infinite mind, as, for instance, Newton and Leibniz thought, or there is the conviction that the world is a manifestation of a supreme mind, or an attribute of God, in the spirit of Spinoza. A creative scientist who would not admit any of these assumptions, maintaining that metaphysical suppositions, such as that the world was created by, or is a manifestation of, a supreme infinite mind, have no place in the realm of science, could not justify his own work except by assuming that the phenomena of nature, even though in themselves chaotic and disordered, lend themselves to the ordering process of the human mind. Even though the world as a thing in itself is not a cosmos in which law and order rule, the world must be thought of as being amenable to law imposed by the human mind; the world is not refractory to a process of unification by the creative mind of man.

Thus, the work of science is impossible without the assumption of one of these three metaphysical ideas: first, that the world was created; second, that it is the manifestation of a supreme being; or, third, that the world, though in itself not orderly, does not resist the imposition of law and order by the human mind, and that man is capable of establishing order out of chaos.

Now, any of these assumptions, without which the work of science is unthinkable, presupposes the possibility of progress, the possibility of growth towards greater unity and towards a more perfect order of the phenomena of nature. But the idea of progress is meaningless in a world in which everything is due to the immediate creation of God. In a world in which God is everything and man is nothing, there can be no growth and development, nor can the idea of progress have any meaning whatsoever.

In order that the idea of progress should have a real function in the ethical creative life of man, whether it be in relation to the scientific work of man or in relation to the political and social life of man striving for an ideal order of society, the idea of progress must be a logically possible idea, that is to say, it must not contradict our concept of the world and our concept of God. In a world view which places in the center the idea of the unfathomable will of God which is the immediate creator of every point of reality, the idea of progress is an impossible idea.

In our time, certain theological schools of thought (Karl Barth, Emil Brunner, etc.) placed the concept of the absolute, the "wholly other," in the center of their thought, leaving no place for man. In the face of the absolute will of God, "the wholly other," manifesting itself in revelation which is essentially an intrusion of the absolute into the relative historical time, there can be no place for the historical man as a being endowed with the faculty of freedom and creative initiative.

The effect of this theology is that God is everything and man is nothing. It is just as impossible to speak of the idea of progress in the "theology of crisis" and in the theology of existentialism, as there is no place for the idea of progress in the school of the Kalam. The motives of their thought may be formally divergent, corresponding to the different problems with which they were respectively concerned and to the different historical situations in which they were placed; the result of their thought is the same, namely, that the unfathomable will of God alone, or the grace of God, is the all-determining factor of all being, and there is nothing left for the "fallen" man but blindly to accept the will of God, to be constantly conscious of it and, through an act of faith (i.e., a leap of faith), subordinate himself to it. Maimonides' criticism of the Kalam is thus equally valid in relation to some of the contemporary theological schools.

Maimonides was critical of the views of the Kalam, who maintained continuous creation and the complete dependence of every point in reality on the immediate act of the divine will. In this connection, it is of great interest to compare the Maimonidean concept of the world in its relation to his God-idea with Newton's view of the world. As is well known, Newton established the universal law of gravitation, from which Kepler's three laws of planetary motion follow, as can be demonstrated by mathematical calculation. Newton thus established greater unity and order in the cosmos, since he required the assumption of only one law, instead of Kepler's three laws. Newton, however, knew of certain "irregularities" in the motions of the planets which could not be accounted for in terms of the law of gravitation. Furthermore, these irregularities, if they were cumulative, could pile up to great deviations and upset the whole balance of the solar system. Newton could not explain the fact that the irregularities do not, after all, upset the balance of our solar system otherwise than by assuming divine intervention. God must intervene from time to time in order to adjust the planets and put them on their proper paths. Leibniz ruled out the possibility of divine intervention in the natural process as incompatible with the idea of God's perfection. He therefore accounted for the fact that the irregularities in the planetary motions do not upset the balance of our solar system in terms of his principle of the "pre-established harmony." At the beginning of creation, the divine mind provided for the proper adjustment of such irregularities. His criticism of Newton's concept of divine intervention in the natural process is summed up by his observation that Newton's God was a mechanic, and a poor one at that. Such a God is like a watchmaker who must intervene from time to time in order to render the watches synchronous in operation. The ideal watchmaker, however, is capable of producing watches the synchronization of which (their operation) does not require any adjustment. (See Leibniz' correspondence with Samuel Clarke, letters 1.4–2.8, and 3.13. Cf. W. T. Stace, *Religion and the Modern Mind.*)

Leibniz' criticism of Newton proceeds along the same lines of thought as that of Maimonides against the Kalam's doctrine of continuous creation. According to the latter, every point of reality is due to an immediate act of divine creation. The Kalam held that there are no natural laws and that every point of reality is the result of the inscrutable divine will. Maimonides' doctrine of the world as an ordered cosmos governed by necessary laws established at the beginning of creation thus, in a way, anticipated Leibniz' doctrine of the pre-established harmony.

Maimonides ruled out the idea of divine intervention in the natural process. The miracles, which cannot be explained as natural phenomena, are to be understood, according to Maimonides, as preordained suspensions of natural law. The individual characteristics of the heavenly bodies with reference to their peculiar motion, their speed and direction, which cannot be explained mechanically, indicate that there is design in nature. This is the only proof for creation adduced by Maimonides. These individual characteristics of the motion of the heavenly bodies have a function, in Maimonides' system of thought, similar to the "irregularities" of the planetary motions in the Newtonian system: they indicate design and a designer. The difference between them, however, consists in that for Newton the "irregularities" indicate intervention by God in the natural process, while for Maimonides the design manifested by the heavenly bodies indicates an act of the divine will at the beginning of creation.

A contemporary author, W. T. Stace, in his book, *Religion and the Modern Mind,* writes about the destructive effect of Newtonian science on religion. He says: "A living religion demands a God who is near to man in the sense that he intervenes in the affairs of man. The belief in miracles is an expression of this sense of present nearness of God. But Newtonian science produced a sense of the remoteness of God. God is no more around us in the world now. But the world as a whole is determined by a system of laws established at the beginning of creation. God is not acting here and now but is far away and long ago at the beginning of time. This concept of God had a destructive effect on the religious sense of man" (*ibid.,* p. 86 ff.). Now Stace is right only with reference to a naïve, superstitious concept of God as cherished by the ignorant masses. And inasmuch as he deals with the religious ideas held by the common man, his analysis is correct. But then his task is really not the investigation of the bearing of science on religion as such, i.e., religion as a body of doctrines concerning the relation of God to the world and to man, as held by intelligent and thinking men, but it is an investigation of the effect of modern science on the religious views held by the masses. This is, in fact, a sociological, not a philosophical problem. The best name for his book would have been: Superstition (or: The Religion of the Common Man) and the Modern Mind.

Many centuries before Newton, Maimonides evolved a concept of God much further "removed" than the God of the masses and much more transcendent than the God of Newton. While Newton still grants a place for intervention by God in the natural process for the adjustment of the "irregularities" in the planetary motion, Maimonides conceived of the world as a completely ordered cosmos governed by laws established at the beginning of creation, ruling out intervention in any shape or form. Even the individual peculiarities of the heavenly bodies, which correspond to the irregularities of the motion of the planets in the Newtonian system, are grounded in the act of creation determined by the divine will and purpose. Creation thus involved a pre-established harmony. This is the religion which Maimonides taught to the masses, for this concept of the world and of God's relation to it found expression even in Maimonides' Halachic works, which are designed as guides for the masses.

Such a religious philosophy will not be shaken by the discoveries of modern science, but rather enhanced and ennobled. The more unity and order the scientific mind establishes in the phenomena of nature, the greater the wonder at the act of creation.

IV

The *Mishneh Torah* begins with a passage defining the first commandment, which consists in the striving for the attainment of knowledge of God. Maimonides then explains the essence of the first commandments as consisting of the intellectual comprehension of the existence, unity, and incorporeality of God. The concluding passage of this great work gives expression to the hope that the knowledge of God will spread over the earth "as the waters cover the sea." Thus the motto of the greatest work of Maimonides in Halachah is the attainment of clear knowledge and the intellectual comprehension of the essence of monotheism.

While the first and the last passages of the *Yad Hachazakah* deal with knowledge of God, the first and the last chapters of the *Moreh Nebuchim* deal with a definition of the essence of man. Man and God thus constitute the two great themes of Maimonides' thought. The first chapter of the *Moreh* defines reason as the *characteristica specifica* of man. By means of the rational capacity, which is the image of God in man, man has the faculty of comprehending the forms of being and the ability of attaining metaphysical knowledge. Man is thus distinct in essence, not merely in degree, from all other forms of being.

The concluding chapter of the *Moreh* presents a scale of values constituting the goals of human striving, the highest value of which consists in *imitatio dei,* i.e., in human striving for the realization of the ethical ideal.

Let us now consider Maimonides' concept of man in relation to the concepts of man prevalent in our time. There are, generally speaking, three classic concepts of the essence of man. First, there is the concept of man which is grounded in the Biblical tradition of creation. Man was created in the image of God; man is thus the counterpart of God. With creation is bound up the story of the paradise and the fall of man.

Second, the whole range of classic Greek thought evolved a concept of man as a being possessing self-consciousness by which he is distinguished from all other forms of life. The essential characteristic of man is his reason, that is, the capacity of comprehension of the forms of being. Man is what he is through the possession of the rational faculty, *logos, ratio, mens. Logos* here means speech as well as the capacity of understanding the forms of reality. The forms of speech and the forms of thought correspond to one another, and they both correspond to the ideas, the forms of reality. Man is, so to say, the counterpart of the cosmos, hence microcosmos and macrocosmos. Closely connected with this conception of man is the doctrine of a universal, superhuman mind in which all the forms of reality are grounded. The universal mind encompasses the fundamental principles of reality, and man alone of all other beings partakes of this universal mind underlying the All.

The third conception of man is bound up with the whole realm of thought as developed by the modern sciences of biology and genetic psychology. According to the views evolved by these sciences, man constitutes the highest form in the series of biological forms which have developed one from the other on the tree of life. Man is the highest peak in the tower of life on our planet, the earth. The form of man is joined with the other forms of life from which this form was generated. It is not different in essence but only in degree from the forms of life in the animal realm. Man is only more complicated by reason of a greater combination of capacities and energies which are to be found in the subhuman realm.

Each of the various schools of contemporary thought is grounded in a different conception of man. Thus, for instance, the various trends of psychoanalysis are predicated upon the conception of man as the last development of the animal realm. An explanation of man's conduct and his mental make-up is sought, therefore, in the discovery of the forces latent in man which have their origin in the lower realm of being.

Some of the contemporary theological schools, with their emphasis on the depravity of man in consequence of which man is incapable of liberating himself from the state of sin except through an act of faith, are rooted in the conception of man as the Augustinian doctrine of original sin developed it on the basis of the Biblical record.

Now, Maimonides' concept of man presents a synthesis of the Greek conception of man as a rational being capable of becoming a part of the universal mind and of the prophetic concept of man as a being endowed with the capacity of creative initiative. Interpreting the Biblical passage about the creation of man in the image of God, Maimonides defines the distinction of man as consisting in his extraordinary ability for intellectual comprehension which is not through the medium of the senses. Just as the divine mind does not operate through an instrument of a sensuous nature, but acts intuitively and spontaneously, so the intellectual comprehension of man is capable of transcending the realm of sensuous perceptions, for he is able to attain concepts not through the medium of percepts. This concept of man determined Maimonides' demand for a belief in certain philosophic principles, even for the ordinary man. The belief in the existence, unity, and incorporeality of God is a necessary requirement for every Jew, according to Maimonides. As every man is capable of attaining a certain degree of metaphysical knowledge, it is a religious commandment to strive for such cognition. Hence, Maimonides' formulation of the principles of faith represents the minimum of philosophic knowledge which is an indispensable requirement.

This, however, is only one aspect of man. The other aspect of man consists in his creative capacity. With reference to the passage in Jeremiah: "Let not the wise man glory in his might, let not the rich man glory in his riches; but let him that glorieth glory in this, that he understandeth and knoweth Me" (9:22–23), Maimonides constructed a scale of values which constitutes the goals of human striving according to the following order: the acquisition of wealth, bodily perfection, wisdom, and mastery over one's passions, and, finally, the intellectual comprehension of the essence of God (*Moreh,* III, 54).

One would have expected of Maimonides, the great rationalist, that the last perfection, namely, the rational comprehension of the essence of God, should be conceived as the highest value for man to strive for. This would be in harmony with Maimonides' conception of human reason as a spark of the divine, infinite mind; it would also be in accord with his view of immortality as the result of the attainment of intellectual perfection. But Maimonides does not consider the intellectual comprehension of the essence of God as the last and the ultimate value. There is still another higher value to which intellectual perfection must lead, namely, the striving for the realization of righteousness and justice.

Maimonides writes: "The prophet does not content himself with stating that the knowledge of God is the highest kind of perfection, for if this had been his intention, he would have said, 'But in this let him who glorieth glory, that he understands and knoweth me,' and would have stopped there; or he would have said, 'that he understandeth and knoweth me that I am one,' or 'that I have not any likeness,' . . . or a similar phrase. He says, however, that man can glory only in the knowledge of God and in the knowledge of His ways and attributes, which are His actions. . . . We are thus told in this passage that the divine acts which ought to be known, and ought to serve as a guide for our actions, are lovingkindness, judgment, and righteousness (חסד משפט וצדקה). Another very important lesson is taught by the additional phrase 'in the earth' (בארץ). It implies a fundamental principle of the Law. . . . It teaches, as has been taught by the greatest of all wise men in the words, 'The earth is the Lord's' (Exod. 9:29), that His providence extends to the earth in accordance with its nature, in the same manner as it controls the heavens in accordance with their nature. This is expressed in the words, 'That I am the Lord which exercise lovingkindness, judgment, and righteousness in the earth' (Jer., *ibid*). The prophet thus, in conclusion, says: . . . 'My object is that you shall practice lovingkindness, judgment, and righteousness in the earth.' In a similar manner we have shown that the object of the enumeration of God's thirteen attributes is the lesson that we should acquire similar attributes and act accordingly" (*Moreh, ibid.*).

The highest ultimate value is thus not the intellectual contemplation of the divine essence, as some of the mystics taught, but the active creative life. This is summed up by Maimonides in the formulation of the highest ideal as *imitatio dei*. The ultimate value for man to strive for consists not in passive contemplation but in active creation.

This is entirely different from Spinoza's formulation of the ultimate value as consisting in the intellectual love of God. The latter is a sort of stoic detachment and philosophic indifference resulting from the recognition that all being is determined by necessary laws and that all reality is the result of the all-determining *causa sui*. Spinoza's concept of the intellectual love of God does not imply activity and creative initiative, but tranquility and quiescence. Just as Spinoza's God is not creative, neither is man. There is a correspondence between the concept of God and that of man: creation is foreign to both of them.

The ultimate value, according to Maimonides, is not aloofness and unconcern, but creative initiative and activity, aiming at the realization of the absolute good, which is an endless goal. Just as God is creative, so is man. God is creative in an absolute sense, not subject to any condition, for the act of creation is *creatio ex nihilo;* man is creative in a limited sense, dependent on conditions and on factors beyond his power and control. With regard to Maimonides, too, there is a correspondence between the concept of God and that of man: creation pertains to both of them.

Maimonides evolves here a concept of ethics which is entirely different from that of Aristotelian ethics. According to the latter, the ethical ideal consists in the attainment of the "golden mean," the middle between the extremes. Maimonides adopted this ethical doctrine of Aristotle and expounded it in the *Mishneh Torah,* thus giving to it the character of *Halachah.* The attainment of the "golden mean" is also a necessary condition for intellectual perfection. Only a person who has achieved mastery over his passions can hope to obtain purity of the mind in the pursuit of truth and knowledge. Self-mastery is an indispensable requirement for clearness and distinctness of thought. But this ethical ideal is not the ultimate ethical goal; it is a preliminary for the attainment of other goals. Such an ethical ideal has the character of finality about it. The characteristic mark of the Aristotelian ethics is its finitude. Its purpose is the harmonization of the various impulses, desires, and inclinations of man, that is to say, the attainment of a proper balance between the different capacities and properties of the human character. This is an attainable end. The "golden mean" is the final goal of the ideal of the proper balance between the various qualities and capacities in the character of man. This ethical perfection, consisting in man's mastery over his passions and the harmonization of his various capacities and impulses, occupies the third place in the scale of values established by Maimonides. It follows the value of the acquisition of wealth and that of the perfection of the human body, its forces and qualities. The rank of the value of moral perfection is higher than the previous ones, but it is subordinated to the value which follows it, namely, the value of the intellectual comprehension of God (השכל וידע אותי).

With the latter value, that is, the attainment of the intellectual comprehension of God, of His essence and attributes, there is bound up a totally different ethical ideal which has the character of infinity. The striving for the realization of the idea of the good on earth is an endless task. The ethical ideal of *imitatio dei,* implying the striving for the actual realization of the will of God, can only be asymptotically approached, but never fully attained. The ethical doctrine of Maimonides, with which the *Moreh* concludes, evolves an infinite ideal, while the Aristotelian ethics is concerned with a finite ethical goal. This places the Aristotelian ethics adopted by Maimonides in its proper light. For Maimonides, the Aristotelian ethics adopted by him is just a preliminary ethical stage. It is bound up with man as a social being, and it is subservient to the value of intellectual perfection. This preliminary Aristotelian ethics is not the highest, ultimate, ethical ideal for Maimonides. Its aim is merely a healthy soul in a healthy body. It is a sort of "medicine of the soul." This is an ethical doctrine within the center of which stands a limited and finite ethical goal.

However, the ultimate ethical value, according to Maimonides, follows the attainment of the metaphysical cognition of God and His attributes. This consists in man's striving for the realization on this earth of the divine, ethical attributes, which is an endless task. Man is thus defined as a being who possesses an endless capacity for creativity commensurate with the endlessness of the ethical task. The ultimate ethical value is not a means for, and subordinated to, the value of intellectual cognition, as Aristotle taught, but it is rather its end and purpose.

Maimonides here reached the climax of the Kantian doctrine of the primacy of the ethical, practical reason. Thus Maimonides' dependence on Aristotle should not be too greatly exaggerated, for in the most important issues, such as in the conception of the infinite character of the ethical ideal and in the conception of the endless ethical goal as the final, ultimate value, Maimonides' deviation from Aristotelianism is clearly pronounced.

Moreover, the concluding chapter of the *Moreh* contains a concept of man as a being endowed with the creative capacity. The idea of the creation of the world now gains new meaning and significance. Maimonides' treatment of the problem of the creation of the world was only to prove its possibility by disproving the Aristotelian arguments for the non-creation, i.e., the eternity, of the world. Maimonides' one and only argument for the creation of the world from the individual characteristics of the heavenly bodies was intended merely to prove its probability. Maimonides did not present it as a conclusive argument. Maimonides thus held that on the basis of rational thought, creation remains an insoluble prob-

lem, an antinomy, to use the Kantian term. Since, however, creation is rationally not impossible, it can become a doctrine of faith,
for faith begins at the point where our reason has its limitations. It
is true that faith cannot embrace a doctrine which is contrary to
reason. But it is wrong to assume, according to Maimonides, that a
doctrine which cannot be proved by reason is *ipso facto* false. It is
dogmatic rationalism to demand that every doctrine of faith which
we hold must be rationally deducible. This was the gross mistake
of Elisha ben Abuyah, according to Maimonides. Elisha was striving for the cognition of metaphysical truth by rational and logical
method. He accepted only those doctrines and tenets of faith
which can be rationally deduced. Elisha did not recognize that our
reason has its limitations in consequence of which our mind is
unable fully to comprehend the realm of metaphysics and to solve
all metaphysical problems. But Maimonides, believing in the power
of the human reason, still held that there are metaphysical problems
which cannot be rationally solved, and that certain metaphysical
ideas transcend the limits of intellectual comprehension. Those
metaphysical ideas, though rationally not deducible, are nonetheless true, because without them the ethical life of man as a creative
being would be impossible.

In spite of the fact that the creation of the world is, from a
rational point of view, only a possibility, the doctrine of the creation
of the world attained for Maimonides a degree of certainty equal
to that of the existence and unity of God. In fact, Maimonides explicitly states that the doctrine of the creation is second in importance to the doctrine of the unity of God. But the unity of God is
for Maimonides a doctrine which can be rationally deduced by
logical methods. We are, therefore, compelled to conclude that the
doctrine of the creation, though not rationally demonstrable, must
nonetheless command a certitude equal in rank to that of the unity
of God.

What kind of certainty is it? It seems to me that its certainty
resides in the ethical realm. The doctrine of the creation is bound
up with the ethical concept of man, in the center of which stands

the idea of freedom. Only in a world which has been created can there be a place for man as an ethical being; only in a world which has its origin in an act of creation can man be thought of as a being endowed with the creative capacity and with freedom of choice. The eternity of the world would imply necessity everywhere. In a world existing eternally and necessarily, there would be no place for man as an ethical being possessing the capacity to acquire freedom and creative initiative and having the power of choice.

The doctrine of the creation of the world is thus an indispensable presupposition for the concept of man as a free agent and as an instrument for the realization of the ethical attributes of God. The formulation of the ultimate value for man, with which Maimonides concludes his treatise, is bound up with a concept of man as a being having the capacity to transcend himself and to transform the world. This is possible only under the assumption that man is endowed with a creative faculty and that this world provides the material for man's ethical creativity. Hence the world itself must be thought of as having its origin in an act of creation, for a world which exists of necessity and from eternity is a static world and everything in it is the same at it has always been. But ethical life can have a place only in a world of non-necessity.

The similarity of Maimonides' position to that of critical philosophy can conclusively be demonstrated. According to Kant, the problem of the creation of the world is antinomy, that is to say, the thesis and the antithesis, the creation and the non-creation of the world, can be equally established by rational arguments. Here reason forsakes us, for it is, in principle, impossible to prove conclusively one position as against the other. Yet Kant's position is that the idea of the creation of the world is a necessary assumption. It is not logically, but ethically, necessary.

The same applies to the idea of God and to the idea of freedom of the will, according to Kant. The problem of the existence or non-existence of a supreme being as well as the dilemma of freedom of the will or absolute necessity constitute antinomies of thought which are, in principle, logically insoluble. For both positions, the thesis and the antithesis, are equally provable by rational methods. However, the existence of a supreme being and the reality of freedom of the will are postulates of pure reason, that is to say, they are necessary assumptions for the possibility of the ethical realm. Man is a citizen of two realms, the realm of *phenomena* and the realm of *noumena*, i.e., the "ought to be." Man cannot be fully defined without taking into account his relation to the "ought to be."

The reality of metaphysical ideas, such as those of God, of freedom of the will, and of creation, is of a different nature and potency from that of the categories of thought, such as causality, substance, and the other categories which are necessary suppositions for the ordering of the natural phenomena. But the metaphysical ideas are not less real than the categories. Now, I would prefer to designate the reality of the metaphysical ideas, such as freedom and creation, as an existential reality, since these ideas are derived from the very existence of man as a creative, ethical being, a being capable of setting for himself aims and goals and possessing a vision of an absolute good, the realization of which requires an infinite time. In the conception of the absolute ideas, such as God, freedom, and creation, man's relation to a noumenal realm is manifest. The existence of man is bound up with his relation to a realm of absolute ideas, transcending the world of phenomena, the realm of experience.

The question whether there is, or whether there is no, metaphysical reality, as a "thing in itself," corresponding to these absolute ideas, remains always an open question; but the existential reality of these ideas is not impaired by it. For by our positing these ideas as suppositions necessary for the creative, ethical life, they acquire a functional value for the existence of man as an ethical being; their existential reality is thus assured. The creative aspect of man demands and posits the reality of these ideas; the existence of man is thus the guarantee of their reality.

I use the term "existential" in a quite different sense from that which is at present in vogue. The philosophy of Existentialism is a philosophy evolved in opposition to rational thought. But the metaphysical ideas of Kant can be designated as "existential" in a quite different sense; they are a superstructure based on the rational. The noumenal realm is conceived as not in opposition to, but as an addition to, the phenomenal world which is rationally expounded.

The metaphysical ideas of God, of freedom, and of creation, which are rationally indeducible, are, however, rationally possible. If they were rationally and logically impossible, they could not become ethical and existential ideas. While for contemporary Existentialism faith embraces doctrines and tenets which are logically contradictory and rationally impossible, there can be no place for metaphysical ideas which are logically impossible and rationally untenable, according to Kant. The logical possibility of the metaphysical ideas must be assured in order that the ideas may become objects of faith, for faith can embrace only doctrines and tenets which are logically and rationally possible, even though not logically deducible.

The same applies to Maimonides' conception of faith and to his doctrines of creation and freedom of the will. These ideas are grounded in the ethical sphere of man; they are derived in a manner similar to the Kantian derivation of the metaphysical ideas which are postulates of pure reason.

The obvious difference between their conceptions of God should not, however, be overlooked. While for Kant the idea of God is included among the metaphysical ideas, i.e., the postulates of practical reason, with Maimonides the existence and unity of God are rationally deducible principles. Only the creation of the world and freedom of the will are for Maimonides assumptions necessary for the ethical realm of man, for without these assumptions man as a being endowed with a creative capacity is unthinkable. And in this respect the similarity of Maimonides' and Kant's positions is clearly discernible.

In order, however, to posit these ideas, they must be logically possible, that is to say, it must be demonstrated that they do not contradict reason, for what is logically contradictory is also untenable as an article of faith. It is worth recalling, in this connection, Maimonides' definition of faith as identical with conviction (*Moreh,* I, 50), and a conviction cannot be incompatible with the laws of logic, i.e., with rational thought. Even those ideas which have their root in the existence of man as a creative being must be logically possible ideas, even though they may not be rationally deducible.

In presenting the different views concerning the origin of the world, Maimonides refers to the view of Plato that the world was created out of an eternal, primeval matter. The philosophers who held such a view maintain that creation out of nothing is a logically impossible idea. They hold that the attribute of the omnipotence of God does not imply that God could do what is logically impossible. Creation out of nothing is just as impossible as it is impossible for God to create a square whose diagonal is equal to any of its sides, or to assume of God's thinking that it could proceed in terms contrary to the logical laws of identity and contradiction.

It is clear that Maimonides admits the validity of the principle implied in the examples cited, namely, that it is unthinkable of God that He could construct a mathematical object contrary to the laws of mathematics, or that God's thought could proceed in terms contrary to the laws of logic. Maimonides disagrees with those philosophers only with regard to the comparison between the doctrine of *creatio ex nihilo,* on the one hand, and the objects that are contrary to the mathematical and logical laws, on the other. While the idea of God's omnipotence could not imply the possible defiance by God of the mathematical and logical laws, *creatio ex nihilo* may be incomprehensible for man, but it is not impossible for God the Omnipotent. While for the philosophers of the Platonic school to whom Maimonides refers (and the same would be true of the Aristotelians who deny creation altogether), the two impossibilities are of an identical nature, Maimonides holds that they are not to be compared.

What is the difference between the two kinds of impossibility? It seems to me that it consists in the distinction between a purely logical impossibility and an experimental and empirical impossibility. While the former is binding for thought as such, including the infinite, divine thought, the latter is confined to human thought. An experiential impossibility is grounded in propositions derived empirically, and empirical propositions are valid only for the realm of experience, not beyond it.

In modern philosophic terms it can be formulated thus: a proposition governed by the laws of logic is an analytic proposition; as such it is valid for thought in general, including that of the infinite mind. A proposition grounded in experience is a synthetic proposition; as such it is valid only in relation to the objects of the synthesis which are objects of experience. An analytic proposition is governed by the laws of identity and contradiction, and is not determined by the nature of the objects involved. The laws of logic are valid for any object of thought as such, quite independent of the nature of the object. But a proposition grounded on experience is determined by the nature of the empirical object; it cannot, therefore, transcend the limits of experience. The application of such a proposition to an object beyond the realm of experience is illegitimate.

Furthermore, a proposition which is determined by the laws of logic is valid also for any thinking subject. Just as it is not dependent on the nature of the particular object, for any object of thought cannot defy the laws of logic, it is also not dependent on the nature of the thinking subject. It is valid for thought as such, that is to say, for all thinking subjects, including the infinite mind. This seems to be the reason for the idea implied by Maimonides that the divine mind must be thought of as being bound by the laws of logic and mathematics, namely, that it is incongruous to assume the possibility that the divine mind could think in terms contrary to the laws of logic and in defiance of the laws of mathematics.

The fact that Maimonides cites examples from the realm of mathematics alongside of those of logic for the illustration of the idea that the attribute of omnipotence has its limitations is sufficient proof that he considered the two realms to be alike in nature, that is to say, that mathematics and logic are rational, not empirical, sciences. Since the laws and principles by which the objects of these sciences are governed are each and all rational, the idea of an object contrary to these laws and principles is not an experiential, but a logical and rational, impossibility.

If it be assumed that Maimonides implied here the "classic" distinction between analytic and synthetic propositions, it would follow that he considered mathematical propositions to be analytic propositions. This was David Hume's view, and this is also the doctrine of modern philosophers of mathematics, such as Bertrand Russell and others.

It would, however, be hazardous and unhistorical to maintain that Maimonides was implying here the distinction between analytic and synthetic propositions. This distinction, which constitutes one of the central issues in modern philosophy, and which Kant characterized as worthy of being called "classic," is of a much later date. It could not possibly have been anticipated by Maimonides. Maimonides' differentiation should rather be understood as implying a distinction between rational thought which is evolved by the pure mind, by way of deduction, without having recourse to the sensuous perceptions, on the one hand, and experiential knowledge which is the result of empirical observation of objects of experience, on the other. While an object of thought which is impossible on the basis of the former, i.e., rational thought, is impossible for any thinking subject, including the divine, an object of thought which is impossible on the basis of the latter, i.e., experiential knowledge, is impossible only for a thinking subject confined to experience, but it is not impossible for an infinite mind, i.e., for God, to whom the attribute of omnipotence is ascribed.

The idea that rational thought by way of pure deduction is valid also for the divine, infinite mind can be predicated only upon the assumption that the human mind is a part of the divine mind. The human mind and the divine mind are of the same kind, though the former is finite and the latter is infinite. Hence, the pure rational concepts evolved by the human mind can claim absolute validity binding also for the infinite mind. But if the divine were defined as the "wholly other" having no relation to the finite, human mind, it would be incongruous to claim absolute validity for the rational concepts, such as the laws of logic and mathematics, and to maintain that they are binding also for the infinite mind.

V

Maimonides' concept of the unity of revelation and philosophy, of Torah and rational thinking, contains the very fruitful idea that the essence of Judaism is grounded in philosophy and not in the revelation of a dogmatic law.

Spinoza and Mendelssohn, each in his own way, denied that Judaism contains a philosophy of its own. Spinoza's whole tendency was to show the essential difference between philosophy and the religious teachings of the Scriptures. The Prophets did not teach any theoretical concept of God and the world, but only obedience, and the moral life was demanded as a means for attaining happiness. The law taught by Moses was a statutory law grounded in a contract made between the people and Moses as the representative of God. It is, therefore, binding only so long as the State was in existence. Since the validity of the law is grounded in a contract, the contracting parties must exist for the law to be valid. Philosophic truth is not the task of religion in general, nor are the religious and ethical teachings of the Prophets bound up in any way with philosophic and metaphysical conceptions of God and the world.

Spinoza's conception of Judaism is, in some of its aspects, in accord with the generally accepted view of some of the traditional schools which are against any attempt to interpret the prophetic teachings and religious doctrines in the light of philosophic thought. In the conception of the law as the very essence of Judaism, Spinoza does not stand alone. He will find support for this view in various circles of traditional Judaism.

The fundamental difference between them consists, however, in the different conceptions of the essence of the law. While for the traditionalist the law is divinely revealed and eternally binding, for Spinoza its validity is closely bound up with the existence of the State. But the view that Judaism in general and the prophetic teachings in particular have no relation to philosophy is common to them all, namely, to Spinoza and to the dogmatic traditionalists alike.

Here again there is, however, a fundamental difference between them which should not be overlooked. This consists in the following. Traditional schools of thought have generally denied the value of philosophy for the understanding of religious doctrines, because of the belief that the absolute value of revelation does not require the light of philosophic thought to illumine it. The cold light of philosophy will not add warmth and lustre to the divine law which radiates a brilliance and warmth of its own. The emotional intensity gained through adherence to the Law and the conviction of faith are, for the traditionalist, of greater value than the conviction arrived at through speculative thought and philosophy.

This is not the case with Spinoza. For him the ideal truth can be attained only by rational or intuitive thought. Consequently, in his maintaining that Scriptures do not teach philosophic ideas about the essence of God, the world, and man, there is implied a degradation of the value of prophetic teachings. The Prophets did not evolve a clear, intellectual concept of the essence of God and the world; their ethical doctrines are not the result of any theoretical comprehension of reality. The Prophets had a deep moral sense; they taught a non-philosophic morality, promising for obedience a happy life in the State and threatening for disobedience the destruction of the State.

The same is true of Mendelssohn's conception of Judaism; its essential characteristic consists in the law. The philosophic ideas which are to be found in the Prophets and in the writings of the later development of Judaism, such as the ideas of God, the soul, and freedom of the will, are common to all monotheistic religions. In addition to these philosophic ideas, Scripture comprises a revealed law given to a particular people.

This conception of Mendelssohn is characteristic of the whole period of the Enlightenment with its belief in the rationality of man. That is to say, in the constitution of the human mind are contained all the eternal *a priori* ideas. Therefore, with respect to philosophy, all monotheistic religions are equal. The pure rational ideas concerning God and man are common to all men, and therefore all religions share equally in this eternal realm of *Ratio*.

A whole world of difference separates Maimonides' conception of Scripture in particular and his conception of Judaism in general from those of Spinoza and Mendelssohn. In a way, Mendelssohn's conception is even more dangerous than that of Spinoza for a possible development of Jewish thought in the light of the developing philosophic thought in general. Spinoza's goal, was, as we have seen, to prove the separation of the teachings of the Prophets from philosophy. But Mendelssohn's conception that the eternal and rational ideas are *a priori* and therefore common to all men, from which it follows that all monotheistic religions are alike with reference to their philosophic content, implies a falsification of the essence of Scripture as well as a misunderstanding of the individual theological doctrines by which each of the monotheistic religions is to be distinguished and characterized.

But Maimonides' conception of the unity of truth, of the identity of philosophy and revelation, and of his view of Judaism, prophetic as well as rabbinic, as containing a philosophy which is in complete harmony with rational thought, opens up new vistas for the possibility of a development of Jewish thought in the light of the further growth of philosophic thought in general. Maimonides laid the basis for the possibility of the development of Jewish religious thought beyond the stage which he had attained. In other words, a proper understanding of the deep motives and tendencies underlying Maimonides' thought allows, yea, even demands, a process of thought leading away from Maimonides. That is to say, *with* Maimonides we can and should go *beyond* Maimonides. The most significant lesson which the understanding of Maimonides' philosophy teaches is that with Maimonides we can supersede Maimonides.

BIOGRAPHICAL NOTES

BIOGRAPHICAL NOTES

ATLAS, SAMUEL (1899-   ), whose rabbinic and secular education was acquired in schools and universities in his native Lithuania, Russia, and Germany, and who taught in Poland and England, came to the United States in 1942 to assume the professorship of Philosophy and Talmud at the Hebrew Union College. His many books and articles include several works dealing with the philosophy of Maimonides.

BAMBERGER, BERNARD (1904-   ), a native of Baltimore and graduate of the Johns Hopkins University, received his rabbinical training at the Hebrew Union College. He has served congregations in Lafayette, Ind., Albany, N.Y., and New York City and has been an active participant in the work of the Central Conference of American Rabbis. Among his works are a popular history, *The Story of Judaism* (1957), and *The Bible: a Modern Jewish Approach* (1955); he is also the writer of an earlier book on *Proselytism in the Talmudic Era* (1939).

BERKOWITZ, HENRY (1857-1924) was a member of the first graduating class at the Hebrew Union College. He served in pulpits in Mobile, Ala., Kansas City, Mo., and Philadelphia. He was the founder, in 1893, of the Jewish Chautauqua Society for the diffusion of knowledge of Judaism. He was active in civic affairs and in the work of the Central Conference of American Rabbis. Editor of *Jewish Comment,* he wrote and published several books, and was deeply concerned with instituting appropriate new ritual forms for the Reform movement.

BETTAN, ISRAEL (1889-1957), a native of Lithuania, came to the United States in 1905 (?) and was graduated from the University of Cincinnati in 1910 and received rabbinical ordination from the Hebrew Union College in 1912. He served as rabbi in Charleston, W. Va., for ten years, after which he was named professor of Homiletics and Midrash at the Hebrew Union College. He wrote a distinguished series of studies in the history of Jewish preaching, as well as studies of modern Responsa.

BLAU, JOSEPH L. (1909-   ), the editor of this collection, received his A.B. (1931), M.A. (1933), and Ph.D. (1945) from Columbia University and has taught at Columbia since 1946, first in the Department of Philosophy and then in the Department of Religion (of which he has been chairman and is now director of graduate studies). His book publications of Jewish interest include *The Christian Interpretation of the Cabala* (1945, 1965), *The Story of Jewish Philosophy* (1962, 1971), *Modern Varieties of Judaism* (1966); other works on American philosophy and philosophy of religion.

BOROWITZ, EUGENE B. (1924-   ), holds a doctorate from Columbia University and rabbinical ordination from the Hebrew Union College. He is Professor of Education and Jewish Religious Thought at the New York School of the Hebrew Union College-Jewish Institute of Religion. He has lectured in various universities, and is the author of several works of general philosophic interest. He is one of the group of younger Jewish theologians whose community of concern crosses the organizational divisions in American Jewish life. His books on Jewish theology are: *A New Jewish Theology in the Making* (1968), and *How Can a Jew Speak of Faith Today?* (1969).

BRAUDE, WILLIAM G. (1907-   ), a native of Lithuania, received his A.B. from the University of Cincinnati in 1929; his M.A. and Ph.D. from Brown University; and his rabbinical ordination from the Hebrew Union College in 1931. After briefly serving as rabbi in Rockford, Ill., he assumed the rabbinate of Temple Beth El, Providence, R.I., where he has remained to the present. He edited and translated the *Midrash on Psalms* (1959-60) and *Pesikta Rabbati* (1968) for the Yale Judaica Series.

COHON, SAMUEL S. (1888-1959) came to the United States from his native Russia in 1904. After ordination from the Hebrew Union College in 1912, he served congregations in Springfield, Ohio, and Chicago until 1923, when he was appointed Professor of Jewish Theology at Hebrew Union College. In 1917, he organized the Chicago Federation of Synagogues. His essays and articles were many. Best known of his many books are *What We Jews Believe* (1931), and *Judaism: A Way of Life* (1948).

FACKENHEIM, EMIL L. (1916-   ), a native of Germany, received his rabbinical ordination from the Hochschule fuer die Wissenschaft des Judentums, Berlin, in 1939. Since 1940 he has lived in

Canada, where he received his Ph.D. from the University of Toronto (1945). He served as rabbi in Hamilton, Ontario, from 1943 to 1948, and since then has been a member of the Department of Philosophy of the University of Toronto. He has published widely his studies in general philosophy and philosophy of religion and also several books of Jewish interest, notably *Paths to Jewish Belief* (1960) and *Quest for Past and Future: Essays in Jewish Theology* (1968).

FREEHOF, SOLOMON B. (1892-   ), born in London, was graduated from the University of Cincinnati and ordained as a rabbi at the Hebrew Union College. He taught at the Hebrew Union College from 1915 to 1924, after which he served congregations in Chicago and Pittsburgh. From 1959 to 1964 he was president of the World Union for Progressive Judaism. His scholarly interests were expressed in a number of books, notably *The Responsa Literature* (1955) and *A Treasury of Responsa* (1963). He was also chairman for many years of the Liturgical Committee of the Central Conference; and the author of *Reform Jewish Practice* (1944), and a number of popular studies in the Bible.

GITTELSOHN, ROLAND B. (1910-   ), a graduate of Western Reserve University, trained for the rabbinate at the Hebrew Union College. Since 1936 he has served as rabbi in Rockville Center, Long Island and in Boston. He has been active on many problems of state and nation as well as in the internal affairs of the Jewish community. His published works include *Modern Jewish Problems* (1943), *Little Lower than the Angels* (1952), and *Man's Best Hope* (1961).

GUTTMANN, ALEXANDER (1904-   ), Hungarian-born scholar, received his doctorate from the University of Breslau in 1924 and was ordained at the Breslau seminary in 1927. After further research and teaching in Germany, he came to the United States in 1940 as professor of Talmud and Rabbinics at the Hebrew Union College-Jewish Institute of Religion. His many books and monographs were, for the most part, written in German, though some shorter studies in Hebrew and English have appeared. Of particular interest to the general reader is his *Enthüllte Talmudzitate* (1930-31), a study of passages in rabbinic literature that have been misinterpreted by antisemites.

HIRSCH, EMIL G. (1851-1923), the son of Samuel Hirsch, one of the outstanding thinkers in German Reform Judaism, was brought to the United States at the age of 15 when his father accepted a pulpit in Philadelphia. The younger Hirsch received his B.A. from the University of Pennsylvania in 1872 and then returned to Germany for graduate study and rabbinical training. He served briefly as rabbi in Philadelphia, Baltimore, and Louisville before election to the rabbinate of Sinai Congregation in Chicago in 1880, where he remained until his death. He was the first American rabbi to have replaced Sabbath services altogether by Sunday services. He was widely acknowledged as a great preacher in the florid style of his era. He taught briefly at the University of Chicago in its early days and was the moving spirit behind the Parliament of Religions at the Chicago World's Fair of 1893. His many publications were chiefly journalistic.

KOHLER, KAUFMANN (1843-1926), a well-trained scholar of German birth and education and a firm advocate of the use of critical ("scientific") methods in Jewish research, came to the United States in 1869 and served as rabbi in Detroit, Chicago, and New York. In 1885 he was the dominant figure in the Reform rabbinical conference that produced the Pittsburgh Platform. In 1903 he became president of the Hebrew Union College, a post he held until his retirement in 1921. Of his many publications, the best known is his *Jewish Theology Systematically and Historically Considered* (1918).

LAUTERBACH, JACOB Z. (1873-1942), born in Galicia, educated at the Universities of Berlin and Göttingen (Ph.D., 1901), ordained to the rabbinate at the Hildesheimer Seminary in Berlin, came to the United States in 1903 as one of the editors of The *Jewish Encyclopedia* for which he wrote most of the articles on Talmudic and rabbinic subjects. After this work was completed he served congregations in Rochester, N.Y., Huntsville, Ala., and Peoria, Ill. In 1911 he was appointed Professor of Talmud and Rabbinic Literature at the Hebrew Union College, a post he held with distinction until his retirement in 1934. He wrote many articles and was the editor and translator of the critical edition of the *Mechilta* in the Jewish Classics Series (1933).

LEVIAS, CASPAR (1860-1934) was a Semitic philologist and lexicographer who was for 10 years (1895-1905) on the faculty of the Hebrew Union College. After a few unsuccessful years in business he returned to teaching in Newark and New York. His many important philological papers appeared in learned journals in the United States and in Europe. His *Grammar of the Aramaic Idiom, Contained in the Babylonian Talmud* (1900) was a pioneering study in this field.

LIEBMAN, JOSHUA LOTH (1907-1948) crowded into his short life a wide range of academic and popular activities and honors. He was born at Hamilton, Ohio, educated at the University of Cincinnati, the Hebrew University, Harvard, and Columbia, ordained rabbi at the Hebrew Union College in 1930, and granted an honorary D.H.L. by Hebrew Union College in 1939. He served as rabbi of Temple Israel, Boston, but his active life as teacher, radio personality, author and lecturer made him, in effect, a national figure. He became even more a public figure after the enormous success of his book, *Peace of Mind* (1946), an exploration of the psychological values of religious belief.

MORGENSTERN, JULIAN (1881-   ) was the first American-born president of the Hebrew Union College. He was graduated from the University of Cincinnati (1901) and ordained at the Hebrew Union College (1902). After post-graduate study in Germany, he received the doctorate from the University of Heidelberg (1904). After three years of congregational service in Lafayette, Ind., he became Professor of Biblical and Semitic Languages at the Hebrew Union College. In 1921 he was named acting president and, in 1922, president. He continued his scholarly studies even while he was a busy and successful administrator of the College; he was a major contributor to biblical studies, to the history of Jewish ceremonial observances, and to the history of religions.

OLAN, LEVI A. (1903-   ), Russian-born, has been in the United States since 1906. He received his B.A. from the University of Cincinnati (1925) and his rabbinical degree from the Hebrew Union College (1929). He has served congregations in Worcester, Mass., and Dallas, Texas, and has taught at the Perkins School of Theology of Southern Methodist University. He is the author of a number of monographic studies of a philosophical nature.

PLAUT, W. GUNTHER (1912-   ), German-born and originally trained in law, came to the United States in 1935 and was graduated from the Hebrew Union College in 1939. He served as rabbi in Chicago and in St. Paul, Minn., before accepting, in 1961, the rabbinical post at the Holy Blossom Temple, Toronto, Canada. His writings include popular and sermonic works, two studies in American Jewish local history, and two fundamental historical anthologies of Reform Judaism, *The Rise of Reform Judaism* (1963) and *The Growth of Reform Judaism* (1965).

RIVKIN, ELLIS (1918-   ), born in Baltimore, earned the B.A.
and Ph.D. degrees from the Johns Hopkins University and a degree
in Hebrew letters from the Baltimore Hebrew College. After three
years as instructor in Jewish history at Gratz College, Philadelphia
(simultaneously post-doctoral research fellow at Dropsie College) he
became a member of the faculty at the Hebrew Union College in
1949, and was named professor of Jewish history in 1953. His publications have been concerned with both general and American Jewish
history and he has developed a personal philosophy of history to
undergird his work.

SCHULMAN, SAMUEL (1864-1955), Russian-born but brought to
the United States at the age of 4, Schulman was graduated from the
College of the City of New York in 1885 and then went to Berlin for
graduate study in the University and rabbinical training at the
Hochschule fuer die Wissenschaft des Judentums. In 1899, after
serving in congregations in New York City, Helena, Mont., and Kansas
City, Mo., Schulman was recalled to New York City as the co-rabbi of
Temple Beth El, and became its senior rabbi when Kaufmann Kohler
was named president of the Hebrew Union College in 1903. In 1927,
Temple Beth El merged with Temple Emanuel; Schulman was named
rabbi of the joint temples, now called Congregation Emanuel. In
1934, he became rabbi emeritus. Schulman was a distinguished pulpit
personality and a leader in many communal activities. He was deeply
imbued with the religious philosophy of classical Reform Judaism and
his occasional writings gave vigorous expression to this position.

SILBERMAN, LOU H. (1914-   ) was born in San Francisco and
graduated from the University of California, Berkeley, in 1934. He
holds three degrees (BHL, MHL, and DHL) from the Hebrew Union
College, where he served as instructor from 1941 to 1943. Then he
held pulpits in Dallas and Omaha before becoming professor of Jewish
literature and thought at Vanderbilt University, Nashville (on faculty
since 1952; Hillel professor since 1955). He has contributed a number of short studies to scholarly journals and written for a number of
encyclopedias. In 1951, he edited a volume of *Rabbinic Essays* by
Jacob Z. Lauterbach.

SILVER, ABBA HILLEL (1893-1963), born in Lithuania, was
brought to the United States at the age of 10. He studied at the University of Cincinnati and the Hebrew Union College, receiving the
B.A. degree and rabbinical ordination simultaneously in 1915. After
two years as rabbi in Wheeling, W. Va., Silver became rabbi of the

Temple, Cleveland, where he remained from 1917 to 1963. He was one of the most active Zionist leaders of his generation and in 1947-48 served the Jewish Agency as representative to the United Nations, where he played a prominent role in the 1947 debates over the Palestine partition plan. Among the many honors, including honorary degrees, that Silver received, the naming after him of the Israeli youth settlement, Kfar Silver, in 1953 deserves special mention. He wrote a number of books of interpretation of Judaism and its place in the modern world. Thoughtful though he was, Silver's greatest distinction came as an activist, a leader in the quest for civil rights in the United States and for justice to the Jew on the world stage.